Navigating Health Information in the Age of Artificial Intelligence

Ashraf Sadat Ahadzadeh
Xiamen University Malaysia, Malaysia

Mansour Amini
Universiti Sains Malaysia, Malaysia

Shin Ling Wu
Sunway University, Malaysia

IGI Global
Scientific Publishing
Publishing Tomorrow's Research Today

Published in the United States of America by
IGI Global Scientific Publishing
701 East Chocolate Avenue
Hershey, PA, 17033, USA
Tel: 717-533-8845
Fax: 717-533-7115
Website: https://www.igi-global.com E-mail: cust@igi-global.com

Library of Congress Cataloging-in-Publication Data

Names: Ahadzadeh, Ashraf, 1980- editor. | Amini, Mansour, 1984- editor. | Wu, Shin Ling, 1987- editor.
Title: Navigating health information in the age of artificial intelligence / edited by Ashraf Ahadzadeh, Mansour Amini, Shin Ling Wu.
Description: Hershey, PA : IGI Global Scientific Publishing, 2025. | Includes bibliographical references and index. | Summary: "This book illuminates the evolving landscape where healthcare intersects with cutting-edge technology. As artificial intelligence (AI) transforms the field, this compilation of expert insights and diverse perspectives explores the dynamic impact on medical practices, patient care, and the broader healthcare ecosystem"-- Provided by publisher.
Identifiers: LCCN 2024053067 (print) | LCCN 2024053068 (ebook) | ISBN 9798369358375 (hardcover) | ISBN 9798369358382 (ebook)
Subjects: LCSH: Communication in medicine--Case studies. | Communication in public health--Case studies. | Artificial intelligence--Medical applications--Case studies.
Classification: LCC R118 .N385 2025 (print) | LCC R118 (ebook) | DDC 362.10285/63--dc23/eng/20250218
LC record available at https://lccn.loc.gov/2024053067
LC ebook record available at https://lccn.loc.gov/2024053068

British Cataloguing in Publication Data
A Cataloguing in Publication record for this book is available from the British Library.

List of Reviewers

Rabiah Adawiah Binti Abu Seman, *School of Psychology and Social Sciences, International Medical University (IMU), Malaysia*

Xiao Yiqing, *School of Communication, Xiamen University Malaysia, Malaysia*

Ali Zahabi, King *Mongkut's University of Technology Thonburi, Bangkok, Thailand*

Wang Mengyao, *School of Communication, Xiamen University Malaysia, Malaysia*

Wu Yushan, *School of Communication and Journalism, The University of Hong Kong (HKU), Hong Kong*

Adam Kah Jjin Wee, *Department of Psychology, School of Medical and Life Science, Sunway University, Malaysia*

Zhou Xianon, *School of Communication, Xiamen University Malaysia, Malaysia*

C.V. Suresh Babu, *Hindustan Institute of Technology and Science, India*

Wen Wenxi, *School of Communication, Xiamen University Malaysia, Malaysia*

Imedla Abas, *Shinawatra International University, Thailand*

Lan Lan, *School of Communication, Xiamen University Malaysia, Malaysia*

Table of Contents

Detailed Table of Contents

Preface

INTRODUCTION

In recent years, artificial intelligence has rapidly transformed numerous aspects of healthcare delivery, research, and patient experience. From diagnostic algorithms to personalized treatment recommendations, from virtual health assistants to automated medical documentation systems, AI technologies are reshaping how health information is created, distributed, consumed, and applied. This transformation brings unprecedented opportunities for improving healthcare outcomes, increasing accessibility, and enhancing efficiency. However, it simultaneously raises profound questions about information integrity, ethical implementation, cultural appropriateness, and psychological impacts.

Due to the rapid technological advancement and digital transformation, the intersection of artificial intelligence and healthcare represents one of the most promising yet challenging frontiers of modern medicine. While technological capabilities advance at a remarkable speed, our frameworks for ensuring these technologies genuinely serve human needs often lag behind. Therefore, the multifaceted challenges and opportunities at the intersection of artificial intelligence and health information should be investigated by bringing together perspectives from diverse disciplines, including healthcare, psychology, ethics, cultural studies, and information science.

Organization of the Book

The book is organized into seven chapters that explore different dimensions of AI's impact on health information ecosystems. These chapters provide a multifaceted examination of how artificial intelligence is transforming health information landscapes and how we might navigate these changes in ways that prioritize human wellbeing, ethical integrity, and equitable access across diverse populations and contexts.

Chapter 1. The "Artificial Intelligence Integration in the Medical Tourism: Medical Breakthroughs: Are We Truly Progressing?" chapter explores how AI technologies are reshaping the landscape of medical tourism. From surgical robots and blockchain to virtual reality and genomics, the chapter investigates transformative trends in cross-border healthcare. While acknowledging the potential benefits of these technologies for improving access to care, the authors raise critical questions about whether technological advances represent genuine progress in patient outcomes, discussing important regulatory, privacy, and ethical considerations.

Chapter 2. This chapter, "Emotionally Intelligent AI - Redefining Wellness in the Digital Age", explores the emerging field of emotional AI and its potential to transform how we understand, monitor, and promote emotional wellness. It examines how these systems can provide real-time emotional support, personalized therapy recommendations, and intelligent self-care guidance. Importantly, the chapter also addresses significant challenges including mental health stigma, privacy concerns, and cross-cultural emotional contexts, while considering the appropriate balance between AI assistance and irreplaceable human therapeutic connections.

Chapter 3. This chapter, "Ethical Considerations in AI-Powered Health Communities to Promote Good Health and Wellbeing: A Narrative Review", employs a narrative review methodology to explore the diverse landscape of AI-powered health communities. It examines their varied functionalities and purposes while identifying key ethical challenges raised by developers, experts, and community participants. The chapter evaluates existing regulatory frameworks governing AI in healthcare, highlighting gaps and opportunities for improvement, and concludes with recommendations for ethical development and implementation of AI in health communities.

Chapter 4. This chapter, "Disinformation through AI", proposes a conceptual model based on dual processes theory that explains why individuals may be susceptible to AI-generated health misinformation. By examining factors at individual, AI, and contextual levels, the authors provide insights into vulnerabilities that make people susceptible to mis- and disinformation from AI systems. The chapter discusses how factors such as trust in AI, AI literacy, analytical mindset, and time pressure influence susceptibility, concluding with practical, legal, and ethical implications.

Chapter 5. This chapter, "Cultural Competence in AI-Driven Health Information", highlights the essential importance of cultural knowledge in creating truly inclusive health information systems. The chapter identifies obstacles including bias, cultural barriers, and dataset heterogeneity that can undermine equitable implementation of AI in healthcare. The authors argue that ensuring cultural competence in AI systems is not merely beneficial but essential for fair and impartial treatment across diverse populations.

Chapter 6. In "From Humans to Humans: Designing Human-centered AI for Better Healthcare", the authors present qualitative case studies of innovative AI healthcare systems including AIDI, SepsisLab, BrainGate, and Neuralink. Through these examples, they illustrate how AI algorithms can learn from human inputs and collaborate with healthcare professionals to deliver more accurate and efficient care. The chapter advocates for AI's evolution from being merely designed by humans to becoming truly human-centered in its approach to healthcare transformation.

Chapter 7. In "Cyberchondria in the Age of Online Health Information", the phenomenon where internet searches for health information paradoxically increase anxiety rather than alleviate concerns was examined. The authors provide a comprehensive overview of cyberchondria, including demographic insights into its prevalence, conceptualization, and psychological impact. The chapter explores factors influencing the development of cyberchondria and discusses potential coping strategies, emphasizing the importance of health education and digital literacy in empowering individuals to use online health resources effectively.

Chapter 8. This chapter, "Timeliness and Appropriateness of Cross-Sectional Study Design in the Study of Online Health Information Seeking Using AI," emphasizes the growing use of AI tools like ChatGPT and Gemini for health consultation, reflecting a shift in how people seek health information. It proposes a cross-sectional study design to explore key factors such as perceived trust, motivation, and satisfaction. A conceptual framework, combining the Planned Risk Information Seeking Model and the Health Belief Model, is introduced to examine how perceived trust, motivation, and perceived accuracy influence users' behavioral intentions in using AI-generated health information.

Acknowledgment

We extend our heartfelt gratitude to the reviewers for their constructive comments. Their thoughtful suggestions and meticulous feedback have been instrumental in shaping and enhancing the quality of the chapters. We deeply appreciate the time and effort they dedicated to the review process, and we are confident that the final work has been significantly strengthened thanks to their invaluable contributions.

Introduction

The integration of Artificial Intelligence (AI) into healthcare represents a paradigm shift, promising to democratize medical access, personalize treatment, and redefine wellness in the digital age. Yet, as this book argues, the transformative power of AI hinges not on its technological sophistication alone, but on our ability to navigate its ethical, cultural, and societal complexities with equal rigor. *Navigating Health Information in the Age of Artificial Intelligence* interrogates this duality, weaving together diverse perspectives—from the ethics of AI-driven health communities to the psychological risks of cyberchondria, to chart a path where innovation aligns with equity, accountability, and human dignity.

At its core, this book confronts a pressing tension: while AI holds immense potential to bridge healthcare disparities, its unregulated adoption risks amplifying existing inequities. For instance, AI-powered tools in medical tourism (**Chapter 1**) promise global access to cutting-edge care through robotic surgery and telemedicine, yet they also raise urgent questions about data sovereignty and the commodification of health. Similarly, emotionally intelligent AI systems (**Chapter 2)** offer revolutionary mental health support but risk depersonalizing care if deployed without safeguards for cultural nuance and human connection. These examples illustrate a recurring theme: technological progress must be tempered by ethical foresight.

Central to this discourse are the ethical foundations of AI. **Chapter 3** exposes vulnerabilities in AI-powered health communities, where algorithmic bias and opaque data governance threaten patient autonomy and trust. These challenges are compounded by AI's role in spreading disinformation (**Chapter 4**), which exploits cognitive biases and information overload to distort public health narratives. Parallel to these risks, **Chapter 5** underscores how culturally incompetent AI systems—trained on homogeneous datasets—perpetuate diagnostic inaccuracies for marginalized groups, exacerbating systemic inequities. Together, these chapters reveal a critical truth: without inclusive design and transparent governance, AI risks replicating the very disparities it seeks to resolve.

Yet, the book also highlights pathways to responsible innovation. Human-centered AI (**Chapter 6**), exemplified by platforms like AIDI and SepsisLab, demonstrates how collaboration between clinicians and algorithms can enhance diagnostic accuracy while preserving the irreplaceable empathy of human care. Meanwhile, **Chapter 7** reframes cyberchondria—a byproduct of AI-driven health searches—as a call to action for digital literacy, advocating for tools that empower users to critically engage with online health information. These solutions are grounded in methodological rigor: **Chapter 8** argues for cross-sectional studies to decode user behavior, ensuring AI systems align with societal values and needs.

Ultimately, this compilation transcends a mere examination of AI's capabilities. It positions cultural competence, ethical governance, and human-AI collaboration not as optional considerations, but as foundational pillars for equitable healthcare. By interrogating AI's role in medical tourism, disinformation, emotional wellness, and beyond, the book challenges stakeholders—developers, policymakers, clinicians, and users—to reimagine progress. True advancement lies not in replacing human judgment with automation, but in designing systems that amplify our collective capacity for care, critical thinking, and compassion.

As AI reshapes the future of health information, this book serves as both a cautionary lens and a visionary guide. It urges readers to confront uncomfortable questions: Who benefits from AI's efficiencies? Who bears the risks? And how do we ensure that the digital age of healthcare uplifts, rather than excludes, the most vulnerable? By weaving together ethical inquiry, cultural critique, and pragmatic solutions, *Navigating Health Information in the Age of Artificial Intelligence* charts a course where technology serves not as a master, but as a partner in the timeless pursuit of health and wellbeing for all.

Chapter 1
Artificial Intelligence Integration in Medical Tourism:
Medical Breakthroughs – Are We Truly Progressing?

Wasswa Shafik
https://orcid.org/0000-0002-9320-3186
Dig Connectivity Research Laboratory (DCRLab), Kampala, Uganda & School of Digital Science, Universiti Brunei Darussalam, Brunei

ABSTRACT

This study explores the future of medical tourism (MT) through the lens of evolving artificial intelligence (AI) technologies, recognizing their profound impact on healthcare. From medical devices and the Internet of Things (IoT) to AI integration, the study examines transformative trends in diagnosis, decision support, and personalized medicine. It scrutinizes technologies like surgery robots, automation, blockchain, virtual and augmented reality, and genomics. Promising the potential of distant healthcare solutions like medical wearables and telemedicine, the study underscores their role in improving access to care are presented. Regulatory, privacy and ethical considerations are addressed, emphasizing the need for ongoing research and robust legislation to unlock the full potential of these technologies in shaping the future landscape of medical tourism.

DOI: 10.4018/979-8-3693-5837-5.ch001

INTRODUCTION

Healthcare and technology integration presents a dynamic environment where the effectiveness of Artificial Intelligence[1] (AI) emerges as a powerful catalyst for change in the field of medical tourism[2,3] (MT) (Rodríguez et al., 2023; Alaziz et al., 2023). The emerging discipline of cross-border healthcare, wherein individuals seek medical services across their national boundaries, recognizes the crucial role of AI in improving patient experiences and outcomes (Yoo et al., 2023). In addition to fostering innovation, AI plays a transformative role in the field of healthcare by fundamentally altering the way healthcare services are delivered. This includes enhancing the processes of diagnoses, treatment planning, and improving the accessibility of patient care. This research investigates the various applications of AI and highlights its potential to significantly transform medical decision-making processes, enhance diagnostic precision, and empower patients on a worldwide scale (Heinz et al., 2023; Fahim et al., 2023). The increasing demand for MT necessitates the integration of AI to ensure the provision of high-quality healthcare services across different geographical locations (Shafk, 2023).

This study investigates the implications of AI-driven medical devices, sensors, and the Internet of Things (IoT) on patient monitoring, safety, and healthcare quality, with a particular focus on the influence of real-time data (Jun et al., 2021). Comprehending these complexities is essential for comprehending how artificial intelligence functions as a catalyst for individualized, patient-centered healthcare (Maulida & Marlina, 2023). The present study aims to examine the profound effects of robotics and automation on surgical procedures, therapeutic interventions, and senior care. Specifically, the focus is on exploring how these technological advancements contribute to improved precision and accelerated recovery periods (Akhavan et al., 2023; Kalinaki et al., 2023). AI offers a comprehensive patient experience, encompassing diagnosis, treatment, and post-treatment care, which is particularly advantageous for individuals seeking efficient medical interventions as medical tourists (Mason et al., 2023).

The significance of blockchain technology[4] in the context of MT is subject to critical examination, with particular emphasis placed on its potential to enhance data security, interoperability, and patient privacy. The applications of virtual and augmented reality in the context of pain management and mental health therapies for those seeking medical treatment abroad (Karadayi-Usta & Serdarasan, 2023; Matinkhah et al., 2019). The integration of genomics and precision medicine, facilitated by genome sequencing, presents personalized healthcare solutions that are in line with the objectives of MT, which seeks to provide state-of-the-art therapies (Kusuma et al., 2023). The potential of emerging technologies such as telemedicine, wearables, and mobile health applications is being investigated to improve access to healthcare and effectively manage chronic illnesses (Wright & Zascerinska, 2023).

Figure 1. Global medical tourism market size, by year, 2023-2032 (Source: precedence research)

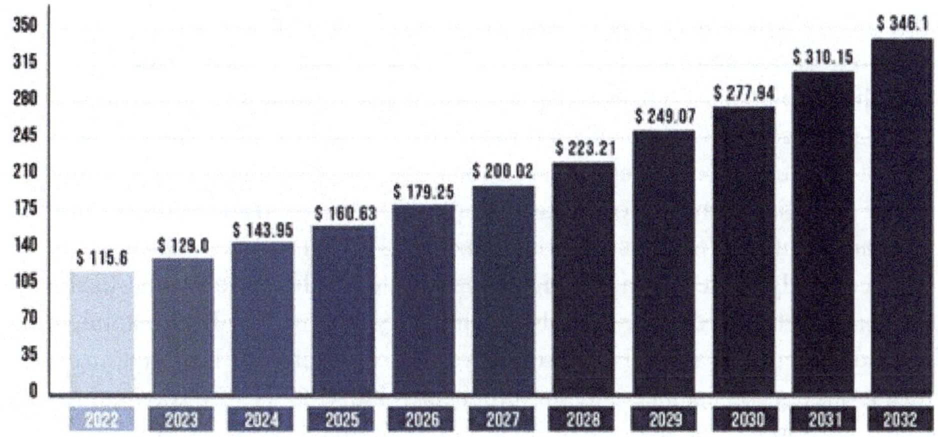

Figure 2. Global medical tourism market size per treatment

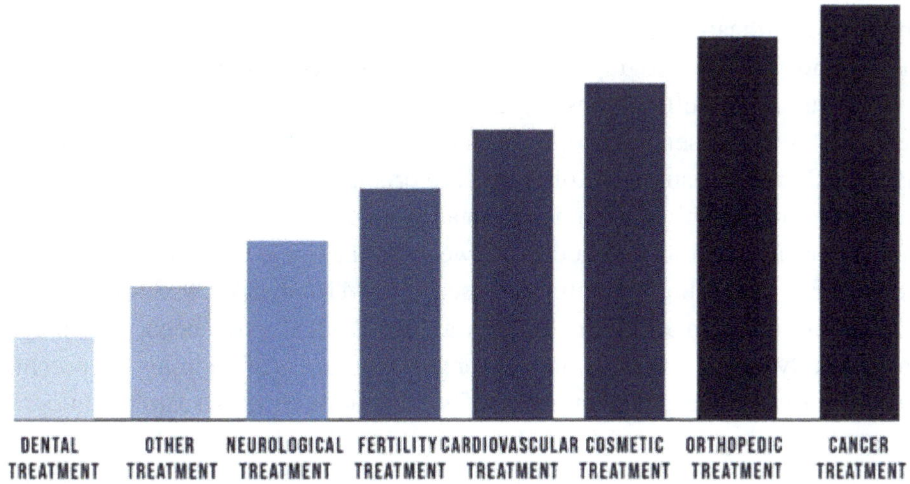

The applications of virtual reality[5] (VR) and augmented reality[6] (AR) in pain management and mental health therapies for those seeking medical treatment abroad. Figure 1 and Figure 2 demonstrate the global MT size by year and treatments that are most sought after as of 2020, respectively (Rodríguez et al., 2023; Shafik, 2023a). VR simulations and AR interventions present novel opportunities to improve the overall welfare of patients who are navigating the intricate realm of MT. These technologies surpass conventional medical interventions by prioritizing the psychological and emotional dimensions of patient care, thereby fostering a more comprehensive approach to healthcare for patients from across the world (Yoo et al., 2023). The significance of this matter is particularly pronounced within the realm of MT, as personalized interventions that are informed by genetic profiles have the potential to provide overseas patients with advanced and highly customized healthcare solutions (Shafik, 2023b; Heinz et al., 2023).

Concurrently, the research investigates nascent technologies for remote healthcare, encompassing telemedicine, wearable technology, and mobile health applications. These advancements are poised to improve the availability of healthcare services, offering ongoing assistance and surveillance to individuals who travel abroad for medical purposes, even upon their repatriation (Zeng et al., 2023; Shafik, 2023c). This study explores the various technologies available and examines their potential in effectively managing chronic illnesses and addressing the issue of limited healthcare access in different geographical areas (Dávila-Aragón & Arrioja-Castrejón, 2021). The advancement of MT is accompanied by the incorporation of telemedicine and wearable technology, which facilitates the ongoing connection between patients and their healthcare providers, thus promoting a seamless continuum of treatment that extends beyond geographical boundaries (Khaksar Shahmirzadi et al., 2022).

The pursuit of fully harnessing the capabilities of AI within the realm of MT necessitates the presence of continuous research, collaborative efforts, and aggressive legislative measures, all of which are crucial catalysts (Dalkıran, 2023). The study continues by highlighting the dynamic character of the industry, underlining the importance of the interaction between sophisticated technology and ethical frameworks in molding the future landscape of MT (Shafik, 2023d; Zhang & Sun, 2019). This transformation aims to create a technologically advanced, patient-centric, and ethically sound environment. The ongoing progress of AI holds the potential to significantly transform the landscape of MT by facilitating its seamless integration, thereby reshaping the provision of healthcare on a worldwide level (Na et al., 2017).

The Contribution of the Chapter

The following are the contributions of the chapter as summarized below:

- Define the function of AI in the broader healthcare sector and discuss the specific issues and potential AI provides in the context of MT.
- This response aims to elucidate diverse uses of AI within the MT business. These applications encompass individualized treatment plans, predictive analytics, virtual consultations, language translation, and more functionalities.
- Present specific instances and empirical analyses to exemplify the pragmatic application of AI within the realm of MT.
- This analysis aims to assess the advantages that AI offers in the context of MT, specifically focusing on the enhancements it provides to patient outcomes, cost optimization, and the overall quality of care.
- This discourse will examine the obstacles associated with the implementation of AI in a given setting. These challenges encompass ethical considerations, data security concerns, and potential limitations of AI technology.
- Incorporate concrete instances wherein AI has been effectively assimilated into the realm of MT, conduct a comprehensive analysis of the outcomes, and derive significant lessons from these particular examples.
- The study further explores the growing trends in AI and their potential implications for the future of MT and examines the ramifications for healthcare providers as well as patients.
- Finally, the study aims to analyze the current regulatory frameworks that regulate the implementation of AI in the healthcare sector and its application in MT and examine the significance of ethical rules and adherence to international standards.

The Organization of the Chapter

The rest of this study is structured as follows. Section 2 presents the contextualization of AI in MT, explaining the role of AI in the broader healthcare landscape. Section 3 presents the applications of AI in MT, detailing numerous applications of AI in the MT sector, for example, predictive analytics, personalized treatment plans, virtual consultations, language translation, and more. Section 4 presents the benefits and challenges encamped with MT, like improved patient outcomes, cost optimization, and enhanced quality of care, and discusses the challenges, including data security, ethical considerations, and potential limitations of AI in this MT context. Section 5 includes practical examples of how AI has been efficaciously integrated into MT practices. Section 6 discusses the emerging research trends in AI and their potential influence on the future of MT. Section 7 examines the existing regulatory frameworks leading AI in healthcare and MT and discusses the reputation of ethical guidelines and compliance with international standards. Section 8 presents the conclusion of the chapter.

CONTEXTUALIZING AI IN MEDICAL TOURISM

The integration of AI is revolutionizing the practice of medical tourism, which involves seeking healthcare services outside of one's own country. The convergence mentioned holds significant potential for enhancing patient experiences, enhancing treatment outcomes, and optimizing healthcare logistics (Dalkıran, 2023). The emergence of AI plays a pivotal role in the advancement of MT, facilitating the intricate aspects of delivering healthcare services on a worldwide scale. This phenomenon signifies a fundamental change in perspective, wherein technology and the endeavor for well-being become intricately interconnected on a worldwide level (Dávila-Aragón & Arrioja-Castrejón, 2021).

Through the analysis of extensive datasets, artificial intelligence algorithms are able to identify complex patterns within the medical histories and genetic information of patients. This enables the customization of treatment programs to cater to the specific needs of each individual (Ananya, 2021). For example, the utilization of AI in diagnostic procedures enables the examination of an individual's genetic composition, hence facilitating the implementation of precision medicine strategies that specifically address the underlying factors contributing to certain diseases. This not only improves health outcomes but also establishes MT as a leading provider of specialized and personalized care to a diverse worldwide clientele (Ryndach et al., 2021).

One of the primary obstacles encountered in the field of MT involves the need to surmount language difficulties and establish efficient communication channels between patients and healthcare providers (Na et al., 2016; Shafik, 2024a)—AI, equipped with sophisticated language translation capabilities, functions as a linguistic intermediary. Real-time translation services, such as those provided by platforms like Google Translate, along with specialized healthcare-specific translation tools, play a crucial role in enabling smooth communication and promoting trust and comprehension between patients and medical personnel in various linguistic environments (Seow et al., 2017). The prioritization of language inclusivity is of utmost importance to improve the accessibility and attractiveness of MT on a worldwide level.

The utilization of AI in conjunction with predictive analytics has brought about a significant transformation in the decision-making process for those seeking medical treatment abroad (Shafik, 2024b). Through the examination of several elements, including previous treatment outcomes, financial considerations, and potential hazards, AI assists individuals in forecasting the probable efficacy of medical operations and enhancing their travel arrangements (Dalkıran, 2023). One illustration of the application of predictive analytics tools is their capacity to evaluate the likelihood of favorable treatment outcomes by analyzing patient profiles, thereby facilitating the making of well-informed decisions (Bhargava et al., 2023; Shafik, 2024b). The utilization of foresight in decision-making processes has a transformative effect, offering a valuable instrument for medical tourists as they navigate intricate options within a progressively globalized healthcare landscape (Zhang & Sun, 2019).

The AI application in virtual health consultations has significantly transformed the nature of pre-travel and post-treatment exchanges. Patients partake in telemedicine consultations with healthcare professionals, facilitating the opportunity to deliberate therapy alternatives, address any apprehensions, and obtain subsequent care without the need for in-person interaction (De Carlo et al., 2021). The utilization of AI-driven telemedicine platforms, such as Teladoc and Doctor on Demand, is facilitating the enhancement of medical expertise accessibility, particularly for individuals involved in MT (Ryndach et al., 2021). The utilization of AI in healthcare delivery not only improves accessibility for medical tourists but also plays a significant role in ensuring the continuity and comprehensiveness of care. This highlights the revolutionary capabilities of AI in the healthcare sector (Khaksar Shahmirzadi et al., 2022).

The consideration of costs plays a crucial role in the decision-making process of MT, and the analytical skills of AI can be used for financial elements, assisting patients in the planning and optimization of their MT journeys (Hassan & Bellos, 2022). Through the provision of precise cost projections and the recommendation of optimization measures, AI plays a crucial role in promoting transparency and facilitating financial readiness. For example, artificial intelligence algorithms examine past cost data pertaining to specific operations and incorporate other factors, like travel charges and hotel costs, in order to generate precise estimations (Subasinghe et al., 2020; Shafik, 2024c). The enhanced analytical capabilities of MT contribute to its attractiveness for those in search of affordable and superior healthcare options.

Quality assurance is of utmost importance within the global realm of MT, and AI assumes a crucial role in upholding and overseeing healthcare standards. AI plays a significant role in promoting compliance with international accreditation standards in healthcare institutions (Arrioja-Castrejón et al., 2023). This is demonstrated through the implementation of systems that effectively monitor and analyze various indicators related to healthcare quality. The provision of transparency in healthcare services instills a sense of trust and assurance among individuals seeking medical treatment abroad, as it guarantees the anticipated level of care and its quality (Hassan & Bellos, 2022). Consequently, AI has emerged as an essential instrument for creating and maintaining a universal benchmark of quality in the provision of healthcare services across international boundaries (Shafik, 2024e).

The incorporation of AI within the field of MT necessitates a meticulous examination of the ethical ramifications. The maintenance of trust necessitates the prioritization of data security, privacy and the appropriate utilization of AI technologies (Beladi et al., 2023). One key aspect involves the rigorous adherence to data protection standards and the full communication regarding the utilization of patient data. Proactively addressing ethical problems is of utmost importance in maintaining the harmonious relationship between AI and the field of MT (Karadayi-Usta & Serdarasan, 2023). This approach is essential for establishing a framework that is both technologically advanced and ethically robust. By effectively addressing these ethical problems, the collaboration between AI and MT can flourish, thereby guaranteeing a sustainable and socially accountable trajectory for the field of global healthcare (Yoo et al., 2023; Shafik & Kalinaki, 2023).

The synergistic interaction between AI and MT represents a significant turning point in the field of global healthcare (Balasubrahmanyam & Prasad, 2024; Beladi et al., 2023). With the ongoing evolution of technology, the role of AI becomes increasingly crucial in providing healthcare solutions that are not only accessible but also tailored to individual needs and of high quality. The integration of AI and MT holds considerable promise in reshaping healthcare paradigms, surpassing the limitations imposed by geographical boundaries (Seow et al., 2018). The seamless incorporation of various components is of utmost importance when considering the increasing need for healthcare services on a worldwide level. As society progresses into the future, the dynamic relationship between AI and MT emerges as a crucial factor in facilitating unparalleled levels of healthcare accessibility, fostering innovation, and providing individualized care (Zhang & Sun, 2019; Wang et al., 2023). Consequently, this symbiotic interaction has the potential to significantly improve the overall well-being of those who seek medical treatments across international borders.

As the progression of this synergy continues, its influence goes beyond the immediate enhancements in patient care. The integration of the practice of MT presents an opportunity to reshape the healthcare industry, combining the utilization of data-driven analysis, precision medicine, and ethical considerations (Kumar et al., 2023). The continuous discourse among technology developers, healthcare providers, and policymakers will play a crucial role in effectively leveraging the capabilities of AI in the field of MT while ensuring responsible implementation (Pereira et al., 2022; Zhao et al., 2023). By cultivating a setting that prioritizes transparency, patient autonomy, and data security, we can guarantee the sustained success of this transformative collaboration, advancing the progression of MT into a domain where state-of-the-art technology converges with empathetic and personalized patient care on a truly worldwide level (Seow et al., 2022). The potential trajectory of MT, influenced by the advancements in artificial intelligence, presents the prospect of a healthcare experience that is more interconnected, readily available, and focused on the needs of patients (Shafik, 2024k).

Figure 3. Contextualizing artificial intelligence in medical tourism

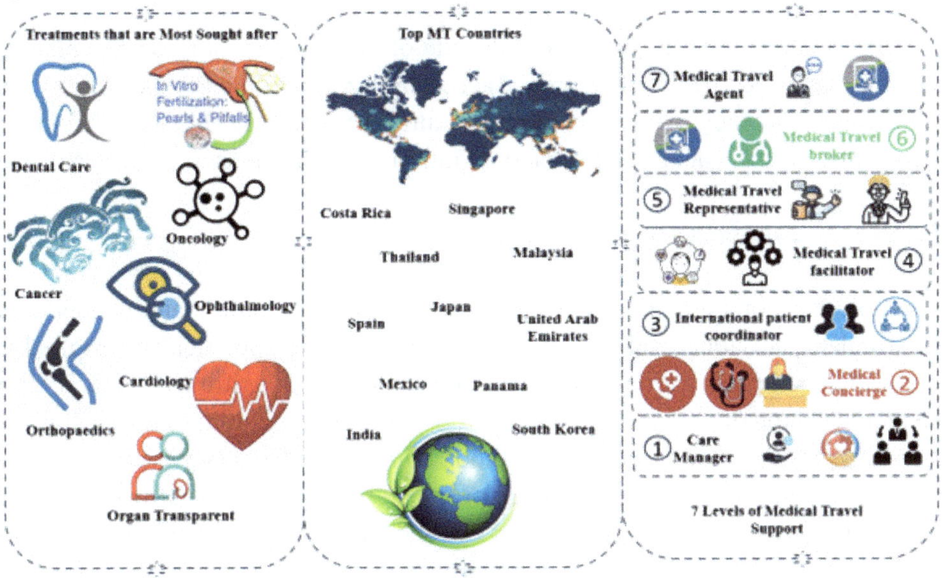

The process of contextualizing AI in the realm of MT entails acknowledging the distinct obstacles and potential advantages that emerge when AI interacts with the worldwide domain of healthcare travel, as demonstrated in Figure 3. Within the domain of MT, which is distinguished by the movement of patients across national borders and the presence of varied healthcare systems, AI catalyzes significant change (Khaksar Shahmirzadi et al., 2022). One of the difficulties that this solution tackles is the issue of language barriers. It achieves this by offering sophisticated translation services, which in turn enables smooth and effective communication between healthcare personnel and patients. The utilization of AI in the field of predictive analytics plays a significant role in enabling medical tourists to make well-informed selections by evaluating various criteria, for example, treatment outcomes and cost concerns (Xiaoling & Xuan, 2022). In addition, AI plays a significant role in upholding quality standards and meeting international certification requirements within healthcare institutions, thereby promoting transparency and encouraging trust (Pereira et al., 2022). The contextualization underscores the significant impact of AI in augmenting the effectiveness, availability, and individualized aspects of MT at a worldwide level (Shafik, 2024d).

APPLICATIONS OF AI IN MEDICAL TOURISM

AI in medical tourism yields a multitude of benefits, encompassing enhanced decision-making capabilities, improved accessibility, individualized patient care, and heightened efficiency in the provision of healthcare services. This section explains these benefits, specifically with practical rationale in the smart medical process.

Personalized Treatment Plans

AI utilizes comprehensive datasets, such as medical records and genetic data, to formulate individualized treatment strategies that are specifically designed for each patient. AI plays a crucial role in aiding healthcare practitioners by facilitating the identification of patterns and correlations, ultimately enabling the development of accurate and personalized care methods (Hu, 2022). This approach guarantees that individuals who engage in MT are provided with tailored healthcare services, thereby maximizing the effectiveness of treatments and fulfilling their unique health requirements (Zhang & Sun, 2019). Tailored interventions have the potential to help patients by decreasing the probability of adverse reactions and enhancing the overall effectiveness of therapies.

Predictive Analytics

AI algorithms forecast health outcomes and evaluate several elements, thereby assisting both patients and healthcare providers in making well-informed decisions regarding medical procedures and travel arrangements. By means of data analysis, AI offers predictive insights into the prospective efficacy of therapies and the corresponding hazards (Hassan & Bellos, 2022). Predictive insights offer significant advantages to medical tourists, as they effectively mitigate potential hazards and enhance the overall efficacy of treatments, all while streamlining their travel arrangements. This predictive capability promotes decision-making, enabling a more efficient and personalized healthcare experience (Shafik, Tufail, et al., 2024).

Virtual Medical Consultations

AI-driven telemedicine technologies enable remote consultations, enabling patients to interact with healthcare practitioners for pre-travel guidance, post-treatment monitoring, and continuous healthcare (Khaksar Shahmirzadi et al., 2022). These systems frequently integrate chatbots and virtual assistants to enhance communication efficiency. Enhanced accessibility, ease, and continuity of healthcare services, facilitating medical tourists' ability to seek consultations with specialized healthcare professionals, irrespective of geographical limitations. Virtual health consultations have been found to improve the overall patient experience by providing healthcare contacts that are both timely and convenient (Hassan & Bellos, 2022).

Language Translation Services

AI-powered language translation services can transcend language obstacles, hence facilitating effective communication between healthcare providers and patients within the varied environment of MT (Pereira et al., 2022). Sophisticated algorithms accurately translate medical information. Improved communication plays a crucial role in cultivating trust, promoting comprehension, and facilitating the precise transmission of medical information, hence leading to enhanced patient safety and satisfaction (Liu et al., 2022). The utilization of language translation services effectively addresses linguistic barriers, hence fostering a healthcare environment that is more inclusive and conducive to patient satisfaction (Shafik, 2024f).

Cost Predictions and Optimization

The AI-enabled system does a comprehensive analysis of many cost elements associated with MT visits, encompassing charges related to medical procedures, travel, and housing (Hu, 2022). It offers precise cost projections and optimization tactics to enhance the efficiency and effectiveness of such excursions. Predictive modeling plays a crucial role in the realm of expense forecasting and the provision of recommendations for cost-efficient options. Patients strategically plan and allocate resources in a manner that fosters transparency and financial readiness, hence potentially mitigating the overall expenses associated with healthcare (Kumar et al., 2023). The utilization of AI-driven algorithms for cost forecasts provides medical tourists with the capacity to make financially educated decisions, hence improving the overall affordability of healthcare services (Dávila-Aragón & Arrioja-Castrejón, 2021).

Figure 4. AI application merits in medical tourism

Diagnostic Assistance

AI technology, such as machine learning algorithms, enhances the diagnostic accuracy of healthcare professionals in the field of medicine (Seow et al., 2022). The algorithms perform an analysis of medical imaging and clinical data with the purpose of assisting in the process of making diagnostic decisions. Enhancements in diagnostic precision have the potential to result in more efficient and prompt treatments, hence augmenting the overall healthcare quality for individuals seeking medical services abroad (Na et al., 2016). The attainment of precise and prompt diagnoses has a crucial role in enhancing patient outcomes and facilitating the timely implementation of suitable medical therapies, as presented in Figure 4.

Robotic Surgery

AI-powered robotic surgical systems have been shown to improve the accuracy and effectiveness of surgical procedures, hence providing enhanced treatment alternatives. Frequently, these technologies integrate machine learning algorithms to facilitate dynamic adaptations in real-time throughout surgical procedures (Li et al., 2023). The enhancement of surgical precision has the potential to result in expedited recovery periods, diminished occurrences of complications, and enhanced overall results for individuals who engage in MT with the intention of undergoing specialized surgical procedures (Seow et al., 2018). Robotic surgical systems have been shown to enhance the safety and efficacy of surgical procedures, hence contributing to an improved overall patient experience (Shafik, 2024f).

Health Monitoring Devices

AI-driven health monitoring systems are capable of remotely tracking patients' vital signs and health parameters. These devices frequently utilize machine learning algorithms for the purpose of analyzing data and identifying anomalies (Karadayi-Usta & Serdarasan, 2023). Following the completion of treatment, individuals who engage in MT have the potential to derive advantages from continuous monitoring, enabling healthcare professionals to swiftly respond in the event of any complications (Wright & Zascerinska, 2023). Continuous health monitoring plays a vital role in improving post-treatment care, as it adopts a proactive stance toward identifying and managing potential health issues, hence safeguarding the overall well-being of medical tourists (Beladi et al., 2023).

Quality Assurance and Accreditation

AI plays a significant role in the monitoring and maintenance of healthcare facilities in MT destinations, hence guaranteeing adherence to international standards and accreditation criteria. AI-enabled systems possess the capability to assess a wide range of quality measures and indicators (Rodríguez et al., 2023). The provision of increased openness and assurance for individuals seeking medical treatment abroad is beneficial, as it allows them to make informed decisions by selecting healthcare facilities that adhere to or beyond established standards of quality (Yoo et al., 2023). The implementation of AI in quality assurance processes plays a significant role in promoting a consistent and superior healthcare encounter, hence cultivating confidence and contentment among individuals seeking medical treatment abroad (Heinz et al., 2023).

Data Security and Privacy

AI is involved in the mitigation of data security and privacy issues, hence guaranteeing the responsible and secure utilization of patient data. AI-assisted cybersecurity systems provide the capability to identify and proactively mitigate possible risks to the confidentiality and integrity of patient data (Kusuma et al., 2023). The establishment of robust safeguards for patient data is crucial in fostering trust and instilling confidence in the utilization of AI technologies within the realm of MT. This, in turn, plays a pivotal role in promoting the ethical and responsible deployment of such tools (Mason et al., 2023). Stringent data security protocols are used to ensure the protection of sensitive medical data, hence upholding the confidentiality and accuracy of patient records within the realm of MT (Yoo et al., 2023).

Genetic Counseling and Genomic Medicine

AI plays a significant role in the field of genomic medicine through its ability to analyze extensive genetic databases, enabling the identification of predispositions and potential inherited risks (Akhavan et al., 2023). Furthermore, genetic counseling platforms that utilize artificial intelligence offer tailored perspectives on an individual's genetic composition, facilitating informed decision-making for both patients and healthcare professionals (Shafik, 2024c). The utilization of modern genetic tests in MT can offer significant advantages to individuals seeking individualized preventative and treatment options (Maulida & Marlina, 2023). The integration of AI into genomic medicine has significantly advanced the comprehension of hereditary disorders, thereby empowering patients to make informed decisions that are in accordance with their genetic profiles (Beladi et al., 2023).

Patient Education and Engagement

AI-driven educational systems offer medical tourists a complete range of information pertaining to their medical issues, available treatment alternatives, and post-treatment care. Chatbots and virtual assistants have been found to significantly boost patient engagement by providing tailored health advice and addressing inquiries (Kusuma et al., 2023). There are several advantages to consider. Enhancing patient comprehension of medical problems and treatment protocols facilitates increased engagement in healthcare decision-making. The utilization of AI-driven patient education facilitates a heightened sense of empowerment, hence promoting a proactive approach among medical tourists in the management of their healthcare (Mason et al., 2023).

Post-Treatment Follow-up and Monitoring

AI further facilitates post-treatment care through the remote monitoring of patient recovery. This entails the examination of data derived from wearable devices, patient-reported outcomes, and several other sources to monitor the progression of recovery and detect potential issues (Yoo et al., 2023). Continuous post-treatment monitoring confers advantages upon medical tourists by facilitating prompt intervention in the event of difficulties. AI improves the efficacy of post-treatment care by facilitating prompt provision of assistance and modifications to patients' treatment regimens, hence enhancing overall efficiency (Heinz et al., 2023). Based on the explained benefits and application of AI in MT, it has some challenges and limitations, as presented in the next section.

CHALLENGES AND LIMITATIONS OF MEDICAL TOURISM

Addressing these problems necessitates a collective endeavor, including various stakeholders, such as healthcare providers, legislators, and industry participants, to establish uniform protocols, improve communication, and guarantee the ethical and secure provision of medical healthcare services across international boundaries.

Cultural Sensitivity and Patient Expectations

Cultural disparities in healthcare practices might potentially result in misinterpretations or unfulfilled patient anticipations, particularly concerning treatment modalities, bedside etiquette, and recovery prognoses (Xu et al., 2023). The experience of MT can be negatively impacted by patient unhappiness and the misalignment of expectations, leading to a decrease in overall satisfaction. The implementation of cultural sensitivity training for healthcare personnel, together with the provision of detailed information to patients regarding cultural subtleties in their desired destination, has the potential to foster greater understanding and promote alignment of expectations (Ediansyah et al., 2023). Effective communication channels can also play a crucial role in the management of patient expectations.

Currency Fluctuations and Financial Risks

The volatility of currency exchange rates can have significant implications on the overall expenses associated with medical treatments, hence presenting financial uncertainties for both patients and healthcare providers. The presence of financial uncertainty has the potential to dissuade prospective medical tourists, hence impacting the affordability and appeal of destinations for MT (Bovsh et al., 2023). The implementation of transparent pricing structures, the provision of financial counseling services, and the exploration of currency-hedging possibilities can effectively limit financial risks for both patients and healthcare providers. Effective communication of future fluctuations in costs is crucial for the purpose of managing and aligning expectations (Thoo et al., 2018).

Limited Availability of Specialized Treatments

Certain MT destinations may have limited availability of specialist therapies or knowledge for rare or difficult medical diseases. The search for appropriate venues might pose difficulties for patients seeking specialist care, constraining the extent of MT (Seow et al., 2022). Collaborative endeavors between healthcare institutions and MT organizations may encompass the establishment of alliances or networks, hence facilitating enhanced accessibility to a wider array of specialist medical interventions (Na et al., 2017). The establishment of centers of excellence facilitates the concentration of expertise within certain disciplines of medicine.

Intellectual Property and Technology Transfer

The adoption of new medical technologies in MT locations may be hindered by concerns surrounding intellectual property rights and knowledge transfer. The limited rate of implementation of state-of-the-art technology has the potential to impede the overall competitiveness and appeal of specific destinations (Hu, 2022). The establishment of collaborative partnerships and agreements that effectively tackle intellectual property issues can effectively allow the transfer of technology and experience in a manner that is advantageous to all parties involved (PATIL, 2021). Promoting activities that facilitate the exchange of knowledge can play a significant role in fostering the sustainable development of healthcare skills in destinations catering to MT (Shafik, 2024l).

Infrastructure and Accessibility Issues

Certain destinations for MT may have difficulties related to infrastructure and accessibility, which can have an impact on the convenience of travel and the overall quality of healthcare services for patients (Kumar et al., 2023). The expansion potential of MT locations may be impeded by limited infrastructure, hence impacting the quality of treatments offered. Investment in the development of infrastructure, encompassing many sectors such as transportation, lodging, and healthcare facilities, has the potential to augment the overall accessibility and desirability of a given place (Dalkıran, 2023). The collaboration between local authorities and business stakeholders can facilitate the enhancement of infrastructure (Shafik, 2025b).

Long-Term Health Record Integration

The process of integrating health records between MT destinations and patients' home countries for long-term follow-up care presents a complex and hard endeavor. The absence of a smooth integration process might lead to the fragmentation of health records, thus impacting the continuity of care and the comprehensiveness of an individual's medical history (Bhargava et al., 2023). The integration of long-term health records can be facilitated through the implementation of standardized electronic health record systems and the promotion of international cooperation aimed at secure data interchange. Participating in global health data interoperability initiatives has the potential to enhance connectivity across the healthcare ecosystem (Khaksar Shahmirzadi et al., 2022).

Medical Quality Variability

Considerable variability exists in the quality of healthcare services across different countries and facilities, hence engendering a sense of unease among medical tourists regarding the standards they are likely to face (Hu, 2022). The presence of inconsistent quality has the potential to lead to treatment outcomes that are less than optimal, resulting in unhappiness among patients. In more severe instances, it may even give rise to problems (Dalkıran, 2023). The implementation of globally recognized accrediting standards and certifications in healthcare institutions can serve as a standardized measure for ensuring quality assurance and fostering patient confidence (Shafik, 2024i).

Lack of Post-Treatment Follow-up

The coordination of post-treatment care and follow-up procedures can present difficulties, given that patients frequently return to their respective home countries. This situation may result in a potential interruption in the provision of continuous healthcare services. The absence of subsequent actions may lead to a delay in identifying difficulties or impede the efficient monitoring of the patient's recuperation (Kumar et al., 2023). The implementation of effective communication channels between healthcare providers in both the destination and home nations, facilitated by telemedicine platforms, can provide uninterrupted post-treatment care and patient data security (Shafik, Kalinaki, et al., 2024).

Insurance Coverage Challenges

A significant number of health insurance policies lack coverage for medical procedures conducted outside the country of residence, placing the onus of the entire financial load on patients. This constraint has the potential to dissuade prospective medical tourists, particularly those lacking the financial resources to afford the costs, from pursuing medical care overseas (Dávila-Aragón & Arrioja-Castrejón, 2021). By establishing partnerships with insurance companies and devising tailored insurance policies for MT, the financial accessibility of this industry can be enhanced.

Inadequate Accessibility for Vulnerable Populations

MT's accessibility may not be uniformly distributed across different socioeconomic groups, which has the potential to worsen existing gaps in healthcare. The potential for MT to exacerbate disparities in healthcare access could result in certain groups being deprived of the ability to avail themselves of medical developments (Khaksar Shahmirzadi et al., 2022). The implementation of measures aimed at ensuring fair and equal access, such as the establishment of subsidized programs for medical travel targeting underprivileged people, can effectively tackle this constraint and foster inclusiveness.

Impact on Local Healthcare Infrastructure

The surge in international patients visiting popular MT locations can potentially impose significant pressure on the local healthcare system. The local populace may encounter difficulties in obtaining healthcare treatments, potentially leading to a compromised standard of care (Liu et al., 2022). The implementation of policies aimed at fostering sustainable development in the field of MT, which encompasses strategic planning of infrastructure and capacity building, has the potential to mitigate the burden placed on local healthcare systems.

MEDICAL TOURISM CASE STUDIES

It is noteworthy that the implementation of AI in healthcare facilities exhibits variations, and obtaining precise information regarding the deployment of AI in these case studies necessitates direct communication with the respective institutions. The potential of AI in the field of MT encompasses various domains, including diagnostics, tailored medicine, language translation, virtual health consultations, and enhancements in operational efficiency (Shafik, 2025a). These apps are in line with the objectives of enhancing patient care, improving outcomes, and delivering a smooth experience for individuals seeking medical treatment abroad, as explained.

Bumrungrad International Hospital, Thailand

Bumrungrad[7], situated in the city of Bangkok, has gained a reputation for its exceptional provision of services to international patients. Medical attention is sought by patients hailing from more than 190 nations at this facility (Subasinghe et al., 2020). The ability of the hospital to attract a wide range of patients highlights Thailand's position as a leading player in the MT sector, underscoring the significance of delivering high-quality healthcare services and ensuring patient contentment. Bumrungrad Hospital has the potential to utilize AI in order to provide individualized patient care (Sakipov & Vikhnin, 2021). This can be achieved by harnessing machine learning algorithms to assess patient data and customize treatment plans accordingly. AI has the potential to improve diagnostic precision, optimize administrative procedures, and enable efficient language translation services for a wide range of foreign patients (Xiaoling & Xuan, 2022).

Apollo Hospitals, India

Apollo Hospitals[8], renowned for its extensive presence throughout India, has emerged as a prominent participant in the field of MT. The institution provides a diverse array of specialized services and has garnered a global patient base (Hassan & Bellos, 2022). The scenario underscores India's status as a prominent destination for MT, characterized by its ability to provide cost-efficient healthcare services without compromising on quality. This has resulted in attracting patients from diverse geographical locations who are in search of reasonably priced and cutting-edge medical treatments. Apollo Hospitals is considering the integration of AI into their diagnostic processes (Subasinghe et al., 2020). This integration would involve the utilization of machine learning techniques for image analysis and predictive analytics. The utilization of AI-powered chatbots or virtual assistants has the potential to increase patient relations by offering valuable insights on treatments, post-operative care, and travel-related inquiries (Subasinghe et al., 2020).

Anadolu Medical Center, Turkey

The Anadolu Medical Center[9], situated in Istanbul, has gained recognition for its extensive range of medical services. The facility has effectively drawn the interest of people from around the world who are seeking medical treatments across a range of disciplines (Akhavan et al., 2023). The case highlights Turkey's growing prominence as a destination for MT, capitalizing on its advantageous geographical position, state-of-the-art healthcare facilities, and cost-effective pricing. The potential implementation of AI in data analytics at Anadolu Medical Center improves patient outcomes and streamlines operational efficiency (Mason et al., 2023). The utilization of language translation services powered by AI could be implemented as a solution to surmount linguistic obstacles, hence facilitating efficient contact with patients from diverse cultural backgrounds.

Singapore Medical Hub

Singapore has strategically established itself as a prominent medical center[10] in the Asian region, drawing patients through its exceptional healthcare infrastructure and renowned expertise in the field of medicine. The case study of Singapore exemplifies the city-state's achievement in integrating advanced medical technologies, proficient healthcare practitioners, and a strong emphasis on enhancing patient satisfaction to attract medical tourists (Maulida & Marlina, 2023). The potential integration of AI with healthcare data analytics inside Singapore's medical hub aims to enhance patient outcomes and treatment methods (Maulida & Marlina, 2023). The utilization of AI-powered chatbots and virtual health platforms has the potential to augment patient interaction and streamline remote consultations for individuals seeking healthcare services across borders.

Medellín, Colombia - Dental Tourism

Medellín[11] has emerged as a prominent hub for dental tourism, attracting patients from North America and Europe who are in search of cost-effective yet superior dental procedures (Heinz et al., 2023). This story serves as an illustration of how particular geographical areas can develop competence in specific medical domains, such as dental treatment, and consequently draw in patients who are seeking specialized knowledge at more affordable prices. Within the realm of dental tourism, dental clinics situated in Medellín possess the potential to employ AI for various purposes like treatment planning, tailored care recommendations, and the creation of AI-powered dental diagnostic tools to augment precision in dental treatments (Heinz et al., 2023).

Mayo Clinic, United States - International Patients Program

The International Patients Program at Mayo Clinic[12], a prominent healthcare institution in the United States, is designed to accommodate individuals from other countries who are in need of specialized medical treatment (Rodríguez et al., 2023).

The Mayo Clinic case study illustrates that healthcare systems in high-cost countries, which have a longstanding reputation for medical competence, actively engage in MT as a means of capitalizing on their established status. The potential utilization of AI in research and diagnostics by the Mayo Clinic could potentially augment its medical skills (Yoo et al., 2023). The utilization of AI-driven predictive analytics has the potential to aid in the development of individualized treatment regimens, while virtual health platforms could potentially enhance the provision of remote consultations for patients residing in different countries (Shafik, Tufail, et al., 2024).

REGULATORY CONSIDERATIONS OF MEDICAL TOURISM

The ability to effectively manage and reconcile these regulatory considerations is crucial in establishing a resilient and reliable MT sector. The establishment and execution of robust regulatory frameworks that prioritize patient safety and well-being necessitate imperative cooperation among nations, international organizations, and healthcare providers, as explained.

Advertising and Marketing Practices

The establishment of regulatory monitoring pertaining to advertising and marketing techniques within the MT industry is of utmost importance in order to uphold openness and mitigate the dissemination of inaccurate or misleading information (Ryndach et al., 2021). Regulations within this domain serve the purpose of ensuring the accuracy of marketing claims and providing medical tourists with dependable information regarding the services that are accessible to them (De Carlo et al., 2021). Through the promotion of ethical advertising methods, these restrictions play a significant role in facilitating informed decision-making among medical tourists, thereby augmenting their capacity to select healthcare providers based on precise depictions of services and outcomes (Zeng et al., 2023).

Public Health and Infection Control

The implementation of regulations pertaining to public health and infection control in the context of MT is of utmost importance in safeguarding the well-being of both medical tourists and the local community. The implementation of rigorous protocols plays a significant role in mitigating the risk of disease transmission and ensuring the preservation of a secure healthcare setting (Xiaoling & Xuan, 2022). The restrictions highlight the dedication of MT destinations to emphasize the well-being of the general population and uphold stringent standards pertaining to hygiene and infection control (Shafik, 2024j).

Continuity of Care and Follow-Up

The establishment of regulatory criteria pertaining to the maintenance of care and subsequent monitoring after treatment is crucial in safeguarding the welfare of those engaging in MT. These regulations serve to enhance the efficiency of transitions between healthcare providers, thereby mitigating the potential for difficulties and guaranteeing that patients receive appropriate and prompt post-treatment care (Ananya, 2021). Through emphasizing the significance of continuous medical assistance, these regulations provide a valuable contribution to the overall experience and satisfaction of patients.

Cross-Border Data Sharing and Privacy

Within the realm of MT, regulatory frameworks play a crucial role in addressing the intricate matters pertaining to the sharing of data and privacy across national borders. The restrictions serve to protect patient information, thereby assuring adherence to data protection legislation and upholding the principle of confidentiality (Liu et al., 2022). The establishment of a delicate equilibrium that enables the essential transmission of medical data while safeguarding patient confidentiality is of utmost importance in cultivating confidence within the global healthcare framework.

Transparent Pricing and Informed Consent

The financial and ethical dimensions of MT are contingent upon the crucial regulatory concerns pertaining to transparent pricing and informed consent. These regulations require the transparent transmission of treatment expenses, thereby mitigating the risk of unforeseen financial burdens for individuals seeking medical care abroad (Liu et al., 2022). Concurrently, they guarantee that patients receive comprehensive information regarding the nature of the procedures, potential hazards, and alternative options, thus fostering shared decision-making and ethical treatment practices.

Professional Qualifications and Licensing of Healthcare Providers

Regulatory agencies are responsible for the establishment and enforcement of criteria pertaining to the professional qualifications and licensing requirements of healthcare practitioners engaged in the practice of MT (Pereira et al., 2022). These restrictions serve the purpose of guaranteeing that patients receive care from experts who possess the necessary qualifications and certifications, hence fostering confidence in the competence of the medical workforce. The prioritization of professional standards has a significant role in enhancing favorable patient outcomes, as it instills a sense of assurance among medical tourists that their medical care is being delivered by proficient healthcare practitioners possessing acknowledged credentials (Khaksar Shahmirzadi et al., 2022).

Insurance and Financial Protections

The implementation of regulations that require insurance coverage and financial safeguards for medical facilities is an essential component in fostering trust and assurance among individuals seeking MT services (Kumar et al., 2023). Healthcare providers incorporate measures to safeguard patients from financial risks arising from unforeseen circumstances, hence enhancing their overall risk management techniques. The implementation of legislation mandating sufficient insurance coverage for facilities diminishes the financial risks faced by patients, thus bolstering the credibility of the MT segment (Dávila-Aragón & Arrioja-Castrejón, 2021).

Malpractice and Liability Laws

The ethical practice of medicine in the context of MT necessitates the presence of regulatory frameworks that specifically address issues related to malpractice and liability. The establishment of explicit standards pertaining to responsibilities and consequences plays a crucial role in enhancing both patient safety and satisfaction (Kumar et al., 2023). These laws serve to build a comprehensive structure for ensuring the accountability of healthcare practitioners in situations where undesirable results occur. By doing so, they aim to instill confidence in medical tourists, assuring them that their well-being is of utmost importance (Dávila-Aragón & Arrioja-Castrejón, 2021). Also, these rules provide a legally recognized means for seeking redress in instances of medical malpractice.

Legal and Ethical Framework

The ability to effectively navigate legal and ethical frameworks is of utmost importance in the context of MT, as it serves to secure the rights of patients, enable the provision of informed consent, and protect the privacy of sensitive data (Hu, 2022). The regulations governing this domain serve as a fundamental basis for ensuring ethical conduct in the field of medicine, thereby building a framework that fosters confidence and accountability between healthcare professionals and individuals seeking medical treatment abroad (Dalkıran, 2023). The authors focus on matters pertaining to the transparency of treatment alternatives, with the aim of ensuring that patients possess adequate knowledge and agency to make decisions that are congruent with their well-being (Graham et al., 2023; Shafik, 2024a).

Accreditation and Licensing

Regulatory bodies play a pivotal role in ensuring the safety and quality of healthcare services in MT by establishing accreditation and licensing standards. International accreditation signifies a commitment to maintaining specific quality benchmarks and fostering trust among medical tourists (PATIL, 2021). These standards often cover areas such as infrastructure, medical staff qualifications, and patient safety protocols, contributing to the overall reliability of MT destinations.

FUTURE RESEARCH TRENDS AND IMPLICATIONS

These observed patterns indicate a forthcoming period marked by the integration of several disciplines, the inclusion of ethical considerations, and a prioritization of efforts toward resolving global issues. In order to effectively conduct their research, scholars must adeptly negotiate intricate ethical terrains, actively engage in responsible innovation, and diligently ensure the inclusivity and equity of the advantages stemming from their endeavors. The dynamic interplay between the ever-changing landscape of technology and the evolving requirements of medical society will influence the trajectory of research in the future.

Artificial Intelligence and Machine Learning

The incorporation of machine learning[13] and AI within the field of MT holds the potential to transform the provision of patient care significantly. This transformation encompasses various aspects, including the development of tailored treatment plans and the utilization of predictive analytics for assessing travel-related risks (Seow et al., 2022). AI algorithms possess the capability to examine extensive datasets, thereby augmenting the accuracy of diagnostics and improving the outcomes of treatments, implying that there is a potential consequence or inference that can be drawn. The potential for MT in the future is rooted in breakthroughs led by artificial intelligence, which aims to enhance administrative procedures, provide accurate diagnosis, and optimize treatment approaches (Zhang & Sun, 2019). This practice not only guarantees a more effective and personalized healthcare encounter for those seeking medical treatment abroad but also plays a significant role in the general expansion and reputation of the MT sector. Nevertheless, it is crucial to prioritize ethical concerns related to the protection of data privacy, the transparency of algorithms, and the autonomy of patients (Bhargava et al., 2023). This necessitates finding a harmonious equilibrium between technical advancements and the implementation of ethical safeguards.

Genomics and Personalized Medicine

The current trend toward genomics and customized medicine is having a transformative impact on the field of MT, as it enables the customization of therapies according to an individual's unique genetic makeup (Bovsh et al., 2023). This phenomenon entails a heightened comprehension of genetic determinants impacting well-being, resulting in more precise and efficacious interventions (Na et al., 2016). This implies that some potential consequences or suggestions can be inferred from the field of MT; the integration of genomics and personalized medicine presents a potential avenue for delivering tailored treatment strategies to patients from other countries (Seow et al., 2021). Advanced genetic assessments have the potential to provide medical tourists with significant advantages, as they enable a more thorough comprehension of their health status and facilitate the tailoring of preventive and therapeutic approaches (Seow et al., 2017).

Climate Change and Sustainability

The rising global attention towards climate change and sustainability is progressively exerting an influence on the field of MT, as there is an increasing recognition of the environmental consequences associated with this profession (Thoo et al., 2020). The incorporation of sustainable and environmentally conscious techniques is increasingly essential in healthcare institutions that serve medical tourists. It may be inferred that the adoption of sustainable practices in the arena of MT will not only make a significant contribution towards achieving global environmental objectives but also serve as a compelling factor in attracting medical tourists who prioritize environmental consciousness (Thoo et al., 2018). The healthcare business is expected to undergo a transition towards environmentally responsible and socially sustainable models, encompassing elements such as green healthcare infrastructure and carbon-neutral activities (Seow et al., 2018).

Biotechnology and Bioengineering

The field of MT is being influenced by the progress made in biotechnology and bioengineering, which are bringing forth innovative therapies and therapeutic strategies (Xu et al., 2023). The incorporation of biotechnological advancements, ranging from individualized biologics to tissue engineering, is revolutionizing the potential scope of medical interventions. The implication can be drawn that the future of MT is expected to incorporate innovative biotechnological advancements, hence providing patients with opportunities to avail themselves of cutting-edge therapeutic interventions. International patients may choose to travel to countries that are leading in the field of biotechnological developments, whether it be for regenerative medicine or gene therapy (Balasubrahmanyam & Prasad, 2024). The appropriate development and deployment of biotechnological breakthroughs in MT requires careful consideration of ethical factors like accessibility, affordability, and equal distribution of improved treatments (Bunduki et al., 2024).

Quantum Computing and Information Science

The potential impact of quantum computing and information science in the field of MT is expected to be significant, particularly in the domains of data security, sophisticated simulations, and optimization algorithms (Zakaria et al., 2023). This implies that some potential consequences or suggestions can be inferred from the potential impact of quantum computing[14] on the processing and security of medical data, which is significant because it brings about a revolutionary transformation (Ediansyah et al., 2023). This technology offers unparalleled computational capacity, enabling the execution of complex tasks like individualized treatment simulations and drug discovery. Within the turf of MT, venues that harness the potential of quantum computing possess the potential to emerge as frontrunners in the world of data-driven healthcare innovation (Xu et al., 2023).

Neuroscience and Brain-Computer Interfaces

Recent developments in the field of neuroscience and the emergence of brain-computer interfaces have opened up novel opportunities for therapies targeting the neurological domain and interactions between humans and machines. The field of MT may experience a rise in demand for advanced neurological therapies and brain-computer interface technology in the future (Giannake et al., 2023). International patients who are in search of cutting-edge treatments for neurological illnesses or upgrades may opt for venues that actively embrace these evolving technologies. The incorporation of ethical considerations will be of utmost importance in the resolution of matters pertaining to privacy, consent, and the potential societal ramifications associated with cognitive advances mediated by brain-computer interfaces (Li et al., 2023). The proper integration of neuroscience breakthroughs in the MT business necessitates the establishment of a delicate equilibrium between medical innovation and ethical precautions.

Global Health and Pandemic Preparedness

The significance of global health and pandemic preparedness has been emphasized by the COVID-19 pandemic[15], hence impacting the priorities of parties involved in MT. This implies that there is a potential consequence or inference that can be drawn. It is anticipated that forthcoming MT practices will incorporate insights gained during the epidemic, with a focus on implementing comprehensive health surveillance, crisis response tactics, and fostering international cooperation (Beladi et al., 2023). International patients who are cautious and value risk awareness may be more inclined to choose MT destinations that focus on health security measures and have strong pandemic readiness. The ethical issues will primarily focus on the promotion of fair and equal access to healthcare resources in times of crisis, as well as the conscientious handling of public health emergencies within the framework of MT (Arrioja-Castrejón et al., 2023). The cultivation of a proactive and collaborative strategy toward addressing global health concerns will be imperative in order to promote the development of a resilient and sustainable MT business.

Cybersecurity and Digital Privacy

The future landscape of MT is being shaped by increasing apprehensions around cybersecurity dangers and digital privacy concerns. The increasing digitization of healthcare necessitates a strong emphasis on safeguarding patient data and upholding privacy (Karadayi-Usta & Serdarasan, 2023). The MT business will be required to allocate resources towards the implementation of comprehensive cybersecurity measures. Destinations that place a high emphasis on safeguarding digital privacy and ensuring the security of healthcare information may possess a distinct advantage in attracting international patients, thus enhancing their competitive position (Wright & Zascerinska, 2023). Ethical considerations in the realm of digital healthcare encompass the protection of patient confidentiality, the prevention of data breaches, and the implementation of appropriate data management methods (Shi & Gan, 2023). The establishment of trust in the digitalized realm of MT will depend significantly on the ability to reconcile technology advancements with ethical considerations effectively.

Social Sciences and Human Behavior

The growing body of research in the field of social sciences and human behavior is contributing to the development of a more sophisticated comprehension of patient preferences, cultural factors, and the influence of societal dynamics on healthcare choices (Akhavan et al., 2023). This statement implies that some potential consequences or suggestions can be inferred from the utilization of social scientific perspectives in future MT practices, have the potential to customize patient experiences, improve cultural competence among healthcare workers, and address the psychological dimensions of medical travel. International patients may show a preference for destinations that stress patient-centered care and culturally relevant offerings (Mason et al., 2023). Ethical considerations encompass the imperative to uphold varied cultural values, guarantee informed consent within diverse cultural contexts, and advocate for inclusive healthcare practices that take into account the social determinants of health in the realm of international MT (Shafik, 2024g, 2024h).

Space Exploration and Astrobiology

The progress made in the field of space exploration and astrobiology is exerting a significant influence on scientific inquiry and the advancement of technology, which in turn has the potential to yield noteworthy repercussions for healthcare advancements here on earth. Although the immediate influence of space exploration on MT may be limited, there is potential for the transfer of breakthroughs, such as telemedicine and remote healthcare technologies, which have been created for space missions, to be applied in the ground of MT (Maulida & Marlina, 2023). Furthermore, the endeavor to develop healthcare remedies for extended space voyages has the potential to generate ancillary technologies that can be advantageous for healthcare on Earth. In this particular context, ethical issues encompass the imperative of facilitating the responsible transfer of space-related medical technologies for the betterment of healthcare on Earth (Maulida & Marlina, 2023). Additionally, it involves the need to address any discrepancies in access to medical innovations inspired by space within the MT corporate.

CONCLUSION

Significant technological advancements and ethical considerations define the outlook for MT. The potential for artificial intelligence and machine learning to significantly transform personalized healthcare by improving the accuracy of diagnoses and the effectiveness of treatments is considerable. The field of genomics and personalized medicine is poised to revolutionize medical interventions by providing worldwide patients with customized and precise healthcare experiences. The sector is being guided by sustainability considerations, leading to the adoption of eco-friendly procedures that are attractive to medical tourists who prioritize environmental consciousness. The fields of biotechnology, quantum computing, and neuroscience hold significant potential for transformative advancements, which revolutionize the domains of diagnoses and interventions. The COVID-19 pandemic has underscored the significant significance of global health and readiness for pandemics in influencing the course of MT. Navigating this growing terrain necessitates a thorough examination of ethical considerations, which encompass a wide range of factors, including data privacy and cultural sensitivity. The future of advanced healthcare hinges upon achieving a harmonious equilibrium between technological expertise and ethical accountability, ensuring that not only is healthcare readily available but also that it is administered with steadfast adherence to ethical principles.

REFERENCES

Akhavan, P., Azizi, N., Akhtari, S., Haass, O., Jan, T., & Sajeev, S. (2023). Understanding critical success factors for implementing medical tourism in a multi-case analysis. *Knowledge Management and E-Learning*, 15(1).

Alaziz, S. N., Albayati, B., El-Bagoury, A. A. A. H., & Shafik, W. (2023). Clustering of COVID-19 Multi-Time Series-Based K-Means and PCA With Forecasting. *International Journal of Data Warehousing and Mining*, *19*(3), 1–25. DOI: 10.4018/IJDWM.317374

Ananya, S. A. (2021). Technology Based Service Offers and Tourist Experience Generation in the Tourism and Hospitality Industry in Bangladesh. In *Technology Application in the Tourism and Hospitality Industry of Bangladesh*. DOI: 10.1007/978-981-16-2434-6_20

Arrioja-Castrejón, E., López-Fernández, A. M., Ramírez-Pérez, H. X., & Dávila-Aragón, G. (2023). Digital consumer behavior and medical tourism: A regional analysis in Mexico. *Contaduría y Administración*, *68*(4), 419. DOI: 10.22201/fca.24488410e.2023.4968

Balasubrahmanyam, S., & Prasad, K. (2024). Disruptive Customer Value Propositions in the Global Health and Medical Tourism Industry. *International Journal of Business and Globalisation*, *1*(1), 10053643. DOI: 10.1504/IJBG.2024.10053643

Beladi, H., Chao, C. C., Ee, M. S., & Hollas, D. (2023). Welfare-improving policy on medical tourism and labor productivity: A theoretical analysis. *Economic Systems*, *47*(1), 101052. DOI: 10.1016/j.ecosys.2022.101052

Bhargava, A., Bhargava, D., & Rana, A. (2023). Edge-AI-empowered blockchain: A game-changer for the medical tourism industry. In *Edge-AI in Healthcare*. Trends and Future Perspectives. DOI: 10.1201/9781003244592-16

Bovsh, L. A., Hopkalo, L. M., & Rasulova, A. M. (2023). *Digital relationship marketing strategies of medical tourism entities*. In Integrating Digital Health Strategies for Effective Administration. DOI: 10.4018/978-1-6684-8337-4.ch008

Dalkıran, G. B. (2023). Health Tourism Components and Intermediary Institutions as Supplier Businesses in the Context of Health 4.0. *In Accounting, Finance, Sustainability, Governance and Fraud*.

Dávila-Aragón, G., & Arrioja-Castrejón, E. (2021). Medical Tourism in Mexico. Analysis of the Economic and Technological Model in the COVID-19 Pandemic Era. *In The Future of Companies in the Face of a New Reality: Impact and Development in Latin America.*

De Carlo, M., Ferilli, G., d'Angella, F., & Buscema, M. (2021). Artificial intelligence to design collaborative strategy: An application to urban destinations. *Journal of Business Research, 129*, 129. DOI: 10.1016/j.jbusres.2020.09.013

Ediansyah, A., Arief, M., Hamsal, M., & Abdinagoro, S. B. (2023). Interplay between Networking Capability and Hospital Performance in Indonesia's Medical Tourism Sector. *International Journal of Environmental Research and Public Health, 20*(1), 374. DOI: 10.3390/ijerph20010374 PMID: 36612699

Fahim, K. E., Kalinaki, K., & Shafik, W. (2023). Electronic Devices in the Artificial Intelligence of the Internet of Medical Things (AIoMT). In *Handbook of Security and Privacy of AI-Enabled Healthcare Systems and Internet of Medical Things* (pp. 41-62). CRC Press.

Giannake, G., Economou, A., Metaxas, T., & Geitona, M. (2023). Medical Tourism in the Region of Thessaly, Greece: Opinions and Perspectives from Healthcare Providers. *Sustainability (Basel), 15*(10), 7864. DOI: 10.3390/su15107864

Hassan, V., & Bellos, G. (2022). COVID-19: Reshaping Medical Tourism through Artificial Intelligence (AI) and Robotics. *Athens Journal of Tourism,* 9(2).

Heinz, T., Eidmann, A., Jakuscheit, A., Laux, T., Rudert, M., & Stratos, I. (2023). Demographics and Trends for Inbound Medical Tourism in Germany for Orthopedic Patients before and during the COVID-19 Pandemic. *International Journal of Environmental Research and Public Health, 20*(2), 1209. DOI: 10.3390/ijerph20021209 PMID: 36673964

Hu, B. (2022). Status Quo and Key Technologies of Artificial Intelligence. *Lecture Notes on Data Engineering and Communications Technologies,* 103.

Jun, Y., Craig, A., Shafik, W., & Sharif, L. (2021). Artificial intelligence application in cybersecurity and cyberdefense. *Wireless Communications and Mobile Computing, 2021*(1), 1–10. DOI: 10.1155/2021/3329581

Kalinaki, K., Fahadi, M., Alli, A. A., Shafik, W., Yasin, M., & Mutwalibi, N. (2023). Artificial Intelligence of Internet of Medical Things (AIoMT) in Smart Cities: A Review of Cybersecurity for Smart Healthcare. *Handbook of Security and Privacy of AI-Enabled Healthcare Systems and Internet of Medical Things*, 271-292.

Karadayi-Usta, S., & Serdarasan, S. (2023). Supplier selection and capacity allocation in medical tourism service supply chain. *OPSEARCH.*

Khaksar Shahmirzadi, E., Saner, T., Attaeyan, A., Abdolahi, S., Mohammadi, M., & Heydari, S. (2022). Evaluation of the use of robotic surgery with remote simulation for use in the field of Medical Tourism and Pro-Tourism development. *In Journal of Simulation and Analysis of Novel Technologies in Mechanical Engineering*, vol. 14(1).

Kumar, S., Sajnani, M., & Chopra, A. (2023). Analysis of RAISA (Robotics, Artificial Intelligence & Service Automation) and Dubai Tourism. *Proceedings of 3rd IEEE International Conference on Computational Intelligence and Knowledge Economy,* 2023. DOI: 10.1109/ICCIKE58312.2023.10131791

Kusuma, A., Praja, A., Chairuddin, B., & Dewi, M. P. (2023). The Role of Stakeholders In Supporting The Hospital Towards Medical Tourism Services. *The Seybold Report,* 17(11).

Li, H., Du, Y., Xue, T., & Jenkins, C. L. (2023). Chinese medical tourism: Review and research agenda. *Journal of Quality Assurance in Hospitality & Tourism*, *24*(5), 663–687. DOI: 10.1080/1528008X.2022.2073939

Liu, Y., Wang, R., & Zhao, T. (2022). Interaction Design in Residence Mode of Health and Tourism. *Lecture Notes in Computer Science (Including Subseries Lecture Notes in Artificial Intelligence and Lecture Notes in Bioinformatics),* 13325 LNCS.

Mason, A., Spencer, E., Barnett, K., & Bouchie, J. (2023). Examining the prominence and congruence of organizational corporate social responsibility (CSR) communication in medical tourism provider websites. *Journal of Hospitality and Tourism Insights*, *6*(1), 1–17. DOI: 10.1108/JHTI-06-2021-0136

Matinkhah, S. M., Shafik, W., & Ghasemzadeh, M. (2019). Emerging artificial intelligence application: reinforcement learning issues on current internet of things. In *2019 16th international Conference in information knowledge and Technology (ikt2019)* (p. 2019).

Maulida, S., & Marlina, L. (2023). Halal Medical Tourism. Halal Tourism and Pilgrimage, 2(2).

Na, S. A., Nee, A. Y. H., & Onn, C. Y. (2017). Medical tourism: The effects of perceived benefits, perceived risks and geographic region. *Pertanika Journal of Social Science & Humanities*, •••, 25.

Na, S. A., Onn, C. Y., & Meng, C. L. (2016). Travel Intentions among Foreign Tourists for Medical Treatment in Malaysia: An Empirical Study. *Procedia: Social and Behavioral Sciences*, *224*, 224. DOI: 10.1016/j.sbspro.2016.05.434

PATIL. (2021). *S.* India–A Pivotal Centre for Medical Tourism. PalArch's Journal of Archaeology of Egypt/Egyptology.

Pereira, T. C., Costa, E., Borges, I., Silva, F. M., Pinto, A. S., & Vázquez-Justo, E. (2022). Health Tourism Monitor System Model. *Smart Innovation, Systems and Technologies,* 284.

Rodríguez, N. R., Cote, L., Fuentes, C., Jaramillo, E., Arana, S., Castro, A., Behrens, E., Ramos, A., & Zerrweck, C. (2023). First National Consensus on the Safe Practice of Medical Tourism for Bariatric Surgery in Mexico. *Obesity Surgery, 33*(4), 1060–1072. DOI: 10.1007/s11695-023-06468-8 PMID: 36729365

Ryndach, M. A., Kargina, L. A., Lebedeva, S. L., & Chernyshova, L. A. (2021). Artificial intelligence in accessible tourism. *CEUR Workshop Proceedings,* •••, 2914.

Sakipov, N., & Vikhnin, O. (2021). The Modern Symbolic Artificial Intelligence and Its Use in Medical Tourism. *15th IEEE International Conference on Application of Information and Communication Technologies,* AICT 2021. DOI: 10.1109/AICT52784.2021.9620321

Seow, A. N., Choong, C. K., Chen, I. C., & Choong, Y. O. (2022). Can protection motivation theory explain the perception of international tourists' on medical tourism? *Journal of Hospitality and Tourism Insights, 5*(2), 394–412. DOI: 10.1108/JHTI-10-2020-0189

Seow, A. N., Choong, Y. O., & Chan, L. M. (2018). What Influences The Behavioural Intention In Medical Tourism? *A Threat and Coping Perspective.Global Business and Management Research, 10*(3).

Seow, A. N., Choong, Y. O., Moorthy, K., & Chan, L. M. (2017). Intention to visit Malaysia for medical tourism using the antecedents of Theory of Planned Behaviour: A predictive model. *International Journal of Tourism Research, 19*(3), 383–393. DOI: 10.1002/jtr.2120

Seow, A. N., Choong, Y. O., Moorthy, K., & Choong, C. K. (2021). Predicting medical tourism behavioural intention using social cognition models. *Tourism Review, 76*(2), 374–391. DOI: 10.1108/TR-06-2019-0267

Shafik, W. (2023a). A Comprehensive Cybersecurity Framework for Present and Future Global Information Technology Organizations. In *Effective Cybersecurity Operations for Enterprise-Wide Systems* (pp. 56–79). IGI Global. DOI: 10.4018/978-1-6684-9018-1.ch002

Shafik, W. (2023b). Artificial intelligence and Blockchain technology enabling cybersecurity in telehealth systems. [IET.]. *Artificial Intelligence and Blockchain Technology in Modern Telehealth Systems, 1*, 285–326. DOI: 10.1049/PBHE061E_ch11

Shafik, W. (2023c). Cyber Security Perspectives in Public Spaces: Drone Case Study. In *Handbook of Research on Cybersecurity Risk in Contemporary Business Systems* (pp. 79–97). IGI Global. DOI: 10.4018/978-1-6684-7207-1.ch004

Shafik, W. (2023d). Making Cities Smarter: IoT and SDN Applications, Challenges, and Future Trends. In *Opportunities and Challenges of Industrial IoT in 5G and 6G Networks* (pp. 73-94). IGI Global.

Shafik, W. (2024a). Predicting Future Cybercrime Trends in the Metaverse Era. In *Forecasting Cyber Crimes in the Age of the Metaverse* (pp. 78–113). IGI Global.

Shafik, W. (2024b). Wearable Medical Electronics in Artificial Intelligence of Medical Things. *Handbook of Security and Privacy of AI-Enabled Healthcare Systems and Internet of Medical Things,* 21-40.

Shafik, W. (2024c). Introduction to ChatGPT. In *Advanced Applications of Generative AI and Natural Language Processing Models* (pp. 1–25). IGI Global.

Shafik, W., & Kalinaki, K. (2023). Smart City Ecosystem: An Exploration of Requirements, Architecture, Applications, Security, and Emerging Motivations. In *Handbook of Research on Network-Enabled IoT Applications for Smart City Services* (pp. 75-98). IGI Global.

Shi, X., & Gan, L. (2023). Equilibrium in Competitive Insurance Markets with Medical Tourism. *Studies in Microeconomics, 11*(2), 246–269. DOI: 10.1177/23210222211051439

Subasinghe, M., Magalage, D., Amadoru, N., Amarathunga, L., Bhanupriya, N., & Wijekoon, J. L. (2020). Effectiveness of artificial intelligence, decentralized and distributed systems for prediction and secure channelling for Medical Tourism. *11th Annual IEEE Information Technology, Electronics and Mobile Communication Conference,* IEMCON 2020.

Thoo, A. C., Khairuddin, A. I. N., Tat, H. H., Sulaiman, Z., Lai, L. Y., & Masâ€T-Mod, A. (2018). Factors Affecting Medical Tourists to Malaysia. *Asia Proceedings of Social Sciences,* 2(3).

Thoo, A. C., Khairuddin, A. I. N., Tat, H. H., Sulaiman, Z., Lai, L. Y., & Mas'od, A. (2020). Why medical tourists must go to Malaysia! *International Journal of Business Continuity and Risk Management, 10*(2–3), 224. DOI: 10.1504/IJBCRM.2020.108510

Wang, Y., Shafik, W., Seong, J. T., Al Mutairi, A., Mustafa, M. S., & Mouhamed, M. R. (2023). Service delay and optimization of the energy efficiency of a system in fog-enabled smart cities. *Alexandria Engineering Journal, 84*, 112–125. DOI: 10.1016/j.aej.2023.10.034

Wright, D. W. M., & Zascerinska, S. (2023). Becoming immortal: Future wellness and medical tourism markets. *Journal of Tourism Futures, 9*(2), 168–195. DOI: 10.1108/JTF-05-2021-0119

Xiaoling, P., & Xuan, Z. (2022). The transformation of artificial intelligence in the 5G era and the impact on education. *2022 IEEE 2nd International Conference on Electronic Technology, Communication and Information,* ICETCI 2022.

Xu, A., Johari, S. A., Khademolomoom, A. H., Khabaz, M. T., Umurzoqovich, R. S., Hosseini, S., & Semiromi, D. T. (2023). Investigation of management of international education considering sustainable medical tourism and entrepreneurship. *Heliyon, 9*(1), e12691. DOI: 10.1016/j.heliyon.2022.e12691 PMID: 36685466

Yoo, B., Thelen, S. T., & Harrison, K. (2023). Patient consideration of local hospital, center of excellence, and medical tourism options for surgery. *Health Marketing Quarterly, 40*(2), 119–140. DOI: 10.1080/07359683.2021.1994171 PMID: 34736359

Zakaria, M., Islam, M. A., Islam, M. K., Begum, A., Poly, N. A., Cheng, F., & Xu, J. (2023). Determinants of Bangladeshi patients' decision-making process and satisfaction toward medical tourism in India. *Frontiers in Public Health, 11*, 11. DOI: 10.3389/fpubh.2023.1137929 PMID: 37200988

Zeng, L., Li, R. Y. M., & Zeng, H. (2023). Weibo users and Academia's foci on tourism safety: Implications from institutional differences and digital divide. *Heliyon, 9*(3), e12306. DOI: 10.1016/j.heliyon.2022.e12306 PMID: 36923855

Zhang, L., & Sun, Z. (2019). The Application of Artificial Intelligence Technology in the Tourism Industry of Jinan. *Journal of Physics: Conference Series, 1302*(3), 032005. DOI: 10.1088/1742-6596/1302/3/032005

Zhao, L., Zhu, D., Shafik, W., Matinkhah, S. M., Ahmad, Z., Sharif, L., & Craig, A. (2022). Artificial intelligence analysis in cyber domain: A review. *International Journal of Distributed Sensor Networks, 18*(4), 15501329221084882. DOI: 10.1177/15501329221084882

ENDNOTES

1 https://www.sas.com/en_us/insights/analytics/what-is-artificial-intelligence.html

2 https://en.wikipedia.org/wiki/Medical_tourism

3 https://www.medicaltourism.com/

4 https://www.simplilearn.com/tutorials/blockchain-tutorial/blockchain-technology

5 https://www.vrs.org.uk/virtual-reality/what-is-virtual-reality.html

6 https://www.investopedia.com/terms/a/augmented-reality.asp

7 https://www.bumrungrad.com/en

8 https://www.apollohospitals.com/

9 https://www.anadolumedicalcenter.com/en

10 https://www.magazine.medicaltourism.com/article/singapore-healthcare-hub-and-medical-marvels

11 https://www.dentaltourismcolombia.com/medellin-dentist

12 https://www.mayoclinic.org/departments-centers/international

13 https://www.ibm.com/topics/machine-learning

14 https://www.ibm.com/topics/quantum-computing

15 https://www.who.int/europe/emergencies/situations/covid-19

Chapter 2
Emotionally Intelligent AI: Redefining Wellness in the Digital Age

Shin Ling Wu
https://orcid.org/0000-0001-8169-5585
Sunway University, Malaysia

Mansour Amini
https://orcid.org/0000-0003-2149-4604
Universiti Sains Malaysia, Malaysia

ABSTRACT

Artificial intelligence shows immense potential to revolutionize how we understand, monitor, and promote emotional wellness. Emotionally intelligent AI systems leverage advanced algorithms and machine learning to recognize, understand, and respond to human emotions. By integrating emotional AI into wellness technologies, novel solutions can provide real-time emotional support, personalized therapy recommendations, and intelligent self-care guidance tailored to each individual's needs. Nevertheless, despite its transformative potential, emotionally intelligent AI faces considerable hurdles such as stigmas surrounding mental health, privacy and security concerns and cross-cultural emotional contexts. As emotionally intelligent AI capabilities mature, the role of AI assistance versus the indispensable human therapeutic connection must be carefully delineated. Therefore, this chapter elucidates the prospects of harnessing emotional AI while providing critical insights into its potential pitfalls.

DOI: 10.4018/979-8-3693-5837-5.ch002

1) EMOTIONAL WELLNESS

Mental health issues are a serious problem globally and have been intensified by the Covid-19 pandemic. According to the World Health Organization (2022), approximately 1 billion people worldwide are living with mental disorders. This is concerning as most of them do not have access to effective care due to various reasons such as lack of services, unaffordable prices, and widespread stigma that prevents individuals from seeking help. Mental health conditions such as depression and anxiety are often intertwined with emotional wellness.

Emotional wellness is a critical component of overall well-being that encompasses the ability to manage and respond to one's emotional state effectively. It is a multi-faceted construct that encompasses an individual's ability to cultivate awareness, acceptance, and regulation of the full range of human emotions. It is a state of being where one can authentically experience and process emotions in a balanced and healthy manner. Emotionally well individuals experience positive feelings and are motivated to perform and be productive (Braun & Kloss, 2017). They have better self-awareness, self-regulation, empathy, and interpersonal skills, which aid in navigating the complexities of life with resilience and adaptability (Ryff & Singer, 1998). On the other hand, individuals who are stressed and overwhelmed fail to regulate their emotions effectively, especially intense emotions like anger, sadness and fear. These intense negative emotions would then disrupt their emotional wellness.

In healthcare settings, emotional wellness is increasingly recognized as essential for enhancing patient outcomes, reducing the burden of chronic diseases, and promoting a healthier lifestyle. Past studies found that there are other psychological challenges that patients are experiencing, such as pain, fatigue, depression and anxiety, are disrupting the treatment plan. Therefore, promoting emotional wellness among patients by providing sufficient support and referring them to mental health professionals is recommended, as patients with higher levels of emotional well-being are more likely to adhere to treatment regimens and experience better health outcomes (Keefer et al., 2022). Patients also experienced a reduction in stress, depression, and anxiety and improved quality of life through the implementation of emotional wellness programs (Russell et al., 2020). Therefore, promoting emotional wellness is important to help patients to overcome their health issues.

Challenges in Maintaining Emotional Wellness

Emotional wellness is important for a person's functioning, however, maintaining it is increasingly challenging in today's fast-paced world. Modern lifestyle encompasses huge daily stressors such as work pressures, financial stress, and relationship and family conflicts. These stressors are overwhelming, and individuals who are unable to cope with them will experience mental health-related issues such as burnout (Maslach & Leiter, 2016), anxiety and depression (Varma et al., 2021). Prolonged exposure to these stressors could lead to chronic stress that would adversely impact one's mental health and cognitive function, and accelerate aging (McEwen, 2007).

Other than daily stressors, there are other factors that challenge individuals' emotional wellness such as social isolation (Clair et al., 2021), lifestyles (Hautekiet et al., 2022), job insecurity and financial concern (Wilson et al., 2020). For instance, many individuals experience a significant lack of meaningful connections which contributes to the feeling of isolation and subjective loneliness. Past studies revealed that social isolation would negatively impact individuals' mental health (Clair et al., 2021). In addition, individuals living an unhealthy lifestyle such as smoking, physical inactivity and poor nutrition are more likely to experience poor mental health with higher odds of developing depressive symptoms, anxiety and suicidal thoughts. On the other hand, a healthy lifestyle is characterized as healthy ageing which could delay ageing and reduce mortality (Hautekiet et al., 2022). Last, economic stressors and fulfilling basic needs are particularly challenging, especially for marginalized communities, which are additional barriers to maintaining emotional wellness (Wilson et al., 2020).

In this modern era, technology overload is another challenge to emotional wellness. Technology has brought numerous benefits to our lives and increased productivity. Nevertheless, overuse of technology could lead to information overload, reduce attention spans and increase anxiety. The constant need for connectivity and the fear of missing out (FoMO) could disrupt sleep patterns and increase restlessness and anxiety. Twenge et al. (2018) highlighted that an increase in screen time has contributed to the increase in depression and suicide.

Despite the rapid development, stigma towards mental illness still exists in the communities. The stigma surrounding mental health continues to be a significant barrier to seeking help and maintaining emotional wellness (Corrigan, 2004). Many individuals hesitate to seek professional support due to fear of judgment, discrimination, or social stigma. This stigma can prevent people from accessing necessary mental health services, exacerbating their conditions and hindering their recovery and well-being. Individuals who are seeking mental health treatment would not fully participate in care and would drop out to avoid the label of mental illness (Corrigan, 2004).

Moreover, traditional healthcare approaches often focus predominantly on physical health, neglecting the crucial aspects of mental and emotional well-being, leaving mental health issues underdiagnosed and undertreated. Subsequently, many patients do not receive the comprehensive care they need, which can lead to a deterioration of emotional wellness and overall health. Therefore, as there is an increasing demand for integrative approaches that address the mind-body connection, there is a growing call for more holistic approaches whereby innovative solutions that could effectively support emotional wellness are crucial (Keefer et al., 2022). For instance, Keefer et al. (2022) proposed an integrated model for patients with Inflammatory Bowel Disease (IBD) that stations mental health professionals directly within the IBD centres. This approach ensures patients receive psychological support alongside their physical treatment, addressing both aspects of their health simultaneously. Such integration of mental health services into primary care settings has shown promising results whereby both the physical and mental health of patients can significantly improve.

Limitations of Traditional Approaches to Emotional Wellness

Traditional approaches to emotional wellness, such as psychotherapy, counselling, and pharmacotherapy, have provided valuable support for many individuals. However, there exist some limitations on the application of these methods. One of the primary limitations is accessibility and availability. Many individuals face barriers such as high costs, long waiting times, and a shortage of mental health professionals, particularly in rural and underserved areas. This lack of accessibility can prevent individuals from receiving timely and appropriate care, leading to worsening mental health conditions (World Health Organization, 2022). The American Psychological Association (2022) revealed that there is an increase in patients with anxiety, depression and stressor-related disorders making the waitlist longer as 60% of psychologists do not have openings for new patients.

The stigma and social barriers associated with mental health issues are another significant limitation. Individuals often fear of discrimination, judgment, or negative perceptions from others, which can discourage them from accessing mental health services. This stigma can also affect the willingness of individuals to discuss their mental health challenges openly, which consequently further isolates them and hinders their recovery (Link & Phelan, 2001). Due to stigma, individuals who require mental health care will opt to face their problems in isolation, which consequently worsens their conditions.

Other limitations of the traditional mental health approach are scalability and efficiency. Traditional mental health interventions, such as face-to-face counselling and psychotherapy, can be time-consuming and resource intensive. These methods may not be scalable to meet the growing demand for mental health services, especially in the context of rising mental health issues worldwide. Many patients struggle with follow-up care as the current system failed to provide consistent, long-term support to the patients (Lattie et al., 2022). Further complicating matters is the tendency of traditional therapeutic approaches to adopt a one-size-fits-all model. This standardized approach often fails to account for individual differences in terms of personality, cultural background, and personal preferences. As a result, the treatment is less effective for some patients. Thus, there is a demand for personalized care, which considers the unique needs and circumstances of each individual (Norcross & Wampold, 2011).

In response to these limitations, the mental health landscape is turning to technological solutions. Technological advancements, such as digital mental health services, which could be delivered via mobile phone or web-based platforms, are emerging tools to expand the accessibility and availability of mental health services (Aboujaoude et al., 2020; Fu et al., 2020; Lattie et al., 2022). These innovative approaches show promising outcomes in addressing mental health issues such as depressive symptoms and anxiety (Kim et al., 2023), and helped patients with substance misuse (Fu et al., 2020). However, the integration of traditional mental health practices with digital tools remains a work in progress. This gap limits our ability to fully utilize the potential of digital health solutions, such as teletherapy, mobile apps, and online support platforms, in enhancing mental health care. Moreover, although there are various applications in the market to help individuals deal with their mental health issues, many lack rigorous testing for their effectiveness and suitability (Anthes, 2016). Therefore, by thoughtfully integrating traditional mental health approaches with Artificial Emotional Intelligence (AEI) technology, we will have the opportunity to create more accessible, convenient and effective mental health services. This integration of human expertise and technological innovative could pave the way for a new era in health care to improve individuals emotional wellness.

2) OVERVIEW OF ARTIFICIAL EMOTIONAL INTELLIGENCE AND ITS APPLICATION

Imagine a world where machines not only understand our words but also our feelings. This is the promise of AEI, a fascinating branch of AI that is pushing the boundaries of how technology interacts with our emotional lives. AEI combines affective computing and artificial intelligence (AI) that teaches machines to recognize, understand, and respond to human emotions (McStay, 2024). Unlike traditional AI which primarily focuses on cognitive tasks such as data analysis and decision-making, AEI integrates human emotional needs and machine responses to create affect-recognizing technology (Picard & Klein, 2002). This involves the integration of various technologies, including natural language processing (NLP), facial recognition, voice analysis, and machine learning (ML) to create systems that can detect and interpret emotional cues of human (Khare et al., 2024).

AEI systems are designed to analyze emotional data from various sources, such as text, speech, and facial expressions, to infer the emotional state of individuals. For instance, an AEI system can analyze the tone, pitch, and pace of a user's voice to detect stress or happiness. Similarly, facial recognition technology can be used to identify expressions of joy, anger, or sadness. By combining these different data points, AEI systems can provide a more comprehensive understanding of a user's emotional state (Picard & Klein, 2002).

The Role of Artificial Emotional Intelligence in Emotional Wellness

AEI represents a significant advancement in the intersection of technology and emotional wellness. It plays an important role in promoting emotional wellness by providing tools and platforms that can assist individuals in managing their mental health. AEI offers several advantages over traditional methods of emotional support.

Firstly, AEI can provide continuous, real-time monitoring and support, which is especially beneficial for individuals who require ongoing assistance. This can be done as AEI systems utilize sensors, wearable devices, and computer vision technologies to continuously gather data on physiological indicators and behavioral cues that reflect emotional states. For example, wearable devices equipped with AI can track physiological indicators such as heart rate variability and skin conductance to detect signs of stress or anxiety and provide immediate feedback or interventions (Gomes et al., 2023; Yang et al., 2016). This real-time monitoring is crucial for early detection of emotional distress and timely intervention.

Furthermore, AEI can enhance the accessibility of mental health support. Many people face barriers to accessing traditional mental health services, such as geographical limitations, stigma, and high costs. AEI can overcome these barriers by offering remote and affordable support through digital platforms. For instance, digital mental health interventions powered by AEI can provide users with personalized feedback and coping strategies, making mental health support more accessible and convenient (Lattie et al., 2022). In addition, virtual mental health assistants such as AI-driven chatbots and virtual therapists can engage users in natural language conversations, providing empathy, support, and therapeutic guidance. By analyzing text inputs and voice tones, AEI systems can recognize emotional cues and respond appropriately, offering comfort, validation, and practical advice (Bickmore et al., 2011).

In addition, AEI can improve the effectiveness of mental health interventions by offering personalized and data-driven insights. Traditional mental health treatments often follow a one-size-fits-all approach, which may not be suitable for everyone. AEI can analyze individual emotional patterns and tailor interventions accordingly, which aids in developing more effective and personalized care. For example, an AEI-powered mental health app can track a user's mood over time and suggest specific activities or therapies that have been shown to improve their emotional well-being (Calvo et al., 2014). Currently, chatbots and virtual assistants like Tess, Woebot, and Wysa offer emotional support to users through pre-programmed expressions of empathy embedded in their systems (Holohan & Fiske, 2021). These AEI technologies deliver conversational mental health support to individuals in need of assistance with their mental health challenges. In addition, Replika, a virtual AI companion, functions as a supportive friend, providing emotional support to a broader audience, particularly to those experiencing loneliness. It engages in friendly conversations, recognizes users' emotions, and responds as though they are interacting with a real person (Ghosh et al., 2023). All in all, by equipping machines with the ability to recognize, interpret, and respond to human emotions, AEI is able to enhance mental health care and emotional support systems in patients.

Benefits of Emotionally Intelligent AI in Promoting Emotional Wellness

AEI offers transformative potential in promoting emotional wellness across various settings, from healthcare to education, workplaces, and daily life. In healthcare, technology and systems equipped with AEI are able to monitor patients' emotional states continuously, providing timely support and interventions. For instance, therapists and psychiatrists can use mobile applications and sensors to monitor patients' changes in symptoms over time and adjust the interventions and medication accordingly (Muetunda et al., 2023). This capability enables mental health professionals to understand patients' unique requirements and develop personalized treatment plans that could promote long-term emotional wellness. These personalized treatment plans would also optimize resource allocation such as mental health professionals' availability, financial support and materials involved (Shimada, 2023).

In educational settings, technology equipped with AEI could support students' learning and increase engagement in class by monitoring their responses and body cues in class. Students have different learning capabilities and speeds, which makes it difficult for educators to track every student's progress and learning interests. With AI technology, educators could also use these technologies to check on students' attention and determine students' understanding in classes by analyzing their responses, body poses, and expressions (Trabelsi et al., 2023). Consequently, students would be prompted to increase engagement, which would help in managing academic pressures and improve overall performance.

AEI also enhances everyday emotional wellness by integrating into personal digital assistants and smart home devices. These devices improve both physical and mental health by offering individualized suggestions to optimize the indoor environment (Yang et al., 2021), comfort levels, and overall well-being (Sequeiros et al., 2022). For the elderly, AEI technologies, such as healthcare smart homes, monitor users' daily activities and wellness through sensors and trackers, as well as encourage social connections. These devices improve the quality of life and promote independence, autonomy and well-being among older adults (Creaney et al., 2021). In conclusion, AEI provides numerous benefits in promoting emotional wellness across various settings, enhancing mental health and emotional well-being through real-time monitoring, personalized interventions, and continuous support.

3) INTEGRATING EMOTIONAL AI INTO DIGITAL HEALTH PLATFORMS AND WEARABLE DEVICES

AI plays a key role in almost every section including health. For example, Sasmal (2024) reported that AI revolutionizes data warehousing, making it faster, more adaptable, and strategically important. AI offers a powerful new approach to environmental monitoring, critical in addressing pressing issues like climate change and biodiversity loss. Advancements in AI-driven solutions require sustainable environmental monitoring. By combining AI with environmental science, its potential to shape a more sustainable future could be unlocked (Saleh & Battseren, 2023).

Furthermore, the examination of data related to human emotional expression through computational methods has a surprisingly extensive past and is now playing an increasingly crucial role in the development of social ML and AI applications (Stark & Hoey, 2019). In this regard, the integration of emotional AI into digital health platforms and wearable devices represents a significant advancement in enhancing senior care within assisted living communities. This innovative approach utilizes AI-powered platforms coupled with wearable devices to monitor and analyze residents' activity and behavior data continuously. Through sophisticated algorithms, these platforms can detect early signs of potential health decline, allowing caregivers and staff to intervene proactively. By leveraging this real-time information, healthcare professionals can implement timely interventions, thereby preventing avoidable health issues and unnecessary hospitalizations (Wilmink et al., 2020). This proactive approach not only improves the quality of care but also enhances the overall well-being of seniors, promoting a healthier and more fulfilling lifestyle.

Moreover, the potential of AI in revolutionizing senior care is further underscored by Loveys et al. (2022), who highlight its applications in long-term care services. While initial studies have shown promising results across various facets of care, there are lingering uncertainties regarding its overall effectiveness due to mixed outcomes and prevalent biases in existing research. Recognizing the potential benefits, researchers emphasize the necessity of conducting more rigorous and inclusive trials, especially in developing regions, to establish the efficacy of AI interventions conclusively. This cautious approach is crucial for ensuring the responsible and beneficial integration of AI technologies in senior care practices globally.

Expanding on the transformative effects of personalized care, Wang and Fan (2022) emphasize the positive impact of home and community care on older adults' health outcomes, particularly for those without disabilities. Their research suggests significant improvements in cognitive function and life satisfaction among this demographic. However, the benefits for older adults with pre-existing disabilities are more nuanced, with notable enhancements observed in cognitive abilities but less pronounced effects on overall health indicators. Interestingly, the study also highlights disparities based on socio-economic status, indicating that individuals from lower socio-economic backgrounds tend to experience more substantial health improvements compared to those with higher socio-economic status. These findings underscore the importance of tailoring care interventions to individual needs and circumstances, leveraging AI-driven insights to optimize outcomes across diverse populations.

Conversational AI Assistants for Emotional Support and Counselling

Conversational AI has surged in popularity, finding applications in diverse areas like customer service. While numerous software platforms support conversational AI development, they share similar objectives yet possess distinct functionalities (Aronsson et al., 2021).

Conversational AI assistants have been extensively researched for emotional support and counselling (Ansari, 2022; Vigneswaran & Aakash, 2022; Meng et al., 2023; Wang et al., 2023). These assistants, also known as conversational agents or chatbots, utilize natural language dialogue to interact with users and offer guidance and support (Cheng et al., 2022). They have demonstrated potential in treating psychological disorders and enhancing mental well-being. Nonetheless, a primary challenge remains in accurately conveying emotional support (ES). Current systems often rely on single-turn interactions and struggle to effectively extract information from previous dialogue data. To tackle this issue, a new emotional support conversational agent named the STEF agent has been proposed. This agent integrates an emotional fusion mechanism to capture emotional fluctuations during a conversation and a strategy tendency encoder to extract underlying strategy semantic embedding. Experimental findings illustrate the effectiveness of the STEF agent when compared to competing baselines. Furthermore, research indicates that incorporating the seeker's persona into the model can significantly enhance personalized emotional support provision.

AI-Driven Therapy Solutions

Advancements in AI-driven solutions are not only reshaping industries but also demanding sustainable environmental monitoring practices. As highlighted by Liao et al. (2022), successful integration of AI in healthcare necessitates robust health system-level governance frameworks. These frameworks should encompass institutional oversight structures, comprehensive deployment pathways considering technological and clinical aspects, continuous monitoring processes to adapt to evolving clinical needs, and ethical guidelines for equitable AI utilization. This approach ensures that AI applications in healthcare are not only effective but also aligned with ethical standards and patient needs.

Mak et al. (2019) showcased the potential of combining crowd innovation and AI to revolutionize cancer treatment through advanced computer programs. These AI tools, developed with inputs from experts worldwide, can perform critical tasks in radiation therapy with precision comparable to highly trained professionals. Such AI innovations not only enhance treatment outcomes but also have the potential to bridge healthcare gaps in underserved regions, bringing advanced medical care to more people globally.

Additionally, AI-based chatbots have emerged as effective tools for delivering personalized and engaging health-promotion interventions, as noted by Aggarwal et al. (2022). Leveraging behavioral change theories and expert consultations, these chatbots facilitate behavior change interventions such as promoting healthy lifestyles, aiding smoking cessation, improving treatment adherence, and reducing substance misuse. Features like goal setting, real-time feedback, and personalized support make AI-driven chatbots valuable assets in promoting individual wellness and public health initiatives. These examples underscore the multifaceted benefits and ethical considerations inherent in leveraging AI for transformative healthcare interventions.

AI-Driven Personalized Recommendations: Therapy Plans and Emotional Self-Care

The integration of AI into healthcare has led to significant advancements, revolutionizing medical practices and patient care. However, as highlighted by Rahman (2023), it is crucial to ensure that AI-powered healthcare solutions align with religious principles such as Halal guidelines, especially in regions where these principles hold significant importance.

AI-driven personalized recommendations are reshaping therapy plans and strategies for emotional well-being, drawing insights from diverse data sources including electronic health records, IoT devices, online platforms, and social media, as noted by Agarwal (2022). In cancer care, AI is playing a pivotal role in virtual care settings and online support groups, tailoring resources to meet patients' psychosocial needs, and thereby improving access to supportive care (Leung et al., 2022). Furthermore, advancements in digital tools and wearable devices allow for remote collection of patient data, facilitating the creation of personalized models using AI techniques specifically for therapies like spinal cord stimulation, as demonstrated by Rauck et al. (2022).

The development of a reinforcement learning psychotherapy AI companion, as discussed by Lin et al. (2023), showcases the potential of AI to enhance therapeutic interventions. This AI companion suggests relevant topics for therapists based on patient interactions, highlighting its ability to deliver personalized and effective therapeutic guidance. These examples underscore the transformative impact of AI in healthcare, from personalized treatment recommendations to enhancing mental health support, while also emphasizing the importance of ensuring cultural and ethical considerations are integrated into AI-powered healthcare solutions.

4) CHALLENGES IN DEVELOPING EMOTIONALLY INTELLIGENT AI

Developing emotionally intelligent AI is a complex endeavor with several challenges, as noted by Assunção et al. (2022). Despite the crucial role of emotions in reinforcement learning, social interactions, and overall human development, AI research often overlooks their significance. Affective computing, which encompasses the recognition, response to, and influence of human emotions, spans multiple research domains but still faces limitations and hurdles, as highlighted by Lee et al. (2022). However, recent advancements in large language models (LLMs) offer promise in understanding and generating human-like text, signaling progress toward artificial empathy and emotional intelligence, as discussed by Patel and Fan (2023). Evaluations of empathy levels and emotional identification in LLMs reveal that newer models like GPT-4 perform at levels close to humans, highlighting the potential of LLMs in emotional intelligence. Nevertheless, further research and development are needed to fully harness empathetic AI capabilities.

AI represents a transformative force akin to the Industrial Revolution, heralding automation and the potential substitution of human tasks across diverse sectors. This rapid progress in ML and decision-making algorithms holds tremendous potential for innovation across industries such as finance, healthcare, and manufacturing, as emphasized by Dwivedi et al. (2021). Studies project significant shifts in job roles due to automation, with estimates suggesting up to one-third of current tasks could be affected by 2030, according to Manyika et al. (2017) and Dwivedi et al. (2021).

This transformation underscores the need for strategic planning, reskilling initiatives, and ethical considerations to navigate the evolving landscape of AI-driven automation and its societal impacts.

Addressing the Stigma Surrounding Mental Health With AI

AI-driven platforms are revolutionizing mental health care by addressing the stigma associated with mental illnesses and providing continuous, tailored support to individuals. Platforms such as the Leora model and Therapy mobile app, powered by AI, engage users in conversations about their mental well-being and offer strategies to improve overall wellness, as highlighted by Timmons et al. (2022). These platforms aim to provide accessible, discreet, and personalized assistance to individuals dealing with mild to moderate symptoms of anxiety and depression, as noted by Kapoor and Goel (2022).

Furthermore, AI applications in mental health care have the potential to mitigate disparities and biases through advanced techniques for assessing and addressing algorithmic bias. By addressing ethical challenges and involving key stakeholders, researchers can ensure the responsible and effective use of AI in mental health care, delivering high-quality assistance as mentioned by Schyff et al. (2023). These AI-powered solutions not only offer convenient and confidential support but also contribute to reducing the stigma surrounding mental health, fostering a more supportive and inclusive environment for individuals seeking help and support.

Data Collection and Privacy

The integration of AI in healthcare brings about significant challenges related to data collection and privacy, stemming from the widespread adoption of electronic health records and digital healthcare data, as highlighted by Galtier and Meadon (2023), and Aryan and Shashank (2023). The use of actual patient data for insights into improving patient outcomes, diagnostics, and treatments raises concerns regarding privacy and regulatory compliance, such as adhering to guidelines like HIPAA and GDPR, as noted by Liu et al. (2023). To address these challenges, leveraging synthetic data generation through generative AI models such as Generative Adversarial Networks (GANs) and Variational Autoencoders (VAEs) emerges as a promising solution. This approach allows for the creation of realistic yet anonymized patient data suitable for research and training purposes, thereby protecting patient privacy, as emphasized by Yousefi (2022).

In addition to synthetic data generation, federated learning (FL) has emerged as an innovative machine-learning technique that addresses privacy concerns in AI health applications. FL ensures that patient data remains securely stored onsite during model training, thus minimizing the risks associated with data sharing and breaches. These strategies not only unlock valuable healthcare insights from data but also uphold patient privacy and trust, paving the way for transformative advancements in healthcare delivery and outcomes.

Privacy and Data Security Concerns

Privacy and data security concerns are paramount in the integration of AI applications within the healthcare sector, as emphasized by Al-Hwsali et al. (2023), and Galtier and Meadon (2023). The use of ML models to analyze vast health datasets raises ethical and legal complexities, particularly concerning patient safety and privacy. Given the sensitive nature of health data, strict regulation and careful handling are essential to ensure compliance and protect patient information (Al-Hwsali et al., 2023). With the increasing availability of health datasets and the integration of AI into healthcare systems, there is a pressing need for robust security and privacy measures, as highlighted by Kabir (2023). Additionally, the proliferation of wearable devices and the Medical Internet of Things (MIoT) further amplifies concerns regarding data security and privacy, as noted by Sankaran et al. (2023).

To address these challenges, various strategies have been proposed, including the adoption of federated learning, which safeguards patient data by keeping it securely stored on-site during model training. Furthermore, innovative protocols like the Secure M-Trust Privacy protocol (SMP) integrate trust, cryptography, and ML techniques to establish secure and private communication channels for medical data.

In a broader context, companies leverage personal data collected online to tailor advertisements to individual preferences, a practice known as online behavioral advertising. Mogaji et al. (2019) introduce a novel model that combines AI and ML techniques to create emotionally compelling advertisements. This approach not only demonstrates the potential of AI in advertising but also underscores the importance of ethical data handling and compliance with data protection regulations. As customer analytics continue to play a vital role in sales and marketing, ethical data practices become increasingly crucial, highlighting the practical implications of responsible data usage for managers and businesses alike.

Context and Cultural Limitations

AI systems often overlook cultural contexts and values, limiting their effectiveness in various applications, as highlighted by Qadri et al. (2023). These technologies, primarily developed in specific nations, tend to embed cultural values and customs specific to those regions, leading to challenges when applied in diverse cultural settings. Moreover, Prabhakaran et al. (2022) point out the lack of fair representation of global cultural diversity in the datasets used to train AI models, further exacerbating the cultural biases in AI applications. This cultural mismatch between AI systems and diverse societies results in difficulties stemming from differing values and interpretive methods, contributing to issues such as bias, as noted by van Noord et al. (2022).

To address these challenges, it is imperative to integrate cultural intricacies such as subjectivity, scalability, contextuality, and temporality into AI research, as suggested by van Noord et al. (2022). This approach enables AI systems to better understand and adapt to diverse cultural contexts, improving their effectiveness and reducing biases in cultural analysis and other applications. Additionally, leveraging AI models' advanced understanding of communication dynamics, especially in responding to emotional cues, as discussed by Vinay et al. (2024), can further enhance AI's capabilities in navigating cultural nuances and optimizing persuasive content generation in culturally diverse settings. These combined efforts can lead to more culturally sensitive and effective AI systems across various domains.

Ethical Considerations in Emotional AI Deployment

AI models utilized for emotion analysis encounter challenges stemming from biased training data that may not accurately capture diverse emotional expressions. These models are primarily developed in select countries, reflecting their cultural values and practices, which can lead to misinterpretations and limitations when interacting with diverse cultural contexts.

The rapid advancements in artificial intelligence (AI) have prompted discussions regarding the ethical and societal implications of socially and emotionally intelligent AI systems, as noted by Ong (2021) and other researchers. Ong (2021) highlights the inevitability of developing AI capable of understanding and responding to human emotions, emphasizing the need for ethical considerations in AI development and deployment. The framework proposed by Ong (2021) underscores the ethical responsibilities of AI developers and operators, focusing on two key pillars: Provable Beneficence, which involves demonstrating AI effectiveness, and Responsible Stewardship, which entails ethical practices in data collection, use, and decision-making processes. This framework serves as a guideline for ensuring that AI technologies are developed and utilized responsibly, considering the potential societal impacts of emotionally intelligent AI systems.

Potential for Emotional Manipulation or Misuse

Emotionally framed queries, especially those employing positive and polite language, significantly influence AI models' propensity to generate disinformation, as highlighted by Vinay et al. (2024). AI systems demonstrate a heightened susceptibility to producing false information when prompted emotionally, showcasing a vulnerability to emotional manipulation. This susceptibility is underscored by the increased success rates of AI models in generating disinformation when exposed to positive emotional prompts, indicating the potential for exploitation of emotional cues in AI systems.

The utilization of AI in potential emotional manipulation or misuse raises substantial ethical concerns, particularly concerning Large Language Models (LLMs) capable of understanding and responding to emotional cues, as noted by Vinay et al. (2024). These capabilities can be harnessed to manipulate emotions, shape opinions, and propagate disinformation, especially when combined with emotional prompts. Such manipulative practices have the potential to amplify misinformation campaigns, leading to societal harm such as confusion, distrust, and heightened social divisions. To mitigate these risks, it is imperative to implement robust ethical guidelines, deploy bias detection tools, ensure transparency in AI processes, and promote responsible AI practices. These measures are essential steps in safeguarding against the potential negative impacts of emotionally intelligent AI systems and fostering ethical AI development and deployment.

Reliance on Technology

Emotional AI sets itself apart from other forms of AI by delving deep into personal feelings through the use of biometric tools, as highlighted by Mantello and Ho (2022). Unlike AI systems that primarily rely on external data sources, emotional AI leverages biometric data to understand and respond to human emotions more effectively. This advanced form of AI utilizes ML algorithms and big data analytics to continuously improve its accuracy and usefulness in interpreting emotional states and providing relevant responses.

By incorporating biometric tools, emotional AI gains insights into physiological signals such as heart rate, skin conductance, facial expressions, and vocal tones, allowing for a more nuanced understanding of human emotions. ML algorithms enable emotional AI systems to learn from these biometric signals over time, refining their ability to recognize and respond to emotional cues accurately. The integration of big data further enhances emotional AI's capabilities by providing a vast pool of diverse data to train and fine-tune these ML models, ultimately improving the overall effectiveness of emotional AI in various applications.

In essence, emotional AI represents a specialized branch of AI that harnesses biometric data, ML techniques, and big data analytics to navigate the complexities of human emotions, offering valuable insights and responses tailored to individual emotional states and needs.

5) FUTURE DIRECTIONS OF AI

AI has transcended its origins in science fiction to become an integral part of everyday reality, deeply embedded in various sectors such as medicine and government on a global scale. This widespread adoption has not only made AI a core component of many businesses but has also elevated its status as a strategic priority across diverse industries. This shift in adoption has catalyzed a corresponding evolution in academic research, moving beyond mere performance measurement to encompass a deeper exploration of AI's broader societal and practical implications, as noted by Dwivedi et al. (2021).

One significant advancement in AI integration is the incorporation of emotional AI into digital health platforms, heralding a new era of personalized care that holds immense promise for transforming senior care, particularly in assisted living communities and beyond. While recognizing the transformative potential of these technologies, it is crucial to address existing research gaps and ensure equitable access to advanced healthcare technologies across different socio-economic strata. Collaborative efforts involving researchers, healthcare providers, and technology developers are paramount in unlocking AI's full potential to enhance the well-being and quality of life for older adults globally. This holistic approach not only fosters innovation but also ensures that AI-driven solutions are ethically developed, inclusive, and accessible to all, ultimately leading to positive outcomes in senior care and healthcare at large.

Future Directions of AI Technology for Researchers

Researchers in artificial emotional intelligence (AEI) have several promising directions to explore, particularly in advancing AEI's application to wellness. A key area of focus is the development of multimodal emotion detection systems that combine voice analysis, facial expression recognition, and physiological signal monitoring to achieve a more comprehensive and accurate understanding of human emotions. Another promising avenue is the refinement of real-time emotional feedback mechanisms, which can provide immediate insights and interventions, particularly in educational and therapeutic contexts. Additionally, creating emotionally aware interfaces that respond empathetically to user sentiment can significantly enhance user experiences. AEI is also being investigated for its potential in personalized mental health support, aiming to design tools capable of delivering tailored emotional assistance and identifying early signs of emotional distress. To ensure responsible development, addressing ethical considerations and mitigating biases in AEI systems remain critical priorities. Advancing these areas can propel the field forward, fostering more effective and empathetic human-AI interactions.

The Future of AI and Wellness

The future of AI in wellness and healthcare is marked by a strategic integration of AI technologies into healthcare systems, aimed at improving user well-being and optimizing healthcare management processes. This integration encompasses leveraging AI capabilities to identify risky behaviors, address health concerns, and provide intelligent interventions for promoting overall well-being, as emphasized by Monlezun (2023). The synergy between AI, ML, edge analytics, IoT, and cloud computing technologies, as highlighted by Xu (2022), has streamlined healthcare management, paving the way for more efficient and effective healthcare services.

AI's potential to revolutionize the healthcare industry is significant, offering benefits such as providing diagnostic and treatment guidelines, improving patient communication and collaboration, and analyzing and predicting health issues across various medical domains including cancer, neurology, and cardiology, as discussed by Vyas et al. (2023). The future healthcare landscape is expected to prioritize the seamless integration of AI technologies while ensuring equity in access and delivery of healthcare services, with a focus on AI-powered well-being initiatives and enterprise-wide AI-driven healthcare solutions, as noted by Arvindhan et al. (2022).

In essence, AI's transformative potential in wellness management and healthcare delivery is substantial, offering innovative approaches and actionable insights to address unique health challenges and improve overall health outcomes for individuals and communities. The strategic deployment of AI technologies across healthcare systems is poised to usher in a new era of personalized, efficient, and equitable healthcare services.

Potential Developments and Innovations

AI presents promising capabilities in supporting and potentially enhancing human emotional intelligence, albeit with limitations in replicating the depth and complexity of human emotions. The key focus should be on leveraging AI's strengths to empower individuals in managing their emotions and interpersonal interactions more effectively.

While AI excels at recognizing emotional indicators such as facial expressions, text sentiment, and speech patterns to infer basic emotions, it often struggles with nuanced understanding and contextual comprehension. This challenge is further compounded by cultural nuances, subtle cues, and the intricate interplay of factors influencing emotions, which can sometimes exceed AI's capabilities.

Despite AI's inability to fully grasp emotional experiences, its capacity to analyze vast datasets enables the identification of emotional patterns, which can be invaluable in various domains such as healthcare for gauging patient sentiments or in behavioral research. Future endeavors in AI research could emphasize the development of AI-powered tools tailored for personalized emotional intelligence training. These tools could provide valuable feedback and exercises aimed at enhancing self-awareness, social interactions, and emotional regulation skills, thus contributing significantly to individual well-being and societal harmony.

Human Touch vs. AI Assistance

AI is revolutionizing our interactions with technology, shifting us from static interfaces to dynamic conversations and engagements with AI systems. These systems possess the ability to comprehend human language, adapt based on behavioral cues, and even predict our preferences and needs. This evolution has led to AI interfaces becoming increasingly personalized and supportive, streamlining various tasks across different facets of life and enhancing overall user experiences. As highlighted by Amershi et al. (2019), the widespread adoption of AI is paving the way for human-AI interactions to become the primary mode of human-computer interaction.

AI-powered chatbots represent a significant advancement in providing initial support to individuals dealing with emotional challenges. However, it is essential to recognize that AI serves as a potent assistant rather than a substitute for genuine human connection and empathy. While AI can augment our understanding of emotions and offer personalized assistance, it cannot replicate the depth of human empathy and emotional intelligence. The optimal approach involves humans leveraging their emotional intelligence in conjunction with AI's capabilities in data analysis, tailored support, and efficient task execution. This synergy ensures a balance between technological advancements and human-centric values, fostering meaningful interactions and holistic well-being in our increasingly AI-driven world.

Integrations of AI in Healthcare Settings

AI is revolutionizing human-computer interactions and is poised to dominate future interactions, particularly through emotional AI tools that encompass algorithms, sensors, and actuators gathering a wide array of data from individuals, as noted by Mantello and Ho (2022).

The integration of AI in healthcare is multifaceted and offers numerous benefits across various critical areas. Firstly, AI-powered diagnostics leverage advanced algorithms to analyze medical images such as X-rays and mammograms, enhancing accuracy and speed in comparison to human radiologists. This capability enables earlier and more precise diagnoses, leading to improved patient outcomes. Secondly, AI-driven treatment recommendations leverage vast medical data to identify patterns and suggest personalized treatment plans for individual patients, thus optimizing treatment approaches.

Additionally, AI-powered virtual assistants and chatbots play a pivotal role in healthcare settings by addressing patient queries, scheduling appointments, and providing basic medical information. This automation streamlines administrative tasks, allowing healthcare providers to focus more on patient care and complex medical procedures. Furthermore, robotic surgical systems controlled by surgeons offer enhanced precision, flexibility, and minimally invasive procedures, revolutionizing surgical interventions.

As AI technology continues to advance, innovative applications are expected to further enhance the quality, efficiency, and accessibility of healthcare services, ultimately benefiting both healthcare providers and patients alike. This ongoing evolution underscores the transformative potential of AI in revolutionizing healthcare delivery and patient outcomes.

In a nutshell, by combining AI's analytical prowess with emotional intelligence insights, healthcare systems can provide personalized and empathetic care, leading to better patient outcomes.

6) CONCLUSION

In conclusion, emotional wellness represents a state of psychological equilibrium characterized by self-confidence, fulfillment, and the capacity to effectively manage life's challenges. It extends beyond the mere absence of mental health disorders to encompass positive emotional experiences and functioning. The maintenance of emotional wellness in contemporary society presents a complex, multifaceted challenge that necessitates a comprehensive approach. This comprehensive approach should address several key factors such as the management of modern lifestyle stressors, coping mechanisms for economic pressures, strategies for navigating technological overload, efforts to overcome mental health stigma, and the adoption of integrative healthcare approaches that prioritize the mind-body connection. In light of these challenges, the integration of innovative solutions, particularly AEI, emerges as a critical component in advancing mental health care and promoting emotional wellness.

The Potential of Artificial Emotional Intelligence to Revolutionize the Health Industry

The potential of AEI to revolutionize the health industry is substantial. It offers numerous benefits, including enhanced patient-provider interactions, personalized mental health interventions, and support for continuous emotional wellness. Through real-time monitoring and feedback, AEI has the capacity to facilitate more effective emotion management, potentially leading to improved mental health outcomes. Furthermore, AEI presents opportunities to improve access to mental health services, reduce healthcare costs, and enhance the overall quality of care.

However, it is crucial to acknowledge the irreplaceable role of human-human interaction in healthcare settings. The empathy, understanding, and personal touch provided by healthcare professionals remain vital components of patient care, particularly in the context of emotional wellness and recovery. Nevertheless, given the increasing demand for healthcare services and the shortage of human resources, AEI can serve a complementary role in the recovery process. The integration of AEI into healthcare systems may ensure continuous emotional support for patients, even in the absence of immediate human interaction.

Aware of the Challenges to Make Informed Decisions About the Implementation of AI Systems

Ultimately, the successful implementation of emotionally intelligent AI in healthcare requires a balanced approach that leverages the strengths of both human and machine interactions. By combining the empathy and intuition of human caregivers with the precision and consistency of AI, a more effective and supportive healthcare environment can be created. However, it is essential to remain cognizant of the challenges and ethical considerations associated with AEI to make informed decisions about its integration into healthcare systems.

In moving forward, careful planning and thoughtful implementation will be critical. To ensure the accuracy of emotional intelligence AI (EMI) diagnoses, doctors and educators should use diverse and high-quality datasets to train the AI, continuously monitor and validate its performance against real-world data, and collaborate closely with the AI to combine human expertise with AI insights. It is crucial to maintain transparency and explainability in the AI's decision-making process, addressing ethical considerations and actively mitigating biases. Regular updates and training on the latest research help keep the AI accurate and relevant, ensuring that it provides reliable and effective diagnoses while enhancing trust and efficacy in its use. With these considerations in mind, emotionally intelligent AI holds significant potential to enhance emotional wellness and transform the health industry. Future research should focus on refining AEI technologies, evaluating their effectiveness in various healthcare settings, and addressing ethical concerns to ensure responsible and beneficial integration of these technologies into mental health care practices.

REFERENCES

Aboujaoude, E., Gega, L., Parish, M. B., & Hilty, D. M. (2020). Editorial: Digital interventions in mental health: Current status and future directions. *Frontiers in Psychiatry, 11*, 111. Advance online publication. DOI: 10.3389/fpsyt.2020.00111 PMID: 32174858

Agarwal, S. (2022). Iot applications for health care. *Advanced Technologies and Societal Change*, 91-97. DOI: 10.1007/978-981-19-0770-8_8

Aggarwal, A., Tam, C. C., Wu, D., Li, X., & Qiao, S. (2022). Artificial intelligence (ai)-based chatbots in promoting health behavioral changes: A systematic review. *Journal of Medical Internet Research, 25*. Advance online publication. DOI: 10.1101/2022.07.05.22277263

Al-Hwsali, A., Alsaadi, B., Abdi, N., Khatab, S., Alzubaidi, M., Solaiman, B., & Househ, M. (2023). Scoping review: Legal and ethical principles of artificial intelligence in public health. *Studies in Health Technology and Informatics*. Advance online publication. DOI: 10.3233/SHTI230579 PMID: 37387113

American Psychological Association. (November, 2022). *Psychologists struggle to meet demand amid mental health crisis: 2022 COVID-19 Practitioner Impact Survey.* Retrieved from https://www.apa.org/pubs/reports/practitioner/2022-covid-psychologist-workload

Amershi, S., Weld, D., Vorvoreanu, M., Fourney, A., Nushi, B., Collisson, P., & Horvitz, E. (2019). Guidelines for human-ai interaction. *Proceedings of the 2019 CHI Conference on Human Factors in Computing Systems*. DOI: 10.1145/3290605.3300233

Ansari, T. M. (2022). Conversational AI assistant. *International Journal for Research in Applied Science and Engineering Technology, 10*(11), 1169–1172. DOI: 10.22214/ijraset.2022.47554

Anthes, E. (2016). Mental health: There's an app for that. *Nature, 532*(7597), 20–23. DOI: 10.1038/532020a PMID: 27078548

Aronsson, J., Lu, P., Strüber, D., & Berger, T. (2021). A maturity assessment framework for conversational AI development platforms. *Proceedings of the 36th Annual ACM Symposium on Applied Computing*. DOI: 10.1145/3412841.3442046

Arvindhan, M., Gupta, R., Priyadharshini, S., & Anbananthen, K. S. M. (2022). The scope and future outlook of artificial intelligence in healthcare systems. *Applications of Artificial Intelligence in E-Healthcare Systems,* 19-36. DOI: 10.1049/PBHE040E_ch2

Aryan, J., & Shashank, K. (2023). Leveraging Generative AI Models for Synthetic Data Generation in Healthcare: Balancing Research and Privacy. *2023 International Conference on Smart Applications, Communications and Networking (SmartNets),* Istanbul, Turkiye, 1-4. DOI: 10.1109/SmartNets58706.2023.10215825

Assunção, G., Patrão, B., Castelo-Branco, M., & Menezes, P. (2022). An overview of emotion in artificial intelligence. *IEEE Transactions on Artificial Intelligence, 3*(6), 867–886. DOI: 10.1109/TAI.2022.3159614

Bickmore, T. W., Schulman, D., & Sidner, C. (2011). A reusable framework for health counseling dialogue systems based on a behavioral medicine ontology. *Journal of Biomedical Informatics, 44*(2), 183–197. DOI: 10.1016/j.jbi.2010.12.006 PMID: 21220044

Braun, P. S., & Kloss, B. (2017). Wellness programs – Emotional wellness. *Employee Benefit Plan Review, 72*(1), 27–28. https://link.gale.com/apps/doc/A504543974/ITOF?u=unilanc&sid=bookmark-ITOF&xid=fc2665b0

Calvo, R. A., D'Mello, S., Gratch, J., & Kappas, A. (2014). *The Oxford handbook of affective computing*. Oxford University Press.

Cheng, J., Sabour, S., Sun, H., Chen, Z., & Huang, M. (2022). Pal: Persona-augmented emotional support conversation generation. *Findings of the Association for Computational Linguistics: ACL, 2023*, 535–554. DOI: 10.18653/v1/2023.findings-acl.34

Clair, R., Gordon, M., Kroon, M., & Reilly, C. (2021). The effects of social isolation on well-being and life satisfaction during pandemic. *Humanities & Social Sciences Communications, 8*(28), 28. Advance online publication. DOI: 10.1057/s41599-021-00710-3

Corrigan, P. W. (2004). How stigma interferes with mental health care. *The American Psychologist, 59*(7), 614–625. DOI: 10.1037/0003-066X.59.7.614 PMID: 15491256

Dwivedi, Y. K., Hughes, L., Ismagilova, E., Aarts, G., Coombs, C., Crick, T., Duan, Y., Dwivedi, R., Edwards, J., Eirug, A., Galanos, V., Ilavarasan, P. V., Janssen, M., Jones, P., Kar, A. K., Kizgin, H., Kronemann, B., Lal, B., Lucini, B., & Williams, M. D. (2021). Artificial intelligence (ai): Multidisciplinary perspectives on emerging challenges, opportunities, and agenda for research, practice and policy. *International Journal of Information Management, 57*, 101994. DOI: 10.1016/j.ijinfomgt.2019.08.002

Fu, Z., Burger, H., Arjadi, R., & Bockting, C. L. H. (2020). Effectiveness of digital psychological interventions for mental health problems in low-income and middle-income countries: A systematic review and meta-analysis. *The Lancet. Psychiatry*, *7*(10), 851–864. DOI: 10.1016/S2215-0366(20)30256-X PMID: 32866459

Galtier, M., & Meadon, D. (2023). *Applying AI to real-world health-care settings and the life sciences: Tackling data privacy, security and policy challenges with federated learning*. In artificial intelligence in science: Challenges, opportunities and the future of research. OECD Publishing. DOI: 10.1787/058a23d0-en

Ghosh, S., Bagai, S., & Westner, M. M. (2023). *Replika: Embodying AI.* Harvard Business School Case 823-090. https://www.hbs.edu/faculty/Pages/item.aspx?num=63508

Gomes, N., Pato, M., Lourenco, A. R., & Datia, N. (2023). A survey on wearable sensors for mental health monitoring. *Sensors (Basel)*, *23*(3), 1330. DOI: 10.3390/s23031330 PMID: 36772370

Hautekiet, P., Saenen, N. D., Martens, D. S., Debay, M., Van der Heyden, J., Nawrot, T. S., & De Clercq, E. M. (2022). A healthy lifestyle is positively associated with mental health and well-being and core markers in ageing. *BMC Medicine*, *20*(1), 328. Advance online publication. DOI: 10.1186/s12916-022-02524-9 PMID: 36171556

Holohan, M., & Fiske, A. (2021). "Like I'm talking to a real person": Exploring the meaning of transference for the use and design of AI-based applications in psychotherapy. *Frontiers in Psychology*, *12*, 720476. Advance online publication. DOI: 10.3389/fpsyg.2021.720476 PMID: 34646209

Kabir, M. (2023). Machine learning-based security and privacy protection approach to handle physiological data. A*rtificial Intelligence for Disease Diagnosis and Prognosis in Smart Healthcare*, 287-304. DOI: 10.1201/9781003251903-16

Kapoor, A., & Goel, S. (2022). *Applications of conversational AI in mental health: A survey.* 2022 6th International Conference on Trends in Electronics and Informatics (ICOEI). DOI: 10.1109/ICOEI53556.2022.9777127

Keefer, L., Bedell, A., Norton, C., & Hart, A. L. (2022). How should pain, fatigue, and emotional wellness be incorporated into treatment goals for optimal management of inflammatory bowel disease? *Gastroenterology*, *162*(5), 1439–1451. DOI: 10.1053/j.gastro.2021.08.060 PMID: 34995528

Khare, S. K., Blanes-Vidal, V., Nadimi, E. S., & Acharya, U. R. (2024). Emotion recognition and artificial intelligence: A systematic review (2014–2023) and research recommendations. *Information Fusion, 102*, 102019. DOI: 10.1016/j.inffus.2023.102019

Kim, J., Aryee, L. M. D., Bang, H., Prajogo, S., Choi, Y. K., Hoch, J. S., & Prado, E. L. (2023). Effectiveness of digital mental health tools to reduce depressive and anxiety symptoms in low- and middle-income countries: Systematic review and meta-analysis. *JMIR Mental Health, 10*, e43066. DOI: 10.2196/43066 PMID: 36939820

Lattie, E. G., Stiles-Shields, C., & Graham, A. K. (2022). An overview of and recommendations for more accessible digital mental health services. *Nature Reviews Psychology, 1*(2), 87–100. DOI: 10.1038/s44159-021-00003-1 PMID: 38515434

Lee, J., Lee, S., & Kim, D. (2022). *Problems and issues of emotional computing and artificial emotional intelligence: A review of Rosalind w. picard's thesis "affective computing: challenges"*. 2022 IEEE/ACIS 7th International Conference on Big Data, Cloud Computing, and Data Science (BCD). DOI: 10.1109/BCD54882.2022.9900683

Leung, Y., Park, B., Heo, R., Adikari, A., Chackochan, S., Wong, J., Alie, E., Gancarz, M., Kacala, M., Hirst, G., de Silva, D., French, L., Bender, J., Mishna, F., Gratzer, D., Alahakoon, D., & Esplen, M. J. (2022). Providing care beyond therapy sessions with a natural language processing–based recommender system that identifies cancer patients who experience psychosocial challenges and provides self-care support: Pilot study. *JMIR Cancer, 8*(3), e35893. DOI: 10.2196/35893 PMID: 35904877

Liao, F., Adelaine, S., Afshar, M., & Patterson, B. W. (2022). Governance of clinical AI applications to facilitate safe and equitable deployment in a large health system: Key elements and early successes. *Frontiers in Digital Health, 4*, 931439. Advance online publication. DOI: 10.3389/fdgth.2022.931439 PMID: 36093386

Lin, B., Cecchi, G., & Bouneffouf, D. (2023, March 13). *Psychotherapy AI Companion with Reinforcement Learning Recommendations and Interpretable Policy Dynamics.* Companion Proceedings of the ACM Web Conference 2023 (WWW '23 Companion). DOI: 10.1145/3543873.3587623

Link, B. G., & Phelan, J. C. (2001). Conceptualizing stigma. *Annual Review of Sociology, 27*(1), 363–385. DOI: 10.1146/annurev.soc.27.1.363

Liu, J., Chen, C., Qu, Y., Yang, S., & Xu, L. (2023). Rass: Enabling privacy-preserving and authentication in online AI-driven healthcare applications. *ISA Transactions, 141*, 20–29. DOI: 10.1016/j.isatra.2023.03.049 PMID: 37059673

Loveys, K., Prina, M., Axford, C., Domènec, Ò. R., Weng, W., Broadbent, E., Pujari, S., Jang, H., Han, Z. A., & Thiyagarajan, J. A. (2022). Artificial intelligence for older people receiving long-term care: A systematic review of acceptability and effectiveness studies. *The Lancet. Healthy Longevity*, *3*(4), e286–e297. DOI: 10.1016/S2666-7568(22)00034-4 PMID: 35515814

Mak, R. H., Endres, M. G., Paik, J. H., Sergeev, R. A., Aerts, H., Williams, C. L., Lakhani, K. R., & Guinan, E. C. (2019). Use of crowd innovation to develop an artificial intelligence–based solution for radiation therapy targeting. *JAMA Oncology*, *5*(5), 654–661. DOI: 10.1001/jamaoncol.2019.0159 PMID: 30998808

Mantello, P., & Ho, T. (2022). Why we need to be weary of emotional AI. *AI & Society*. Advance online publication. DOI: 10.1007/s00146-022-01576-y

Manyika, J., Chui, M., Miremadi, M., Bughin, J., George, K., Willmott, P., & Dewhurst, M. (2017). A future that works: AI, automation, employment, and productivity. *McKinsey Global Institute Research. Tech. Rep*, *60*, 1–135.

Maslach, C., & Leiter, M. P. (2016). Understanding the burnout experience: Recent research and its implications for psychiatry. *World Psychiatry; Official Journal of the World Psychiatric Association (WPA)*, *15*(2), 103–111. DOI: 10.1002/wps.20311 PMID: 27265691

McEwen, B. S. (2007). Physiology and neurobiology of stress and adaptation: Central role of the brain. *Physiological Reviews*, *87*(3), 873–904. DOI: 10.1152/physrev.00041.2006 PMID: 17615391

McStay, A. (2024). *Automating empathy: Decoding technologies that gauge intimate life*. Oxford University Press., DOI: 10.1093/oso/9780197615546.001.0001

Meng, J., Rheu, M., Zhang, Y., Dai, Y., & Peng, W. (2023). *Mediated social support for distress reduction: ai chatbots vs. human.* Proceedings of the ACM on Human-Computer Interaction, 7(CSCW1), 1-25. DOI: 10.1145/3579505

Mogaji, E., Olaleye, S. A., & Ukpabi, D. C. (2019). Using AI to personalise emotionally appealing advertisement. *Digital and Social Media Marketing*, 137-150. DOI: 10.1007/978-3-030-24374-6_10

Monlezun, D. (2023). The future's (ai) thinking healthcare system. *The Thinking Healthcare System,* 263-303. DOI: 10.1016/B978-0-443-18906-7.00008-8

Muetunda, F., Jamil, M. L., Pais, S., Sabry, S., Dias, G., Pombo, N., & Cordeiro, J. (2023). Exploring the role of artificial intelligence in mental health. *2023 IEEE International Conference on Data Mining Workshops (ICDMW)*, 1289–1298. DOI: 10.1109/ICDMW60847.2023.00166

Norcross, J. C., & Wampold, B. E. (2011). Evidence-based therapy relationships: Research conclusions and clinical practices. *Psychotherapy (Chicago, Ill.)*, *48*(1), 98–102. DOI: 10.1037/a0022161 PMID: 21401280

Ong, D. C. (2021, September). An ethical framework for guiding the development of affectively-aware artificial intelligence. *9th International Conference on Affective Computing and Intelligent Interaction (ACII)*, Nara, Japan, 2021, 1-8. DOI: 10.1109/ACII52823.2021.9597441

Patel, S., & Fan, J. (2023). Identification and description of emotions by current large language models. *bioRxiv*. DOI: 10.1101/2023.07.17.549421

Peuter, S. D., Oulasvirta, A., & Kaski, S. (2023). Toward AI assistants that let designers design. *AI Magazine*, *44*(1), 85–96. DOI: 10.1002/aaai.12077

Picard, R. W., & Klein, J. (2002). Computers that recognize and respond to user emotion: Theoretical and practical implications. *Interacting with Computers*, *14*(2), 141–169. DOI: 10.1016/S0953-5438(01)00055-8

Prabhakaran, V., Qadri, R., & Hutchinson, B. (2022). *Cultural incongruencies in artificial intelligence*. arXiv. https://doi.org//arXiv.2211.13069DOI: 10.48550

Qadri, R., Shelby, R., Bennett, C. L., & Denton, E. (2023). AI's regimes of representation: a community-centered study of text-to-image models in South Asia. *2023 ACM Conference on Fairness, Accountability, and Transparency*. DOI: 10.1145/3593013.3594016

Rahman, M. M. (2023). Ensuring halal compliance in AI-driven healthcare solutions. *Advances in Healthcare Information Systems and Administration*, •••, 298–320. DOI: 10.4018/979-8-3693-1082-3.ch015

Rauck, R., Loudermilk, E., Paez, J., Bojrab, L., Noles, J., Turley, T., Ibrahim, M., Patwardhan, A., Scowcroft, J., Przkora, R., Miller, N., Chaiban, G., Hershey, B., Lechleiter, K., Woon, R., Huynh, D., Tchrakian, T., Rodgers, J., & McDonald, M. (2022). O045 / #626 artificial intelligence-driven closed-loop SCS: Early patient feedback on personalized therapy recommendations from a digital-health assistant. *Neuromodulation*, *25*(7), S72–S73. DOI: 10.1016/j.neurom.2022.08.083

Russell, R. D., Black, L. J., Pham, N. M., & Begley, A. (2020). The effectiveness of emotional wellness programs on mental health outcomes for adults with multiple sclerosis: A systematic review and meta-analysis. *Multiple Sclerosis and Related Disorders*, *44*, 102171. DOI: 10.1016/j.msard.2020.102171 PMID: 32554283

Ryff, C. D., & Singer, B. (1998). The contours of positive human health. *Psychological Inquiry*, *9*(1), 1–28. DOI: 10.1207/s15327965pli0901_1

Saleh, S., & Battseren, B. (2023). Ai-driven solutions for sustainable environment monitoring. *Embedded Selforganising Systems, 10*(8), 1-2. https://doi.org/DOI: 10.14464/ess.v10i8.615

Sankaran, K. S., Tai-Hoon, K., & Renjith, P. N. (2023). An improved AI-based secure m-trust privacy protocol for medical internet of things in smart healthcare system. *IEEE Internet of Things Journal, 10*(21), 18477–18485. DOI: 10.1109/JIOT.2023.3280592

Sasmal, S. (2024). Data warehousing revolution: AI-driven solutions. International Research *Journal Of Engineering & Applied Sciences, 12*(1), 01-06. https://doi.org/DOI: 10.55083/irjeas.2024.v12i01001

Schyff, E. L. d., Ridout, B., Amon, K. L., Forsyth, R., & Campbell, A. (2023). *Providing self-led mental health support through an artificial intelligence–powered chatbot (leora) to meet the demand of mental health care* (preprint). DOI: 10.2196/preprints.46448

Sequeiros, H., Oliveira, T., & Thomas, M. A. (2022). The impact of IoT smart home services on psychological well-being. *Information Systems Frontiers, 24*(3), 1009–1026. DOI: 10.1007/s10796-021-10118-8

Shimada, K. (2023). The role of artificial intelligence in mental health: A Review. *Science Insights, 43*(5), 1119–1127. DOI: 10.15354/si.23.re820

Stark, L., & Hoey, J. (2019). The ethics of emotion in AI systems. *AoIR Selected Papers of Internet Research.* DOI: 10.5210/spir.v2019i0.11039

Timmons, A. C., Duong, J. B., Fiallo, N. S., Lee, T., Vo, H. P. Q., Ahle, M. W., & Chaspari, T. (2022). A call to action on assessing and mitigating bias in artificial intelligence applications for mental health. *Perspectives on Psychological Science, 18*(5), 1062–1096. DOI: 10.1177/17456916221134490 PMID: 36490369

Trabelsi, Z., Alnajjar, F., Parambil, M. M. A., Gochoo, M., & Ali, L. (2023). Real-time attention monitoring system for classroom: A deep learning approach for student's behavior recognition. *Big Data and Cognitive Computing, 7*(48), 48. Advance online publication. DOI: 10.3390/bdcc7010048

Twenge, J. M., Joiner, T. E., Rogers, M. L., & Martin, G. N. (2018). Increases in depressive symptoms, suicide-related outcomes, and suicide rates among US adolescents after 2010 and links to increased new media screen time. *Clinical Psychological Science, 6*(1), 3–17. DOI: 10.1177/2167702617723376 van Noord, N., Wevers, M., Blanke, T., Noordegraaf, J., & Worring, M. (2022). *An Analytics of Culture: Modeling Subjectivity, Scalability, Contextuality, and Temporality.* arXiv. https://doi.org//arXiv.2211.07460DOI: 10.48550

Varma, P., Junge, M., Meaklim, H., & Jackson, M. L. (2021). Younger people are more vulnerable to stress, anxiety and depression during COVID-19 pandemic: A global cross-sectional survey. *Progress in Neuro-Psychopharmacology & Biological Psychiatry*, *109*, 110236. DOI: 10.1016/j.pnpbp.2020.110236 PMID: 33373680

Vigneswaran, A. J. G., & Aakash, B. (2022). Artificial intelligence-based voice assistant. *International Journal for Research in Applied Science and Engineering Technology*, *10*(12), 1130–1133. DOI: 10.22214/ijraset.2022.48147

Vinay, R., Spitale, G., Biller-Andorno, N., & Germani, F. (2024). *Emotional manipulation through prompt engineering amplifies disinformation generation in AI large language models.* arXiv. https://doi.org//arXiv.2403.03550DOI: 10.48550

Vyas, S., Gupta, S., & Shukla, V. K. (2023). Towards edge AI and varied approaches of digital wellness in healthcare administration: a study. *2023 International Conference on Computational Intelligence and Knowledge Economy (ICCIKE)*. DOI: 10.1109/ICCIKE58312.2023.10131857

Wang, Q., Fan, K., & Li, P. (2022). Effect of the use of home and community care services on the multidimensional health of older adults. *International Journal of Environmental Research and Public Health*, *19*(22), 15402. DOI: 10.3390/ijerph192215402 PMID: 36430119

Wang, Q., Peng, S., Zha, Z., Han, X., Deng, C., Hu, L., & Hu, P. (2023). Enhancing the conversational agent with an emotional support system for mental health digital therapeutics. *Frontiers in Psychiatry*, *14*, 1148534. Advance online publication. DOI: 10.3389/fpsyt.2023.1148534 PMID: 37139323

Wilmink, G., Dupey, K., Alkire, S., Grote, J., Zobel, G., Fillit, H., & Movva, S. (2020). Artificial intelligence–powered digital health platform and wearable devices improve outcomes for older adults in assisted living communities: Pilot intervention study. *JMIR Aging*, *3*(2), e19554. DOI: 10.2196/19554 PMID: 32723711

Wilson, J. M., Lee, J., Fitzgerald, H. N., Oosterhoff, B., Sevi, B., & Shook, N. J. (2020). Job insecurity and financial concern during the COVID-19 pandemic are associated with worse mental health. *Journal of Occupational and Environmental Medicine*, *62*(9), 686–691. DOI: 10.1097/JOM.0000000000001962 PMID: 32890205

Xu, X. (2022). *Towards future health and well-being: bridging behavior modeling and intervention.* Adjunct Proceedings of the 35th Annual ACM Symposium on User Interface Software and Technology. DOI: 10.1145/3526114.3558524

Yang, T., Zhao, L., Li, W., Wu, J., & Zomaya, A. Y. (2021). Towards healthy and cost-effective indoor environment management in smart homes: A deep reinforcement learning approach. *Applied Energy*, *300*, 117335. DOI: 10.1016/j.apenergy.2021.117335

Yang, Z., Zhou, Q., Lei, L., Zheng, K., & Xiang, H. (2016). An IoT-cloud based wearable ECG monitoring system for smart healthcare. *Journal of Medical Systems*, *40*(286), 286. Advance online publication. DOI: 10.1007/s10916-016-0644-9 PMID: 27796840

Yousefi, Y. (2022). Data sharing as a debiasing measure for AI systems in healthcare: new legal basis. *15th International Conference on Theory and Practice of Electronic Governance*. DOI: 10.1145/3560107.3560116

Chapter 3
Ethical Considerations in AI-Powered Health Communities to Promote Good Health and Wellbeing:
A Narrative Review

Chin Siang Ang
https://orcid.org/0000-0003-1868-7827
Nanyang Technological University, Singapore

Kam-Fong Lee
SEGi University, Malaysia

ABSTRACT

The proliferation of Artificial Intelligence (AI) use not only has transformed the health communities but also raised concerns about its ethical implications. Employing a narrative review method, this chapter explores the different types of AI-powered health communities to examine the functionalities and purposes each community serves. This review also delves into identifying the key ethical considerations and its challenges associated raised by developers, experts and participants in the health communities. Besides, it will examine the existing regulations and frameworks governing the use of AI in the healthcare industry in relation to their effectiveness, potential gaps and areas for improvement in addressing the identified ethical concerns. Finally, it will propose recommendations for the ethical development and implementation of AI-powered health communities by synthesizing existing literature.

DOI: 10.4018/979-8-3693-5837-5.ch003

Findings from this narrative review will offer insights for addressing the identified ethical concerns to propose best practices for data governance.

1. INTRODUCTION

The advent of Web 2.0 technologies has driven the rise and widespread adoption of online health communities (OHCs) (Le et al., 2023). OHCs fulfil various roles (Zhao et al., 2022); some function as communities of practice where healthcare professionals share insights, while others offer peer support to patients and their families or connect healthcare professionals with the public for health-related initiatives. These specialized social networks act as hubs for exchanging healthcare information, enhancing communication, delivering services, and providing emotional support. The growth of these communities has been fuelled significantly by advances in Artificial Intelligence (AI). Historically, AI has evolved from its inception in the mid-20 century to become a powerful tool with diverse applications across various sectors, including healthcare (Bohr & Memarzadeh, 2020). As Drukker et al. (2020) suggest, AI holds transformative potential in healthcare by generating new insights and innovative ideas through data analysis. Recognising this, the World Health Organization (WHO) has highlighted the benefits of AI in public health and medicine (WHO, 2021).

AI, defined by its ability to mimic intelligent human actions, offers numerous applications within OHCs (Zhang, 2024). For example, AI can simplify complex medical guidance, making it accessible to a broader audience, including marginalized communities with limited healthcare access. AI-driven chatbots, such as Noom, Orbita, and Buoy Health, can provide personalized advice on medication, diet, and lifestyle changes, potentially improving patient compliance. Additionally, AI has the potential to enhance diagnostic capabilities (Taddeo & Floridi, 2018), increased operational efficiency in healthcare (Nelson et al., 2019), and optimised patient care (Sujan et al., 2019). AI-powered health communities can also foster patient engagement and participation in their own care.

However, several challenges hinder the equitable implementation of AI in OHCs. Achieving equitable access to AI resources for marginalized populations remains a significant hurdle due to factors like limited exposure and low digital literacy (Marzo, 2024). Moreover, the inadequate design of digital health information for underprivileged groups (Ouédraogo, 2024) further exacerbates this issue. Additionally, the ethical implications of AI in healthcare, such as privacy concerns, algorithmic bias, and the potential for misuse, warrant careful consideration (Haleem et al., 2022).

These ethical concerns encompass moral considerations, responsibilities, and the consequences associated with AI use in healthcare. Although research on OHCs is extensive, AI-driven platforms remain underexplored in the literature. Ensuring these AI-powered platforms adhere to human ethics and values is critical (Redrup Hill et al., 2023). This chapter seeks to address this gap by conducting a comprehensive literature review to examine the ethical considerations of AI in OHCs and identify areas requiring further study.

2. RESEARCH OBJECTIVES

This study seeks to address the identified gap through the following objectives:

1. Explore AI-powered platforms and their applications.
2. Investigate ethical concerns and risks associated with AI integration in health communities.
3. Identify key ethical considerations related to AI technologies in healthcare.
4. Examine existing regulations and frameworks governing AI use in healthcare to address ethical concerns.
5. Propose recommendations for the ethical development and implementation of AI-powered health communities.

These objectives clarity the study's focus on critical variables. Objective 1 provides insights into the types and applications of AI-powered platforms. Objectives 2 and 3 examine ethical concerns, risks, and considerations, while Objectives 4 and 5 focus on regulatory frameworks and actionable recommendations to foster ethical AI practices. Together, these objectives address the pressing ethical challenges associated with AI use in healthcare communities.

3. METHODOLOGY

A narrative synthesis approach was employed to integrate findings from empirical studies on AI in healthcare, presented them in a structured narrative format. The review focused on studies published between 2019 and April 21, 2024, to capture recent advancements. To ensure high-quality evidence, grey literature was excluded, and only peer-reviewed articles were considered. Searches were conducted using Scopus and Web of Science, two leading academic databases known for their comprehensive coverage (Pranckuté, 2021), to minimize the risk of missing relevant studies due to database variability.

The screening process consisted of two stages. First, duplicate entries were eliminated to streamline the dataset, followed by the remaining articles were evaluated based on the following criteria:

- Inclusion Criteria:
  - o Focus on AI and health communities with explicit mention of ethical considerations.
  - o Application of AI in health communities.
  - o Articles published in English.
- Exclusion Criteria:
  - o Studies unrelated to the review objectives (e.g., not addressing AI, health, or ethics).
  - o Non-research publications (e.g., editorials, commentary, conference abstracts).
  - o Articles in languages other than English.

These criteria ensured the inclusion of relevant, robust empirical evidence, while minimizing irrelevant materials (Chaney, 2021; Sukhera, 2022). Following data extraction, a thematic narrative synthesis approach was adopted. This involved organizing data into conceptual categories and subcategories using structured feature maps (Pautasso, 2019; Strauss & Corbin, 1990). The findings were synthesized to align with the study's research objectives.

4. RESULTS

The search strategy identified a total of 2,866 articles, comprising 1,034 from Web of Science and 1,832 from Scopus (see Table 1). These articles were imported into Endnote, where duplicate removal reduced the dataset to 1,967 unique articles. During the article screening process, approximately 95% of the articles were excluded based on title and abstract relevance, leaving 101 articles for full-text review. Eight articles were inaccessible, and 71 were further excluded based on the predetermined inclusion and exclusion criteria. This process resulted in a final set of 22 articles deemed relevant to the review.

Table 1. Search queries employed in database searches

Databases used	Search field	Keywords	No. of publications
Web of Science	Topic	((“artificial intelligen*” OR “artificial neural network*” OR “machine learn*” OR “deep learn*”) AND (communi* OR “health communit*” OR forum*) AND (ethic* OR bioethic*))	1034
Scopus	Title, abstract, keywords		1832
Provisory N total			2866

4.1 Characteristics of Included Studies

This review comprises 22 studies, the majority were published in recent years, highlighting growing interest in the topic. 2023 was the most common publication year (n = 10), followed by 2022 (n = 4), 2019 (n = 3), and 2020 and 2021 (n = 2 each). One study was published in 2024. A word cloud analysis of the literature identified frequently occurring terms, including “intelligence” (13 occurrences), “artificial” (12), “health” (7), and “AI” (7), reflecting the focus of the studies. The studies represent contributions from 11 countries, with the United States leading (n = 9). Other contributors included the United Kingdom, Australia, and Switzerland (n = 2 each). Additionally, Finland, China, Spain, Canada, Norway, Mexico, and Saudi Arabia each contributed one study. In terms of publication type, 14 studies appeared in academic journals, while the remainder were published as conference papers (n = 5) and book chapters (n = 3).

4.2 AI-Powered Platforms and Their Application Areas

This review identifies a range of AI-powered platforms employed across the included studies. Conversational agents such as chatbots were the most frequently discussed (n = 6; Balcombe, 2023; Brown & Halpern, 2021; Denecke et al., 2021; Fournier-Tombs & McHardy, 2023; Kurian, 2023; Sedlakova & Trachsel, 2023). Two studies utilized multiple platforms, including mobile apps, virtual agents, and robotics (Castañeda-Garza et al., 2023; Gamble, 2020). Ten studies focused on platforms with specific designations, such as language technologies (Diaz-Asper et al., 2024), information and communication technologies (Bouderhem, 2022), virtual agents (Maharjan et al., 2019), augmented intelligence systems (Crigger, 2022), eHealth technologies (Chatterjee et al., 2019), telemedicine systems (Kaas et al., 2023), healthcare applications (Goirand et al., 2023), message generation technology (Schmälzle & Wilcox, 2022), social media platforms (Leung, 2023), and human-centered AI technologies (Ozmen Garibay et al., 2023). Four studies did not specify the platforms used (McCradden et al., 2020; Subasi et al., 2023; Vellido, 2019; Zhang & Zhang, 2023).

Most studies focused on applications within the broader healthcare sector (n = 10; Bouderhem, 2022; Crigger et al., 2022; Fournier-Tombs & McHardy, 2023; Goirand et al., 2023; Kaas, 2023; Leung, 2023; McCradden et al., 2020; Subasi et al., 2023; Vellido, 2019; Zhang & Zhang, 2023), addressing areas such as: disease diagnosis, treatment planning, drug discovery, patient monitoring, and healthcare administration. Six studies specifically targeted mental health (Balcombe, 2023; Brown & Halpern, 2021; Castañeda-Garza et al., 2023; Denecke et al., 2021; Gamble, 2020; Sedlakova & Trachsel, 2023), using platforms for teletherapy, digital cognitive behavioral therapy programs, and AI-driven emotional support systems. Two studies explored individual health or wellness management, with applications supporting chronic disease management and promoting healthy lifestyles (Chatterjee et al., 2019; Maharjan et al., 2019). Other studies highlighted diverse applications, including psychological science (Diaz-Asper et al., 2024), early childhood and care (Kurian, 2023), and health communication (Schmälzle & Wilcox, 2022). One study did not specify its application area (Ozmen Garibay et al., 2023).

4.3 Ethical Concerns and Associated Risks

The 22 reviewed studies highlight critical ethical concerns arising from the integration of AI into health communities. These issues, encompassing potential risks and adverse outcomes, are categorised into six key areas: algorithm bias and discrimination, data breaches and privacy issues, lack of transparency, technical limitations and associated harm, overconfidence and misplaced trust in AI, and lack of regulation and standards (see Table 2).

- ***Algorithm Bias and Discrimination (n=13):*** A prominent concern was the risk of AI perpetuating biases and discrimination. Zhang and Zhang (2023) emphasized the impact of unstructured medical data and inconsistent annotation on algorithm quality. Insufficient sampling during AI training can lead to biased predictions and potentially harmful recommendations (Balcombe, 2023; Denecke et al., 2021; Goirand et al., 2023; Leung, 2023; Vellido, 2019). Sociocultural variations in language further expose underrepresented groups to inaccurate assessments, reinforcing stereotypes (Diaz-Asper et al., 2024). Fournier-Tombs and McHardy (2023) warned that sociodemographic factors might inadvertently propagate stereotypes or exclude marginalized populations. Kurian (2023) noted that societal biases embedded in training data could undermine users' rights to equitable interactions, while Gamble (2020) cautioned that poor adaptation to specific populations may exacerbate disparities. Crigger et al. (2022) observed that AI could neglect the needs of historically marginalized groups, widening healthcare inequalities. Brown and Halpern (2021) highlighted risks to self-advocacy for individuals facing mental health challenges or social marginalization. Finally, Chatterjee et al. (2019) pointed out how insufficient data for certain groups could lead to sub-optimal solutions.

- ***Data Breaches and Privacy Issues (n=8)***: Data security emerged as a significant ethical challenge, especially given the reliance of AI systems on extensive personal data. Risks of hacking, misuse, or repurposing were highlighted by Goirand (2023) and Vellido (2019), while Leung (2023) expressed concerns about social media data collection compromising patient identity. Chatterjee et al. (2019) discussed unauthorised access to sensitive data and privacy violations like non-consensual photography. Legal gaps in chatbot user privacy protection were flagged by Denecke et al. (2021). The absence of clear data protection measures, as noted by Castañeda-Garza et al. (2023), poses a further risk to user identity. Fournier-Tombs (2023) and Balcombe (2023) underlined the dangers of inadequate data governance, which could lead to stigmatization from data misuse.
- ***Lack of transparency (n = 4)***: The "black box" nature of AI present another major challenge, complicating users' understanding of AI-driven decisions (Diaz-Asper et al., 2024; Vellido, 2019). Zhang and Zhang (2023) stressed that this opacity undermines trust and hinders the detection or correction of biases. In healthcare, such lack of transparency can jeopardize patient safety, as comprehending clinical decisions is vital. Schmälzle and Wilcox (2022) noted that individuals unfamiliar with AI might find AI-generated content both captivating and unsettling, further complicating trust.
- ***Technical limitations and associated harm (n=7)***: Technical deficiencies, particularly in AI's ability to engage empathetically, pose significant risks. Brown and Halpern (2021) discussed the absence of non-verbal cues critical to patient interactions. Kurian (2023) emphasized AI's limited capacity for emotional depth, which can lead to misinterpretations. Sedlakova and Trachsel (2023) warned of the dangers of over-quantification in therapeutic settings, which may diminish personal insights. Schmälzle and Wilcox (2022) highlighted that AI's reliance on language patterns, rather than context, can result in irrelevant outputs. Concerns about AI learning autonomously without human oversight were raised by Crigger et al. (2022), while Denecke et al. (2021) and Zhang and Zhang (2023) flagged risks to patient safety from

AI's autonomous decision-making, particularly when accountability for errors is unclear.

- ***Overconfidence and Misplaced Trust in AI (n=5)***: Excessive reliance on AI systems pose significant risks. Fournier-Tombs (2023) and Denecke et al. (2021) noted that overconfidence in AI could erode trust in human professionals and result in adverse outcomes if AI errors occur. Sedlakova and Trachsel (2023) highlighted the complexities of human-AI relationships, warning of unrealistic expectations from interactions with AI systems lacking genuine therapeutic capabilities (Gamble, 2020). Schmälzle and Wilcox (2022) added that AI's human-like responses might create a false sense of intelligence and understanding.
- ***Lack of Regulation and Standards (n=4)***: The absence of robust regulatory standards for AI remains a critical concern. Gamble (2020) observed that many AI tools lack strict oversight, raising concerns about safety and ethical use. Denecke et al. (2021) noted that many chatbots operate without an evidence-based foundation, potentially leading to unreliable information. Diaz-Asper et al. (2024) highlighted how informational chatbots often evade the ethical scrutiny applied to clinical tools. Castañeda-Garza et al. (2023) emphasized the need for regulations to adapt to AI's role as a support tool rather than a replacement for mental health professionals.

Table 2. Ethical concerns and risks

First author, year	Types of ethical concerns and risks						Short description of ethical concerns and risks
	Bias	Data	Trans	Harm	Trust	Standards	
Balcombe, 2023	•	•					• Algorithmic biases, misinformation, deep fakes. • Unauthorized data access, emotional distress.
Bouderhem, 2022							• Not specified
Brown, 2021	•			•			• Impact on marginalized groups. • Non-verbal attunement issues; loss of special benefits in clinical settings.
Castañeda-Garza, 2023		•				•	• Data privacy safeguarding issues. • AI not replacing professionals.
Chatterjee, 2019	•	•					• Illegitimate data access; violation of privacy without consent. • Compromised solution validity.
Crigger, 2022	•			•			• Exclusion of marginalized groups. • AI systems evolve outside human observation.

continued on following page

Table 2. Continued

First author, year	Types of ethical concerns and risks						Short description of ethical concerns and risks
	Bias	Data	Trans	Harm	Trust	Standards	
Denecke, 2021	•	•		•	•	•	• AI decisions are out of control. • Bias towards population groups. • Lack of evidence-based interaction. • Lack of legal protection for privacy. • Over-reliance on AI.
Diaz-Asper, 2024	•		•			•	• Information use only. • "Black box" challenges. • Sociocultural factors impact.
Fournier-Tombs, 2023	•	•			•		• Recommendations based on sociodemographic groups. • Improper data governance. • Overconfidence in AI.
Gamble, 2020	•				•	•	• Trust exploitation. • Lack of informed approach. • Safety and efficacy untested.
Goirand, 2023	•	•					• Hacking and misuse concerns. • Entrenchment of inequities.
Kaas, 2023							• Not specified
Kurian, 2023	•			•			• Societal biases in AI output. • Limit in emotion and language processing.
Leung, 2023	•	•					• Privacy concerns in data collection. • Bias in predictive functions.
Maharjan, 2019							• Not specified
McCradden, 2020							• Not specified
Ozmen Garibay, 2023							• Not specified
Schmälzle, 2022			•	•	•		• Misunderstanding AI capabilities. • Human-like but flawed AI outputs. • Inaccurate information.
Sedlakova, 2023				•	•		• Quantification of emotions; unclear norms in digital relationships. • Deception in AI relationships; no moral responsibilities.
Subasi, 2023							• Not specified
Vellido, 2019	•	•	•				• "Black box" issues. • Data misuse risks. • Reinforcement of stereotypes.
Zhang, 2023	•		•	•			• Unstructured medical data issues; bias in clinical predictions. • Opacity affects trust; security vulnerabilities; • Unclear responsibility.

Source: Authors' work

Note: Bias = Algorithm bias and discrimination; Data = Data breaches and privacy issues; Trans = Lack of transparency; Harm = Technical limitations and associated harm; Trust = Overconfidence and misplaced trust in AI; Standards = Lack of regulation and standards

4.4. Ethical Considerations

Our data extraction revealed that ethical considerations were a prominent focus across the studies. These considerations included principles and values essential for the responsible development, deployment, and evaluation of AI technologies in healthcare. They emphasized proactive integration of safeguards and adherence to best practices to ensure ethical AI implementation. An analysis of the studies showed that most relied on secondary sources for ethical guidance, including academic reviews and grey literature (Balcombe, 2023; Castañeda-Garza et al., 2023; Denecke et al., 2021; Leung, 2023; McCradden et al., 2020; Subasi et al., 2023; Vellido, 2019). Frequently cited frameworks included the Principles of Biomedical Ethics (Brown & Halpern, 2021; Fournier-Tombs & McHardy, 2023; Zhang & Zhang, 2023) and guidelines from entities such as the WHO, European Union, and American Psychological Association (Bouderhem, 2022; Crigger et al., 2022; Diaz-Asper et al., 2024). A smaller subset of studies used alternative approaches, such as philosophical framework (Sedlakova & Trachsel, 2023), participatory engagement (Goirand et al., 2023), or expert consensus (Ozmen Garibay et al., 2023). Notably, five studies did not disclose their ethical sources (Chatterjee et al., 2019; Gamble, 2020; Kurian, 2023; Maharjan et al., 2019; Schmälzle & Wilcox, 2022).

From these findings, we categorized the ethical considerations into eight thematic groups (see Table 3):

- ***Beneficence and Non-Maleficence (n=10):*** Studies underscored the necessity of designing AI systems that prioritize patient outcomes while minimizing harm (Brown & Halpern, 2021; Fournier-Tombs & McHardy, 2023; Goirand et al., 2023; Kaas et al., 2023; Zhang & Zhang, 2023). Kurian (2023) emphasized placing user needs and vulnerabilities at the forefront of AI system design through human-centered approaches. Ozmen Garibay et al. (2023) advocated for AI tools that enhance lives, while Gamble (2020) focused on safety measures for addressing suicidality. Balcombe (2023) highlighted the importance of equipping vulnerable individuals with informed guidance to self-manage their mental health when using AI chatbots to access resources and treatments. To mitigate risks, Sedlakova and Trachsel (2023) recommended limiting AI's psychotherapeutic functions to non-rational tasks, while Kurian (2023) stressed ongoing monitoring of AI performance and risk management.
- ***Autonomy and Human Agency (n=7):*** Maintaining human agency and empowering individuals to make autonomous healthcare decisions were recurring themes (Kaas et al., 2023; Diaz-Asper et al., 2024; Ozmen Garibay et al., 2023). Brown and Halpern (2021), Fournier-Tombs and McHardy (2023),

Goirand et al. (2023), and Zhang and Zhang (2023) emphasized the critical roles of informed consent, transparency in AI functions, and fostering self-determination in patient care.

- ***Justice, Fairness, and Equity (n=8):*** Justice in AI-focused healthcare necessitated equitable access and unbiased treatment outcomes (Kaas et al., 2023). Studies highlighted the creation of inclusive AI systems to mitigate healthcare disparities, particularly for disadvantaged populations (Bouderhem, 2022; Brown & Halpern, 2021; Crigger et al., 2022; Fournier-Tombs & McHardy, 2023; Vellido, 2019; Zhang & Zhang, 2023). Diaz-Asper et al. (2024) stressed the importance of respecting individual rights and dignity to avoid discriminatory predictions.
- ***Transparency and Explainability (n=9):*** Transparency was identified as fundamental to building trust in AI, emphasizing traceability (documentation) and explainability (clear in decision-making processes) (Diaz-Asper et al., 2024; Goirand et al., 2023; Kaas et al., 2023). urian (2023), Leung (2023), and Vellido (2019) advocated for clear communication of AI system functionality and decision-making to help healthcare providers and patients understand and trust AI-based recommendations, thus enabling informed decisions (Subasi et al., 2023). This transparency also fostered trust in AI adoption, influenced by perceived utility, reliability, and professional oversight (McCradden et al., 2020; Subasi et al., 2023). Furthermore, communicating the limitations and realistic capabilities of AI systems, such as therapeutic contexts, was essential to managing expectations, particularly regarding emotional support or complex conversations (Sedlakova & Trachsel, 2023).
- ***Privacy and Security (n=11):*** Safeguarding patient privacy and securing data were critical due to sensitive nature of health information (Ozmen Garibay et al., 2023; Subasi et al., 2023). Privacy considerations included protocols for data collection, usage, sharing, and storage (Castañeda-Garza et al., 2023). Studies by Chatterjee et al. (2019) and McCradden et al. (2020) emphasized securing personal data and ensuring informed, voluntary consent. Data anonymization was highlighted as a key measure for privacy protection, preventing unauthorized sharing or misuse (Leung, 2023; Vellido, 2019). Protecting confidentiality was particularly critical for mental health data, as Denecke et al. (2021) noted, to reduce fears of stigma. Ensuring trust in data security was further linked to minimizing about stigmatization (Gamble, 2020). Robust security protocols were advocated to prevent data breaches, with calls for adherence to principles such as data minimization, fairness, transparency, integrity, and accountability (Bouderhem, 2022; Crigger et al., 2022).
- ***Accountability. Regulation, and Efficacy (n=9):*** Defining clear accountability and implementing robust regulatory frameworks were deemed essential

for addressing ethical challenges in AI healthcare applications. Researchers highlighted the importance of assigning responsibility to AI developers, healthcare providers, and institutions to uphold ethical standards (Balcombe, 2023; Goirand et al., 2023; Leung, 2023; McCradden et al., 2020; Ozmen Garibay et al., 2023; Subasi et al., 2023). For example, developers of mental health chatbots bore the ethical obligation to ensure competent care, protect user confidentiality, and adhere to evidence-based therapeutic practices (Denecke et al., 2021). Scientific validation of AI systems, including content informed by medical guidelines and expertise, was emphasized as critical (Crigger et al., 2022; Maharjan et al., 2019).

- ***Public Engagement and Trust (n=2):*** Public engagement was identified as essential to fostering trust and ethical alignment in AI systems. McCradden et al. (2020) and Ozmen Garibay et al. (2023) called for transparency and open communication to ensure alignment with societal values and expectations.
- ***Human-Centered Design and Accessibility (n=3):*** Human-centered design was emphasized to ensure AI technologies were accessible, particularly for individuals with limited digital literacy or resources (Maharjan et al., 2019; Castañeda-Garza et al., 2023; Ozmen Garibay et al., 2023). Such design aimed to enhance usability and inclusivity across patient demographics.

The synthesis of these studies provided a comprehensive view of the ethical dimensions of AI in healthcare. These themes underscored the importance of adopting a multifaceted approach to AI ethics, encompassing fairness, transparency, privacy, accountability, and engagement. As AI technologies continue to evolve, collaboration among developers, healthcare professionals, regulators, and the public is imperative to ensure that AI systems are designed and implemented ethically. By prioritizing these considerations, healthcare can maximize the benefits of AI while minimizing potential harms, ensuring alignment with ethical standards and societal values.

Table 3. Ethical considerations

Authors, year	Types of ethical considerations								Short description of ethical considerations
	Benefit	Autonomy	Justice	Transparent	Privacy	Account	Trust	Access	
Fournier-Tombs, 2023	•	•	•						• Promote patients' welfare and avoid harm. • Respect patients' self-determination, informed consent, and confidentiality. • Ensure fair and equitable treatment.
Diaz-Asper, 2024		•	•	•					• Maintain human control over AI decisions. • Provide clear documentation and explanations. • Avoid discrimination, uphold ethical principles.
Brown, 2021	•	•	•						• Provide empathetic, individualized care. • Respect patients' personhood. • Ensure inclusive, fair care.
Bouderhem, 2022			•		•				• Ensure health products are available, affordable, and acceptable. • Minimize data risks, prioritize safety and fairness.
Kurian, 2023	•			•					• Clearly inform users about AI interactions. • Consider user needs and vulnerabilities in AI design; regularly audit and improve AI.
Maharjan, 2019						•		•	• 24/7 access to tailored nutrition info. • Use verified, guideline-based knowledge.
Gamble, 2020	•				•				• Provide appropriate resources, especially for emergencies. • Protect confidentiality to reduce stigma and encourage help-seeking; ensure technology is rigorously tested.
Castañeda-Garza, 2023					•			•	• Control over the collection, use, and storage of personal information; protecting data from unauthorized access and breaches. • Reducing stigma and structural barriers for equitable mental healthcare access.
Balcombe, 2023	•					•			• Guide vulnerable individuals in using AI chatbots for mental health; enhance social media resources with AI support. • Research and monitor AI efficacy, implement safety measures, and collaborate on standards.
Sedlakova, 2023	•			•					• Clarify AI's limitations and expected goals to prevent unrealistic user expectations. • Limit AI to specific, non-critical tasks in therapy, avoiding areas requiring rational and moral judgment.

continued on following page

Table 3. Continued

Authors, year	Types of ethical considerations								Short description of ethical considerations
	Benefit	Autonomy	Justice	Transparent	Privacy	Account	Trust	Access	
Crigger, 2022			•		•	•			• Incorporate ethics throughout AI design and implementation, ensuring privacy and consent. • Adhere to high scientific standards in AI development. • Ensure eHealth system access for all, regardless of socioeconomic background.
Chatterjee, 2019					•				• Ensure informed consent for managing personal health data.
Kaas, 2023	•	•	•	•					• Ensure system benefits for patients, clinicians, and developers; avoid causing unjustified harm. • Support individuals' control over their own decisions. • Equitably distribute benefits, risks, and constraints. • Provide clear and accessible information.
Goirand, 2023	•	•		•		•			• Respect patients' rights to make informed healthcare decisions. • Ensure AI decisions are understandable; openly disclose AI development and implementation processes. • Clearly define accountability for AI use among developers, providers, and institutions. • Design AI to benefit all patient populations equally.
Schmälzle, 2022									• Not specified
Leung, 2023				•	•	•			• Protect personal data through anonymization. • Make AI algorithms comprehensible to users. • Hold social media companies accountable for AI outcomes.
McCradden, 2020				•	•	•	•		• Ensure agreement is informed and free from coercion. • Maintain control over personal information; safeguard entrusted information; foster reliability and consistency. • Take ownership of decisions; ensure answerability and proper accounting. • Promote meaningful societal participation.
Ozmen Garibay, 2023	•	•			•	•	•	•	• Prioritize human-centered AI design to enhance life quality. • Ensure ethical AI development. • Protect privacy in data collection and AI use. • Develop frameworks for human control over AI. • Implement independent oversight across sector. • Align AI with human values and cognitive capabilities.

continued on following page

Table 3. Continued

Authors, year	Types of ethical considerations								Short description of ethical considerations
	Benefit	Autonomy	Justice	Transparent	Privacy	Account	Trust	Access	
Vellido, 2019			•	•	•				• Models must be interpretable to ensure decisions in medicine are understandable. • Protect personal information while analyzing data; ensure data anonymity. • Ensure AI respects autonomy, non-maleficence, beneficence, and justice.
Zhang, 2023	•	•	•						• Act in patients' best interests to improve health outcomes; avoid causing harm to patients. • Respect patients' rights to make informed healthcare decisions. • Ensure fair distribution of healthcare resources and equitable access.
Subasi, 2023				•	•	•			• Encourage healthcare professionals and patients to embrace AI, influenced by trust and utility; help clinicians and patients understand AI decisions, enhancing trust; Build trust by making AI capabilities and limitations clear. • Define accountability for AI errors, with oversight and regulations. • Obtain consent for data use and protect personal data.
Denecke, 2021					•	•			• Use evidence-based approaches in mental health chatbots for effective support; developers must provide competent care and uphold ethical standards beyond legal requirements. • Protect sensitive mental health information.

Source: Authors' work

Note. Benefit = Beneficence and Non-Maleficence; Autonomy = Autonomy and Human Agency; Justice= Justice, Fairness, and Equity; Transparent = Transparency and Explainability; Privacy = Privacy and Security; Account = Accountability. Regulation, and Efficacy; Trust = Public Engagement and Trust; Human-Centered Design and Accessibility.

4.5 Existing Regulations and Frameworks

The rapid evolution of AI technology has amplified ethical concerns, particularly in AI-powered health communities, necessitating robust regulatory frameworks and ethical guidelines. Scholars like Vellido (2019) underscore the need for these frameworks, particularly as AI's ethical challenges continue to grow. Various paradigms—association-driven, regulatory-driven, principles-driven, and ethics-driven—have been developed to address these challenges.

- ***Association-Driven (n=10):*** Association-driven approaches emphasized guidelines and standards established by professional bodies and institutions.

Research highlighted the role of ethical rules and regulatory frameworks across diverse contexts, including medical treatment (Fournier-Tombs & McHardy, 2023), mental health services (Gamble, 2020), health communication (Schmälzle & Wilcox, 2022), psychotherapy (Sedlakova & Trachsel, 2023), healthcare settings (Kaas, 2022) and digital experiences for children (Kurian, 2023). These studies collectively demonstrated the impact of governance frameworks on ethical outcomes, particularly for vulnerable populations such as children. Notable examples included: the American Medical Association (AMA) Code of Medical Ethics, the European Commission's Ethics Guidelines for Trustworthy AI, and the FDA's Digital Health Innovation Action Plan, as identified by Crigger et al. (2022). Laws like the Health Insurance Portability and Accountability Act (HIPAA) in the United States played a pivotal role in safeguarding patient data privacy and security by imposing penalties for non-compliance. Collectively, these association-driven frameworks fostered a fair, inclusive, and patient-centered healthcare environment.

- ***Regulatory-Driven (n= 7):*** Regulatory-driven frameworks underscored the importance of legal and institutional mandates in governing AI use. Bouderhem (2022) proposed updates to the WHO International Health Regulations (IHR) to include AI governance, aligning with existing treaties supported by the WHO. These updates complemented global frameworks such as the General Data Protection Regulation (GDPR) in Europe, which regulated cybersecurity and ethical AI use, particularly for vulnerable populations, as noted by Kurian (2023), Chatterjee et al. (2019), Castañeda-Garza et al. (2023), and Leung (2023). In the United States, HIPAA served as a regulatory benchmark by mandating stringent management of electronic protected health information (ePHI) and enforcing penalties for violations (Brown & Halpern, 2023; Diaz-Asper, 2024). Such measures ensured accountability and mitigated risks associated with AI in healthcare, providing a robust mechanism for maintaining ethical standards and data security.
- ***Principles-Driven (n=5):*** Principles-driven frameworks focused on embedding core ethical principles, such as privacy, fairness, and accountability, into AI technologies. Kaas et al. (2023) introduced the ethics assurance argument pattern, integrating policymaking, ethics, and technology to reduce risks and uphold ethical standards. Other frameworks included the Belmont Report, the APA Ethics Code, and the WHO AI Ethics and Governance Guidelines, which provided actionable strategies for addressing ethical concerns in clinical and research settings (Diaz-Asper et al., 2024). Studies by Balcombe (2023), Gamble (2020), and Ozmen Garibay et al. (2023) further advocated

for responsible AI deployment, emphasizing the need for safeguards to protect patient welfare while improving the effectiveness of AI applications.

- ***Ethics-Driven (n=9):*** Ethics-driven frameworks prioritized human values and societal well-being as central to AI governance. This paradigm sought to address fundamental ethical issues such as data privacy, transparency, and fairness in AI applications. Gamble (2023) explored legislative gaps in regulating AI-driven mental health tools, highlighting the urgency of robust frameworks to ensure clinical safety and user trust. Additional studies, including Brown and Halpern (2023), Crigger et al. (2022), and Marharjan (2018) emphasized safeguarding patient rights, promoting informed consent, and ensuring confidentiality. These findings were in accordance with Ozmen Garibay et al. (2023) and Sedlakova and Trachsel (2023), who advocated for establishing and updating regulatory frameworks to manage AI in a manner that prioritizes human values and societal well-being. In addition to these aspects, other scholars proposed the development and deployment of regulations and frameworks that regulate AI in healthcare must prioritise patient rights (Schmälzle & Wilcox, 2022), informed consent (Brown & Halpern, 2023), human-centered (Marharjan, 2018), fairness and confidentiality (Diaz-Asper, 2023). These ethics-driven frameworks ensured patient-centered AI applications aligned with broader societal values, fostering equitable and sustainable healthcare practices.

4.6 Recommendations for Ethical Development and Implementation of AI Technology

Despite substantial efforts to develop and comply with existing regulations and frameworks within AI-powered health communities globally, several healthcare challenges remained inadequately addressed. The review revealed diverse scholarly perspectives on integrating ethical practices across community members. These recommendations highlighted four key aspects: adoption of reliable and well-established AI-powered technologies, implementation of stringent regulatory measures, thorough evaluations of AI applications, and active engagement of stakeholders. These considerations were shaped by key stakeholders in healthcare, including AI health application developers, policymakers, users, and collaborators.

- ***Well-established and Dependable AI-Powered Technologies (n=13):***McCradden et al. (2020) emphasized in their studies the importance of prioritizing reliable and well-established AI programs with clear, and actionable plans to raise awareness about ethical considerations. They further highlighting the need to equip healthcare communities with the capacities to address ethical challenges effectively. The study emphasized the necessity of ensuring that AI tools are dependable and transparent, enabling users to assess the trustworthiness of the information produced by AI models. Key suggestions included maintaining data privacy, ensuring transparency, and incorporating patient perspectives to sustain an ethical AI-powered healthcare ecosystem. Furthermore, AI design must be resilient and incorporate standardized procedures to support consistent ethical practices (Crigger et al., 2022). Continuous monitoring of AI systems' effectiveness (Kaas, 2022; Kurian, 2022; Sedlakova, 2020) and ongoing ethical oversight inAI development (Brown & Halpern, 2021) are critical to ensuring safety and reliability in healthcare applications. Ethical principles such as transparency and accountability are essential for the advancement of AI-driven technologies in the healthcare sector (Balcombe, 2023; Chatterjee, 2023; Ozlem, 2018). Compliance with ethical guidelines established by policymakers (Kurian, 2022), the implementation of AI algorithms that prioritize accuracy (Leung, 2024), and an ethics-focused design in AI applications (Goirand et al., 2023) further enhance the integrity of AI systems. Lastly, regularly updating AI applications based on user feedback is vital. This iterative process enables AI technology developers to refine their systems to better meet user requirements and expectations, thereby fostering improved ethical and practical outcomes (Maharjan, 2019).

- ***Stringent Measures (n=16):***Castañeda-Garza et al. (2023) emphasized the need for robust security measures and legislation to govern the ethical application of AI in mental health settings, ensuring safety, fairness, and equitable utilization of AI technology. Similarly, Diaz-Asper et al. (2024) underscored the significant efforts to design AI ethical guidelines for application in psychological settings, given the complexity of these technologies. Subasi et al. (2023) stressed the importance of transparent AI use, arguing that stringent rules are imperative to integrate reliable and trustworthy AI systems, thereby fostering societal trust and enhancing patient experiences. Additional recommendations focused on the necessity of establishing explicit guidelines that are clear (Fournier-Tombs & Mchardy, 2023; Leung, 2024), consistently updated (Kaas, 2022), rigorous (Gamble, 2020; Goirand et al., 2023; Ozlem, 2018), comprehensive in scope (Sedlakova & Trachsel, 2023), ethically sound (Balcombe, 2023; Schmälzle, 2023; Vellido, 2018), and specialized (Diaz-Asper, 2023). Furthermore, stringent policies and data protection measures are essential for the effective deployment of AI in healthcare (Bouderhem, 2022; Zhang & Zhang, 2023).
- ***Critical Evaluations of AI Use (n=6):*** Castañeda-Garza (2023) advocated for ensuring that users from all demographic groups can assess AI applica-

tions. Chatbots, widely recognized in healthcare communities, exemplify this need. For example, Denecke et al. (2021) asserted that while chatbots offer multiple benefits to the mental health community, a more critical evaluation of their potential risks is necessary. Balcombe (2023) supported this observation, noting that incorporating AI chatbots could improve mental health treatment and expand access to digital services. However, users must be aware of both the benefits and limitations of these technologies. Kurian (2022) further highlighted the importance of educating children and caregivers about the limitations of engaging with AI as younger users may struggle to discern the reliability of AI-generated outputs. Furthermore, it is crucial to promote autonomous use of AI, equipping users with the skills to make informed, AI-driven decisions (Gamble, 2020; Ozlem, 2018)

- ***Active Stakeholders Engagement (n=7):*** In contrast to Balcombe (2023), Goirand et al. (2023) and Zhang and Zhang (2023) emphasized the critical roles of three key stakeholders—practitioners, policymakers, and researchers—in advancing the ethical use of AI. Practitioners were encouraged to develop ethics-based AI applications and provide guidelines for healthcare professionals using AI tools in clinical settings. Policymakers were urged to implement frameworks that incorporate stakeholder feedback, regulate AI use, and enforce stringent ethical guidelines. Researchers, in turn, were called upon to engage actively in ethical AI development and identify future research directions that prioritize ethical practices in healthcare. These findings align with studies by Gamble (2020), McCradden et al. (2020), and Leung (2024), which highlighted the importance of incorporating diverse stakeholder perspectives in ethical decision-making. Goirand et al. (2023) proposed utilizing methodologies like Soft Systems Methodology (SSM) and Critical Systems Heuristics (CSH) to better understand ethical uses of AI, particularly in public health crises. Leung (2023) highlighted the importance of stakeholder involvement, particularly policymakers in enhancing regulatory frameworks and AI application developers in improving AI-ML algorithms. Such advancement could yield more accurate medical analyses and improve patient interactions. The study also advocated for collaboration between educational institutions, healthcare professionals, policymakers, and AI developers to address challenges in integrating AI into healthcare systems, ultimately benefiting both providers and patients (Leung, 2024). Finally, researchers are encouraged to investigate the broader implications of AI use (Castañeda-Garza, 2023), assess the feasibility of voice-based technologies for diverse population groups (Maharjan, 2019), and explore future directions for ethical compliance and regulation (Zhang & Zhang, 2023).

5. DISCUSSION

In the AI-driven healthcare sector, online health communities (OHCs) play an integral role in improving health outcomes by facilitating knowledge exchange, peer support, and collaborative learning. These communities are uniquely positioned to promote the ethical use of AI, a critical factor for ensuring transparency and accountability in AI applications (Iniesta, 2023). By incorporating ethical considerations into their practices, such communities can effectively address potential ethical issues and enhance trust among users tasked with evaluating AI operations (WHO Guidance, 2021).

While AI has revolutionized healthcare, its reliance introduces significant risks, particularly concerning patient data privacy and informed decision-making. Marginalized populations, in particular, face barriers such as limited digital literacy and the lack of tailored digital solutions to meet their needs (Marzo, 2024; Ouédraogo, 2024). These disparities hinder equitable access to AI-enabled technologies and compromise their utility for underserved groups. An ethics-first approach, prioritizing inclusivity and equity, is therefore essential to mitigate these challenges. Moreover, concerns about the reliability of AI systems and their potential misuse remain prominent. Risks include unauthorized data access, misinterpretation of health information, and overreliance on AI at the expense of human expertise (Schmälzle & Wilcox, 2022; Fournier-Tombs & McHardy, 2023). These issues underscore the necessity of stringent ethical safeguards and robust security measures.

AI technologies have shown considerable potential in addressing healthcare disparities. For instance, AI-powered conversational agents and chatbots provide immediate support and improve accessibility (Balcombe, 2023; Brown & Halpern, 2021). Language technologies have bridged communication gaps in healthcare delivery (Diaz-Asper et al., 2024), while telemedicine systems have expanded healthcare access for underserved communities (Kaas et al., 2023). These innovations demonstrate how AI can advance healthcare equity, provided ethical standards are maintained. Applications in mental health, chronic disease management, and wellness have further highlighted AI's transformative impact. Teletherapy platforms and AI-driven emotional support systems enhance mental health care (Castañeda-Garza et al., 2023; Gamble, 2020), while virtual agents improve patient monitoring and lifestyle management (Chatterjee et al., 2019; Maharjan et al., 2019). Despite their promise, these technologies require continuous evaluation to address risks related to data security, system reliability, and user trust.

To ensure safe and equitable AI applications, several ethical frameworks and guidelines have been developed. These include the WHO's International Health Regulations, the AMA Code of Medical Ethics, and the European Commission's Ethics Guidelines for Trustworthy AI (Crigger et al., 2022). These frameworks emphasize critical principles such as data security, patient privacy, and informed consent. They also stress the importance of protecting vulnerable populations, such as those with limited digital access or young users (Kurian, 2023; Ozmen Garibay et al., 2023). The principles-based assurance argument pattern proposed by Kaas et al. (2023) outlines key criteria for ethical AI deployment, including transparency, accountability, and equitable access. Adherence to such standards minimizes legal and ethical risks while fostering trust in AI systems.

Collaboration between policymakers, developers, researchers, and healthcare professionals is vital for fostering ethical AI use in healthcare communities (Goirand et al., 2023; Zhang & Zhang, 2023). Effective human-AI collaboration ensures that AI complements, rather than replaces, human expertise. For example, in online health communities, AI chatbots handle routine tasks like patient screening, allowing healthcare professionals to focus on complex decision-making and emotional support (Brown & Halpern, 2021). Similarly, in mental health applications, AI provides continuous support between therapy sessions, enhancing care delivery (Castañeda-Garza et al., 2023). Despite progress, the effective implementation of AI in healthcare requires rigorous regulatory oversight, robust security measures, and clearly defined ethical guidelines. Researchers must focus on developing reliable, transparent, and user-centered AI applications that align with these standards. By addressing ethical, legal, and social implications (ELSI), AI technologies can be deployed responsibly to maximize their benefits while minimizing potential harms (Pullman & Etchegary, 2021).

6. CONCLUSION

The advent of AI has profoundly transformed healthcare systems, revolutionizing the operations and objectives of OHCs. Upholding ethical standards in these AI-powered ecosystems is paramount for fostering trust, fairness, safety, and accountability in healthcare. AI-driven practices within these communities must prioritize core ethical principles, including data privacy, patient autonomy, transparency, and well-being. This is particularly crucial in healthcare contexts, where the advanced and complex nature of AI technologies can exacerbate vulnerabilities, particularly for marginalized populations. To address these challenges, the development of effective, context-specific guidelines and regulatory frameworks is indispensable. These measures are critical for mitigating risks such as data breaches, safeguarding patient rights, and minimizing errors in AI-based health decision-making processes. They also provide a robust foundation for ethical regulation, ensuring secure and trustworthy healthcare environments. Frameworks such as the WHO's International Health Regulations and the AMA Code of Medical Ethics play a pivotal role in guiding AI's ethical integration into healthcare practices. Furthermore, fostering professionalism among key stakeholders—healthcare providers, policymakers, AI developers, researchers, and educators—is essential. A collective commitment to ethical principles not only enhances patient well-being but also aligns with broader global health goals, such as the Sustainable Development Goals (e.g., Goal 6; Verdejo Espinosa et al., 2021). This collaborative effort ensures that AI technologies are deployed equitably and sustainably, addressing health disparities while promoting global health equity. Ultimately, integrating ethical considerations into AI-driven healthcare practices strengthens the quality, credibility, and integrity of healthcare systems. It ensures that these systems operate within robust ethical frameworks, supporting equitable advancements that benefit all stakeholders and reinforcing trust in the ongoing digital transformation of healthcare.

7. IMPLICATIONS OF THE REVIEW

This review offers a timely and thorough examination of the ethical considerations surrounding AI-powered health communities. By synthesizing previous research on this emerging field, it provides a nuanced understanding of the ethical tensions that define this evolving landscape. Key takeaways for stakeholders include:

- Healthcare Professionals: This review emphasizes the importance of ethical awareness in delivering AI-integrated health services. It equips healthcare professionals with insights to help navigate the ethical complexities of AI adoption in clinical practice.
- AI Developers: The findings highlight the need for developers to embed ethical considerations into the design and functionality of AI health applications, ensuring safer and more ethical user experiences.
- Policymakers: The review emphasizes the critical role policymakers play in creating regulations that address the impact of AI on healthcare and patient outcomes. Thoughtful policymaking can support the responsible integration of AI technologies into healthcare systems.
- Collaborative Discourse: The study calls for sustained dialogue and collaboration among stakeholders to address ethical dilemmas in AI-driven health communities. Such collective efforts are essential for identifying gaps in current ethical frameworks and proposing solutions that align technological advancements with principles of fairness, trust, and user protection.

This review's systematic approach also reveals areas where current ethical frameworks for AI fall short, offering opportunities to refine these structures. These insights can inform the development of clinical guidelines and health policies that prioritize patient and provider safety in AI interactions. In conclusion, this review serves as a roadmap for fostering ethical innovation in healthcare, providing actionable recommendations for building user-centered, ethically sound digital health systems. By balancing AI's benefits with the imperative to safeguard user rights and well-being, this work contributes to developing healthcare technologies that are effective, equitable, and trustworthy.

8. LIMITATIONS AND RECOMMENDATIONS FOR FUTURE STUDIES

While this review provides comprehensive insights, several limitations warrant acknowledgment. First, the narrative review methodology focuses exclusively on existing literature and AI ethical frameworks in healthcare. This approach may introduce selection bias, favouring regions such as the United States or European countries while overlooking others. Consequently, the findings may have limited generalizability (Kundu et al., 2024). Future research could broaden its scope to include frameworks from more diverse settings, as contextual factors and sociocultural differences may shape distinct requirements for AI implementation in healthcare. Second, there is a potential for researcher bias. Despite employing multiple safeguards—such as initial screening, article categorization, researcher collaboration, and the use of "blind mode" features in the literature review system to limit access to screening and filtering results—bias may still arise. Familiarity with the content, personal interest, or pre-existing assumptions could lead to confirmation bias, influencing the selection of specific articles. Engaging external reviewers to evaluate findings could help mitigate such biases and enhance the study's rigor. Lastly, the use of predetermined selection criteria resulted in a limited sample size of articles, potentially excluding other significant AI ethical frameworks. Future studies should consider expanding the selection criteria and incorporating a broader range of publications, particularly those covering underrepresented regions. This approach would yield more comprehensive and impactful findings, enriching the understanding of ethical frameworks for AI in healthcare.

REFERENCES

Balcombe, L. (2023, October). AI chatbots in digital mental health. [). MDPI.]. *Informatics (MDPI), 10*(4), 82. DOI: 10.3390/informatics10040082

Bouderhem, R. (2022, December). AI regulation in healthcare: new paradigms for a legally binding treaty under the World Health Organization. In *2022 14th International Conference on Computational Intelligence and Communication Networks (CICN)* (pp. 277-281). IEEE. DOI: 10.1109/CICN56167.2022.10008303

Brown, J. E., & Halpern, J. (2021). AI chatbots cannot replace human interactions in the pursuit of more inclusive mental healthcare. *SSM. Mental Health, 1*, 100017. DOI: 10.1016/j.ssmmh.2021.100017

Castañeda-Garza, G., Ceballos, H. G., & Mejía-Almada, P. G. (2023). Artificial Intelligence for Mental Health: A Review of AI Solutions and Their Future. *What AI Can*, 373-399.

Chaney, M. A. (2021). So you want to write a narrative review article? *Journal of Cardiothoracic and Vascular Anesthesia, 35*(10), 3045–3049. DOI: 10.1053/j.jvca.2021.06.017 PMID: 34272117

Chatterjee, A., Gerdes, M. W., & Martinez, S. (2019, October). eHealth initiatives for the promotion of healthy lifestyle and allied implementation difficulties. In *2019 International Conference on Wireless and Mobile Computing, Networking and Communications (WiMob)* (pp. 1-8). IEEE. DOI: 10.1109/WiMOB.2019.8923324

Crigger, E., Reinbold, K., Hanson, C., Kao, A., Blake, K., & Irons, M. (2022). Trustworthy augmented intelligence in health care. *Journal of Medical Systems, 46*(2), 12. DOI: 10.1007/s10916-021-01790-z PMID: 35020064

Denecke, K., Abd-Alrazaq, A., & Househ, M. (2021). Artificial intelligence for chatbots in mental health: opportunities and challenges. *Multiple perspectives on artificial intelligence in healthcare: Opportunities and challenges*, 115-128.

Diaz-Asper, C., Hauglid, M. K., Chandler, C., Cohen, A. S., Foltz, P. W., & Elvevåg, B. (2024). A framework for language technologies in behavioral research and clinical applications: Ethical challenges, implications, and solutions. *The American Psychologist, 79*(1), 79–91. DOI: 10.1037/amp0001195 PMID: 38236217

Drukker, L., Noble, J. A., & Papageorghiou, A. T. (2020). Introduction to artificial intelligence in ultrasound imaging in obstetrics and gynecology. *Ultrasound in Obstetrics & Gynecology, 56*(4), 498–505. DOI: 10.1002/uog.22122 PMID: 32530098

Fournier-Tombs, E., & McHardy, J. (2023). A medical ethics framework for conversational artificial intelligence. *Journal of Medical Internet Research, 25*, e43068. DOI: 10.2196/43068 PMID: 37224277

Gamble, A. (2020). Artificial intelligence and mobile apps for mental healthcare: A social informatics perspective. *Aslib Journal of Information Management, 72*(4), 509–523. DOI: 10.1108/AJIM-11-2019-0316

Goirand, M., Austin, E., & Clay-Williams, R. (2023). Mapping the flow of knowledge as guidance for ethics implementation in medical AI: A qualitative study. *PLoS One, 18*(11), e0288448. DOI: 10.1371/journal.pone.0288448 PMID: 37917735

Guidance, W. H. O. (2021). *Ethics and governance of artificial intelligence for health*. World Health Organization.

Haleem, A., Javaid, M., Singh, R. P., & Suman, R. (2022). Medical 4.0 technologies for healthcare: Features, capabilities, and applications. *Internet of Things and Cyber-Physical Systems, 2*, 12–30. DOI: 10.1016/j.iotcps.2022.04.001

Iniesta, R. (2023). The human role to guarantee an ethical AI in healthcare: A five-facts approach. *AI and Ethics*, 1–13.

Kaas, M. H., Porter, Z., Lim, E., Higham, A., Khavandi, S., & Habli, I. (2023, July). Ethics in conversation: Building an ethics assurance case for autonomous AI-enabled voice agents in healthcare. In *Proceedings of the First International Symposium on Trustworthy Autonomous Systems* (pp. 1-13). DOI: 10.1145/3597512.3599713

Kundu, R., Shi, X., Morrison, J., Barrett, J., & Mukherjee, B. (2024). A framework for understanding selection bias in real-world healthcare data. *Journal of the Royal Statistical Society. Series A, (Statistics in Society), 187*(3), qnae039. DOI: 10.1093/jrsssa/qnae039 PMID: 39281782

Kurian, N. (2023). AI's empathy gap: The risks of conversational Artificial Intelligence for young children's well-being and key ethical considerations for early childhood education and care. *Contemporary Issues in Early Childhood*, 14639491231206004.

Le, L. H., Hoang, P. A., & Pham, H. C. (2023). Sharing health information across online platforms: A systematic review. *Health Communication, 38*(8), 1550–1562. DOI: 10.1080/10410236.2021.2019920 PMID: 34978235

Leung, R. (2023, June). Using ai–ml to augment the capabilities of social media for telehealth and remote patient monitoring. [). MDPI.]. *Health Care, 11*(12), 1704. PMID: 37372822

Maharjan, B., Li, J., Kong, J., & Tao, C. (2019, October). Alexa, what should I eat?: A personalized virtual nutrition coach for native American diabetes patients using Amazon's smart speaker technology. In *2019 IEEE International Conference on E- health Networking, Application & Services (HealthCom)* (pp. 1-6). IEEE. DOI: 10.1109/HealthCom46333.2019.9009613

Marzo, R. R. (2024). Bridging the Digital Divide: AI Solutions for Health Literacy in Underserved Populations. In *Modern Management Science Practices in the Age of AI* (pp. 151-180). IGI Global.

McCradden, M. D., Baba, A., Saha, A., Ahmad, S., Boparai, K., Fadaiefard, P., & Cusimano, M. D. (2020). Ethical concerns around use of artificial intelligence in health care research from the perspective of patients with meningioma, caregivers and health care providers: A qualitative study. *CMAJ Open*, *8*(1), E90–E95. DOI: 10.9778/cmajo.20190151 PMID: 32071143

Nelson, G. S. (2019). Bias in artificial intelligence. *North Carolina Medical Journal*, *80*(4), 220–222. DOI: 10.18043/ncm.80.4.220 PMID: 31278182

Ouédraogo, I. (2024). *Mobile technology and artificial intelligence for improving health literacy among underserved communities* (Doctoral dissertation, Université de Bordeaux; Université Nazi Boni (Bobo-Dioulasso, Burkina Faso)).

Ozmen Garibay, O., Winslow, B., Andolina, S., Antona, M., Bodenschatz, A., Coursaris, C., Falco, G., Fiore, S. M., Garibay, I., Grieman, K., Havens, J. C., Jirotka, M., Kacorri, H., Karwowski, W., Kider, J., Konstan, J., Koon, S., Lopez-Gonzalez, M., Maifeld-Carucci, I., & Xu, W. (2023). Six human-centered artificial intelligence grand challenges. *International Journal of Human-Computer Interaction*, *39*(3), 391–437. DOI: 10.1080/10447318.2022.2153320

Pautasso, M. (2019). The structure and conduct of a narrative literature review. *A guide to the scientific career: Virtues, communication, research and academic writing*, 299-310.

Pranckuté, R. (2021). Web of science (WoS) and Scopus: The titans of bibliographic information in today's academic world. *Publications/MDPI*, *9*(1), 12. DOI: 10.3390/publications9010012

Pullman, D., & Etchegary, H. (2021). Ethical, legal, and social issues (ELSI) in clinical genetics research. *Clinical Epidemiology: Practice and Methods*, 65-82.

Redrup Hill, E., Mitchell, C., Brigden, T., & Hall, A. (2023). Ethical and legal considerations influencing human involvement in the implementation of artificial intelligence in a clinical pathway: A multi-stakeholder perspective. *Frontiers in Digital Health*, *5*, 1139210. DOI: 10.3389/fdgth.2023.1139210 PMID: 36999168

Schmälzle, R., & Wilcox, S. (2022). Harnessing artificial intelligence for health message generation: The folic acid message engine. *Journal of Medical Internet Research*, *24*(1), e28858. DOI: 10.2196/28858 PMID: 35040800

Sedlakova, J., & Trachsel, M. (2023). Conversational artificial intelligence in psychotherapy: A new therapeutic tool or agent? *The American Journal of Bioethics*, *23*(5), 4–13. DOI: 10.1080/15265161.2022.2048739 PMID: 35362368

Strauss, A., & Corbin, J. (1990). *Basics of qualitative research* (Vol. 15). Newbury Park, CA: sage.

Subasi, A., Ozaltin, O., Mitra, A., Subasi, M. E., & Sarirete, A. (2023). Trustworthy artificial intelligence in healthcare. In *Accelerating Strategic Changes for Digital Transformation in the Healthcare Industry* (pp. 145–177). Academic Press. DOI: 10.1016/B978-0-443-15299-3.00015-4

Sujan, M., Furniss, D., Grundy, K., Grundy, H., Nelson, D., Elliott, M., White, S., Habli, I., & Reynolds, N. (2019). Human factors challenges for the safe use of artificial intelligence in patient care. *BMJ Health & Care Informatics*, *26*(1), e100081. DOI: 10.1136/bmjhci-2019-100081 PMID: 31780459

Sukhera, J. (2022). Narrative reviews: Flexible, rigorous, and practical. *Journal of Graduate Medical Education*, *14*(4), 414–417. DOI: 10.4300/JGME-D-22-00480.1 PMID: 35991099

Taddeo, M., & Floridi, L. (2018). How AI can be a force for good. *Science*, *361*(6404), 751–752. DOI: 10.1126/science.aat5991 PMID: 30139858

Vellido, A. (2019). Societal issues concerning the application of artificial intelligence in medicine. *Kidney Diseases*, *5*(1), 11–17. DOI: 10.1159/000492428 PMID: 30815459

Verdejo Espinosa, A., Lopez, J. L., Mata Mata, F., & Estevez, M. E. (2021). Application of IoT in healthcare: Keys to implementation of the sustainable development goals. *Sensors (Basel)*, *21*(7), 2330. DOI: 10.3390/s21072330 PMID: 33810606

World Health Organization. (2021). Ethics and governance of artificial intelligence for health: WHO guidance: executive summary.

Xafis, V., Schaefer, G. O., Labude, M. K., Brassington, I., Ballantyne, A., Lim, H. Y., Lipworth, W., Lysaght, T., Stewart, C., Sun, S., Laurie, G. T., & Tai, E. S. (2019). An ethics framework for big data in health and research. *Asian Bioethics Review, 11*(3), 227–254. DOI: 10.1007/s41649-019-00099-x PMID: 33717314

Zaidan, A. M. (2023). The leading global health challenges in the artificial intelligence era. *Frontiers in Public Health, 11*, 1328918. DOI: 10.3389/fpubh.2023.1328918 PMID: 38089037

Zhang, J., & Zhang, Z. M. (2023). Ethics and governance of trustworthy medical artificial intelligence. *BMC Medical Informatics and Decision Making, 23*(1), 7. DOI: 10.1186/s12911-023-02103-9 PMID: 36639799

Zhang, Q. (2024). Online health communities provide important support in China. *Nature Human Behaviour, 8*(1), 8–8. DOI: 10.1038/s41562-023-01766-8 PMID: 37923912

Zhao, Y., Chen, K., Peng, J., Wang, J., & Song, N. (2022). Diverse needs and cooperative deeds: Comprehending users' identities in online health communities. *Information Processing & Management, 59*(5), 103060. DOI: 10.1016/j.ipm.2022.103060

Chapter 4
Disinformation Through AI

Adam Kah Jjin Wee
Sunway University, Malaysia

Mei Hua Lin
https://orcid.org/0000-0002-2873-5426
Sunway University, Malaysia

Michael John Jenkins
https://orcid.org/0000-0003-2394-9019
Sunway University, Malaysia

Shu En Lee
https://orcid.org/0009-0008-6325-9884
HELP University, Malaysia

ABSTRACT

The rise of artificial intelligence (AI) has amplified spreading falsified, misleading information, and the difficulty to detect manipulated content, warranting the need to identify determinants of user susceptibility toward mis-and-disinformation from AI in the public health contexts. Adopting a three-stage dual processes theory, this chapter proposed a conceptual model that explains user susceptibility toward mis-and-disinformation from AI as the results of courtesy type 2 processing. From the individual-level, individuals who reflect higher trust in AI, AI literacy, analytical mindset, bullshit receptivity, and prior experience with AI are more vulnerable to AI mis-and-disinformation. From the AI-level, people are more susceptible to mis-and-disinformation from AI with higher automation levels and if the content produced is aligned with people's prior knowledge. From the contextual-level, people are more susceptible to disinformation from AI if they are more pressed for time and overloaded

DOI: 10.4018/979-8-3693-5837-5.ch004

with extra information. Practical, legal, and ethical implications were discussed.

INTRODUCTION

Following the widespread use of the internet which enables great exposure and accessibility of information, deceptive, falsified, inaccurate and misleading information has also been accumulated in massive amounts. The consequences of the spread of this deceptive, falsified information either with or without malicious intention (i.e., misinformation and disinformation respectively) range in severity and scale across various contexts. Politically, foreign actors have been deploying information operations to manipulate the formation of public opinion, discredit political leadership, degrade public trust, deepen societal divides, and influence citizens' voting decisions (Kertysova, 2018). Also, mis-and-disinformation on science, technology, engineering and maths related topics such as vaccine resistance and climate change have also encountered political repercussions (Curiel & Ramirez, 2021; Sylvester, 2021). Worryingly, an Ipsos (2020) poll showed that over 83 percent of people are very concerned about the spread of mis-and-disinformation, with about 69 percent of people believing that the information encountered on social media is inaccurate. Regardless, it is remarkable that the spread of misinformation and disinformation always comes hand in hand with the acceleration and adoption of technology (Naja, 2018).

How AI Alters the Spread of Mis-and-Disinformation?

To date, artificial intelligence (AI) is affecting people's life tremendously due to its highly prevalence in various industries and education fields. While AI acts as a popular tool in simplifying workflow, generating solutions, and elevating productivity, its convenience comes at the cost of vague transparency, limited accountability, and systematic discrimination (Möller et al., 2018). These in turn contribute to the amplification of mis-and-disinformation. As Gordon Crovits, the co-chief executive of NewsGuard, an organisation that tracks online misinformation once made a comment about AI:

This tool is going to be the most powerful tool in spreading misinformation that has never been on the internet. Crafting a new false narrative can now be done at dramatic scale, and much more frequently — it's like having AI agents contributing to disinformation. (Thompson & Tsu, 2023)

Indeed, the rise of AI has altered how misinformation and disinformation is spread in at least two ways. First, advancements in machine learning enable AI to identify individual's unique attributes, weaknesses, and needs, in which highly personalised, falsified content would be delivered to influence targeted vulnerable populations with maximum effectiveness (Whyte, 2020). These user profiling and micro-targeting techniques may pose threats on democracy, people's decisions, and public debates (Monteleone, 2019). That is, while people may view information presented by AI as spontaneous, objective, universally encountered, and citizen-generated, it is in fact the AI algorithms that determine what views and contents they come across (Sodiya et al., 2024). For instance, during the United States presidential election in 2016, both Trump and Hillary Clinton, the presidential candidates, utilised demographic segmentation techniques through AI to map different groups of voters (Bayer et al., 2021). As such, data through AI is often stripped from its initial objective and might be used for purposes that users are unaware of (Bayer et al., 2021).

Second, deep fakes - digitally manipulated visual and audio material that is virtually indistinguishable and highly realistic from real materials, also becomes a means where mis-and-disinformation is spread through AI (Karnouskos, 2020). Scholars at the United Nations have also developed an AI model that produces realistic speeches on a variety of debated topics within thirty hours (Aylett-Bullock & Luengo-Oroz, 2019). Following the advancement of AI technology, the growing ease of generating falsified video and audio content elevated opportunities for blackmail, intimidation, and sabotage beyond the scope of political and international affairs (Chesney & Citron, 2019). Bayer et al. (2021) claimed that by 2030, deepfakes can become much easier to produce and nearly impossible for people to detect the difference between the falsified content from the genuine information. Politically, these fake contents could discredit leaders and institutions, incite violence and tilt cities towards civil unrest, exacerbate existing divisions in society, or influence the outcome of elections (Chesney & Citron, 2019).

The proliferation of the spread of mis-and-disinformation through AI warrants further need to dive deeper into users' susceptibility towards mis-and-disinformation through AI for more effective implications and regulations. Yet, existing literature circled around the general and social media contexts (Bryanov & Vziatysheva, 2021; Doss et al., 2023; Rubin, 2019, 2022), with AI contexts receiving less attention. While this paper recognises the values of past interventions and strategies to combat mis-and-disinformation, this still poses a problem. Past work that established manoeuvres, findings, and interventions to combat mis-and disinformation under the general and social media contexts may not be applicable to the AI contexts, given that AI alters the way information is disseminated. For instance, Bryanov and Vziatysheva (2021)'s presented that negative comments on social media, social media flags, bandwagon cues on social media, and sources credibility are significant predictors of people's proneness towards mid-and-disinformation. Yet, due to the nature of AI-generated content, information might be crafted anonymously and based on biases and errors, and humans play a relatively passive role in consuming and spreading information. This eventually bypasses traditional social cues and credibility markers in the social media environments.

AI MIS-AND-DISINFORMATION IN PUBLIC HEALTH SETTINGS

Among various domains, AI has been widely applied in the public health domain, defined as all organised measures that preclude disease, promote health, and prolong life among the entire population (World Health Organisation [WHO], n.d.). Indeed, AI has been used in facilitating clinical documentation, generating discharge summaries, creating clinical operations and procedural notes, and answering questions from patients regarding their health concerns or data (Mesko & Topol, 2023). Concurrently, AI also assists physicians in diagnosing health conditions based on laboratory findings, medical records, and images, as well as suggesting alternative treatments (Mesko & Topol, 2023). Systematic reviews also suggested the benefits of AI in streamlining healthcare workflow, saving medical costs, enhancing medical research equity, and improving personalised learning in medical education (Li et al., 2023; Sallam, 2023). Also, patients could have more autonomy in obtaining individual assessment of their healthcare concerns, data, and symptoms (Bohr & Memarzadeh, 2020; Jiang et al., 2017). However, with the wide applications of AI due to its benefits in the public health domain, it is not without concerns.

Public Health Issues Caused by AI Mis-and-Disinformation

The Institution of Safe Medication Practice (2017) presented the following real incident that illustrated the dangers of misinformation through AI in the healthcare practice:

A pharmacy staff member accidentally selected the wrong medication (I.E., dilTIAZem instead of Dilantin). Despite noticing the difference between the medication administration record (i.e., listing Dilantin) and the AI dispensing cabinets (i.e., listing dilTIAZem), the nurse, who trusted the information on AI dispensing cabinets, did not correct the error. Consequently, the patient who received the incorrect medication experienced significant hypotension and bradycardia.

Apart from healthcare practice as described above, there were also cases where AI disseminated public-health related mis-and-disinformation that dangers the well-being of the community. For example, driven by AI-algorithms, one post went viral that misrepresented a TED Talk by Tal Zaks, the chief medical officer of Moderna, confirming that MRNA vaccines alter human DNA, with the headline, "Bombshell: Moderna Chief Medical Officer admits MRNA alters DNA". Meanwhile, during Covid-19 period, there was also AI-generated content spread on social media that hydroxychloroquine and ivermectin are effective in combating Covid symptoms though being unproven, where population who consumed the two drugs were risky to have side effects like heart rhythm problems and seizures (Gonzalez et al., 2022; Perlis et al., 2023).

Alarmingly, as a result, these misrepresented scientific findings regarding alleged harms of vaccines would elevate the vaccine resistance among the general population (Rubin, 2022). Another pertaining issue involves the misuse of AI self-diagnosis tools. For example, using the WebMD, a AI self-diagnosis tool, users with mild symptoms of coughing and headache were suggested with serious medical conditions like lung cancer or brain tumour, which resulted in seeking for unnecessary treatments (Mahlknecht et al., 2023). Ultimately, there were also cases where AI misinterpreted the symptoms and provided generic or inaccurate advice without having full information of patients' medical history (Wimbarti et al., 2024). Not only this may delay proper treatments and worse patient's symptoms, it may also lead to misuse or overuse of medications and supplements which is life-risking (Shahsavar & Choudhury, 2023). In sum, mis-and-disinformation through AI seems to be a hazard and requires effective regulation in the domain of public health.

Altogether, AI has altered the way mis-and-disinformation is consumed and disseminated. Due to the recent rise of AI usage, effective regulations, interventions, or strategies to combat users' susceptibility to mis-and-disinformation through AI are still absent at the current stage, given that past work mostly focused on traditional and social media contexts. This chapter has main branches of focus. First, this chapter first delves into the psychology aspects of the intricate manoeuvres of users' susceptibility toward the consumption and dissemination of mis-and-disinformation through AI. Second, this chapter will delve into some practical solutions that can be applied in public health contexts to combat the AI dis-or-misinformation. Third, given the wide application of AI in public health domains, which could potentially lead to harmful consequences to the community wellbeing, especially with past work mostly focusing for general and political implications, this chapter will focus the discussion in the public health domains and extent their theoretical, practical, legal, and ethical implications in regard to the effective detection and mitigation strategies to combat mis-and-disinformation through AI.

WHAT MAKES ONE BEING PRONE TO AI MIS-AND-DISINFORMATION?

While diving into the mechanism of people's proneness to mis-and-disinformation, literature has been adopting the dual process theory as the framework (Bryanov & Vziatysheva, 2021; Doss et al., 2023; Rubin, 2019, 2022). Particularly, dual process theory describes humans' reasoning and decision making (i.e., whether information should be viewed as true or false) as the results of two distinct types of process (Evans, 2008). Type 1 thinking refers to a heuristic system that does not require much attention, characterised as instant, effortless, and unaffected by intellect, alertness, and motivation; type 2 thinking is characterised as mental operations requiring effort, motivation, concentration, and the execution of learned rules (Thompson, 2013). Specifically, type 1 thinking is described as providing default output which acts upon explicit representations manipulated in working memory via type 2 processing (Evans & Stanovich, 2013). In brief, literature established consensus that the operation of type 1 and 2 thinking increases and reduces one's vulnerability towards mis-and-disinformation respectively. But, the detailed explanation of how it operates may differ based on the two existing perspectives of this theory.

One perspective claims that type 2 thinking monitors the output from type 1 thinking, which could be biassed. Yet, the notion that type 2 thinking is responsible for the instantiation of type 2 thinking themselves is problematic. Two, the parallel theorists assert that both types of thinking operate in parallel, where biases are results of type 1 thinking processing the output before type 2 thinking completes, albeit additional type 2 thinking may process if conflicts occur between both types of thinking. But, this poses an issue, as the parallel theorists highlight conflict detection as a source of later Type 2 thinking, but still assume that the monitoring of conflict is a type 2 thinking. That is, neither of the major dual-process theories adequately explain important aspects of cognitive architecture. This is a problem, as the utility and explanatory value of dual-process theories largely depends on our understanding of the sources of analytic reasoning - the main key that explains one's proneness towards mis-and-disinformation (Evans & Stanovich, 2013; Thompson, 2013). Hence, the three-stage dual process theory (TSDPT), developed to complement this, would be adopted as the main framework of this conceptual review.

TSDPT

TSDPT describes information processing as duan processes (type 1 and 2 processes) that involve three stages (Figure 1). In the first stage, the autonomous type 1 process generates intuitive or initial responses, which is often cued by features of stimulus and do not require executive functioning and operate in parallel. Some stimuli will cue multiple, potentially competing type 1 outputs. Notably, some initial responses are generated faster and more fluently than others. For example, research found that stereotypical information is formed more quickly and fluently than base-rate information (i.e., clearer illustration of the mechanism could be referred to the scenario latter). The second stage is then to monitor the conflict between type 1 outputs. If there is no conflict detected, the first initial response will then proceed to the third stage where cursory type 2 analysis is involved. This is prototypically where biases arise (i.e., one is more prone to mis-or-disinformation)- unimpeded and with little effort. However, if conflict is detected, a more substantive type 2 reasoning will be involved, in which conflict detection becomes the bottom-up source of analytical engagement (Pennycook et al., 2015).

The third stage then branches two distinguished type 2 reasoning, with each having different implications on the ultimate degree of biases displayed. One, rationalisation refers to the process where, albeit successful conflict detection, humans focus on justifying the first initial responses without seriously alternative type 1 output cued by the stimulus which do not come as fast and as fluent as the first initial response. This process would typically result in biases that are bolstered by analytical engagement (i.e., when people justify and accept mis-or-disinformation as true). That is, additional consideration is focused on verifying rather than falsifying type 1 output. Two, decoupling, the most prototypical analytic process, refers to the additional process that inhibits and overrides the first initial response with two components involved: (1) Suppressing the first initial response rather than the alternative type 1 output, which, upon reflection, could emerge as stronger alternative, or (2) generating alternative responses that represent novel amalgamation of all the type 1 output. As such, the decoupling process usually reflects greater analytical processes that increase one's scepticism on the information presented (Pennycook et al., 2015).

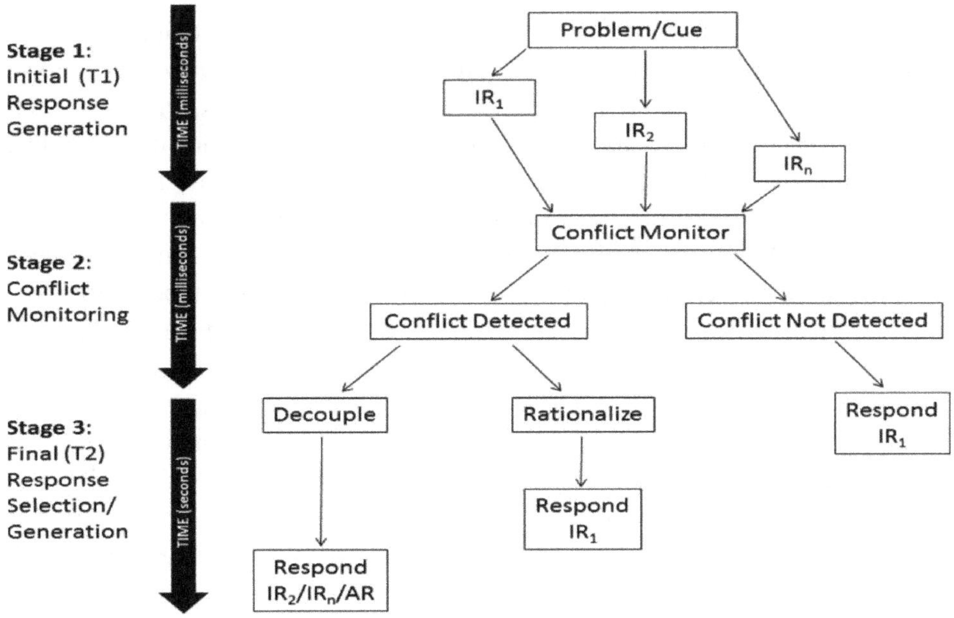

TSDPT Framework by Pennycook et al. (2015)

To illustrate the three-stage dual processes better, a problem is shown below:

In a study 1000 people were tested. Among the participants there were 995 nurses and five doctors. Paul is a randomly chosen participant of this study. Paul is 34 years old. He lives in a beautiful home in a posh suburb. He is well spoken and very interested in politics. He invests a lot of time in his career. What is most likely? (a) Paul is a nurse. (b) Paul is a doctor. (Pennycook et al., 2015)

The problem consisted of two pieces of information: (1) The base-rate probability (i.e., five doctors versus 995 nurses) that indicates a Paul has a 99.5% of chances to be a nurse, and (2) the stereotypical information with personality description that favours Paul to be more likely a doctor (Pennycook et al., 2015). In line with the description mentioned earlier, research found that people are more likely to favour stereotypical information, which is a more intuitive source of information, than base-rate probability (Barbey & Sloman, 2007).

Even when detection of conflict between base-rate and stereotypical information occurs (i.e., typically reflected by increased reaction time), there are cases that participants still give responses that are intuitively salient. Rectifying this, DeNeys and Glucimic (2008) found greater activation in participants' anterior cingulate cortex, which is associated with conflict detection for stereotypical responses for incongruent problems than congruent problems. Given the stereotypical responses despite type 2 processing, this supports the notion of rationalisation, which often leads to effortful beliefs or acceptance of false information. On the other hand, DeNeys and Glucimic (2008) also found cases where increase in reaction time in incongruent problems in relative to congruent problems occurred when participants responded with base-rate probability. DeNeys and Glucimic (2008) reported that when participants showed base-rate responses for incongruent problems, an increase in activation was shown in both anterior cingulate cortex and right prefrontal lateral cortex, where the latter is often associated with response inhibition. This supports the notion of decoupling with an additional deliberative process being applied in type 2 processes.

In relation to one's susceptibility to mis-or-disinformation, either in general contexts or through AI, the gist of TSDPT is that as one fails to detect conflict between type 1 output or further one engages in rationalisation under the type 2 process if conflict is detected, one is more susceptible to accept mis-or-disinformation. In contrast, the greater one engages in decoupling under the type 2 process, the less susceptible for one towards mi-or-disinformation (Pennycook et al., 2015). In line with this, Bryanov and Vziatysheva (2021) has suggested applying the TSDPT as a framework in analysing one's proneness to mis-or-disinformation. In their scope review, Bryanov and Vziatysheva (2021) not only identified various factors that strongly influence one's proneness to mis-or-disinformation but also broken them into three categories, individual level, message level, and ecological factors. However, they may not be as applicable as the review focused in the general contexts.

Yet, to fit into the contexts of mis-or-misinformation through AI, this book chapter will focus on both general factors that are applicable to the AI context and break it down into three levels, following Bryanov and Vziatysheva (2021)'s suggestions.

Individual Level

Trust in AI. Trust in AI has been defined as humans' psychological mechanisms that expect AI to help mitigate risks and uncertainty and increase the likelihood of successful interactions occurring with entities of the environment (Lukyanenko et al., 2022). Indeed, trust facilitates congruence in humans' cognition while processing information, which often leads to the confirmation biases, humans' tendency to look for information that is consistent with their pre-existing information (Lockey et al., 2021). Concurrently, people with high trust in AI tend to believe that AI will act in the best interest of the users and that people accept or disregard the flaws of AI (Choung et al., 2022). Literature postulated that in the AI contexts, distrust, which is functionally equivalent to trust, elevates one's ability in navigating misinformation through AI (Stanton & Jensen, 2021). In contrast, studies provided a consensus that trust in AI often impedes individuals from discovering the true information, as trust in AI reduces the need for humans to further invest in cognitive resources by reducing complexity of cognition.

In this case, two scenarios are anticipated to occur during the information processing in accordance to TSDPT. First, people who invest high trust in AI tend to exhibit low conflict monitoring while processing incoming information, for they may believe that whatever output AI generates is congruent and will result in the best outcome for them, despite being aware that AI output might not be accurate (Lukyanenko et al., 2022). This is because high trust increases confidence in AI that AI is competent in solving problems for them, with general belief that AI is more effective and competent than humans (Jacovi et al., 2021) Alternatively, as trust in AI increases the congruence of information processing (i.e.,, it is more likely for one to engage in rationalisation to justify the first initial responses cued by the AI output (i.e., the idea is similar to confirmation bias; Ha & Kim, 2023). Supporting this, studies found that trust reduces one's scepticism, which is then likely to prompt ones to reassure that their first intuitive responses are correct (Baghramian & Panizza, 2022; Harding et al., 2016). Intriguingly, both cases result in processing that are prone to biases and errors. All these form the following proposition.

Proposition 1. Trust in AI positively predicts one's susceptibility to mis-or-disinformation through AI, such that the greater trust in AI one possesses, the more susceptible one to mis-or-disinformation through AI.

AI literacy. AI literacy refers to a set of skills in using AI, specifically focusing on four dimensions: (1) Knowing the basic functions of AI and understanding the use of AI applications, (2) applying AI knowledge, concepts, and applications in different scenarios, (3) evaluating and creating AI applications, and (4) taking AI ethics into considerations (Ng et al., 2021). Due to greater knowledge and understanding about how AI systems and its algorithms work, people with greater AI literacy tend to be sceptical of over-sensationalized claims and the sources of the output, being more critical while evaluating the AI output (Beretta, 2024; Hristovska, 2023). That is, people with greater AI literacy tend to take potential biases and errors into account while processing AI output, which strengthens the conflict monitoring processes due to greater amount of intuitive responses generated in type1 processing contributed by existing AI knowledge (Giustini & Dastyar, 2024). Therefore, conflicts between AI output seem more likely to be detected with additional deliberative evaluations (Pennycook et al., 2015).

Empirical findings indirectly corroborated the mechanism in the media contexts by postulating that media literacy heightens people's criticism by offering knowledge and skills to resist and critically interpret and against the detrimental effects of fake news (Flynn et al., 2017). In line with this, a meta-analysis suggested that increase in knowledge and understanding of media production systems tend to exhibit greater scepticism and realistic expectancies about media messages (Jeong et al.,, 2012). Also, Jones-Jang et al. (2019) found that information literacy, an intellectual framework in understanding, evaluating, using, and finding information, is positively associated with identification of falsified information. Coiro et al. (2010) asserted that the ability to navigate and locate information is the key to adapt in the information presented by the ever-changing technologies, with evidence that the ability to locate fact-checking websites and other relevant tools contributes to one's ability in discerning fake news (Mihailidis & Viotty, 2017). Though existing studies were not under the AI contexts, it seems reasonable to apply the same manoeuvre to AI literacy. Thus, proposition 2 is formed.

Proposition 2. AI literacy negatively predicts one's susceptibility to mis-or-disinformation through AI, such that the greater AI literacy one possesses, the less susceptible one to mis-or-disinformation through AI.

Analytical mindset. Despite the engagement in type 2 processes (i.e., the analytical process) being equipped by people in nature according to TSDPT, the extent to which one is prone in accepting false information as true is subject to individual differences in analytical mindset (Pennycook et al., 2015; Stanovich & West, 1998, 2000), defined as one's propensity to engage in analytical reasoning, specifically referring to the decoupling process in this context. To elucidate, studies found that people with a high analytical mindset tend to report high reflective openness, which is characterised as (1) having high willingness to think, (2) engaging in and enjoying more effortful cognitive abilities, (3) more likely to accept incoming information as false (Pennycook & Rand, 2019; Petty et al., 2009). That is, people with greater analytical mindset are more likely to compare different type 1 output generated in the first stage of information processing and detect conflicts between output, who then are more likely to further the information to the decoupling processes (i.e., more cognitively effortful in nature).

Extensively, Pennycook & Rand (2019) found that people with a greater analytical mindset performed better in discerning fake and real news headlines in the contexts of accuracy judgements, regardless of whether the participants' political ideology is consistent with the content or not. This suggests that one with a high analytical mindset tends to decouple information presented, rather than to rationalise first initial response (i.e., consistent political ideology in this case). Indirectly supporting this, Martel et al. (2020) found that induced emotionality (i.e., as opposed of analytical mindset) is strongly associated with increased beliefs in fake news, with Fernández-López and Perea (2020) replicated the same finding in the Spanish samples. Despite these studies mostly being conducted under the media and political contexts, the same mechanism seems applicable to the AI contexts as well, given that one's analytical mindset, as a trait, operates across all contexts. As such, it is likely people with a high analytical mindset tend to evaluate and decouple information presented by AI greater. Hence, the following proposition is formed.

Proposition 3. Analytical engagement negatively predicts one's susceptibility to mis-or-disinformation through AI, such that the greater analytical engagement one possesses, the less susceptible one to mis-or-disinformation through AI.

Bullshit receptivity. Bullshit receptivity refers to the degree of receptiveness of one towards bullshit (i.e., both in terms of consuming and generating it). While bullshit generally is constructed absent concern for the truth (Frankfurt, 2005), which is conceptually distinct from misinformation and disinformation, research found that bullshit receptivity is strongly associated with failure to detect falsified information and high willingness to accept falsified claim (Pennycook et al., 2015). Studies also reported that bullshit receptivity is linked with increased beliefs in religious, paranormal, conspiracy, and doubtful claims (Evans et al., 2020). In the contexts of deep fakes, Iacobucci et al. (2021) also reported that people with high bullshit receptivity are more susceptible to information priming and have less ability in discerning fake content. Indirectly supporting this, people who perform well on the cognitive reflection task (i.e., a measure that reflects analytical thinking) tend to report less bullshit receptivity, implying that bullshit receptivity kind of deactivates one's type 2 process during information processing (Baptista, et al., 2022).

Extending on it, it is likely that individuals with high bullshit receptivity have weaker conflict monitoring, which then results in greater likelihood to detect conflicts between type 1 output while processing information presented by AI (i.e., they might disregard the conflicts even if any), with courtesy type 2 processing involved (Pennycook et al., 2015; Pennycook & Rand, 2019). In favour of this, research found that bullshit receptivity increases reflexive openness and overclaiming (Paulhus et al., 2003), where both have been found to reflect high tendency to rate fake information as accurate due to overconfidence to indicate knowledge even if they do not have it. These could also in turn contribute to lack of scepticism toward information encountered, which has been observed in non-analytic individuals (Pennycook & Rand, 2017). As literature asserts that the influence of bullshit receptivity in information detection is similar across contexts in general (Iacobucci & Cicco, 2022), it thus seems logical to assume that people with high bullshit receptivity are less likely to detect mis-or-information through AI. Thus, forming the following proposition:

Proposition 4. Bullshit receptivity positively predicts one's susceptibility to mis-or-disinformation, such that the greater the tendency for one to debunk, the less susceptible one to mis-or-disinformation through AI.

User's positive experience of using AI. This refers to the user's experience of achieving small success by using AI to solve problems (Nicolescu & Tudorache, 2022). When users are provided with positive feedback while using AI, it arouses positive emotions toward AI usage, who in turn invest more trust and efficacy in AI in providing quality content (Sidaoui et al., 2020). The heightened trust and efficacy might reduce one's scepticism and critical thinking, making users accept information provided by AI without verifying its reliability (Lukyanenko et al., 2022). In support of this, studies found that when people experience positive emotions, they are more likely to rely on their intuition and heuristics, which might also result in confirmation biases toward AI content (Dunne, 2016; Ha & Kim, 2023). Lun et al. (2023) provided evidence that participants experiencing negative mood performed better in critical thinking assessment than participants experiencing positive mood, implying that people under positive emotions may not scrutinise information as thoroughly as people under negative emotions.

Alternatively, to maintain the positive experience interacting with AI, users might favour information provided by AI in lieu of risking to evaluate and challenge information that has suggested mastery feedback, which is likely to result in rationalisation (Zhao et al., 2020). Meanwhile, positive emotions also can elevate one's level of satisfaction toward AI, which reduces the perceived need to engage in effortful analysis (i.e., type 2 process, specifically decoupling) and increases the likelihood to consume and disseminate misleading information presented by AI (Bhatnagr et al., 2024; Rastogi et al., 2022). Also, users who have mastery experience of using AI might increase their engagement and exposure to AI. With the larger exposure to a wider pool of AI information, the chance to encounter false information also increases (Kertosy, 2018). All these sort of inform that positive emotions are related to the activation of type 1 process (i.e., then later proceed to either rationalisation or cursory analysis) and the deactivation of type 2 decoupling process. Hence, proposition 5 is formed.

Proposition 5. User's positive experience with AI positively predicts one's susceptibility to mis-or-disinformation, such that the greater positive experience with AI one has, the more susceptible one to mis-or-disinformation through AI.

AI-Content Level

AI-content alignment. If the AI content is consistent with the information one has exposed to earlier, one is more likely to believe the AI content despite its accuracy. Though not under the AI contexts, studies established that repetition of information increases perceptions of accuracy (Dechene et al., 2010; Fazio et al., 2015). Pennycook et al. (2018) found that simply reading a news headline is adequate enough to increase its perceived accuracy at the later stage, with Pennycook and Rand. (2017) reporting that a single exposure to a news headline "Trump to Ban All TV Shows that Promote Gay Activity Starting with Empire as President" increased the fraction of accuracy rate as double in the following week where participants were shown the same title and to rate the accuracy again. Allen et al. (2023) showed that participants who were shown twice about a deepfaked video tend to rate it as a real video compared to participants who were only shown once. All these inform that if AI produces information that is aligned with user's or aligned with past AI content, it increases people's susceptibility in detecting false information from it.

To elucidate, exposure to similar information facilitates the rapid and fluency processing, where the information is likely to be taken as accurate (Westerman & Bonnet, 2015). Pennycook et al. (2018) further explained that low-level fluency heuristic (i.e., type 1 processing) influences one's accuracy judgements for even greatly intense and implausible partisan and entirely fabricated stories. The sped up type 1 processing later decreases one's scepticism on information encountered, impairing one's ability to detect and identify falsified information (Duke et al., 2014), even in the AI contexts. In this case, people would fail to detect conflicts between type 1 output and proceed the first initial response to the cursory type 2 processing while encountering information presented by AI that is aligned with what they have exposed earlier, given that the first initial response has been processed before in the earlier exposures (Oberauer, 2018). This is because humans would minimise cognitive resources in additional deliberation to process information that has been processed earlier (Mandler, 2008). All these justify the following proposition.

Proposition 6. AI-content alignment positively predicts one's susceptibility to mis-or-disinformation, such that the greater the alignment between AI-content and user's knowledge, the more susceptible one to mis-or-disinformation through AI.

AI automation. AI automation is defined as the extent to which AI can perform a task in the absence of human intervention. Following the increase in training datasets, as AI automation becomes higher and the automated fact-checking system advances, AI will keep humans out-of-the-loop by eventually replacing humans' oversight (Srinivasan, 2020). Highly automated AI systems usually require less interaction with humans, where humans are usually the passive receiver of information, risking users to accept falsified information in the absence of proper scrutiny (Xu et al., 2022). As such, users might be more likely to trust the information presented by AI without questioning its accuracy or sources (Araujo et al., 2020). This is due to users automatically "assuming" that whatever information presented by AI is correct, hence having less involvement in the tasks (Bader & Kaiser, 2019). While processing information presented by highly automated AI, users are more likely to rely on their first initial response from type 1 processing or rationalisation due to stronger belief that highly automated AI produces high quality content (Pennycook et al., 2015).

Legaspi et al. (2019) explained this as the result of reduced human's agency and increased AI agency. Further, diminished human's agency has been found to result in overreliance on AI; following the impaired predictive ability of humans, this rules out humans' cognitive input (i.e., questioning, evaluating, and verifying) from the tasks (Awad & Wagoner, 2015; Mishima et al., 2023). In line with this, Ghost et al. (2019) claimed that one's intuitive analysis is getting out from problem-solving processes while engaging with highly automated AI. Supporting this, studies found that reduced agency in humans impairs one's ability in detecting errors, understanding information, and determining following actions (Pagliari et al., 2022; Victor et al., 2018; Wen et al., 2021). Kertysova (2018) indirectly rectified this by asserting that keeping humans in the loop of information processing facilitates questioning the AI decisions as well as scrutinising. Given that humans' role depletes following the increase in AI automation which depletes one's cognitive functions, proposition 7 is formed.

Proposition 7. AI automation positively predicts one's susceptibility to mis-or-disinformation, such that the greater the AI automation, the more susceptible one to mis-or-disinformation through AI.

Contextual Level

Overloaded with Information. Human's cognitive capacity is limited. When the information processed exceeds the limits of one's cognitive capacity, humans are overloaded with information (Laato et al., 2020). Given the rise of AI usage in recent years, the context to which humans are overloaded with information under the use of AI has gained more attention in the literature (Gandhi et al., 2023). Studies formed a consensus that individuals overloaded with information tend to make careful or unintellectual decisions (i.e., including consuming mis-or-disinformation) due to the inability in processing incoming information with depleted self-control (Samson & Kostyszyn, 2015; Sweller, 2011). That is, when one is stressed with a huge amount of information, their motivation to search and sense new information depletes, who later recoil from exerting more effort to verify the accuracy of it (Whelan et al., 2020). In line with this, research found that people overwhelmed with information on social media consume and share falsified information without completely processing it due to the influx of additional information (Khan et al., 2024).

Concurrently, research found that overloaded with information results in fatigue, which further reduces humans' ability in processing and verifying information (Whelan et al., 2020). Literature suggested that fatigue conditions could lead to failure in detecting the conflict between type 1 output or biases where the first initial response is correct, hence either proceeding the information to cursory type 2 process or rationalisation (i.e., more likely to result in biases and errors; Bryanov & Vziatysheva, 2021; Pennycook et al., 2015). Talwar et al. (2019) further explained this as humans' tendency to avoid extra cognitive resources to verify information sources with additional deliberative analysis under fatigue conditions. Apuke et al. (2022) exhibited that this not only leads to consumption but also proliferation of misinformation, with evidence that showed a positive relationship between information-induced stress and fake news sharing (Huang et al., 2022). It thus seems that when people are overloaded with information, their ability to detect mis-or-disinformation reduces, thus forming the following proposition:

Proposition 8. Overloaded with information positively predicts one's susceptibility to mis-or-disinformation, such that the greater the time constraint, the more susceptible one to mis-or-disinformation through AI.

Time constraint. The amount of time one has also influences the identification of mis-or-disinformation, especially in the contexts of AI. Ling et al. (2021)'s systematic review reported that perceived timeliness is strongly associated with AI usage in a concurrent workflow, where people tend to follow AI decisions without their own input under timely conditions (Tejeda et al., 2022). Baron et al. (2015) found that under timely conditions, people reflect strong reflexive impulsivity (i.e., lack of willingness to think analytically, or in other words, lack of engagement to proceed information to type 2 processing while sticking with the first initial response), which often results in inaccurate intuitive responses (Pennycook & Rand, 2019). Similarly, Roberts and Newton (2010) found that when participants were to give an answer within a short period of time, their type 2 processing is differentially inhibited. Ergo, it seems that when one is under a timely condition, their analytical mindset (i.e., Type 2 processing, especially decoupling) is usually suppressed, which results in biases and errors and failure to detect mis-or-disinformation through AI.

Several lines of research established findings that support this mechanism. Evans and Curtis-Holmes (2005) found that in rapid-responding conditions, the amount of belief biases (i.e., the tendency to verify the validity of an argument based on whether one agrees on the conclusion or not, rather than whether the conclusion follows the premises logically) significantly increased, followed by the reduced number of logically correct decisions. In addition, studies also showed a significant increase in matching biases (i.e., a non-logical tendency to choose cards which match the explicit content of certain conditional statements, regardless the presence of negations) in the rapid-response version of the selection task compared to a free-time version (Roberts & Newton, 2010). Moreover, Zhang et al. (2016) found that participants were less likely to detect misinformation presented in the task under time constraint conditions. All these indirectly imply that the more timely the condition is, the less likely for one to detect inaccurate information, even in the AI context. Henceforth, the following proposition is generated.

Proposition 9. Time constraint positively predicts one's susceptibility to mis-or-disinformation, such that the greater the time constraint, the more susceptible one to mis-or-disinformation through AI.

Taken together, adopting the TSDPT, this book chapter presented a conceptual framework that explains users' susceptibility toward mis-or-disinformation through AI with nine propositions proposed (Figure 2). Specifically, following Bryanoz and Vziatysheva (2021)'s method, the framework is broken down into three categories. The first category concerns factors that fall under individual level, including trust in AI, AI literacy, analytical mindset, bullshit receptivity, and user's positive experience in using AI. The second category involves factors that lie under AI-related level, such as AI-content alignment and AI automation. The third category concerns factors that are under the contextual level, which include being overloaded with information and time constraints. Worth to mention, while some of these factors are AI context-specific (e.g., AI-content alignment, AI automation, trust in AI, and AI literacy), there are some generic factors that work across all contexts (e.g., analytical mindset, bullshit receptivity, time constraints, and overloaded with information).

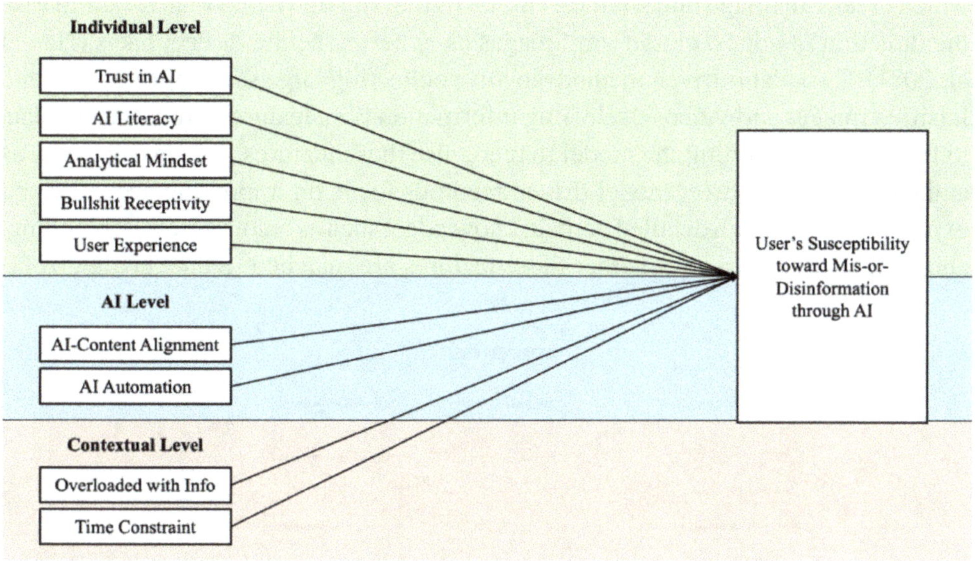

The Book Chapter's Illustration of the Conceptual Framework

Practical Cases Studies that Combat AI Dis-and-Misinformation

The earlier section of this chapter delved into the psychology aspects of one's susceptibility in consuming and disseminating mis-and-disinformation through AI in general. However, it is also essential to review some existing practical solutions that combat AI dis-or-misinformation to scrutinise whether those psychological aspects have been considered. Hence, this session will review some practical strategies that combat AI-driven dis-or-misinformation and could potentially be applied under the public health contexts.

AI Against AI

Not only AI plays a role in spreading dis-and-misinformation, but AI has also been used in combating AI-driven dis-and-misinformation. An example is the use of edge-based features in detecting and combating deepfakes. It involves using machine learning models that rely on three methods (see Figure 3; Gilbert & Gilbert, 2024), to detect, process, and analyse the edges in videos and images automatically, which enables devices to recognise patterns, objects, and shapes. One, neural classifier for feature anonymisation system (NC-FAS) focuses on anonymising personal data to train detection algorithms while ensuring edge-based features could still be utilised to detect deepfakes. It is based on the histogram of gradients techniques, which breaks an image into smithereens, turns the data into a historian to summarise the direction of edges, classifying images as either authentic or deepfakes (Han et al.,2021). Two, data-driven methods involve collecting large samples (e.g., real and falsified images and videos), selecting information (i.e., features) from the raw data to find patterns, training the model to recognise these features and classify them as authentic or fake. Three, model-driven methods focus on improving accuracy and explainability through detailed domain knowledge, such as colours, noises, blending, and edge maps, to assess whether those features are matched (Siegel et al., 2021).

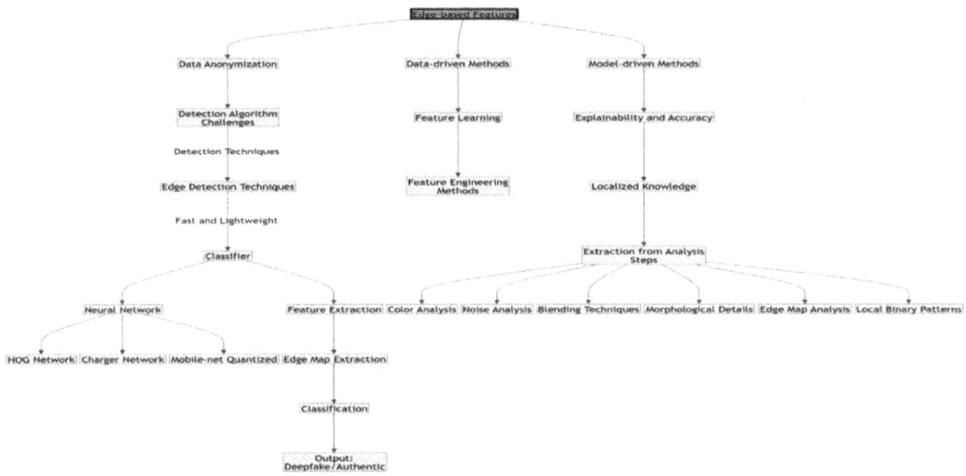

Edge-Based Features (AI Technologies) for Detecting Deepfakes by Gilbert & Gilbert (2024)

While edge-based features act as a AI technique to identify fake images or videos, natural language processing (NLP) is another AI technique that analyses falsified content. NLP involves computational models that solves practical problems for manipulating and understanding human languages. It has six primary stages of analysis (see Figure 4). Stage 1 involves the segmentation by tokenisation, which transforms each contiguous sentence into tokens. Stage 2 involves lexical analysis, in which orthographic features, such as punctuations and special characters are eliminated. Stage 3 involves syntactic analysis, focusing on the relationship between words (i.e., structural role of each word in the sentence). Stage 4 involves semantic analysis, which distils the meanings of words, fixed expressions, sentences and resolves ambiguity. Stage 5 involves pragmatic analysis, which comprehends sentences and observes pronominal references as well as the textual accuracy of the structure of the adjacent sentences. Lastly, stage 6 involves either stemming or lemmatization, which refers to reduction of possible variants or plurals of the same work by transferring each word into its radical and to the same lemma respectively (Oliveira et al., 2021).

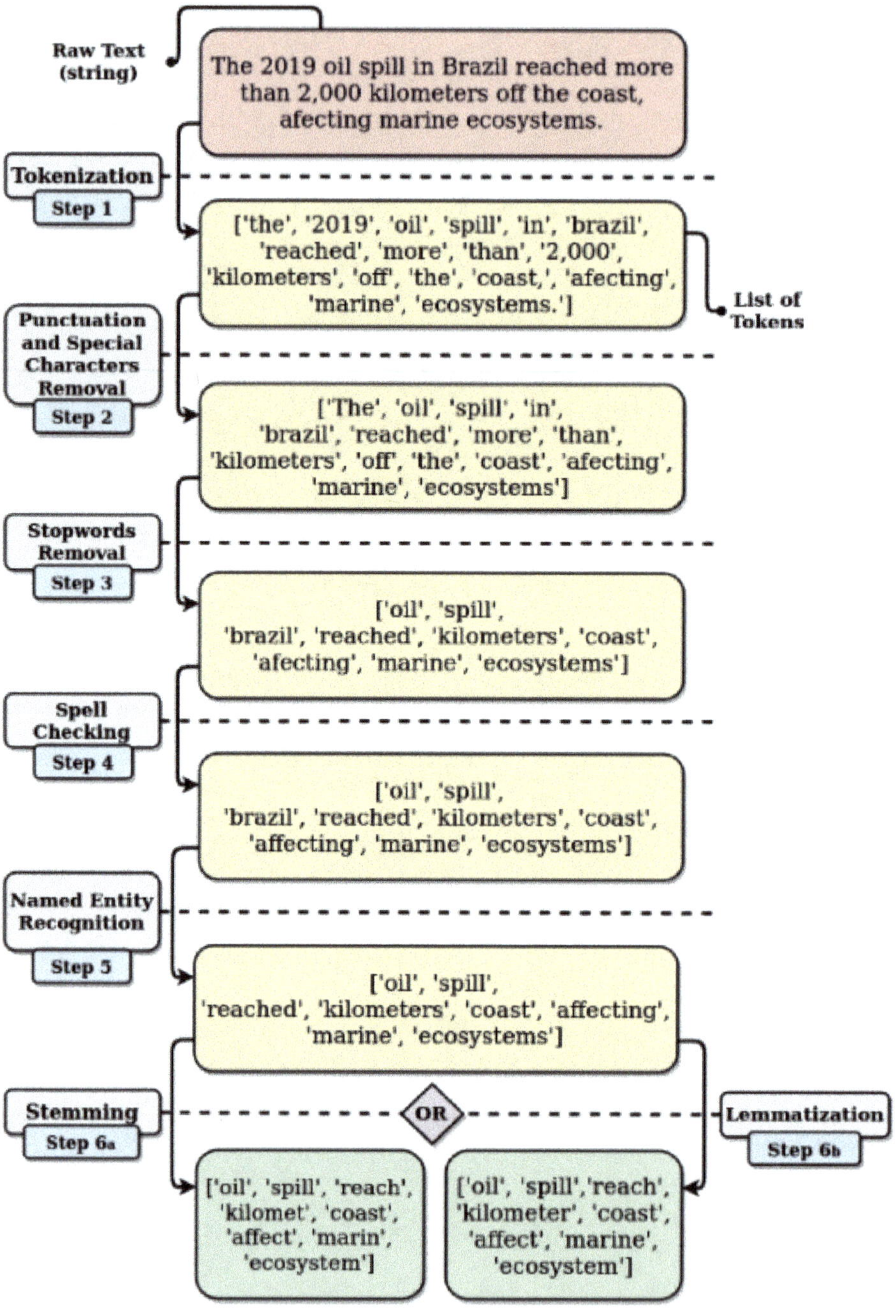

Edge-Based Features (AI Technologies) for Detecting Deepfakes by Gilbert & Gilbert (2024)

By these stages, NLP could identify and combat dis-or-misinformation through several means. One, sentiment analysis is done to detect emotionally charged or biased language that typically manipulates audiences', flagging exaggerated or sensationalist sentiment to detect potential manipulative or misleading content (Saquete et al., 2020). Two, NLP can evaluate the patterns of network of how dis-or-misinformation is spread. One example of NLP is Latent Dirichlet Allocation, which tracks emerging keywords or topics associated with fake news or information, enabling earlier strategies to stop the spread (Alonso et al., 2021). Three, comparisons between diverse contents that are either distorted or taken out of contexts with more reliable, recent sources are made through some semantic similarity tools, detecting misleading, outdated, or recycled information (Saquete et al., 2020). Four, as mentioned, reductions of content are done in stage 6 of NLP, of which automated summarization tools rely on. It highlights factual claims, provides a more concise, accurate, and clear, and removes unnecessary exaggerations, clarify misleading content (Oliveira et al., 2021).

Keeping Human-In-The-Loop

While AI-based methods have been used in combating dis-or-misinformation, it is also important to incorporate human-based approach for better fact-checking processes. Human-in-the-loop AI framework has been proposed to leverage three parties in fighting dis-or-misinformation, including AI, fact-checking experts (i.e., could be healthcare professionals in this context, and crowdsourcing workers (see Figure 5; Dermatini et al., 2020). This approach leverages the positive aspects of these parties: (1) the experts that factcheck and correctly identify the truthfulness level of verified content in a fair and transparent means, (2) the capability of crowdsourcing to manually process large amount of data, and (3) AI's scalability to efficiently process large datasets (Dermatini et al., 2020). That is, AI tools, such as NLP, will search and verify content via the mechanism mentioned. Concurrently, the crowdsourcing workers will provide judgements to the trustworthy level of the verified content, where the experts will then fact check the content in a transparent, open, fair, and honest way. This approach could result in improved trust on the outcomes over purely AI-based methods by leveraging embedded human dimension to elevate the transparency of the truthfulness labels attached (i.e., elucidating why certain pieces of content is labelled as fake or authentic; Daniel et al., 2021).

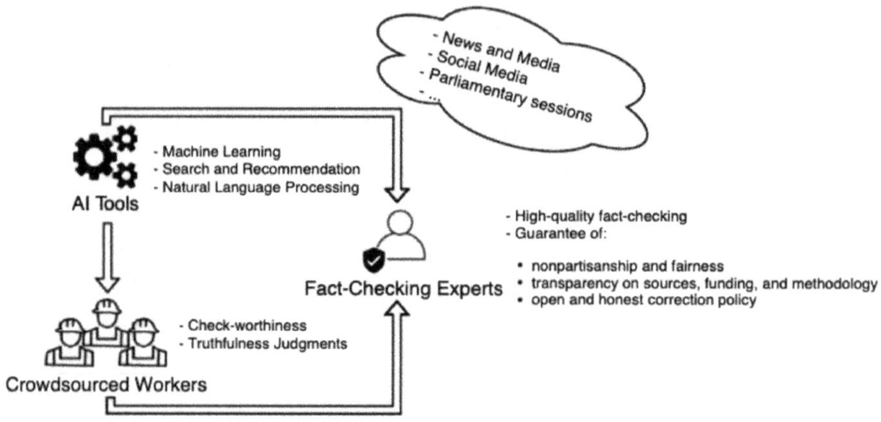

Human-In-The-Loop AI Framework by Demartini et al. (2020)

To dive deep, given the workload of dis-or-misinformation tasks, with constraints like deadline, costs, and maintaining quality, a cascade model is utilised to identify a task allocation solution to satisfy constraints with maximum values while balancing the trade-offs between the parties in the system (see Figure 6; Dermatini et al., 2020). For instance, for the trade-off between urgency and quality, as soon as the content is labelled as needing fact-check, the AI model will be adopted to provide a truthfulness label which then is replaced later once the experts have concluded their investigations of available evidence to identify if the content is true (Daniel et al., 2021). This cascade of annotation task, in which all labels are estimated quickly and automatically, with solely a small subset of content being sent to the crowd for quick verification. After this, only very few contents left will be then sent to experts to scrutinise in depth, where the core is to leverage different levels of size-quality-cost trade-offs provided by different methodologies. Also, AI and crowdsourcing could be adopted to scale up the annotation effort to huge content to provide a truthfulness labels, where experts can then be utilised on content where both AI and crowds have difficulty to identify (Dermatini et al., 2020).

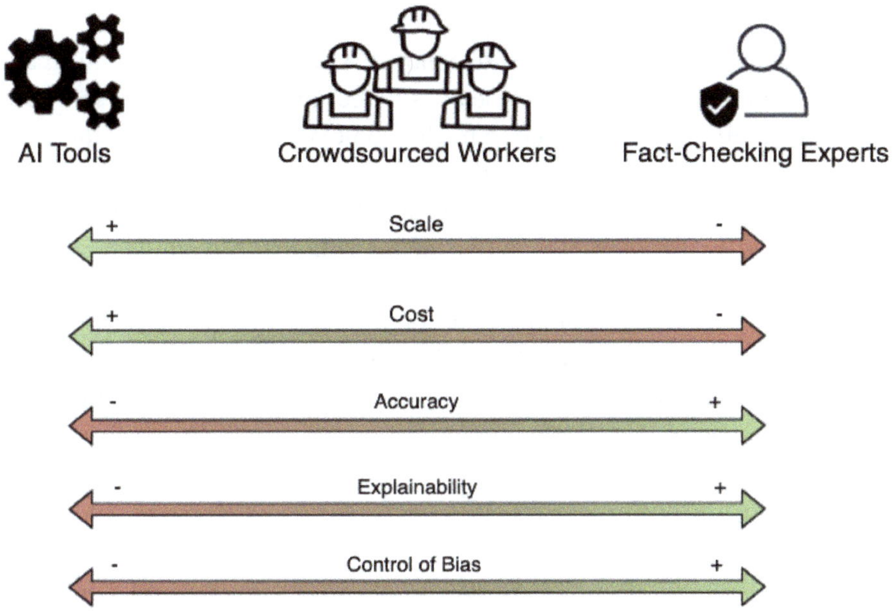

Trade-offs between the Parties in Human-In-The-Loop AI

Blockchain

Another method to combat AI-driven dis-or-misinformation is the blockchain, a decentralised, distributed ledger technology that provides proof of authenticity (PoA) for digital content to identify trusted sources and hence combating deepfakes (Fraga-Lamas & Fernández-Caramés, 2020). To explain, blockchain-solution uses Ethereum smart contracts (i.e., automatically enforce regulations and permissions attached to content, e.g., when a content is uploaded, the contract records the creator's Ethereum address, terms of use, and permissions, ensuring that only authorised people can edit the content, of which being recorded on the blockchain if edits occur) and the Interplanetary File System (i.e., to store content in a decentralised channel to ensure that the content is accessible even when individual servers shut down; Petratos & Faccia, 2023). At the same time, decentralised reputation systems (i.e., to verify the credibility of the creators as in if the AI sources consistently generate and upload trustworthy contents, the reputation increases) and Ethereum Name Services (i.e., allows creators to use human-readable names instead of cryptographic addresses, which is easier to associate AI content with trustworthy sources) are embedded (Wang et al., 2023). As such, users can refer to and rely on these to determine if AI content associated with the source is valid.

What Can Be Done in the Public Health Sectors?

Indeed, there are existing methods to conquer AI-driven dis-or-misinformation. However, several points are worth to be considered. First, they are not specifically designed and applied under the public health contexts, where most of them focus on the general AI-driven dis-or-misinformation. Two, they are mostly designed from a machine or technology-advancement standpoint, in which the psychological aspects of people's vulnerability to dis-or-misinformation through AI might not be fully accounted for. As such, this section will extend the discussions to mitigating strategies or intervention to debunk and combat people's susceptibility towards mis-and-disinformation in the public health domains, from *practical*, *legal*, and *ethical* perspectives, apart from the existing combating solutions being applied in the healthcare contexts.

Practical Perspectives

Several practical implications are suggested in regard to the existing challenges contributed by mis-and-disinformation through AI and the conceptual model proposed in the public health contexts. At the individual level, public health initiatives could initiate educational programs to improve one's AI literacy among general population and healthcare workers (Kasinidou, 2024). For the general population, the programs should explain the mechanism of how AI works, as well as the benefits, potential biases, and limitations of AI in conveying public-health related messages. General population could also be taught to be sceptical and verify information presented by AI from various reliable public health sources, instead of blindly trusting whatever content AI presented. On the other side, for the healthcare workers, the campaigns could target content that focuses on the integration of AI in their daily workflows, with practical tips to cross-check AI output. In addition, a guideline or checklist on verifying AI output against traditional records and for common tasks could be distributed to validate AI output.

At the AI level, public health authorities should make efforts in correcting public health related, misleading, falsified information through AI repeatedly. Specifically, established, verified, and latest public-health related content could be updated regularly to deemphasis and flag false content through leveraging similar platforms in which misinformation is prevalent to match correct, updated information with what general public and healthcare workers typically encounter. Concurrently, AI systems should be developed to include humans' oversight in both the public health and healthcare sectors, where large bodies of medical professionals and experts could continuously work on verifying and auditing public health-related information through AI. That is, any AI information regarding important medical decisions should be double-checked and verified with multiple healthcare experts, with healthcare workers being trained to effectively utilise AI while balancing the effectiveness of AI automation and keeping their critical judgement.

At the contextual level, given the intense schedule of healthcare workers, they could be provided with training that focuses on identifying and processing information through AI critically and making timely decisions. Also, healthcare professionals could be trained with techniques to filter irrelevant information from AI output. In detail, some case studies and real-life scenarios to train healthcare professionals on evaluating AI information under timely and information overloaded contexts could be provided. At the same time, in case where general public is overloaded with information and under a timely setting which might result in inability to evaluate the accuracy of AI-driven health-related information, resources, such as help desks and hotlines (i.e., with groups of medical, healthcare, and AI experts) could be established to provide assistance and sources to individuals to evaluate and verify AI contents. Online resource hubs could also be set up to provide a wide range of information or tools to evaluate AI-driven health content to the public.

Legal Perspectives

A review also informs several legal implications. The first concerns the issues of regulatory oversight. Pesapane et al. (2021) noted a list of legislation obligations for AI-based medical systems: (1) supervising medical organisations with AI-generated medical solutions, (2) preventing uniformity in the process of developing AI-based medical systems, (3) certifying and confirming the quality and effectiveness of AI-based healthcare systems, and (4) creating experimental legal regimes and regulatory sandboxes. While several legal systems have enhanced their framework to reach the obligations stated, more stringent standards are still needed to establish. For example, a risk-based approach could be adopted to regulate AI systems. In the healthcare sectors, high-risk AI systems (i.e., the usage for biometric identification, sorting patients based on medical record, and for management of public healthcare services) must be mandated under risk management and data governance. For low-risk AI (e.g., chatbots that interact with humans in healthcare services), they must be regulated under code of conduct for reliable and safe services (Hoek et al. 2024).

Further, liability issues are not clearly addressed from a legal perspective. It is complex to determine the liability for misinformation or disinformation disseminated through AI systems especially in the public health domains (Bottomley & Thaldar, 2023). Due to the "black box" nature of AI, where the decision-making is not as transparent, if an AI system provides misleading information that results in harmful consequences to both the general community or patients, the liability attribution is complicated as to who is responsible, the AI system, the AI developers, or healthcare providers (Khullar et al., 2021). For instance, harms caused to patients due to AI errors, such as inaccurate medical or health information presented, are not yet considered as negligence (i.e., established by the duty of care and causality between the suffered harm and the breach) under the legal systems in the United Kingdom (Schonberger, 2019). The European Union has also mentioned their aims to highlight responsibility and liability of notified bodies and competent authorities in regard to mis-and-disinformation through AI in the public health sector (Pesapane et al., 2021).

Practically, platforms that disseminated AI-driven health information, such as Youtube, Facebook, and Twitter, should be given legal obligations to control for malicious content and to hold accountable for the AI-driven health-related mis-and-disinformation. In detail, legislation parties could establish stringent standards and ensure that those platforms are in compliance with health information regulations (Qureshi & Khan, 2024). For instance, those platforms could be required to implement advanced detection technologies that identify and eliminate misleading AI-driven health information, with regular auditing conducted by the authorities (Davey & Sauerwein, 2023). Concurrently, platforms must also be made mandatory to provide transparency reporting about the approaches to mitigate false health information through AI (Land & Aronson, 2020). Apart from this, healthcare providers should also hold accountable not only for regulating the accuracy of AI-generated health information but also consequences of misleading information by AI (Alam et al., 2023). In this case, healthcare providers are required to verify the reliability of sources and content used for generating health and medical decisions (Bernal & Mazo, 2022).

Delving further, open-source policies could also be promoted through the legislation processes. Open-source licences that include assurances of transparency, accountability, collaboration, and prevention of misuse of AI-generated health information could be developed (Paton & Kobayashi, 2019). Regulatory bodies could also be established to monitor compliance with open-source licences (Calonzone et al., 2023). At the same time, organisations could be required to use open-source AI tools to make regular reports for public health information (Solanki et al. 2023). Regular audits of open-source AI should be mandated to evaluate their adherence to ethical guidelines, safeness, and effectiveness (Rajpurkar et al., 2022). The report should include details of how the AI tools are used and any detected mis-and-disinformation. Next, laws that encourage sharing of public health data within the open-source community could also be enacted under stringent guidelines and privacy to train and improve AI models for public health uses (Kiseleva et al., 2020).

Ethical Perspective

Ethical implications are proposed to inform codes of ethics regarding issues of mis-and-disinformation through AI. First, truthfulness and accuracy of AI-generated health information must be ensured (Kim et al., 2021). AI developers and other public health stakeholders have the responsibility to ensure that AI-generated health information is based on reliable sources and free from biases or errors that might mislead the public. Meanwhile, transparency about the sources of AI-generated information should be promoted to ensure that users have the knowledge of the basis for the recommended information (Mensah, 2023). Second, harmful influences through misleading health information by AI must be prevented while ensuring individual safety (Kiseleva, 2020). Notably, public health authorities must also prioritise well-being and safety by coming out with ethical guidelines, which make sure that the community has access to safe and reliable health information (Kempton & Vassilakopoulou, 2021). This could also be done by implementing measures that identify and correct false information promptly, especially in the public health settings (Al-Tamimi & Aziz, 2022).

Third, informed healthcare or medical related decision-making must be promoted (Lysaght et al., 2019). Individuals should be equipped with adequate knowledge and information to make informed decisions in accordance with public health information by AI (Bjerring & Busch, 2020). For instance, clear, understandable explanations of the way AI algorithms generate information and the potential limitations (e.g., risks, biases, and errors) should be provided to the users (Amann et al., 2020). That is, promoting AI literacy and analytical skills among the community and healthcare workers are also ethically imperative. Fourth, fairness and biases should be addressed to the greatest degree (Angerschmid et al., 2022). Regular assessments could be mandated by ethical guidelines to identify and address biases that might result discriminatory health-related outcomes (Celi et al., 2022). Ethical responsibility to ensure that health disparities are not reinforced through unequal information should be equipped among AI developers, public health authorities, and healthcare workers as well (Moore, 2022).

Fifth, individuals' privacy and autonomy must be safeguarded (Murdoch, 2021). To elucidate, it is important to ensure that individuals' personal health data and information will not be misused or exploited by AI systems (Gerke et al., 2020). Individual's health data must be protected from unauthorised access, and individuals must have full control over their health information (Tom et al., 2020). At the same time, individuals' or healthcare workers' autonomy in making decisions should be supported but not replaced by AI, especially individuals should be allowed to have control over their health choices (Williamson & Prybutok, 2024). Sixth, accountability and responsibility should be fostered among AI developers, policymakers, and

REFERENCES

Al-Tamimi, F., & Aziz, A. M. (2022). Evaluating the impact of transparency and accountability measures on the ethical implementation of artificial intelligence applications in healthcare. *International Journal of Responsible Artificial Intelligence, as*(as), 27–34.

Alam, M. N., Kaur, M., & Kabir, M. S. (2023). Explainable AI in healthcare: Enhancing transparency and trust upon legal and ethical consideration. *International Research Journal of Engineering and Technology, 10*(6), 828–835.

Allen, C., Payne, B., Abegaz, T., & Robertson, C. (2023). What you see is not what you know: Studying deception in deepfake video manipulation. *Journal of Cybersecurity Education Research and Practice, 2024*(1). Advance online publication. DOI: 10.32727/8.2023.25

Amann, J., Blasimme, A., Vayena, E., Frey, D., & Madai, V. I. (2020). Explainability for Artificial Intelligence in healthcare: A multidisciplinary perspective. *BMC Medical Informatics and Decision Making, 20*(1), 310. Advance online publication. DOI: 10.1186/s12911-020-01332-6 PMID: 33256715

Angerschmid, A., Zhou, J., Theuermann, K., Chen, F., & Holzinger, A. (2022). Fairness and explanation in AI-informed decision making. *Machine Learning and Knowledge Extraction, 4*(2), 556–579. DOI: 10.3390/make4020026

Apuke, O. D., Omar, B., Tunca, E. A., & Gever, C. V. (2022). Information overload and misinformation sharing behaviour of social media users: Testing the moderating role of cognitive ability. *Journal of Information Science, 016555152211219*. Advance online publication. DOI: 10.1177/01655515221121942

Araujo, T., Helberger, N., Kruikemeier, S., & de Vreese, C. H. (2020). In ai we trust? perceptions about automated decision-making by Artificial Intelligence. *AI & Society, 35*(3), 611–623. DOI: 10.1007/s00146-019-00931-w

Awad, S. H., & Wagoner, B. (2014). Agency and creativity in the midst of social change. *Constraints of Agency*, 229–243. DOI: 10.1007/978-3-319-10130-9_14

Bader, V., & Kaiser, S. (2019). Algorithmic decision-making? the user interface and its role for human involvement in decisions supported by Artificial Intelligence. *Organization, 26*(5), 655–672. DOI: 10.1177/1350508419855714

Baghramian, M., & Caprioglio Panizza, S. (2022). Scepticism and the value of distrust. *Inquiry (Oslo, Norway)*, •••, 1–28. DOI: 10.1080/0020174X.2022.2135821

Baptista, J. P., Gradim, A., & Correla, E. (2022). Bullshit receptivity: What matters is who said it, not what is said. *Journal of Digital Media & Interaction*, *5*(12), 7–23. DOI: 10.34624/jdmi.v5i12.28717

Barbey, A. K., & Sloman, S. A. (2007). Base-rate respect: From ecological rationality to dual processes. *Behavioral and Brain Sciences*, *30*(3), 241–254. DOI: 10.1017/S0140525X07001653 PMID: 17963533

Baron, J., Scott, S., Fincher, K., & Emlen Metz, S. (2015). Why does the Cognitive Reflection Test (sometimes) predict utilitarian moral judgment (and other things)? *Journal of Applied Research in Memory and Cognition*, *4*(3), 265–284. DOI: 10.1016/j.jarmac.2014.09.003

Bayer, J., Bitiukova, N., Bard, P., Szakács, J., Alemanno, A., & Uszkiewicz, E. (2021). Disinformation and propaganda – impact on the functioning of the rule of law in the EU and its Member States. SSRN *Electronic Journal*. DOI: 10.2139/ssrn.3409279

Beretta. (2024). *The impact of AI literacy on the emotional reaction to AI mistakes in human-AI collaboration* (thesis). *University of Twente*. Retrieved 2024, from https://essay.utwente.nl/98115/

Bernal, J., & Mazo, C. (2022). Transparency of artificial intelligence in Healthcare: Insights from professionals in computing and Healthcare Worldwide. *Applied Sciences (Basel, Switzerland)*, *12*(20), 10228. DOI: 10.3390/app122010228

Bhatnagr, P., Rajesh, A., & Misra, R. (2024). Continuous intention usage of artificial intelligence enabled Digital Banks: A review of expectation confirmation model. *Journal of Enterprise Information Management*, *37*(6), 1763–1787. Advance online publication. DOI: 10.1108/JEIM-11-2023-0617

Bjerring, J. C., & Busch, J. (2020). Artificial Intelligence and patient-centered decision-making. *Philosophy &amp. Philosophy & Technology*, *34*(2), 349–371. DOI: 10.1007/s13347-019-00391-6

Bohr, A., & Memarzadeh, K. (2020). The rise of Artificial Intelligence in healthcare applications. *Artificial Intelligence in Healthcare*, 25–60. DOI: 10.1016/B978-0-12-818438-7.00002-2

Bonnet, G. W. and D. (2015, February 18). *Revamping your business through Digital Transformation*. MIT Sloan Management Review. https://sloanreview.mit.edu/article/revamping-your-business-through-digital-transformation/

Bottomley, D., & Thaldar, D. (2023a). Liability for harm caused by ai in Healthcare: An overview of the core legal concepts. *Frontiers in Pharmacology*, *14*, 1297353. Advance online publication. DOI: 10.3389/fphar.2023.1297353 PMID: 38161692

Bottomley, D., & Thaldar, D. (2023b). Liability for harm caused by ai in Healthcare: An overview of the core legal concepts. *Frontiers in Pharmacology*, *14*, 1297353. Advance online publication. DOI: 10.3389/fphar.2023.1297353 PMID: 38161692

Bryanov, K., & Vziatysheva, V. (2021). Determinants of individuals' belief in fake news: A scoping review determinants of belief in fake news. *PLoS One*, *16*(6), e0253717. Advance online publication. DOI: 10.1371/journal.pone.0253717 PMID: 34166478

Calanzone, D., Coppari, A., Tedoldi, R., Olivato, G., & Casonato, C. (2023). *An open source perspective on AI and alignment with the EU AI Act*. CEUR Workshop Proceedings. https://halixness.github.io/assets/pdf/calanzone_coppari_tedoldi.pdf

Celi, L. A., Cellini, J., Charpignon, M.-L., Dee, E. C., Dernoncourt, F., Eber, R., Mitchell, W. G., Moukheiber, L., Schirmer, J., Situ, J., Paguio, J., Park, J., Wawira, J. G., & Yao, S. (2022). Sources of bias in artificial intelligence that perpetuate healthcare disparities—A global review. *PLOS Digital Health*, *1*(3), e0000022. Advance online publication. DOI: 10.1371/journal.pdig.0000022 PMID: 36812532

Chesney, R., & Citron, D. (2019). Deepfakes and the new disinformation war: The coming age of post-truth geopolitics. *Foreign Affairs*, *98*(1), 147.

Choung, H., David, P., & Ross, A. (2022). Trust and ethics in ai. *AI & Society*, *38*(2), 733–745. DOI: 10.1007/s00146-022-01473-4

Coiro, J. (2010). *Handbook of Research on new literacies*. Lawrence Erlbaum Associates.

Crossnohere, N. L., Elsaid, M., Paskett, J., Bose-Brill, S., & Bridges, J. F. (2022a). Guidelines for Artificial Intelligence in Medicine: Literature Review and Content Analysis of Frameworks. *Journal of Medical Internet Research*, *24*(8), e36823. Advance online publication. DOI: 10.2196/36823 PMID: 36006692

Crossnohere, N. L., Elsaid, M., Paskett, J., Bose-Brill, S., & Bridges, J. F. (2022b). Guidelines for Artificial Intelligence in Medicine: Literature Review and Content Analysis of Frameworks. *Journal of Medical Internet Research*, *24*(8), e36823. Advance online publication. DOI: 10.2196/36823 PMID: 36006692

Curiel, R. P., & Ramirez, H. G. (2021). Vaccination strategies against covid-19 and the diffusion of anti-vaccination views. *Scientific Reports*, *11*(1), 6626. Advance online publication. DOI: 10.1038/s41598-021-85555-1 PMID: 33758218

Davey, O. M., & Sauerwein, L. (2023). Deepfake in online fraud cases: The haze of artificial intelligence's accountability based on the international law. *Sriwijaya Crimen and Legal Studies*, *1*(2), 89–99. DOI: 10.28946/scls.v1i2.2654

De Neys, W., & Glumicic, T. (2008). Conflict monitoring in dual process theories of thinking. *Cognition*, *106*(3), 1248–1299. DOI: 10.1016/j.cognition.2007.06.002 PMID: 17631876

Dechene, A., Stahl, C., Hansen, J., & Wänke, M. (2010). The truth about the truth: A meta-analytic review of the truth effect. *Personality and Social Psychology Review*, *14*(2), 238–257. DOI: 10.1177/1088868309352251 PMID: 20023210

Doss, C., Mondschein, J., Shu, D., Wolfson, T., Kopecky, D., Fitton-Kane, V. A., Bush, L., & Tucker, C. (2023). Deepfakes and scientific knowledge dissemination. *Scientific Reports*, *13*(1), 13429. Advance online publication. DOI: 10.1038/s41598-023-39944-3 PMID: 37596384

Duke, D., & Fiacconi, C. M., & KÃ¶hler, S. (. (2014). Parallel effects of processing fluency and positive affect on familiarity-based recognition decisions for faces. *Frontiers in Psychology*, *5*. Advance online publication. DOI: 10.3389/fpsyg.2014.00328 PMID: 24795678

Dunne, R. (2016). *Decision making is caused by information processing and emotion: A synthesis of two approaches to explain the phenomenon of confirmation bias* (thesis). Belfield.

Evans, A., Sleegers, W., & Mlakar, Ž. (2020). Individual differences in receptivity to scientific bullshit. *Judgment and Decision Making*, *15*(3), 401–412. DOI: 10.1017/S1930297500007191

Fazio, L. K., Brashier, N. M., Payne, B. K., & Marsh, E. J. (2015). Knowledge does not protect against illusory truth. *Journal of Experimental Psychology. General*, *144*(5), 993–1002. DOI: 10.1037/xge0000098 PMID: 26301795

Fernández-López, M., & Perea, M. (2020). Language does not modulate fake news credibility, but emotion does. *Psicológica Journal*, *41*(2), 84–102. DOI: 10.2478/psicolj-2020-0005

Flynn, D. J., Nyhan, B., & Reifler, J. (2017). The nature and origins of misperceptions: Understanding false and unsupported beliefs about politics. *Political Psychology*, *38*(S1), 127–150. DOI: 10.1111/pops.12394

Frankfurt, H. G. (2005). *On bullshit*. Princeton University Press. DOI: 10.1515/9781400826537

Gandhi, T. K., Classen, D., Sinsky, C. A., Rhew, D. C., Vande Garde, N., Roberts, A., & Federico, F. (2023). How can artificial intelligence decrease cognitive and work burden for front line practitioners? *JAMIA Open*, *6*(3), ooad079. Advance online publication. DOI: 10.1093/jamiaopen/ooad079 PMID: 37655124

Gerke, S., Minssen, T., & Cohen, G. (2020a). Ethical and legal challenges of artificial intelligence-driven healthcare. *Artificial Intelligence in Healthcare*, 295–336. DOI: 10.1016/B978-0-12-818438-7.00012-5

Gerke, S., Minssen, T., & Cohen, G. (2020b). Ethical and legal challenges of artificial intelligence-driven healthcare. *Artificial Intelligence in Healthcare*, 295–336. DOI: 10.1016/B978-0-12-818438-7.00012-5

Giustini, D., & Dastyar, V. (2024). *Critical AI literacy for interpreting in the age of AI*. Interpreting and Society., DOI: 10.1177/27523810241247259

Gonzalez, J. L. B., González Gámez, M., Mendoza Enciso, E. A., Esparza Maldonado, R. J., Hernández Palacios, D., Dueñas Campos, S., Robles, I. O., Macías Guzmán, M. J., García Díaz, A. L., Gutiérrez Peña, C. M., Martinez Medina, L., Monroy Colin, V. A., & Arreola Guerra, J. M. (2022). Efficacy and safety of ivermectin and hydroxychloroquine in patients with severe COVID-19: A randomized controlled trial. *Infectious Disease Reports*, *14*(2), 160–168. DOI: 10.3390/idr14020020 PMID: 35314650

Guan, J. (2019). Artificial Intelligence in Healthcare and medicine: Promises, ethical challenges, and governance. *Chinese Medical Sciences Journal*, *0*(0), 99. DOI: 10.24920/003611 PMID: 31315747

Ha, T., & Kim, S. (2023). Improving trust in AI with mitigating confirmation bias: Effects of explanation type and debiasing strategy for decision-making with explainable AI. *International Journal of Human-Computer Interaction*, •••, 1–12. DOI: 10.1080/10447318.2023.2285640

Habli, I., Lawton, T., & Porter, Z. (2020). Artificial Intelligence in health care: Accountability and safety. *Bulletin of the World Health Organization*, *98*(4), 251–256. DOI: 10.2471/BLT.19.237487 PMID: 32284648

Hagendorff, T. (2020). The ethics of AI Ethics: An evaluation of guidelines. *Minds and Machines*, *30*(1), 99–120. DOI: 10.1007/s11023-020-09517-8

Harding, N., Azim, M. I., Jidin, R., & Muir, J. P. (2016). A consideration of literature on trust and distrust as they relate to auditor professional scepticism. *Australian Accounting Review*, *26*(3), 243–254. DOI: 10.1111/auar.12126

Hoek, S., Metselaar, S., Ploem, C., & Bak, M. (2024). Promising for patients or deeply disturbing? the ethical and legal aspects of Deepfake Therapy. *Journal of Medical Ethics*, jme-2024-109985. Advance online publication. DOI: 10.1136/jme-2024-109985 PMID: 38981659

Hristovska, A. (2023). Fostering media literacy in the age of AI: Examining the impact on digital citizenship and ethical decision-making. *Media and Communication Review, 2*(2).

Huang, Q., Lei, S., & Ni, B. (2022). Perceived information overload and unverified information sharing on WeChat amid the covid-19 pandemic: A moderated mediation model of anxiety and perceived herd. *Frontiers in Psychology, 13*, 837820. Advance online publication. DOI: 10.3389/fpsyg.2022.837820 PMID: 35185742

Iacobucci, S., & Cicco, R. D. (2022). A literature review of bullshit receptivity: Perspectives for an informed policy making against misinformation. *Journal of Behavioral Economics for Policy, 6*(1), 23–40.

Iacobucci, S., De Cicco, R., Michetti, F., Palumbo, R., & Pagliaro, S. (2021). Deepfakes Unmasked: The effects of information priming and bullshit receptivity on deepfake recognition and sharing intention. *Cyberpsychology, Behavior, and Social Networking, 24*(3), 194–202. DOI: 10.1089/cyber.2020.0149 PMID: 33646046

Institution of Safe Medication Practice. (2017). (rep.). *Understanding human over-reliance on technology* (Vol. 5, Ser. 5).

Ipsos. (2020). *More than 1 in 3 Americans believe a 'deep state' is working to undermine Trump.* https://www.ipsos.com/en-us/news-polls/npr-misinformation-123020

Jacovi, A., Marasović, A., Miller, T., & Goldberg, Y. (2021). Formalizing trust in artificial intelligence. *Proceedings of the 2021 ACM Conference on Fairness, Accountability, and Transparency*. DOI: 10.1145/3442188.3445923

Jeong, S.-H., Cho, H., & Hwang, Y. (2012). Media Literacy Interventions: A meta-analytic review. *Journal of Communication, 62*(3), 454–472. DOI: 10.1111/j.1460-2466.2012.01643.x PMID: 22736807

Jiang, F., Jiang, Y., Zhi, H., Dong, Y., Li, H., Ma, S., Wang, Y., Dong, Q., Shen, H., & Wang, Y. (2017). Artificial Intelligence in healthcare: Past, present and future. *Stroke and Vascular Neurology, 2*(4), 230–243. DOI: 10.1136/svn-2017-000101 PMID: 29507784

Jobin, A., Ienca, M., & Vayena, E. (2019). The global landscape of AI ethics guidelines. *Nature Machine Intelligence, 1*(9), 389–399. DOI: 10.1038/s42256-019-0088-2

Jones-Jang, S. M., Mortensen, T., & Liu, J. (2019a). Does Media Literacy help identification of fake news? information literacy helps, but other literacies don't. *The American Behavioral Scientist, 65*(2), 371–388. DOI: 10.1177/0002764219869406

Jones-Jang, S. M., Mortensen, T., & Liu, J. (2019b). Does Media Literacy help identification of fake news? information literacy helps, but other literacies don't. *The American Behavioral Scientist*, *65*(2), 371–388. DOI: 10.1177/0002764219869406

Karnouskos, S. (2020). Artificial Intelligence in digital media: The Era of Deepfakes. *IEEE Transactions on Technology and Society*, *1*(3), 138–147. DOI: 10.1109/TTS.2020.3001312

Kasinidou, M. (2024). Development of personalised educational tools for AI literacy using participatory design. *Adjunct Proceedings of the 32nd ACM Conference on User Modeling, Adaptation and Personalization*. DOI: 10.1145/3631700.3664917

Kertysova, K. (2018). Artificial Intelligence and disinformation. *Security and Human Rights*, *29*(1–4), 55–81. DOI: 10.1163/18750230-02901005

Khan, M. A., Asadi, H., Zhang, L., Qazani, M. R., Oladazimi, S., Loo, C. K., Lim, C. P., & Nahavandi, S. (2024). Application of artificial intelligence in cognitive load analysis using functional near-infrared spectroscopy: A systematic review. *Expert Systems with Applications*, *249*, 123717. DOI: 10.1016/j.eswa.2024.123717

Khullar, D., Casalino, L. P., Qian, Y., Lu, Y., Chang, E., & Aneja, S. (2021). Public vs physician views of liability for Artificial Intelligence in health care. *Journal of the American Medical Informatics Association : JAMIA*, *28*(7), 1574–1577. DOI: 10.1093/jamia/ocab055 PMID: 33871009

Kim, B., Xiong, A., Lee, D., & Han, K. (2021). A systematic review on fake news research through the lens of news creation and consumption: Research efforts, challenges, and Future Directions. *PLoS One*, *16*(12), e0260080. Advance online publication. DOI: 10.1371/journal.pone.0260080 PMID: 34882703

Kiseleva, A. (2020). Ai as a medical device: Is it enough to ensure performance transparency and accountability? *European Pharmaceutical Law Review*, *4*(1), 5–16. DOI: 10.21552/eplr/2020/1/4

Kompton, A. M., & Vassilakopoulou, P. (2021). *Accountability, Transparency and Explainability in AI for Healthcare*. DOI: 10.18420/ihc2021_018

Laato, S., Islam, A. K., Islam, M. N., & Whelan, E. (2020). What drives unverified information sharing and cyberchondria during the covid-19 pandemic? *European Journal of Information Systems*, *29*(3), 288–305. DOI: 10.1080/0960085X.2020.1770632

Land, M. K., & Aronson, J. D. (2020). Human Rights and Technology: New challenges for justice and Accountability. *Annual Review of Law and Social Science*, *16*(1), 223–240. DOI: 10.1146/annurev-lawsocsci-060220-081955

Legaspi, R., He, Z., & Toyoizumi, T. (2019). Synthetic Agency: Sense of agency in Artificial Intelligence. *Current Opinion in Behavioral Sciences*, *29*, 84–90. DOI: 10.1016/j.cobeha.2019.04.004

Li, J., Dada, A., Kleesiek, J., & Egger, J. (2023). *Chatgpt in Healthcare: A Taxonomy and Systematic Review*. DOI: 10.1101/2023.03.30.23287899

Ling, E. C., Tussyadiah, I., Tuomi, A., Stienmetz, J., & Ioannou, A. (2021). Factors influencing users' adoption and use of conversational agents: A systematic review. *Psychology &amp. Psychology and Marketing*, *38*(7), 1031–1051. DOI: 10.1002/mar.21491

Lockey, S., Gillespie, N., Holm, D., & Someh, I. A. (2021a). A review of trust in artificial intelligence: Challenges, vulnerabilities and future directions. In *54th Hawaii International Conference on System Sciences*. DOI: 10.24251/HICSS.2021.664

Lockey, S., Gillespie, N., Holm, D., & Someh, I. A. (2021b). A review of trust in artificial intelligence: Challenges, vulnerabilities and future directions. In *54th Hawaii International Conference on System Sciences*. DOI: 10.24251/HICSS.2021.664

Lukyanenko, R., Maass, W., & Storey, V. C. (2022). Trust in artificial intelligence: From a foundational trust framework to emerging research opportunities. *Electronic Markets*, *32*(4), 1993–2020. DOI: 10.1007/s12525-022-00605-4

Lun, V. M.-C., Yeung, J. C., & Ku, K. Y. (2023a). Effects of mood on critical thinking. *Thinking Skills and Creativity*, *47*, 101247. DOI: 10.1016/j.tsc.2023.101247

Lun, V. M.-C., Yeung, J. C., & Ku, K. Y. (2023b). Effects of mood on critical thinking. *Thinking Skills and Creativity*, *47*, 101247. DOI: 10.1016/j.tsc.2023.101247

Lysaght, T., Lim, H. Y., Xafis, V., & Ngiam, K. Y. (2019). Ai-assisted decision-making in Healthcare. *Asian Bioethics Review*, *11*(3), 299–314. DOI: 10.1007/s41649-019-00096-0 PMID: 33717318

Mahlknecht, A., Engl, A., Piccoliori, G., & Wiedermann, C. J. (2023). Supporting primary care through symptom checking artificial intelligence: A study of patient and physician attitudes in Italian general practice. *BMC Primary Care*, *24*(1), 174. Advance online publication. DOI: 10.1186/s12875-023-02143-0 PMID: 37661285

Mandler, G. (2008). Familiarity breeds attempts: A critical review of dual-process theories of recognition. *Perspectives on Psychological Science*, *3*(5), 390–399. DOI: 10.1111/j.1745-6924.2008.00087.x PMID: 26158957

Martel, C., Pennycook, G., & Rand, D. G. (2020). Reliance on emotion promotes belief in fake news. *Cognitive Research: Principles and Implications*, *5*(1), 47. Advance online publication. DOI: 10.1186/s41235-020-00252-3 PMID: 33026546

Mensah, G. B. (2024). Ai ethics. *Africa Journal For Regulatory Affairs*. DOI: 10.62839/AJFRA/2024.v1.I1.32-45

Mesko, B., & Topol, E. J. (2023). The imperative for regulatory oversight of large language models (or generative AI) in healthcare. *NPJ Digital Medicine*, *6*(1), 120. Advance online publication. DOI: 10.1038/s41746-023-00873-0 PMID: 37414860

Mihailidis, P., & Viotty, S. (2017). Spreadable spectacle in Digital Culture: Civic expression, fake news, and the role of media literacies in "Post-fact" society. *The American Behavioral Scientist*, *61*(4), 441–454. DOI: 10.1177/0002764217701217

Mishima, M., Hayashida, K., Fukasaku, Y., Ogata, R., Ohsawa, K., Iwai, K., Wen, W., & Morioka, S. (2023). Adaptability of the sense of agency in healthy young adults in sensorimotor tasks for a short term. *Behavioral Sciences (Basel, Switzerland)*, *13*(2), 132. DOI: 10.3390/bs13020132 PMID: 36829361

Möller, J., Trilling, D., Helberger, N., & van Es, B. (2018). Do not blame it on the algorithm: An empirical assessment of multiple recommender systems and their impact on content diversity. *Information Communication and Society*, *21*(7), 959–977. DOI: 10.1080/1369118X.2018.1444076

Monteleone, S. (2019). Artificial Intelligence, data protection, and elections. *Ser.*, *637*, 952.

Moore, C. M. (2022). The challenges of health inequities and ai. *Intelligence-Based Medicine*, *6*, 100067. DOI: 10.1016/j.ibmed.2022.100067

Murdoch, B. (2021). Privacy and artificial intelligence: Challenges for protecting health information in a new era. *BMC Medical Ethics*, *22*(1), 122. Advance online publication. DOI: 10.1186/s12910-021-00687-3 PMID: 34525993

Naik, N., Hameed, B. M., Shetty, D. K., Swain, D., Shah, M., Paul, R., Aggarwal, K., Ibrahim, S., Patil, V., Smriti, K., Shetty, S., Rai, B. P., Chlosta, P., & Somani, B. K. (2022). Legal and ethical consideration in artificial intelligence in Healthcare: Who takes responsibility? *Frontiers in Surgery*, *9*, 862322. Advance online publication. DOI: 10.3389/fsurg.2022.862322 PMID: 35360424

Naja, B. (2018). (rep.). *Computation propaganda techniques*. *Ser.*, *628*, 284.

Ng, D. T., Leung, J. K., Chu, S. K., & Qiao, M. S. (2021). Conceptualizing ai literacy: An exploratory review. *Computers and Education: Artificial Intelligence*, *2*, 100041. DOI: 10.1016/j.caeai.2021.100041

Nicolescu, L., & Tudorache, M. T. (2022). Human-Computer Interaction in Customer Service: The experience with AI Chatbots—a systematic literature review. *Electronics (Basel)*, *11*(10), 1579. DOI: 10.3390/electronics11101579

Oberauer, K. (2018). On the automaticity of familiarity in short-term recognition: A test of the dual-process assumption with the PRP paradigm. *Journal of Cognition*, *1*(1), 20. Advance online publication. DOI: 10.5334/joc.21 PMID: 31517194

Okoro, Y. O., Ayo-Farai, O., Maduka, C. P., Okongwu, C. C., & Sodamade, O. T. (2024). A review of health misinformation on Digital Platforms: Challenges and countermeasures. *International Journal of Applied Research in Social Sciences*, *6*(1), 23–36. DOI: 10.51594/ijarss.v6i1.689

Pagliari, M., Chambon, V., & Berberian, B. (2022). What is new with Artificial Intelligence? human–agent interactions through the lens of Social Agency. *Frontiers in Psychology*, *13*, 954444. Advance online publication. DOI: 10.3389/fpsyg.2022.954444 PMID: 36248519

Paton, C., & Kobayashi, S. (2019). An open science approach to artificial intelligence in Healthcare. *Yearbook of Medical Informatics, 28*(01), 047–051. DOI: 10.1055/s-0039-1677898

Paulhus, D. L., Harms, P. D., Bruce, M. N., & Lysy, D. C. (2003). The over-claiming technique: Measuring self-enhancement independent of ability. *Journal of Personality and Social Psychology*, *84*(4), 890–904. DOI: 10.1037/0022-3514.84.4.890 PMID: 12703655

Pennycook, G., Cannon, T. D., & Rand, D. G. (2018). Prior exposure increases perceived accuracy of fake news. *Journal of Experimental Psychology. General*, *147*(12), 1865–1880. DOI: 10.1037/xge0000465 PMID: 30247057

Pennycook, G., Fugelsang, J. A., & Koehler, D. J. (2015). What makes us think? A three-stage dual-process model of analytic engagement. *Cognitive Psychology*, *80*, 34–72. DOI: 10.1016/j.cogpsych.2015.05.001 PMID: 26091582

Pennycook, G., & Rand, D. G. (2017). Assessing the effect of "disputed" warnings and source salience on perceptions of fake news accuracy. SSRN *Electronic Journal*. DOI: 10.2139/ssrn.3035384

Pennycook, G., & Rand, D. G. (2019). Who falls for fake news? the roles of bullshit receptivity, overclaiming, familiarity, and analytic thinking. *Journal of Personality, 88*(2), 185–200. DOI: 10.1111/jopy.12476 PMID: 30929263

Perlis, R. H., Lunz Trujillo, K., Green, J., Safarpour, A., Druckman, J. N., Santillana, M., Ognyanova, K., & Lazer, D. (2023). Misinformation, trust, and use of ivermectin and hydroxychloroquine for covid-19. *JAMA Health Forum, 4*(9), e233257. Advance online publication. DOI: 10.1001/jamahealthforum.2023.3257 PMID: 37773507

Pesapane, F., Bracchi, D. A., Mulligan, J. F., Linnikov, A., Maslennikov, O., Lanzavecchia, M. B., Tantrige, P., Stasolla, A., Biondetti, P., Giuggioli, P. F., Cassano, E., & Carrafiello, G. (2021). Legal and regulatory framework for AI solutions in Healthcare in EU, US, China, and Russia: New scenarios after a pandemic. *Radiation, 1*(4), 261–276. DOI: 10.3390/radiation1040022

Petty, R. E., Brinol, P., McCaslin, M. J., & Loerch, C. (2009). The need for cognition. In *Handbook of individual differences in social behavior* (pp. 318–329). essay.

Qureshi, J., & Khan, S. (2024). *Artificial Intelligence (AI) Deepfakes in Healthcare Systems: A Double-Edged Sword? Balancing Opportunities and Navigating Risks.* DOI: 10.20944/preprints202402.0176.v1

Rajpurkar, P., Chen, E., Banerjee, O., & Topol, E. J. (2022). Ai in Health and Medicine. *Nature Medicine, 28*(1), 31–38. DOI: 10.1038/s41591-021-01614-0 PMID: 35058619

Rastogi, C., Zhang, Y., Wei, D., Varshney, K. R., Dhurandhar, A., & Tomsett, R. (2022). Deciding fast and slow: The role of cognitive biases in AI-assisted decision-making. *Proceedings of the ACM on Human-Computer Interaction, 6*(CSCW1), 1–22. DOI: 10.1145/3512930

Roberts, M. J., & Newton, E. J. (2010). Inspection Times, the change task, and the rapid-response selection task. *The Quarterly Journal of Experimental Psychology. A, Human Experimental Psychology, 54*(4), 1031–1048. DOI: 10.1080/713756016 PMID: 11765731

Rubin, V. L. (2022). *Misinformation and disinformation: Detecting fakes with the eye and ai.* Springer. DOI: 10.1007/978-3-030-95656-1

Sallam, M. (2023). *The Utility of Chatgpt as an Example of Large Language Models in Healthcare Education, Research and Practice: Systematic Review on the Future Perspectives and Potential Limitations.* DOI: 10.1101/2023.02.19.23286155

Samson, K., & Kostyszyn, P. (2015a). Effects of cognitive load on trusting behavior – an experiment using the Trust game. *PLoS One*, *10*(5), e0127680. Advance online publication. DOI: 10.1371/journal.pone.0127680 PMID: 26010489

Samson, K., & Kostyszyn, P. (2015b). Effects of cognitive load on trusting behavior – an experiment using the Trust game. *PLoS One*, *10*(5), e0127680. Advance online publication. DOI: 10.1371/journal.pone.0127680 PMID: 26010489

Schonberger, D. (2019). Artificial Intelligence in healthcare: A critical analysis of the legal and ethical implications. *International Journal of Law and Information Technology*, *27*(2), 171–203. DOI: 10.1093/ijlit/eaz004

Shahsavar, Y., & Choudhury, A. (2023). User intentions to use CHATGPT for self-diagnosis and health-related purposes: Cross-sectional survey study. *JMIR Human Factors*, *10*, e47564. Advance online publication. DOI: 10.2196/47564 PMID: 37195756

Sidaoui, K., Jaakkola, M., & Burton, J. (2020). Ai feel you: Customer experience assessment via chatbot interviews. *Journal of Service Management*, *31*(4), 745–766. DOI: 10.1108/JOSM-11-2019-0341

Smith, H. (2020). Clinical AI: Opacity, accountability, responsibility and liability. *AI & Society*, *36*(2), 535–545. DOI: 10.1007/s00146-020-01019-6

Sodiya, E. O., Amoo, O. O., Umoga, U. J., & Atadoga, A. (2024). AI-driven personalization in web content delivery: A comparative study of user engagement in the USA and the UK. *World Journal of Advanced Research and Reviews*, *21*(2), 887–902. DOI: 10.30574/wjarr.2024.21.2.0502

Solanki, P., Grundy, J., & Hussain, W. (2022). Operationalising Ethics in Artificial Intelligence for Healthcare: A framework for AI developers. *AI and Ethics*, *3*(1), 223–240. DOI: 10.1007/s43681-022-00195-z

Srinivasan, V. (2020, April 2). *Context, language, and reasoning in AI: Three key challenges*. MIT Technology Review. https://www.technologyreview.com/2016/10/14/156968/context-language-and-reasoning-in-ai-three-key-challenges/

St. Evans, J. (2008). Dual-processing accounts of reasoning, judgment, and social cognition. *Annual Review of Psychology*, *59*(1), 255–278. DOI: 10.1146/annurev.psych.59.103006.093629 PMID: 18154502

St. Evans, J., & Curtis-Holmes, J. (2005). Rapid responding increases belief bias: Evidence for the dual-process theory of reasoning. *Thinking &amp. Thinking & Reasoning*, *11*(4), 382–389. DOI: 10.1080/13546780542000005

St. Evans, J., & Stanovich, K. E. (2013). Dual-process theories of higher cognition. *Perspectives on Psychological Science*, *8*(3), 223–241. DOI: 10.1177/1745691612460685 PMID: 26172965

Stanovich, K. E., & West, R. F. (1998). Individual differences in rational thought. *Journal of Experimental Psychology. General*, *127*(2), 161–188. DOI: 10.1037/0096-3445.127.2.161

Stanovich, K. E., & West, R. F. (2000). Individual differences in reasoning: Implications for the rationality debate? *Behavioral and Brain Sciences*, *23*(5), 645–665. DOI: 10.1017/S0140525X00003435 PMID: 11301544

Stanton, B., & Jensen, T. (2021). Trust and artificial intelligence. *National Institute of Standards and Technology*. https://doi.org/https://doi.org/10.6028/NIST.IR.8332-draft

Sweller, J. (2011). Cognitive load theory. *Psychology of Learning and Motivation*, *55*, 37–76. DOI: 10.1016/B978-0-12-387691-1.00002-8

Sylvester, S. M. (2021). Covid-19 and motivated reasoning: The influence of knowledge on covid-related policy and Health Behavior. *Social Science Quarterly*, *102*(5), 2341–2359. DOI: 10.1111/ssqu.12989 PMID: 34226771

Talwar, S., Dhir, A., Kaur, P., Zafar, N., & Alrasheedy, M. (2019). Why do people share fake news? associations between the Dark Side of social media use and fake news sharing behavior. *Journal of Retailing and Consumer Services*, *51*, 72–82. DOI: 10.1016/j.jretconser.2019.05.026

Tejeda, H., Kumar, A., Smyth, P., & Steyvers, M. (2022). Ai-assisted decision-making: A cognitive modeling approach to infer latent Reliance Strategies. *Computational Brain &amp. Computational Brain & Behavior*, *5*(4), 491–508. DOI: 10.1007/s42113-022-00157-y

Thompson, S. A., & Tsu, T. (2023, February 8). *Disinformation researchers raise alarms about A.I. Chatbots*. The New York Times. https://www.nytimes.com/2023/02/08/technology/ai-chatbots-disinformation.html

Thompson, V. A. (2013). Why it matters. *Perspectives on Psychological Science*, *8*(3), 253–256. DOI: 10.1177/1745691613483476 PMID: 26172968

Tom, E., Keane, P. A., Blazes, M., Pasquale, L. R., Chiang, M. F., Lee, A. Y., & Lee, C. S. (2020). Protecting data privacy in the age of ai-enabled ophthalmology. *Translational Vision Science &amp. Technology*, *9*(2), 36. DOI: 10.1167/tvst.9.2.36 PMID: 32855840

Victor, T. W., Tivesten, E., Gustavsson, P., Johansson, J., Sangberg, F., & Ljung Aust, M. (2018). Automation expectation mismatch: Incorrect prediction despite eyes on threat and hands on wheel. *Human Factors*, *60*(8), 1095–1116. DOI: 10.1177/0018720818788164 PMID: 30096002

Wen, W., Ishii, H., Ohata, R., Yamashita, A., Asama, H., & Imamizu, H. (2021). Perception and control: Individual difference in the sense of agency is associated with learnability in sensorimotor adaptation. *Scientific Reports*, *11*(1), 20542. Advance online publication. DOI: 10.1038/s41598-021-99969-4 PMID: 34654878

Whelan, E., Islam, A. K. M. N., & Brooks, S. (2020a). Applying the SOBC paradigm to explain how social media overload affects academic performance. *Computers &amp. Computers & Education*, *143*, 103692. DOI: 10.1016/j.compedu.2019.103692

Whelan, E., Islam, A. K. M. N., & Brooks, S. (2020b). Applying the SOBC paradigm to explain how social media overload affects academic performance. *Computers &amp. Computers & Education*, *143*, 103692. DOI: 10.1016/j.compedu.2019.103692

Whyte, C. (2020). Deepfake News: AI-enabled disinformation as a multi-level public policy challenge. *Journal of Cyber Policy*, *5*(2), 199–217. DOI: 10.1080/23738871.2020.1797135

Williamson, S. M., & Prybutok, V. (2024). Balancing privacy and progress: A review of privacy challenges, systemic oversight, and patient perceptions in AI-driven healthcare. *Applied Sciences (Basel, Switzerland)*, *14*(2), 675. DOI: 10.3390/app14020675

Wimbarti, S., Kairupan, B. H., & Tallei, T. E. (2024). Critical review of self-diagnosis of mental health conditions using artificial intelligence. *International Journal of Mental Health Nursing*, *33*(2), 344–358. DOI: 10.1111/inm.13303 PMID: 38345132

World Health Organisation. (n.d.). *Constitution of the World Health Organization*. World Health Organization. https://www.who.int/about/governance/constitution

Xu, W., Dainoff, M. J., Ge, L., & Gao, Z. (2022). Transitioning to human interaction with AI systems: New challenges and opportunities for HCI professionals to enable human-centered AI. *International Journal of Human-Computer Interaction*, *39*(3), 494–518. DOI: 10.1080/10447318.2022.2041900

Zhang, H., Kuhnle, A., Zhang, H., & Thai, M. T. (2016). Detecting misinformation in online social networks before it is too late. *2016 IEEE/ACM International Conference on Advances in Social Networks Analysis and Mining (ASONAM)*. DOI: 10.1109/ASONAM.2016.7752288

Zhao, H., Fu, S., & Chen, X. (2020). Promoting users' intention to share online health articles on social media: The role of Confirmation Bias. *Information Processing &amp. Management*, *57*(6), 102354. DOI: 10.1016/j.ipm.2020.102354 PMID: 32834400

Chapter 5
Cultural Competence in AI-Driven Health Information

Ali Zahabi
https://orcid.org/0000-0002-8632-4553
King Mongkut's University of Technology, Thonburi, Thailand

Imedla Hermilinda Abas
Shinawatra University, Thailand

ABSTRACT

John McCarthy is credited as the first person to use the term artificial intelligence (AI) in 1956. The debate regarding replacing humans with AI has become increasingly plausible due to technological advancements. The application of AI in healthcare has expanded, enhancing quality, diminishing expenses, and preserving lives. Ensuring inclusion in AI-driven health systems requires the utmost importance of cultural knowledge. Obstacles encompass prejudice, cultural obstacles, and heterogeneity in datasets. Gaining a comprehensive understanding of cultural diversity in healthcare is crucial for successfully adopting AI. Researchers and policymakers must emphasise cultural competence in AI systems to ensure fair and impartial treatment for all individuals.

DOI: 10.4018/979-8-3693-5837-5.ch005

1. BRIEF OVERVIEW OF THE INCREASING ROLE OF AI IN HEALTHCARE

According to Kostic et al. (2019), John McCarthy introduced the term artificial intelligence (AI) in 1956. Artificial intelligence (AI) primarily depends on analysing extensive databases, identifying interconnections, comparing intricate symptoms and indicators, and formulating algorithms to address issues (Jiang et al., 2017). In recent decades, there has been a notable rise in the number of peer-reviewed papers on artificial intelligence (AI), which can be attributed to the growing interest in this field (Tran et al., 2019).

AI's use in the healthcare sector is expected to experience significant expansion (Gerke et al., 2020). Current applications encompass disease diagnostics, pharmaceutical advancements, individualised treatment approaches, supportive healthcare services, and genetic manipulation. AI's application in medicine can be categorised into two broad domains: visual and physical. The scope of Visual AI encompasses electronic medical records, reminders for outpatient appointments, and applications for health tracking. On the other hand, physical AI includes activities like robotic surgeries and robotic drug dispensers. AI has experienced a substantial enhancement in its capabilities. Technological singularity (TS) is an alternative term for AI-enabled systems. TS refers to a theoretical scenario wherein artificial intelligence (AI) develops an unmanageable superintelligence that is anticipated to exceed human intelligence, leading to unpredictable consequences (Solez et al., 2013; Smolin, 2020). This scenario is projected to unfold between 2040 to 2050 (Solez et al., 2013).

At its most fundamental level, TS in healthcare will necessitate the substitution of human physicians with peripheral systems and AI-enabled robotics. An instance of TS in the future of healthcare was demonstrated during the production of the American science fiction series Star Trek Voyager (1995-2001). The programme featured an AI hologram of a physician who attended to the personnel of the spaceship. With the current rate of technological advancements in AI, the argument about the potential of AI replacing humans has evolved from fictitious to realistic. Some scientists think AI in healthcare can perform on par with humans. Others remain sceptical regarding the substantial transition in healthcare towards Artificial Intelligence and its subsequent advancement. Artificial Intelligence has seen significant growth over time since it can enhance the calibre of healthcare, diminish expenses, and save lives. Nevertheless, it is imperative to guarantee the ethical and transparent use of artificial intelligence (AI) in the healthcare sector while safeguarding patients' privacy and to thoroughly evaluate these advancements' potential socio-legal and moral implications and equip society to adopt and accommodate such transformations when they occur effectively.

1.1 Role of AI in Healthcare

The application of artificial intelligence (AI) in healthcare has expanded significantly in recent years. This has led to transformative improvements in healthcare delivery and better patient outcomes (Pannu, 2015). AI-driven health information systems can potentially improve the efficiency, accuracy, and accessibility of healthcare services. However, understanding and integrating cultural competence in these AI-based systems is essential to ensuring inclusivity and equity for individuals across diverse cultural backgrounds (Shinners et al., 2019).

As such, policymakers, scholars, and healthcare practitioners must recognise the importance of cultural competence in developing and implementing AI-driven health information systems. Cultural competence means healthcare providers and systems can effectively communicate and interact with individuals from diverse cultural backgrounds. When applied to AI in healthcare, cultural competence promotes that these technologies are responsive to diverse populations' unique needs and preferences.

Embedding cultural competence in designing and deploying AI-based health information systems helps policymakers tackle healthcare access and outcome disparities among different cultural groups. Additionally, researchers play a crucial role in advancing cultural competence in AI-driven systems through studies and evaluations of how these technologies impact different communities. Prioritising cultural competence in AI-powered health information systems is essential for promoting equity, inclusivity, and high standards of care.

Ultimately, when policymakers, researchers, and healthcare practitioners collaborate to prioritize cultural competence, they ensure that AI-driven health information systems are fair and effective for all individuals, regardless of cultural background. The application of Artificial Intelligence (AI) in the healthcare sector has experienced substantial growth in recent years, leading to a notable transformation in healthcare delivery methods and resulting in better patient outcomes (Pannu, 2015). The use of AI-driven health information systems promises to transform the healthcare sector by enhancing healthcare services' efficiency, accuracy, and accessibility. Understanding cultural competence in AI-driven health information systems is essential to guarantee inclusivity and equity for individuals, irrespective of their cultural heritage (Shinners et al., 2019).

Therefore, policymakers, academics, and healthcare practitioners need to acknowledge the significance of cultural competency in the advancement and execution of health information systems driven by artificial intelligence. Cultural competence pertains to the aptitude of healthcare personnel and systems to proficiently communicate and interact with people from varied cultural backgrounds. Cultural competence is essential in AI-driven health information systems to ensure that these technologies are attuned to the distinct requirements and preferences of individuals from diverse cultural backgrounds.

Policymakers can contribute to resolving gaps in healthcare outcomes and access among various populations by integrating cultural competency into designing and deploying AI-driven health information systems. Researchers can also help advance cultural competence in AI-driven health information systems by conducting studies and reviews on how these technologies affect different cultural groups. Understanding cultural competence in AI-powered health information systems is critical for encouraging equity, inclusiveness, and excellence in healthcare delivery. Policymakers, researchers, and healthcare practitioners may help promote that AI-driven health information systems serve all people, regardless of cultural background, by prioritising cultural competency in their development and implementation.

1.2 The Need for Cultural Competence in AI Systems in Healthcare

Cultural competence refers to an individual's and systems' capacity to interact effectively with people of diverse cultural origins. Cultural competence is essential in AI-driven health information systems to guarantee precise and pertinent information to persons from various cultural backgrounds. Recognising and comprehending the distinct cultural beliefs, values, and behaviours of diverse groups of individuals constitutes a fundamental element of cultural competency. By understanding this concept, healthcare providers and AI-driven systems can customise their services and recommendations to align with individual patients' specific requirements and preferences.

Cultural competency is especially crucial in healthcare settings since people from different cultures may have different perspectives on health and well-being and diverse treatment and care preferences. Healthcare practitioners can promote culturally sensitive treatment to all patients, irrespective of their background, by integrating cultural competence into AI-driven health information systems. Moreover, since cultural diversity in healthcare refers to patients of various socioeconomic, ethnic, cultural, and linguistic backgrounds, it influences individuals' perceptions of health, interactions with healthcare practitioners, and healthcare decision-making is substantial (Hall et al., 2015). In order to achieve effectiveness and fairness, AI and digital health technologies need to adjust to the various cultural contexts surrounding them. Ensuring patients receive high-quality, effective care that respects their cultural beliefs and customs is critical. Therefore, it is safe to say that cultural competence is essential in AI-driven health information systems since these technologies can perpetuate or help overcome healthcare access and outcomes inequities.

Comprehending cultural competency in AI-driven health information systems is vital for policymakers, academics, and healthcare professionals by putting diversity, equity, and inclusion first when creating and deploying these technologies. Policymakers have the power to guarantee that AI systems are trained on a variety of datasets and that user interfaces are sensitive to cultural differences (Amiri, 2024). Additionally, policymakers possess the capacity to mitigate bias and enhance the efficacy of AI-powered health information systems for individuals hailing from various cultural backgrounds. Researchers must also prioritise cultural competence while working on AI-powered health information systems. Researchers can contribute to the inclusivity and effectiveness of AI technologies by investigating cultural aspects' impact on health outcomes and by designing algorithms that consider cultural variations in healthcare preferences and practices. Healthcare professionals must have cultural competence to provide the highest quality of care. This necessitates comprehending and valuing the ideas, values, and traditions that influence the health practices of their patients. Healthcare practitioners can enhance trust and health outcomes for all patients by actively listening, inquiring about cultural backgrounds, and developing individualised treatment plans.

Comprehending this concept is of utmost importance to ensuring the efficient delivery of modern technologies to diverse populations. By incorporating cultural competency into the design and deployment of AI-driven systems, stakeholders have the potential to address gaps in healthcare outcomes and improve the overall quality of treatment for all patients.

1.3 Enhancing Cultural Competence in Healthcare: Bridging Gaps for Inclusive Care

Cultural competence in healthcare has become a vital area of emphasis, especially as societies grow more varied. The concept of cultural competence emerged from acknowledging differences in health outcomes across various ethnic and racial groups. The necessity for culturally competent care is emphasised by the observation that minority communities frequently encounter elevated morbidity and mortality rates relative to their majority counterparts (Kim-Godwin et al., 2001). This discrepancy is intensified by a healthcare system that has not adequately adjusted to the cultural and language requirements of these groups (Razzaq, 2023). The advancement of cultural competency in healthcare has been propelled by the need to close these disparities and enhance health outcomes for all patients.

Previous studies have continuously emphasised the significance of cultural competence training for healthcare practitioners. Research demonstrates that good cultural competency training can improve communication between physicians and patients, enhancing patient satisfaction and adherence to treatment regimens

(Čebron & Huber, 2020). A systematic evaluation by Govere and Govere (2016) demonstrated that cultural competency training significantly enhanced healthcare personnel's knowledge and sensitivity towards various populations, which is essential for cultivating collaborative patient interactions. Jongen et al. (2018) assert that evaluating the results of cultural competence training is essential for proving its efficacy in mitigating healthcare disparities. Despite the favourable results, a significant deficiency exists in the literature concerning the long-term effects of such training on actual health outcomes, as numerous studies concentrate mainly on immediate behavioural modifications rather than enduring enhancements in patient health (Harrison et al., 2019).

Incorporating artificial intelligence (AI) in healthcare offers distinct prospects to improve cultural competence. AI applications can scrutinise extensive datasets to discern health patterns and inequities across varied populations, guiding targeted actions (Razzaq, 2023). AI-driven solutions can enhance language translation services, improving healthcare accessibility for non-English-speaking patients (Yunus et al., 2021). Moreover, AI can facilitate the creation of individualised treatment plans that consider cultural ideas and customs, enhancing patient participation and satisfaction (Trivedi, 2023). The implementation of AI in culturally competent care remains nascent, necessitating research to assess the efficacy of these technologies in practical environments (Handtke et al., 2019).

Notwithstanding the progress in cultural competence training and the capabilities of AI, substantial deficiencies persist. A significant problem is the inconsistency in implementing cultural competence training across healthcare organisations, resulting in differences in care quality (McCalman et al., 2017). Furthermore, there is an absence of standardised assessment instruments to measure cultural competence among healthcare practitioners (Balachandran et al., 2022). This variability impedes the assessment of training programs' efficacy and their influence on patient outcomes. Moreover, although there is an expanding corpus of literature on cultural competency, numerous studies fail to sufficiently consider the intersectionality of diverse cultural characteristics, including ethnicity, gender identity, and socioeconomic status, which might affect health outcomes (Nowaskie & Najam, 2022). Rectifying these deficiencies is crucial for establishing a more resilient foundation for cultural competency in healthcare.

In summary, the historical backdrop of cultural competency in healthcare highlights its significance in mitigating health inequities among varied people. Although prior research has shown the advantages of cultural competency training and the possibilities of AI applications, substantial gaps persist in the literature concerning the long-term effects of these treatments. Future research must prioritise the standardisation of training programs, the creation of assessment tools, and the investigation of cultural intersectionality to improve the efficacy of culturally competent care.

2. INTERSECTIONALITY OF CULTURAL COMPETENCE IN HEALTHCARE

Socioeconomic status, gender, age, and cultural differences are just a few intersecting factors that influence the multifaceted construct of cultural competence in healthcare. This section explores how these dimensions influence healthcare experiences and outcomes, emphasising the importance of culturally competent care in mitigating health disparities. Additionally, case studies that illustrate these intersections examine the role of community engagement in developing AI systems tailored for diverse populations.

The intersectionality of cultural competency is essential for comprehending how many social identities affect health outcomes. Socioeconomic status (SES) significantly influences access to healthcare services. Individuals from lower socioeconomic status backgrounds frequently encounter obstacles, including insufficient insurance coverage, restricted access to quality healthcare, and elevated prevalence of chronic diseases (McCalman et al., 2017). This imbalance is exacerbated by cultural variations that may influence communication and trust between patients and healthcare providers (Čebron & Huber, 2020). Cultural views around health and illness can affect patients' readiness to pursue care, comply with treatment, and participate in preventative practices (Arestad et al., 2017).

Gender overlaps with cultural competency, as healthcare experiences might vary markedly between males and females. Studies demonstrate that women, especially those from minority groups, may encounter biases in pain management and treatment suggestions (Nowaskie & Najam, 2022). Moreover, age constitutes a significant variable, as older individuals may possess distinct cultural expectations and health literacy levels compared to younger demographics. The generational divide may result in misconceptions and miscommunications within therapeutic environments, ultimately impacting patient outcomes (Balachandran et al., 2022).

2.1 Patient Outcomes Related to Culturally Competent Care

Culturally competent care has significantly improved patient outcomes, as evidenced by various studies. Research indicates that training healthcare personnel in cultural competency increases patient satisfaction and enhances adherence to treatment regimens (Govere & Govere, 2016). A systematic evaluation has shown that culturally competent care fosters better communication, increases patient compliance, and ultimately leads to superior health outcomes (Lomiguen et al., 2020). Furthermore, culturally adapted therapies have proven beneficial in managing specific health conditions, such as diabetes control among ethnic minorities (Pettersson et al., 2021).

However, despite these positive findings, there remain notable gaps in the literature regarding the long-term effects of cultural competence training on health inequalities. Many studies focus on immediate behavioural changes rather than sustained improvements in health outcomes (McCalman et al., 2017). The lack of longitudinal data limits the ability to thoroughly evaluate the effectiveness of cultural competence initiatives in addressing health disparities.

Cultural competency is a vital strategy for mitigating health inequities. The ability of healthcare personnel to understand and respect diverse cultural backgrounds can lead to more equitable healthcare provision (Čebron & Huber, 2020). Culturally competent care can also help reduce the stigma associated with certain health issues, encouraging individuals from marginalized communities to seek medical assistance (Balachandran et al., 2022). Organizations that prioritize cultural competence are better equipped to meet the unique needs of diverse populations, thereby promoting enhanced health equity (McCalman et al., 2017).

Despite the importance of cultural competence training, its implementation varies across healthcare settings, which may inadvertently perpetuate inequities. A comprehensive evaluation has highlighted the need for standardized training programs and assessment tools to measure the effectiveness of cultural competency initiatives (McCalman et al., 2017). Addressing these deficiencies is crucial to support the idea that all healthcare practitioners are adequately prepared to deliver culturally competent care.

Alongside cultural competency, addressing the ramifications of data privacy and security, algorithmic bias, and transparency in healthcare AI systems is crucial. Data privacy and security are essential for safeguarding sensitive patient information from unauthorised access and breaches, ensuring patients feel secure in sharing their health data. Algorithmic bias may occur when AI systems are trained on unrepresentative datasets, resulting in inequities in healthcare recommendations and results among various demographic groups. Transparency in AI algorithms is essential for fostering confidence between patients and healthcare professionals, as it enables stakeholders to comprehend decision-making processes and to ensure accountability for system recommendations. By considering these variables in conjunction with cultural competence, healthcare systems can strive for a more equitable and effective approach to patient treatment.

2.2 Role of Community Engagement in Developing AI Systems

Community engagement is essential in creating AI systems that adequately meet the demands of varied communities. Engaging community people in designing and implementing AI technologies enables healthcare organisations to guarantee that these systems are culturally pertinent and attuned to the distinct issues encountered by various groups (Gulati & Weir, 2022). AI apps integrating language translation services can improve communication between healthcare personnel and patients from non-English speaking backgrounds (Gulati & Weir, 2022).

Case studies demonstrate the effective incorporation of community involvement in AI development. An example is the implementation of AI-driven health monitoring systems in underprivileged regions, where local input customised the technology to address particular cultural and language requirements (Gulati & Weir, 2022). This method enhances patient participation and cultivates trust between healthcare providers and their communities.

In conclusion, the intersectionality of cultural competency, including factors such as socioeconomic status, gender, and age, profoundly impacts healthcare experiences and outcomes. Culturally competent care is vital for mitigating health inequities and enhancing patient satisfaction. Moreover, community involvement is essential in creating AI systems that address the needs of varied communities. Future research must prioritise the standardisation of cultural competence training and investigate the long-term effects of these activities on health outcomes, thereby fostering a fairer healthcare system.

3. CHALLENGES IN ACHIEVING CULTURAL COMPETENCE IN HEALTHCARE

The progress of AI-powered health information systems unquestionably accompanies a multitude of challenges. Policymakers, researchers, and healthcare practitioners must comprehend and tackle these challenges to effectively adopt culturally competent approaches in designing and utilising AI-driven health information systems.

The lack of diversity and representation in AI algorithms and technologies is an important challenge to gaining cultural competence in healthcare (Sun & Zhou, 2023). Numerous AI systems are created and trained using datasets that fail to accurately reflect the variety of populations they are intended to cater to. Such circumstances might result in prejudiced results and inaccurate projections, especially for minority or marginalised communities (Nazer et al., 2023). To effectively tackle this matter, it is imperative to undertake a collaborative endeavour to broaden the range of data sets, engage a broader array of stakeholders in the development process, and conduct thorough testing of AI technologies to ascertain their bias and fairness.

Another challenge is the cultural and linguistic gaps between healthcare personnel and patients (Hudelson, 2005). Effective communication is imperative to establish trust and provide high-quality treatment. However, disparities in linguistic and cultural interpretations may impede this process. In order to effectively address these obstacles and deliver patient-centred care, healthcare workers must possess the requisite cultural understanding and communication skills (Hudelson, 2005).

Furthermore, there are issues with healthcare laws and policies that might not fully meet the requirements of certain groups. It is imperative for policymakers to carefully contemplate the cultural ramifications of their actions and strive towards establishing a more inclusive healthcare system, placing a high emphasis on cultural competence. Attaining cultural proficiency in AI-powered health information systems necessitates a comprehensive strategy that tackles diversity, communication, and policy matters. Therefore, it is crucial to acknowledge and overcome these issues to ensure the effective design and implementation of healthcare technologies that cater to the requirements of all persons, regardless of their cultural background.

3.1 Ethical Considerations in AI-Driven Health Information Systems

Integrating artificial intelligence (AI) into healthcare presents many ethical implications that necessitate careful consideration, particularly in data privacy and algorithmic transparency. As AI technologies become increasingly prevalent in clinical settings, the ethical challenges surrounding these systems have garnered significant attention from scholars and practitioners alike. As AI is utilized to improve patient outcomes and streamline processes, it is crucial to carefully consider the ethical implications of these technologies, especially concerning cultural proficiency. Ensuring cultural proficiency is crucial to prevent AI-driven healthcare systems from perpetuating biases or disparities in treatment.

Data privacy is one of the primary ethical concerns in AI-driven healthcare systems. AI in healthcare often involves collecting and analysing vast amounts of sensitive patient data, raising questions about how this information is stored, used, and protected. AI-driven health information systems raise various ethical concerns, including but not limited to data privacy and security, algorithmic bias, and transparency (Keshta, 2022). Research indicates that exploiting privacy regulations can lead to a deterioration of public trust in AI systems, as companies may prioritise proprietary interests over patient confidentiality (Abdullah et al., 2021). The possibility of algorithmic bias, stemming from the datasets used to train AI models, intensifies the ethical implications of data handling. The AI systems may perpetuate existing health disparities if these datasets do not represent diverse patient populations (Elendu, 2023). Thus, ensuring robust data privacy measures and addressing biases in AI training datasets are critical to maintaining ethical standards in healthcare AI applications (Familoni, 2024). It is incumbent upon legislators, researchers, and healthcare professionals to guarantee that AI technologies are created and implemented in a manner that maintains the utmost ethical principles.

The possibility of algorithm bias is a significant ethical concern in AI-driven health information systems. The efficacy of AI systems is contingent upon the quality of the data on which they are trained. The presence of bias or incompleteness in this data can result in inequities in healthcare provision for marginalised communities. Therefore, it is crucial that we thoroughly assess the data sets utilised for training AI models and implement measures to reduce bias whenever feasible. Ensuring transparency and accountability are vital ethical considerations in AI-driven health information systems. Patients have the right to be informed about how their data is utilized in AI-driven healthcare systems. Algorithmic transparency is another significant ethical consideration. The "black box" nature of many AI systems complicates the ability of healthcare professionals and patients to understand how decisions are made, which can undermine trust and accountability (Murphy et al., 2021). Transparency in AI algorithms is essential for fostering patient trust and enabling healthcare providers to make informed decisions based on AI recommendations. Furthermore, the development of AI systems must include mechanisms for accountability, allowing stakeholders to address potential errors or biases in AI-driven decisions (Familoni, 2024).

To navigate these ethical challenges, it is imperative to adopt comprehensive ethical frameworks and guidelines that promote culturally competent AI systems. Culturally competent AI systems are designed to respect and integrate the diverse cultural contexts of patients, which is essential for equitable healthcare delivery. Recommendations for developing such frameworks include incorporating cultural competence training for healthcare professionals, which has been shown to enhance engagement with ethnic minority consumers (Harrison et al., 2019; Pettersson et al., 2021). Additionally, establishing partnerships with community organizations and conducting regular cultural assessments can help ensure that AI systems are sensitive to the needs and values of diverse populations. By prioritizing cultural competence in developing and implementing AI systems, healthcare providers can work towards reducing disparities and improving health outcomes for all patients. Healthcare organisations should establish interdisciplinary teams that include ethicists, data scientists, and cultural representatives to guide the development and implementation of AI technologies, ensuring that diverse perspectives are considered throughout the process (Gulati & Weir, 2022).

In conclusion, AI's ethical implications in healthcare are multifaceted, encompassing critical data privacy issues, algorithmic transparency, and cultural competence. Addressing these concerns through strong ethical frameworks and guidelines is crucial to building trust and ensuring that AI technologies positively impact patient care and health equity.

3.2 Cultural Bias in AI Algorithms

Artificial intelligence (AI) algorithms in healthcare information systems have demonstrated significant potential for enhancing patient outcomes and optimising operational procedures in recent times. Nevertheless, an important concern is the cultural bias inside these algorithms (Keshta, 2022). Cultural bias pertains to the inclination of artificial intelligence (AI) systems to exhibit a preference for specific cultural groups over others, resulting in discrepancies in healthcare results that are influenced by characteristics such as race, ethnicity, or other cultural considerations.

This bias can be observed in diverse manners, ranging from underrepresenting particular cultural groups in training datasets to utilising unfamiliar or objectionable vocabulary or terminology when referring to specific populations. For instance, a research article published in the Journal of the American Medical Association revealed that an artificial intelligence algorithm employed to forecast healthcare expenses frequently underestimated the requirements of black patients, resulting in inequalities in the availability of healthcare and medical intervention (Burgess et al., 2019; Williams & Mohammed, 2009).

It is necessary for policymakers, researchers, and healthcare professionals to possess an understanding of the inherent cultural bias present in AI algorithms and to implement measures to alleviate its influence proactively. This may involve implementing strategies to promote the diversity and representativeness of training data sets to the populations being served and establishing tools to monitor and actively eliminate bias in real-time. This may include ensuring that training data sets are diverse and representative of the populations served and implementing mechanisms for monitoring and addressing bias in real time.

In addition, academics must develop AI algorithms that possess cultural competence, thereby considering varied people's distinct requirements and viewpoints. Collaborating with community stakeholders and cultural specialists may be necessary to ensure that algorithms are attuned to the cultural nuances that can influence healthcare outcomes. Mitigating cultural bias in AI algorithms can contribute to developing more equitable and efficient healthcare information systems, enhancing their ability to cater to individuals from diverse cultural backgrounds.

3.3 Trends in AI Adoption in Healthcare and Evolving Understanding of Cultural Competence

The integration of artificial intelligence (AI) in healthcare is rapidly transforming the landscape of medical practice, particularly as patient populations become increasingly diverse. Concurrently, the understanding of cultural competence is evolving, recognizing the need for healthcare providers to be equipped with the skills necessary to address the unique needs of varied patient demographics. This chapter discusses current trends in AI adoption in healthcare, the implications of increasing diversity in patient populations, and the evolving understanding of cultural competence, supported by relevant statistics and case studies.

AI technologies are being adopted across various healthcare domains, including diagnostics, treatment planning, and patient management. A notable trend is the development of AI algorithms that enhance diagnostic accuracy, particularly in imaging and pathology. For instance, AI-assisted mammography has shown promise in improving breast cancer detection rates, with studies indicating that AI algorithms can outperform traditional methods in certain contexts (Lee et al., 2020). However, the effectiveness of these AI systems is contingent upon their validation in diverse patient populations to facilitate generalizability and equity in healthcare delivery (Lee et al., 2020).

Moreover, the increasing reliance on AI in clinical settings raises concerns about biases inherent in the data used to train these systems. Research has highlighted that AI models may exhibit structural biases based on the demographics of the training datasets, which can exacerbate existing health disparities (Drukker et al., 2023). For example, suppose an AI algorithm is primarily trained on data from a homogenous population. In that case, its performance may diminish when applied to patients from diverse backgrounds, leading to unequal care outcomes (Hadjiiski et al., 2023). Thus, there is a pressing need for AI developers to prioritize inclusivity in data collection and model training processes to mitigate these biases (Drukker et al., 2023).

Cultural competence in healthcare refers to providers' ability to understand and respect the cultural differences that influence patient care. The evolving understanding of cultural competence emphasizes recognizing the intersectionality of various factors, including socioeconomic status, gender, and age, in shaping health outcomes (Campinha-Bacote, 2018). For instance, a study found that individuals from lower socioeconomic backgrounds often experience barriers to accessing quality healthcare, which can be exacerbated by cultural misunderstandings between providers and patients (Gopichandran & Chetlapalli, 2013).

As healthcare systems become more aware of the diverse needs of their patient populations, there is a growing recognition that cultural competence must extend beyond mere awareness of cultural differences. It requires an active engagement with patients to understand their unique health beliefs and practices ("Committee Opinion No. 493: Cultural Sensitivity and Awareness in the Delivery of Health Care", 2011). This shift towards a more holistic approach to cultural competence is reflected in integrating self-reflection strategies in training programs, encouraging healthcare professionals to examine their biases and assumptions (Kwiatkoski et al., 2017).

The increasing diversity in patient populations necessitates reevaluating how AI systems are developed and implemented in healthcare. As demographic shifts occur, healthcare providers must adapt their practices to meet the needs of a broader range of patients. This includes recognizing the cultural factors influencing health behaviours and outcomes (Campinha-Bacote, 2018). For example, a case study involving a community health initiative to improve diabetes management among Hispanic populations demonstrated the effectiveness of culturally tailored interventions incorporating traditional health beliefs into treatment plans (González-Prendes et al., 2011).

Statistics indicate that minority populations often face higher rates of chronic diseases, underscoring the need for culturally competent care. According to the Centers for Disease Control and Prevention (CDC), African Americans and Hispanics are disproportionately affected by conditions such as diabetes and hypertension (Huñis, 2023). This disparity highlights the importance of integrating cultural competence into AI systems to ensure they are responsive to the unique needs of diverse populations.

4. STRATEGIES FOR ENSURING CULTURAL COMPETENCE IN AI-DRIVEN HEALTH INFORMATION SYSTEMS

Policymakers, researchers, and healthcare practitioners can employ various essential measures to guarantee cultural competence in AI-driven health information systems. Catering to varied communities' distinct cultural requirements and preferences can enhance the efficacy and inclusivity of health information systems.

An essential approach involves emphasising diversity and inclusion when building and implementing health information systems driven by artificial intelligence. To support the system's sensitivity to the requirements and preferences of many cultural groups, it is necessary that it actively seeks input and feedback from these groups. Integrating multiple viewpoints into the development process enables researchers to enhance systems' inclusivity and cultural competence.

An additional crucial approach is allocating resources to enhance cultural competence and diversity among healthcare professionals through training and education. Equipping professionals with the requisite knowledge and competencies to manage cultural disparities effectively may enhance their ability to cater to various patient populations and guarantee the cultural competence of AI-driven health information systems.

Furthermore, policymakers play a crucial role in fostering cultural competency by implementing laws and regulations emphasising diversity and inclusion within healthcare environments. Policymakers can promote the accessibility and effectiveness of culturally competent AI-driven health information systems by implementing incentives that encourage their development. This approach ensures that these systems are accessible to persons from diverse cultural backgrounds.

To enhance healthcare outcomes for individuals of all cultural backgrounds, policymakers, researchers, and healthcare professionals can collaborate by employing these strategies and prioritising cultural competence when designing, developing, and implementing AI-driven health information systems.

4.1 Case Studies of Cultural Competence in AI-Driven Health Information Systems

A relevant case study is presented by a research team that has successfully created an artificial intelligence (AI)--based health information system tailored for a community characterised by a substantial immigrant population. Considering these individuals' cultural norms and preferences, the system offered tailored healthcare advice that effectively connected with the community members. Consequently, there was a notable rise in user involvement with the system, resulting in enhanced health results for the populace. This led to an increase in overall well-being and quality of life within the community.

Numerous case studies illustrate the convergence of AI implementation with cultural competence in healthcare. A prominent instance is deploying AI-powered telemedicine services in rural areas with significant minority populations. These services have enhanced care accessibility by integrating language translation capabilities for non-English speaking patients (Robertson et al., 2023). This method improves patient involvement and cultivates confidence between healthcare providers and their communities.

A separate case study pertains to creating an AI system for breast cancer detection, validated among various populations. Researchers discovered that the algorithm's efficacy was markedly enhanced when evaluated on a more representative dataset, underscoring the significance of inclusivity in AI model training (Lee et al., 2020). This case highlights the necessity of rectifying AI system biases to guarantee equitable healthcare provision.

Akter et al. (2021) examine the significant concerns of data bias, procedure bias, and societal bias within the context of artificial intelligence (AI) in healthcare. These biases can profoundly impact the efficacy and fairness of AI applications, resulting in inequities in healthcare delivery and results. Data bias pertains to the flaws and disparities in the datasets utilised for training AI algorithms. Akter et al. emphasise that if the training data primarily reflects specific demographics—such as white males within a particular age bracket—the AI systems derived from this data will likely exhibit suboptimal performance for under-represented groups, including women and individuals from diverse ethnic backgrounds (Hulsen, 2021). The absence of representativeness may lead to misdiagnoses or insufficient treatment recommendations for these populations, worsening health inequities (Queiroz & Wamba, 2021). Akter et al. (2021) underscore the necessity for varied and extensive datasets that accurately represent the demographics of the general population to reduce data bias successfully. Procedure Bias pertains to the procedures utilised in developing and implementing AI systems. The methodologies employed in building AI algorithms can unintentionally favour some groups, typically stemming from the assumptions established during the algorithmic design phase (Luca et al., 2021). If methods prioritise efficiency over fairness, the emerging AI systems may neglect the specific demands of marginalised communities. This prejudice may result in diminished trust in AI technology among healthcare providers and patients, exacerbating the challenges of integrating AI into healthcare environments (Vilela et al., 2021). Societal bias includes the societal factors influencing perceptions and interactions with AI in healthcare. Akter et al. (2021) contend that societal norms and values influence the adoption and utilisation of AI technologies in healthcare systems. If social attitudes towards specific demographic groups are unfavourable, AI systems may mirror and reinforce these biases, resulting in discriminatory behaviours in healthcare delivery (Jung et al., 2021).The study by Akter et al. (2021) seeks to investigate the origins of algorithmic biases in artificial intelligence (AI) through a comprehensive survey of existing literature, theme analysis, and a specific examination of the Robo-Debt scheme in Australia. The results indicate that algorithmic bias can be attributed to three primary sources: data bias, procedure bias, and societal bias. The findings shed light on the theoretical significance of dynamic managing competence in mitigating different biases and offer recommendations for eliminating algorithmic biases, specifically emphasising data, methodologies, and managerial competencies. The research findings have practical consequences that underscore the significance of continuous monitoring and evaluation of artificial intelligence (AI) systems to uphold fairness and equity principles. Furthermore, the research emphasises the importance of placing diversity and inclusion as top priorities in data gathering and algorithm development procedures to successfully address biases.

The view is further supported by Murphy et al. (2021) research that examines ethical concerns associated with artificial intelligence (AI) in the healthcare sector. The study identified several prevalent ethical considerations on privacy, trust, accountability, responsibility, and bias. The analysis indicates that introducing AI should be approached cautiously and optimistically. It also highlights the urgent requirement for additional research on the ethical ramifications of AI in the context of global and public health. This research is crucial to ensuring that the development and implementation of AI are ethically sound for all individuals, regardless of location.

Hoop et al. (2008) described the ethics and culture in mental health care. The significance of cultural disparities between patients and physicians has escalated in the context of mental health care due to the rising diversity observed in Western countries. This study aims to demonstrate the positive impact of considering cultural variations on ethical considerations within the field of mental health care. Additionally, it explores how cultural competency contributes to the ethical treatment of individuals seeking mental health services. To possess cultural competence, a clinician must demonstrate sensitivity, expertise, and empathy towards cultural disparities and therapeutically employ these abilities. Cultural competency can be understood as a tangible and pragmatic manifestation of bioethics principles. Mental health professionals adhere to ethical concepts such as beneficence, nonmaleficence, fairness, and respect for humans as they strive to comprehend, value, and empathise with their patients' cultural values. They employ these skills to deliver exceptional patient care.

These case studies highlight the significance of integrating cultural competence into AI-driven health information systems. By comprehending and valuing varied people's cultural backgrounds and beliefs, these systems can enhance their ability to cater to their users and eventually improve health outcomes for all individuals. To foster equitable and effective care for all individuals, policymakers, academics, and healthcare practitioners must give utmost emphasis on cultural competence while designing and deploying AI-driven health information systems.

4.2 Policy Considerations for Promoting Cultural Competence in AI-Driven Health Information Systems

Enhancing cultural competence in AI-driven health information systems is crucial for guaranteeing equitable healthcare provision and meeting the varied needs of patient demographics. To effectively cultivate cultural competency within these systems, politicians, academics, and healthcare professionals must contemplate several critical policy consequences.

Policymakers must prioritise formulating ethical norms that explicitly address cultural competency in AI applications. These criteria must be grounded in established ethical frameworks, such as the Belmont Report, which underscores the concepts of beneficence, nonmaleficence, autonomy, and justice (Abdullah et al., 2021). By incorporating these principles into AI development, stakeholders may guarantee that AI systems uphold patient rights and foster equal treatment among varied populations (Elendu, 2023). Furthermore, frameworks such as the European Commission's guidelines on trustworthy AI can exemplify the development of culturally attuned AI systems that conform to ethical healthcare standards (de-Manuel-Vicente, 2024).

Comprehensive data governance standards must be established to reduce biases and guarantee equity in AI-driven health information systems. This entails setting standards for data gathering, guaranteeing that datasets accurately represent various populations, and fostering transparency in algorithmic decision-making processes (Murphy et al., 2021; Reddy et al., 2019). Policymakers ought to promote using varied training datasets to mitigate the likelihood of reinforcing current health inequities and biases in AI algorithms (Huriye, 2023). Moreover, transparency initiatives must mandate AI developers to provide the methodology employed in algorithm creation, allowing healthcare providers and patients to comprehend the decision-making processes (Reddy et al., 2019).

Healthcare practitioners and academics must work across disciplines to improve cultural competence in AI systems. This partnership may encompass interdisciplinary teams comprising ethicists, cultural representatives, and data scientists to guarantee that AI technologies are built with cultural sensitivity (Salih, 2024; Baigi et al., 2023). Healthcare professional training programs must prioritise cultural competence to effectively engage with AI technologies and comprehend its consequences for various patient groups (McKivigan, 2020).

Establishing public confidence in AI-driven health information systems is essential for effective implementation. Policymakers should promote public engagement programs that inform patients about AI technology, including its advantages and potential hazards (Mays et al., 2021). By promoting an informed public discourse, stakeholders may tackle privacy, prejudice, and transparency issues, therefore improving AI adoption in healthcare environments (Jobin & Ienca, 2019).

Implementing methods for the ongoing evaluation and adaptation of AI systems is crucial to guaranteeing their cultural competence and ethical integrity. This entails systematic evaluations of AI efficacy among various demographic cohorts and integrating insights from heterogeneous patient populations (Familoni, 2024; BOŽIĆ, 2023). Policymakers ought to endorse research endeavours that investigate the cultural adaptability of AI systems and their effects on health outcomes, hence promoting continuous advancements in AI technology (Salih, 2024).

5. RECOMMENDATIONS FOR IMPLEMENTING CULTURAL COMPETENCE IN AI-DRIVEN HEALTH INFORMATION SYSTEMS

The ongoing integration of artificial intelligence (AI) in the healthcare sector necessitates policymakers, academics, and healthcare practitioners prioritising cultural competency in AI-driven health information systems. By comprehending and using cultural competency, these relevant parties can guarantee AI technologies' efficacy, ethicality, and inclusivity for all individuals.

In order to facilitate the successful integration of cultural competency into AI-driven health information systems, it is necessary to take into account the following recommendations:

1. Inclusive Data Collection: AI developers must prioritise the acquisition of diverse datasets that accurately represent the demographics of the populations they intend to serve. This will help alleviate biases and enhance the generalisability of AI models (Drukker et al., 2023). The importance of varied data collection lies in training AI algorithms on diverse and representative datasets, encompassing information from many cultural backgrounds. This strategy would make it easier to prevent biases within the system and improve the accuracy of diagnoses and treatment recommendations for people from different cultural backgrounds.
2. Cultural Competence Training: Healthcare organisations must establish extensive cultural competency training programs for healthcare providers, including self-reflection and bias awareness (Kwiatkoski et al., 2017). This training must be continuous and responsive to the evolving demographics of patient populations. Offer healthcare practitioners and AI developers comprehensive training in cultural competence to enhance their knowledge and comprehension of the cultural elements that can potentially influence healthcare decisions and results. This will improve their ability to effectively cater to patients from all backgrounds and customise AI technology to meet their specific requirements.
3. Community Engagement: It is essential to involve communities in the creation and execution of AI systems. This may entail gathering input from patients and community leaders to guarantee that AI technologies are culturally pertinent and meet the distinct requirements of varied groups (Robertson et al., 2023). Engage individuals from many cultural communities in designing, developing, and testing health information systems powered by artificial intelligence. This will aid in guaranteeing that the technologies are culturally suitable, widely accepted, and efficacious for the intended demographics.

4. Monitoring and Evaluation: AI systems must be monitored and assessed continuously to evaluate their effects on health outcomes among various demographic groups. This will assist in pinpointing areas for enhancement and guarantee that AI technologies aid in mitigating health inequities (Hadjiiski et al., 2023). Establish and uphold ethical rules for using artificial intelligence (AI) in healthcare, focusing on cultural competence and safeguarding patient privacy. This approach will facilitate the establishment of trust among patients and communities while promoting responsible and respectful utilisation of AI technologies.

By implementing these guidelines, policymakers, academics, and healthcare practitioners can enhance cultural competence in AI-driven health information systems. This results in a more fair and inclusive healthcare system for everyone, regardless of cultural background.

5.1 Benefits and Limitations of AI in Healthcare

In healthcare, it is imperative to have a comprehensive understanding of the benefits and limitations associated with incorporating artificial intelligence (AI) into health information systems. Understanding cultural competency in AI-driven health information is of utmost importance for policymakers, academics, and healthcare practitioners, enabling them to make well-informed decisions and adopt practical solutions.

AI in healthcare offers a key advantage by optimising operations and enhancing efficiency. Health information systems powered by artificial intelligence can evaluate extensive quantities of data in significantly less time than human analysis, resulting in faster and more precise diagnoses (Ponnusamy et al., 2022). This can provide significant advantages for individuals from various ethnic backgrounds who may encounter linguistic obstacles or possess distinct healthcare requirements necessitating individualised treatment.

Moreover, AI can assist healthcare personnel in remaining abreast of the most recent medical research and guidelines, guaranteeing that they deliver optimal patient care. Health information systems powered by artificial intelligence can also aid in detecting patterns and trends in patient data, resulting in more efficient treatment plans and enhanced outcomes (Ponnusamy et al., 2022).

Nevertheless, it is imperative to recognise artificial intelligence's constraints in the healthcare sector. A significant obstacle is guaranteeing that AI algorithms are impartial and do not sustain current inequalities in healthcare. The absence of adequate control and regulation in AI-driven health information systems can unintentionally perpetuate cultural prejudices and result in disparities in healthcare accessibility.

Furthermore, AI is incapable of substituting human influence in the healthcare sector. Artificial intelligence (AI) in diagnosing and treating patients necessitates healthcare providers to uphold a compassionate and culturally competent attitude while engaging with patients from various cultural backgrounds.

Ultimately, the use of AI in healthcare presents many advantages, including enhanced efficacy and tailored health services. Understanding the constraints and difficulties linked to health information systems powered by artificial intelligence (AI) ensures that every patient receives fair and culturally sensitive healthcare.

5.2 Future Directions for Research and Practice

When considering the future of cultural competency in AI-driven health information systems, researchers and practitioners should prioritise three crucial aspects to guarantee these systems' effectiveness, fairness, and inclusivity for all individuals.

An essential avenue for future investigation involves advancing artificial intelligence algorithms tailored to exhibit cultural sensitivity and responsiveness towards the requirements of heterogeneous communities. This entails integrating a wide range of cultural viewpoints into the creation and instruction of AI models and devising techniques to assess the cultural proficiency of these systems. Mitigating healthcare outcome gaps and enhancing the quality of care for all people is imperative to ensure that AI-driven health information systems include cultural competence.

An additional crucial domain for future investigation involves formulating protocols and optimal approaches for incorporating cultural proficiency into AI-powered health information systems. This includes creating tools and resources that developers and practitioners may use while creating and implementing these systems. Additionally, it involves offering training and assistance to healthcare professionals to support their proficient use of these tools in their professional endeavours. Creating explicit rules and best practices for cultural competency is crucial to foster ethical, courteous, and successful use of AI-driven health information systems.

The prospects for cultural competence in AI-driven health information systems appear promising. Numerous prospects exist for collaboration among researchers, practitioners, and policymakers to establish equity, inclusivity, and efficacy systems for all individuals. By prioritising these crucial domains of investigation and application, we can guarantee that AI-powered health information systems are genuinely revolutionary in enhancing healthcare results for individuals, irrespective of their cultural heritage.

5.3 Final Thoughts on the Future of Cultural Competence in AI-Driven Health Information Systems

In the culmination of our investigation into cultural competency within AI-driven health information systems, it becomes evident that the forthcoming period presents considerable potential and notable challenges. The potential impact of incorporating artificial intelligence (AI) technologies into the healthcare sector is significant, as it can transform the delivery and reception of medical services, leading to enhanced efficiency, accuracy, and outcomes. Suppose we are genuinely able to utilise the potential of AI in the field of healthcare. Therefore, we must guarantee the cultural competence of these systems.

Policymakers are responsible for formulating rules and laws that place cultural competency as a top priority in developing and implementing health information systems driven by artificial intelligence. This entails guaranteeing that these systems acknowledge and honour the variety of beliefs, practices, and values that influence the health outcomes of individuals and communities. Policymakers can prevent the unintentional perpetuation of inequities in healthcare access and outcomes by establishing explicit criteria for cultural competence in AI systems.

Researchers play a vital role in furthering our comprehension of the integration of cultural competency into AI-driven health information systems. By examining cultural factors' influence on the efficiency of these systems, researchers can establish best practices for ensuring that AI technologies are responsive to the requirements and preferences of varied patient populations. This study can also contribute to advancing algorithms and technologies that exhibit greater inclusivity and equity.

To support the future of cultural competence in AI-driven health information systems, healthcare providers must demonstrate a steadfast dedication to continuous education and training. By keeping themselves informed about the latest research and best practices in cultural competency, healthcare practitioners can ensure their ability to effectively negotiate the complexity of delivering care in a diverse and globalised society. Adopting cultural competency within AI-driven health information systems makes it possible to strive towards a future in which every individual is provided with exceptional and tailored healthcare to which they are entitled.

REFERENCES

Abdullah, Y., Schuman, J., Shabsigh, R., Caplan, A., & Al-Aswad, L. (2021). Ethics of artificial intelligence in medicine and ophthalmology. *Asia-Pacific Journal of Ophthalmology*, *10*(3), 289–298. DOI: 10.1097/APO.0000000000000397 PMID: 34383720

Akter, S., McCarthy, G., Sajib, S., Michael, K., Dwivedi, Y. K., D'Ambra, J., & Shen, K. N. (2021). Algorithmic bias in data-driven innovation in the age of AI. *International Journal of Information Management*, *60*, 102387. Advance online publication. DOI: 10.1016/j.ijinfomgt.2021.102387

American College of Obstetricians and Gynecologists. (2011). Committee opinion no. 493: Cultural sensitivity and awareness in the delivery of health care. *Obstetrics and Gynecology*, *117*(5), 1258–1261. DOI: 10.1097/AOG.0b013e31821d7db0

Amiri, Z. (2024). Ai-Driven Decision-Making in Healthcare Information Systems: A Comprehensive Review. Available at *SSRN* 4756316. DOI: 10.2139/ssrn.4756316

Arestad, K., MacPhee, D., Lim, C., & Khetani, M. (2017). Cultural adaptation of a pediatric functional assessment for rehabilitation outcomes research. *BMC Health Services Research*, *17*(1), 658. Advance online publication. DOI: 10.1186/s12913-017-2592-6 PMID: 28915817

Baigi, S., Sarbaz, M., Ghaddaripouri, K., Ghaddaripouri, M., Mousavi, A., & Kimiafar, K. (2023). Attitudes, knowledge, and skills towards artificial intelligence among healthcare students: A systematic review. *Health Science Reports*, *6*(3), e1138. Advance online publication. DOI: 10.1002/hsr2.1138 PMID: 36923372

Balachandran, P., Karuveettil, V., & Janakiram, C. (2022). Development and validation of cultural competence assessment tool for healthcare professionals, India. *Frontiers in Public Health*, *10*, 919386. Advance online publication. DOI: 10.3389/fpubh.2022.919386 PMID: 36081476

BOŽIĆ, V. (2023). Integrated risk management and artificial intelligence in hospital. *Journal of AI*, *7*(1), 63-80. DOI: 10.61969/jai.1329224

Burgess, D. J., Bokhour, B. G., Cunningham, B. A., Do, T., Gordon, H. S., Jones, D. M., Pope, C., Saha, S., & Gollust, S. E. (2019). Healthcare providers' responses to narrative communication about racial healthcare disparities. *Health Communication*, *34*(2), 149–161. DOI: 10.1080/10410236.2017.1389049 PMID: 29068701

Campinha-Bacote, J. (2018). Cultural competemility: A paradigm shift in the cultural competence versus cultural humility debate – part i. *Online Journal of Issues in Nursing, 24*(1). Advance online publication. DOI: 10.3912/OJIN.Vol24No01PPT20

Čebron, U., & Huber, I. (2020). Cultural competence and healthcare. *Etnološka Tribina, 50*(43), 68–88. DOI: 10.15378/1848-9540.2020.43.02

de-Manuel-Vicente, C. (2024). A development framework for trustworthy artificial intelligence in health with example code pipelines. DOI: 10.1101/2024.07.17.24310418

Drukker, K., Chen, W., Gichoya, J., Gruszauskas, N., Kalpathy–Cramer, J., Koyejo, S., Myers, K., Sá, R. C., Sahiner, B., Whitney, H., Zhang, Z., & Giger, M. (2023). Toward fairness in artificial intelligence for medical image analysis: Identification and mitigation of potential biases in the roadmap from data collection to model deployment. *Journal of Medical Imaging (Bellingham, Wash.), 10*(06). Advance online publication. DOI: 10.1117/1.JMI.10.6.061104 PMID: 37125409

Elendu, C., Amaechi, D. C., Elendu, T. C., Jingwa, K. A., Okoye, O. K., John Okah, M., Ladele, J. A., Farah, A. H., & Alimi, H. A. (2023). Ethical implications of AI and robotics in healthcare: A review. *Medicine, 102*(50), e36671. DOI: 10.1097/MD.0000000000036671 PMID: 38115340

Familoni, B.Babajide Tolulope Familoni. (2024). Ethical frameworks for AI in healthcare entrepreneurship: A theoretical examination of challenges and approaches. *International Journal of Frontiers in Biology and Pharmacy Research, 5*(1), 57–65. DOI: 10.53294/ijfbpr.2024.5.1.0032

Gerke, S., Minssen, T., & Cohen, G. Ethical and legal challenges of artificial intelligence-driven health care In: *Artificial Intelligence in Health Care*. 1st ed. 2020:295–336. DOI: 10.2139/ssrn.3570129

González-Prendes, A., Hindo, C., & Pardo, Y. (2011). Cultural values integration in cognitive-behavioral therapy for a Latino with depression. *Clinical Case Studies, 10*(5), 376–394. DOI: 10.1177/1534650111427075

Gopichandran, V., & Chetlapalli, S. (2013). Factors influencing trust in doctors: A community segmentation strategy for quality improvement in healthcare. *BMJ Open, 3*(12), e004115. DOI: 10.1136/bmjopen-2013-004115 PMID: 24302512

Govere, L., & Govere, E. (2016). How effective is cultural competence training of healthcare providers on improving patient satisfaction of minority groups? A systematic review of literature. *Worldviews on Evidence-Based Nursing, 13*(6), 402–410. DOI: 10.1111/wvn.12176 PMID: 27779817

Gulati, S., & Weir, C. (2022). Cultural competence in healthcare leadership education and development. *Societies (Basel, Switzerland)*, *12*(2), 39. DOI: 10.3390/soc12020039

Hadjiiski, L., Cha, K., Chan, H., Drukker, K., Morra, L., Näppi, J., Sahiner, B., Yoshida, H., Chen, Q., Deserno, T. M., Greenspan, H., Huisman, H., Huo, Z., Mazurchuk, R., Petrick, N., Regge, D., Samala, R., Summers, R. M., Suzuki, K., & Armato, S.III. (2023). Aapm task group report 273: Recommendations on best practices for AI and machine learning for computer-aided diagnosis in medical imaging. *Medical Physics*, *50*(2). Advance online publication. DOI: 10.1002/mp.16188 PMID: 36565447

Hall, W. J., Chapman, M. V., Lee, K. M., Merino, Y. M., Thomas, T. W., Payne, B. K., Eng, E., Day, S. H., & Coyne-Beasley, T. (2015). Implicit Racial/Ethnic Bias Among Health Care Professionals and Its Influence on Health Care Outcomes: A Systematic Review. *American Journal of Public Health*, *105*(12), 60–76. DOI: 10.2105/AJPH.2015.302903 PMID: 26469668

Handtke, O., Schilgen, B., & Mösko, M. (2019). Culturally competent healthcare – a scoping review of strategies implemented in healthcare organizations and a model of culturally competent healthcare provision. *PLoS One*, *14*(7), e0219971. DOI: 10.1371/journal.pone.0219971 PMID: 31361783

Harrison, R., Walton, M., Chauhan, A., Manias, E., Chitkara, U., Latanik, M., & Leone, D. (2019). What is the role of cultural competence in ethnic minority consumer engagement? An analysis in community healthcare. *International Journal for Equity in Health*, *18*(1), 191. Advance online publication. DOI: 10.1186/s12939-019-1104-1 PMID: 31801565

Hoop, J. G., DiPasquale, T., Hernandez, J. M., & Roberts, L. W. (2008). Ethics and Culture in Mental Health Care. *Ethics & Behavior*, *18*(4), 353–372. DOI: 10.1080/10508420701713048

Hulsen, T. (2021). Literature analysis of artificial intelligence in biomedicine. https://doi.org/DOI: 10.20944/preprints202105.0056.v1

Huñis, A. (2023). Addressing cancer disparities in the Hispanic population in the US and LMICs. *Acta Scientific Cancer Biology*, *7*(6), 8–21. DOI: 10.31080/ASCB.2023.07.0428

Huriye, A. (2023). The ethics of artificial intelligence: Examining the ethical considerations surrounding the development and use of AI. *American Journal of Technology*, *2*(1), 37–45. DOI: 10.58425/ajt.v2i1.142

Jiang, F., Jiang, Y., Zhi, H., Dong, Y., Li, H., Ma, S., Wang, Y., Dong, Q., Shen, H., & Wang, Y. (2017). Artificial intelligence in health care: Past, present and future. *Stroke and Vascular Neurology*, *2*(4), 230–243. DOI: 10.1136/svn-2017-000101 PMID: 29507784

Jobin, A., Ienca, M., & Vayena, E. (2019). The global landscape of AI ethics guidelines. *Nature Machine Intelligence*, *1*(9), 389–399. DOI: 10.1038/s42256-019-0088-2

Jongen, C., McCalman, J., & Bainbridge, R. (2018). Health workforce cultural competency interventions: A systematic scoping review. *BMC Health Services Research*, *18*(1), 232. Advance online publication. DOI: 10.1186/s12913-018-3001-5 PMID: 29609614

Jung, W., Lee, K., Suh, B., Seok, H., & Lee, D. (2021). Deep learning for osteoarthritis classification in temporomandibular joint. *Oral Diseases*, *29*(3), 1050–1059. DOI: 10.1111/odi.14056 PMID: 34689379

Kim-Godwin, Y., Clarke, P., & Barton, L. (2001). A model for the delivery of culturally competent community care. *Journal of Advanced Nursing*, *35*(6), 918–925. DOI: 10.1046/j.1365-2648.2001.01929.x PMID: 11555040

Kostic, E. J., Pavlović, D. A., & Živković, M. D. (2019). Applications of artificial intelligence in medicine and pharmacy – ethical aspects. *Acta Medica Medianae*, *58*(3), 128–137. DOI: 10.5633/amm.2019.0319

Kwiatkoski, D., Mantovani, M., Pereira, E., Bortolato-Major, C., & Peres, A. (2017). Translation and cross-cultural adaptation of the clinical competence questionnaire for use in Brazil. *Revista Latino-Americana de Enfermagem*, *25*(0). Advance online publication. DOI: 10.1590/1518-8345.1757.2898 PMID: 28591303

Lee, C., Houssami, N., Elmore, J., & Buist, D. (2020). Pathways to breast cancer screening artificial intelligence algorithm validation. *The Breast : Official Journal of the European Society of Mastology*, *52*, 146–149. DOI: 10.1016/j.breast.2019.09.005 PMID: 31540699

Lomiguen, C., Rosete, I., & Chin, J. (2020). Providing culturally competent care for covid-19 intensive care unit delirium: A case report and review. *Cureus*. Advance online publication. DOI: 10.7759/cureus.10867 PMID: 33178520

Luca, C., Casu, F., Manunta, M., Onorato, G., & Lanari, R. (2021). Comment on "Study of systematic bias in measuring surface deformation with SAR interferometry" by Ansari et al. (2021). DOI: 10.36227/techrxiv.14691333

Mays, K., Lei, Y., Giovanetti, R., & Katz, J. (2021). AI as a boss? A national US survey of predispositions governing comfort with expanded AI roles in society. *AI & Society*, *37*(4), 1587–1600. DOI: 10.1007/s00146-021-01253-6

McCalman, J., Jongen, C., & Bainbridge, R. (2017). Organisational systems' approaches to improving cultural competence in healthcare: A systematic scoping review of the literature. *International Journal for Equity in Health*, *16*(1), 78. Advance online publication. DOI: 10.1186/s12939-017-0571-5 PMID: 28499378

McKivigan, J. (2020). Evaluation of the American physical therapy association's guidelines for training culturally competent physical therapists. *Higher Education Research*, *5*(4), 154. DOI: 10.11648/j.her.20200504.16

Murphy, K., Ruggiero, E., Upshur, R., Willison, D., Malhotra, N., Cai, J., & Gibson, J. (2021). Artificial intelligence for good health: A scoping review of the ethics literature. *BMC Medical Ethics*, *22*(1), 14. Advance online publication. DOI: 10.1186/s12910-021-00577-8 PMID: 33588803

Nazer, L. H., Zatarah, R., Waldrip, S., Ke, J. X. C., Moukheiber, M., Khanna, A. K., Hicklen, R. S., Moukheiber, L., Moukheiber, D., Ma, H., & Mathur, P. (2023). Bias in artificial intelligence algorithms and recommendations for mitigation. *PLOS Digital Health*, *2*(6), e0000278. DOI: 10.1371/journal.pdig.0000278 PMID: 37347721

Nowaskie, D., & Najam, S. (2022). Lesbian, gay, bisexual, and/or transgender (lgbt) cultural competency across the intersectionalities of gender identity, sexual orientation, and race among healthcare professionals. *PLoS One*, *17*(11), e0277682. DOI: 10.1371/journal.pone.0277682 PMID: 36367906

Pannu, A. (2015). Artificial intelligence and its application in different areas. *Artificial Intelligence*, *4*(10), 79–84.

Patricia, H. (2005). Improving patient–provider communication: Insights from interpreters. *Family Practice*, *22*(3), 311–316. DOI: 10.1093/fampra/cmi015 PMID: 15805131

Pettersson, S., Holstein, J., Jirwe, M., Jaarsma, T., & Klompstra, L. (2021). Cultural competence in healthcare professionals, specialised in diabetes, working in primary healthcare—A descriptive study. *Health & Social Care in the Community*, *30*(3). Advance online publication. DOI: 10.1111/hsc.13442 PMID: 34145649

Ponnusamy, V., Vasuki, A., Clement, J. C., & Eswaran, P. (2022). AI-Driven Information and Communication Technologies, Services, and Applications for Next-Generation Healthcare System. Smart Systems for Industrial Applications, 1-32.

Queiroz, M., & Wamba, S. (2021). A structured literature review on the interplay between emerging technologies and covid-19 – insights and directions to operations fields. *Annals of Operations Research, 335*(3), 937–963. DOI: 10.1007/s10479-021-04107-y PMID: 34226781

Razzaq, N., Farzeen Khan, E., & Razzaq, S. (2023). Analyzing the role of language and religion in culturally competent healthcare: An interdisciplinary perspective. *AIM, 1*(3). Advance online publication. DOI: 10.59652/aim.v1i3.61

Reddy, S., Allan, S., Coghlan, S., & Cooper, P. (2019). A governance model for the application of AI in health care. *Journal of the American Medical Informatics Association : JAMIA, 27*(3), 491–497. DOI: 10.1093/jamia/ocz192 PMID: 31682262

Robertson, C., Woods, A., Bergstrand, K., Findley, J., Balser, C., & Slepian, M. (2023). Diverse patients' attitudes towards artificial intelligence (AI) in diagnosis. *PLOS Digital Health, 2*(5), e0000237. DOI: 10.1371/journal.pdig.0000237 PMID: 37205713

Salih, S. (2024). Perceptions of faculty and students about use of artificial intelligence in medical education: A qualitative study. *Cureus*. Advance online publication. DOI: 10.7759/cureus.57605 PMID: 38707183

Shinners, L., Aggar, C., Grace, S., & Smith, S. (2019, September 30). Exploring healthcare professionals' understanding and experiences of artificial intelligence technology use in the delivery of healthcare: An integrative review. *Health Informatics Journal, 26*(2), 1225–1236. DOI: 10.1177/1460458219874641 PMID: 31566454

Smolin, V. S. (2020). The prospects of the mankind in the era of technological singularity. *Epistemol Philos Sci, 57*(2), 192–207. DOI: 10.5840/eps202057230

Solez, K., Bernier, A., Crichton, J., Graves, H., Kuttikat, P., Lockwood, R., Marovitz, W. F., Monroe, D., Pallen, M., Pandya, S., Pearce, D., Saleh, A., Sandhu, N., Sergi, C., Tuszynski, J., Waugh, E., White, J., Woodside, M., Wyndham, R., & Zakus, D. (2013). Bridging the gap between the technological singularity and mainstream medicine: Highlighting a course on technology and the future of medicine. *Global Journal of Health Science, 5*(6), 112–125. DOI: 10.5539/gjhs.v5n6p112 PMID: 24171879

Sun, G., & Zhou, Y.-H. (2023). AI in healthcare: Navigating opportunities and challenges in digital communication. *Frontiers in Digital Health, 5*, 1291132. DOI: 10.3389/fdgth.2023.1291132 PMID: 38173911

Tran, B. X., Vu, G. T., Ha, G. H., Vuong, Q.-H., Ho, M.-T., Vuong, T.-T., La, V.-P., Ho, M.-T., Nghiem, K.-C. P., Nguyen, H. L. T., Latkin, C. A., Tam, W. W. S., Cheung, N.-M., Nguyen, H.-K. T., Ho, C. S. H., & Ho, R. C. M. (2019). Global evolution of research in artificial intelligence in health and medicine: A bibliometric study. *Journal of Clinical Medicine*, *8*(3), 360. DOI: 10.3390/jcm8030360 PMID: 30875745

Trivedi, B., Mares, A. C., & Mukherjee, D.. (2023). Effectiveness of a social justice curriculum intervention on cultural competency among internal medicine residents. *Research Square*. DOI: 10.21203/rs.3.rs-3426316/v1

Vilela, A., Costa, C., Souza, M., Fiaccadori, F., Leles, C., & Costa, N. (2021). Validity and reliability of immunochromatographic IGM/IGG rapid tests for covid-19 salivary diagnosis. *Oral Diseases*, *28*(S2), 2465–2473. DOI: 10.1111/odi.14059 PMID: 34695290

Williams, D. R., & Mohammed, S. A. (2009). Discrimination and racial disparities in health: Evidence and needed research. *Journal of Behavioral Medicine*, *32*(1), 20–47. DOI: 10.1007/s10865-008-9185-0 PMID: 19030981

Yunus, S., Puteh, S., Ali, A., & Daud, F. (2021). The covid impact to public healthcare utilization among urban low-income subsidized community in Klang Valley Malaysia. *Health Services Research and Managerial Epidemiology*, *8*, 23333928211002407. https://doi.org. DOI: 10.1177/23333928211002407 PMID: 33796627

Chapter 6
From Humans to Humans:
Designing Human-Centered AI for Better Healthcare

Yushan Wu
Xiamen University Malaysia, China

ABSTRACT

Artificial intelligence (AI) is transforming healthcare through advancements in service platforms, decision-making processes, and biomedical technologies, while adhering to humanistic principles. In the era of digital transformation and Healthcare 4.0, this chapter examines how AI algorithms enable systems to learn from human inputs and collaborate with professionals to deliver accurate and efficient care. Adopting a qualitative approach, this chapter provides comprehensive literature reviews and explores in-depth case studies, including AIDI, the AI-powered service platform enhancing patient experiences and hospital operations; SepsisLab, improving diagnoses and decision-making through AI-human collaboration; and BrainGate and Neuralink, the state-of-the-art brain-computer interfaces aiding neural communication and autonomous movement. Potential ethical issues are also addressed. Ultimately, the chapter advocates for AI's evolution from being purely designed by humans to more human-centered solutions, where AI revolutionizes healthcare and contributes to a promising future.

DOI: 10.4018/979-8-3693-5837-5.ch006

1. INTRODUCTION TO ARTIFICIAL INTELLIGENCE IN HEALTHCARE

Artificial Intelligence (AI) has been generally defined by academia as systems that mimic human's cognitive functions in learning, speech, and problem-solving (Russell & Norvig, 2016). A more detailed elaboration explains that AI possesses the capability of independently interpreting and learning from external data to achieve specific outcomes through flexible adaptation, which usually involves utilizing big data to design algorithms to deliver excellent performance for specific tasks and displays a more pragmatic trend of effectively translating human thoughts and emotions (Dwivedi et al., 2021).

What is noteworthy is that AI is not an isolated technology but rather a spectrum of algorithms and functionalities processed and generated by machines and computers (Chen & Decary, 2020). AI is closely associated with machine learning, natural language processing (NLP), voice technology, assistants, and chatbots. Among them, machine learning along with its subfield deep learning, the most prevailing method in AI fields, entails a system training a predictive model by discerning primarily data patterns from inputs, subsequently utilizing this model to generalize their judgment to new observations (Barbierato & Gatti, 2024). The capability of machine learning epitomizes the essence of AI by autonomously studying from experience and making enhancements without explicit programming, which display extensive applications and interactions across various other AI domains as well, such as NLP, AI voice technology, and AI chatbots. Natural language processing (NLP), usually relying on machine learning, refers to the interplay between computers and humans through the utilization of natural language, focusing on the computer's capacity to deprive meaning from human language in an AI discipline (Sun et al., 2020). Coupled with those capabilities mentioned above, AI, encompassing a sophisticated and interactive system, has become a powerful solution to many real-world problems, including the AI-based human-centered healthcare, which is the subject of this chapter.

2. HUMAN-CENTERED AI AND ITS THREE DIMENSIONS TO BOOST HEALTHCARE

With significant shifts brought by AI in many sectors of human life, the field of healthcare also benefits from this increasingly advanced and human-centered intricacy. It is reported by Shaban-Nejad et al. (2022) that since the onset of COVID-19 pandemic, AI tools and technologies have displayed an important role in the healthcare area, including but not limited to "disease surveillance, screening, diagnostics, case detection, prediction, risk stratification, drug and vaccine development, resource allocation, and socioeconomic interventions." With an increasing amount of data about human input and experience, human-centered AI is continuously evolving through testing, debugging, and upgrading, which pushes previously limited boundaries to further effective solutions (Lee et al., 2023).

Scientists have put forward potential advancements of AI technologies in five directions: collaborative AI (cooperation, competition, or coordination among human and machines), multimodal AI (analyze complex associations and relationships between various biological processes, health indicators, risk factors, and health outcomes, and developing models), equitable AI (collecting more precise and inclusive data among g under-represented and marginalized communities), ethical and value-based AI (understanding individuals' concerns and respecting their personal autonomy and right to informed consent, and dissent), and human-centered AI (Shaban-Nejad et al., 2022). The last direction of AI's future, aligning with this chapter, demonstrates AI's intention to "amplify and augment rather than display human abilities", which means that human-centered AI focuses on including the human in the loop of the transparent, fair, accountable, reliable, and explainable AI systems with respect to human rights and interests.

Therefore, human-centered AI in healthcare basically includes prioritizing patients' needs, conforming to humane value, involving medical professionals' efforts, and respecting human trust and comprehensibility. Scholars suggested that with the rise of Internet of Things, and wearable devices, health systems have experienced a digital transformation from antient medication to human-centered Healthcare 4.0, of which the latest version is featured by remote monitoring, remote diagnostics, recommender systems, and personalized healthcare services (Sharma et al., 2023). Great significance has been attached to AI and related machine learning algorithms, of which the ability to process extensive data sets and generate suitable treatment suggestions within several seconds or minutes can help doctors and physicians make better decisions at lower costs. This indeed manifests a more patient-centric approach, in other words, the human-centered principle. With such advantages and demands, the integration of AI and the healthcare domain is no longer a predictive future, but an unfolding reality (Turchi et al., 2024).

Nowadays, the application of AI can be characterized from three key dimensions. Firstly, AI is increasingly being viewed as a service product or platform, with small and medium-sized enterprises following the trend and providing cloud-based AI service platforms tailored to their specific needs. These services have even been given a unique name: "Artificial Intelligence as a Service" (AIaaS), of which the essence of AIaaS combines AI with the cloud computing model (Lins et al., 2021). Secondly, AI is more commonly seen as a useful tool for augmenting decision-makers' capabilities in the Big Data era (Duan et al., 2019). However, as more opportunities arise for improved data-driven decision-making, innovation, and organizational agility, decision makers should adapt by remaining professional lucidity and independence, developing a comprehensive understanding of AI applications, fostering an AI-ready organizational culture, and ensuring ethical and regulatory compliance (Chong et al., 2023). Thirdly, AI's latest advancements in its fusion with brain-computer interface (BCI) have garnered significant attention from academia, modern industry, and healthcare. These sectors aim to optimize electronic integrated chips and neuro-ergonomic systems, facilitate robot-assisted surgeries, minimize surgical wounds, and extend the durability of devices in safe life scenarios (Asgher et al., 2023).

As for the outline, this chapter serves as a comprehensive exploration of the principles of human-centered design in healthcare, emphasizing the pivotal role of user involvement in shaping AI-powered health technologies. Delving into the intricacies of implementation, the chapter examines both challenges and solutions associated with integrating human-centered design approaches in the development of healthcare technologies. By presenting different case studies, the author aims to illustrate AI's role in healthcare from three aspects: AI as service platform, AI as decision-making process, and AI as biomedical technology. It endeavors to offer valuable insights into successful projects which have effectively embraced and applied human-centered principles throughout design and practice phases.

3. APPLICATION OF AI

3.1 AI as a Service Platform

3.1.1 Conceptualization

AI as a service platform in healthcare aligns with the concept presented by Benlian et al. (2018), which emphasizes the role of Platform-as-a-Service (PaaS) providers in designing cloud-based platforms that facilitate access and interaction among a diverse ecosystem of consumers, complementors, and other stakeholders. This concept opened the door to the Application Programming Interfaces (APIs) economy, allowing platforms to offer value-adding components like AI, analytics, and blockchains, and enabling integration across platforms via APIs with other open services from the programmable web to provide the best-of-breed solutions. In the context of healthcare, the AI-embedded service platform can be viewed as a model that enables access to AI capabilities without the need for developing AI systems in-house. The integration of AI into existing patient use systems and medical workers' workflows is specialized in areas such as Machine Learning,

Natural Language Processing, and computer vision and robotics, which are crucial to enhancing patients' user experience and efficiency of the management system.

3.1.2 Necessity and Significance

The application of AI in the service platform of the hospital usually embodies the chatting box, health dataset, and hospital's management system. AI-powered chatbots nowadays are widely applied in healthcare, which can interact with patients, gather their information, and intelligently make appointments based on doctors' availability and patient preferences. In addition, it can provide patients with highly personalized services, including health guidance, medication reminders, and appointment scheduling. Furthermore, on the hospital's management side, this AI automation system can manage the inventory, bill, and bed occupancy, which helps to improve efficiency and optimize resource distribution with computer algorithms (Pillai, 2023).

Powered by AI, the service platforms have brought benefits to real world. It is widely accepted that AI tools will assist in and amplify the efficiency of human work, rather than serve as a substitute for the crucial roles played by physicians and other healthcare professionals (Bohr & Memarzadeh, 2020). To facilitate a higher level of healthcare services, AI largely relies on NLP, which is the computer's autonomy to process and comprehend the natural language of human, and then output filtered data for specific uses. Therefore, the AI service platforms can make the billing process more efficient by extracting pertinent information from physician's notes to accurately assign medical codes. Additionally, in the authoritative approval process, the AI-embedded platforms will learn automatically and subsequently leverage information contained in physician's notes to mitigate delays and administrative errors. On a higher level, the AI platforms can analyze medical policy documents and generate evaluation correspondingly, which further consolidates good clinical practices and formulate apt care guidelines. This will be a win-win situation for both patients and hospitals.

Despite the great convenience brought by AI-assisted service platforms, managers should not ignore the underlying issues regarding patients' privacy. It is crucial to avoid revealing sensitive information such as specific diseases, including contagious diseases (i.e., HIV, syphilis, and hepatitis B), and mental health disorders (i.e., depression, anxiety, and bipolar disorder). While these diseases can be detrimental to public health of which the cases should be immediately reported to the local health system agencies, the situation also indicates the virus carrier's vulnerability. Thus, preserving or revealing what degree of medical history requires the right and informed consent from individuals and the conformity to local medical regulations as well. And in what kind of necessary condition should the AI service platforms provide some pivotal information, with only a small handful of people having access to it? The more convenient the technology is, the greater the risk of private information leakage is. These questions remain further discussions as AI evolves and reshapes the routine of healthcare industry.

3.2 AI as Decision-Making Process

3.2.1 Conceptualization

In the context of hospital operations, medical professionals are continually required to make critical decisions that will have significant consequences. Given the vast expanse of health-related data, AI has the potential to exponentially enhance the efficiency of resource analysis, pattern recognition, and risk assessment, with NLP, and Machine Learning algorithms, thereby facilitating the identification of the most economically viable and clinically prudent medical interventions from the standpoint of both patient welfare and healthcare provider efficacy. In addition, there is an emerging consensus on the optimal integration of human-AI interaction, necessitating a human-in-the-loop approach to decision-making while leveraging computational capabilities for data processing. This paradigm underscores the necessity for explainable AI (XAI), an important feature of AI systems, to ensure the interpretability and transparency of the collaborative human-AI partnership and involved reasoning processes (Ferreira & Monteiro, 2021). Such an approach is essential for bolstering the credibility and trustworthiness of AI within the healthcare sector

3.2.2 Necessity and Significance

With its great potentiality in healthcare, AI has evolved at a rapid pace to help make clinical decisions based on big data evidence and achieve personalized care based on human values. Healthcare field requires a wide range of public and private data collection, of which the information is usually not structured and relational. Scholars elaborated that data exists in various aspects, such as clinical data, genomic data, and behavioral data, as shown in Figure 1 (Kaur & Mann, 2018). The database can serve as background information like diagnosis, family history, statistics, opinions, etc., and then provide valuable suggestions for the individuals.

Figure 1. Healthcare data sources (Kaur & Mann, 2018)

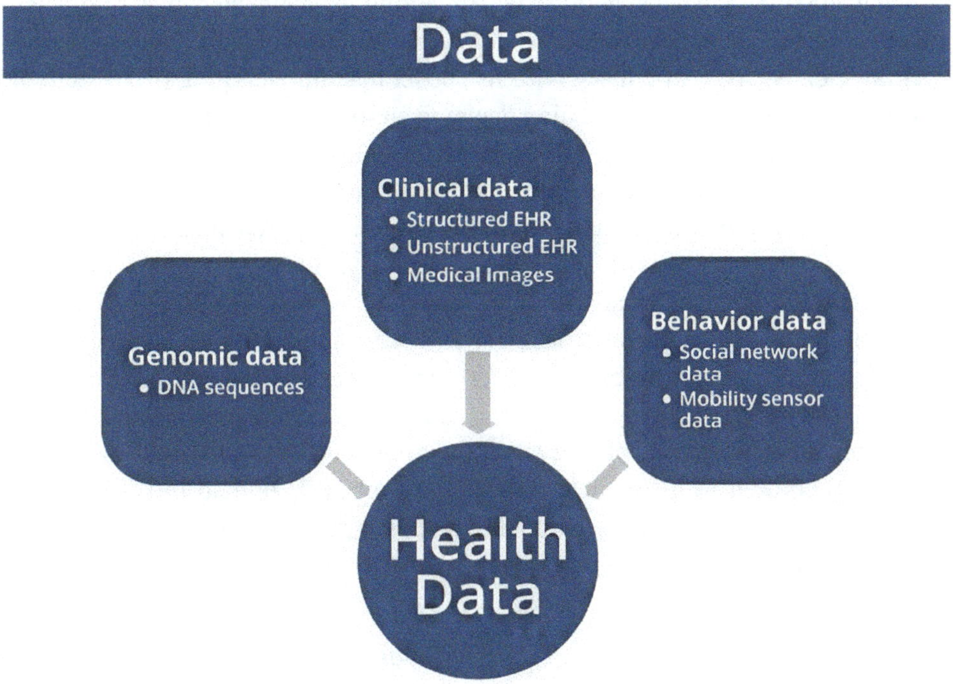

With such a massive amount of data, it is too difficult for mankind to process all the information and make the right decisions. Similarly, doctors will have problems deciding the right treatment methods for the right patients at the right time, which will slow down personalized healthcare for individuals. Therefore, great significance is attached to the development of a new system which can help doctors to detect precisely the origin and spread of certain diseases and reduce the treatment costs as much as possible, protecting the health and interests of patients.

3.2.3 Explanation of the Decision-Making Process

The emerge of AI has brought disruption to conventional decision-making paradigms by shifting the cognitive and strategic processes (Kaggwa et al., 2024).

Cognitively, traditional decision-making method used to be merely human involved, where now the AI technology embedded within the digital information system of the hospital can noticeably enhance the internal efficiency and effectiveness. To elaborate further, within the internal environment of the organization, AI-driven digital frameworks will be seamlessly integrated into the decision-making process with varying levels of involvement, either participating in a specific phase, the concluding stage, or the entire process. The harmonious collaboration between AI and human would then yield a synergy effect, resulting in an elevated level of precision and concurrently an accelerated pace in making and implementing decisions.

Strategically, AI, particularly with its subset machine learning (ML) technologies, is crucial in providing clinician decision support, early illness detection, and personalized treatment plans. ML-based AI technologies can scan and analyze satellite data, news and social media reports, and even video sources to detect early indicators of an epidemic or pandemic. This proactive approach enables healthcare professionals to respond swiftly and effectively, minimizing the impact of subsequent disease outbreaks (Javaid et al., 2022). Furthermore, AI's capabilities extend beyond immediate healthcare warnings, as it can automatically conduct market research and analyze profitability and competitive forces, thereby providing long-term benefits for hospitals.

Furthermore, the quality of AI evaluation is only one side of the decision-making process. According to different weight of AI input and human involvement, the decision-making process may fall into three types as presented in Figure 2 (Meissner & Keding, 2021).

Figure 2. Three types of AI involved decision-making process (Meissner & Keding, 2021)

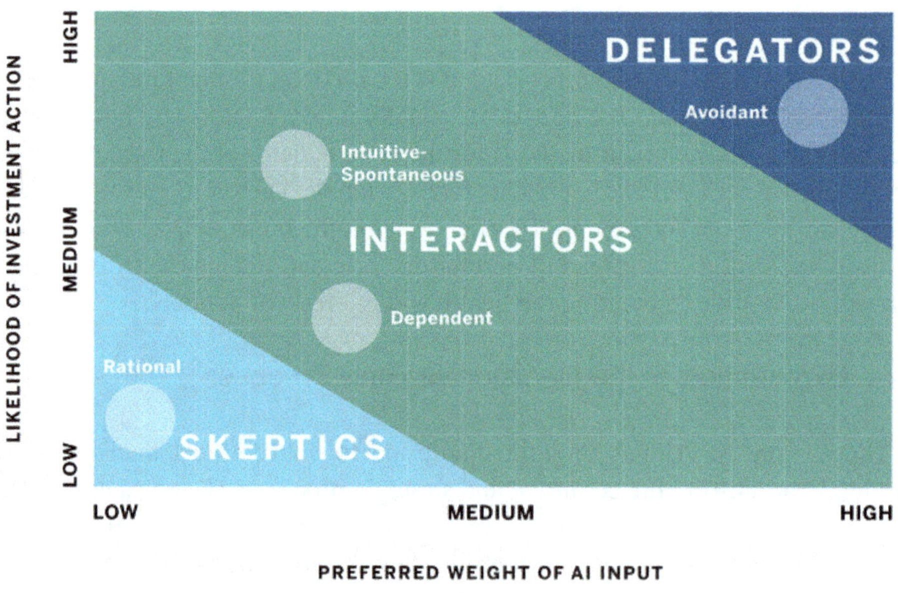

Skeptics give little trust to the black box of AI-based recommendations, preferring to comprehend details and keep analytical control over the process themselves. However, skeptics can fall prey to a false illusion of control, causing them to be excessively confident in their own judgment and underestimate AI.

Interactors strike a balance between human perception and algorithms' advice. They are open to the use of AI but do not rely on it entirely. When AI-based analyses are available, interactors are willing to trust and make decisions based on these recommendations.

Delegators largely cede their decision-making authority to AI in order to reduce perceived individual risk. For delegators, AI significantly accelerates the strategic decision-making process and can break a potential gridlock. However, delegators may also misuse AI to avoid personal responsibility; they might rely on its recommendations as a personal insurance policy in case something goes wrong. This transfer of risk from the decision-maker to the machine could lead to an unwarranted assumption of risk for the organization.

3.2.4 Improved Diagnostic Accuracy and Effectiveness

Applications of AI models can contribute to improved clinical outcomes with a higher degree of diagnostic accuracy and effectiveness, which is achieved by risk stratification, patient outcome optimization, and early warning of acute decompensation (Giordano et al., 2021).

Rish stratification refers to stratifying patients of different diseases and stages, helping clinicians to identify high risks, and making resources optimization and designing best treatment plans. Rish stratification can work throughout the treatment process, from preoperative preparations, perioperative reactions, to postoperative complications. The proactive AI models utilized by doctors can alleviate such destructive effects. Results suggested that these machine learning models can predict more accurate mortality rate for liver cancer surgery, aortic aneurysm surgery, and cardiac surgery, and provide more human value-based care. In addition, AI models enable continuing calculations of risks in the longitudinal period, which can warn doctors about some sudden changes, such as hypotension. By incorporating risk stratification data during the whole phases, identifying potential risks, and detecting complications, AI models can maximize the benefits of patients and provide more timely, accurate, efficient, and relatively affordable healthcare.

It is crucial to optimize each patient's outcome in the decision-making process and patient care procedures. Despite good intentions, human errors may sometimes deviate from established protocols in the complex patient care environment. However, based on multi-dimensional data, machine learning and analysis models can optimize objective functions, such as determining the best medication dosage. Tools like decision trees, which combine expert opinions with systematic algorithms for disease and treatment models, have been used in various scenarios ranging from optimizing surgical outcomes to improving the management of chronic diseases and acute conditions.

Acute decompensation is not a frequent phenomenon, but once come, much more severe results follow. This attaches significance to avoiding being involved in vicious physiological circles. In fact, there are six to eight hours before the acute decompensation to take intervening measures. The AI early-warning systems can study the data from electronic health records and therefore monitor subtle alarms of patients' decompensation. One application example is the algorithm used in operating room, known as the Hypotension Prediction Index, which had been integrated into the Edwards monitoring system. This model is designed to detect impending hypotension signs, and pinpoint the causes for the estimated hypotension phenomenon, such as vasoplegia, hypovolemia, and cardiac contractility. In essence, with AI-equipped monitoring systems, handling large volumes of electronic health records becomes seamless, allowing early detection and treatment for high-risk patients, of which the task surpasses what clinicians and physicians typically achieve (Wijnberge et al., 2020).

3.2.5 Potential Biases and Ethical Considerations

Concerns about potential biases arose with the growing popularity of AI in personal and public healthcare domain, where AI solutions led to inadvertent biases due to the data used for training and testing, and even the mechanism of the model itself (O'Reilly-Shah et al., 2020). To be more specific, common biases intervene AI model are the failure to consider genders, ages, and races differences. The findings by Weber et al. (2017), for instance, suggested that the strategy of data "completeness" in the adoption of electronic health records could bring about pernicious effects, causing biases towards those elderly female patients. Researchers find that some datasets largely consist of white people, or the light-skinned patients, leaving intrinsic biases and disadvantages for public health system (Buolamwini & Gebru, 2018).

These AI models lack linearities and extensive interactions among potential variables and constraints, thus exposing flaws and challenges in real-life scenarios. Being able to cater to every individual has always been a constant goal for human-centered AI. Future AI algorithms can work on improving their adaptability and flexibility, which can be achieved by initial programming, supervised or unsupervised machine learning, and reinforcement learning (RL) to widen the database.

The double-edged AI's participation can be a disruption to people's decision-making process, where the trust and transparency can be compromised (Kaggwa et al., 2024). The research of Meske and Bunde (2020) put forward the concept of

"Black Box", which indicated the complicated AI algorithms led to the lack of trust and transparency, whereas this issue could be addressed by the "Explainable AI" (XAI) principle for human-AI collaboration. This principle can greatly enhance the sense of security and accountability, therefore, facilitating more practical applications of AI.

Figure 3. The waxing and waning explainability and accuracy of black box, grey box, and white box (Ali et al., 2023)

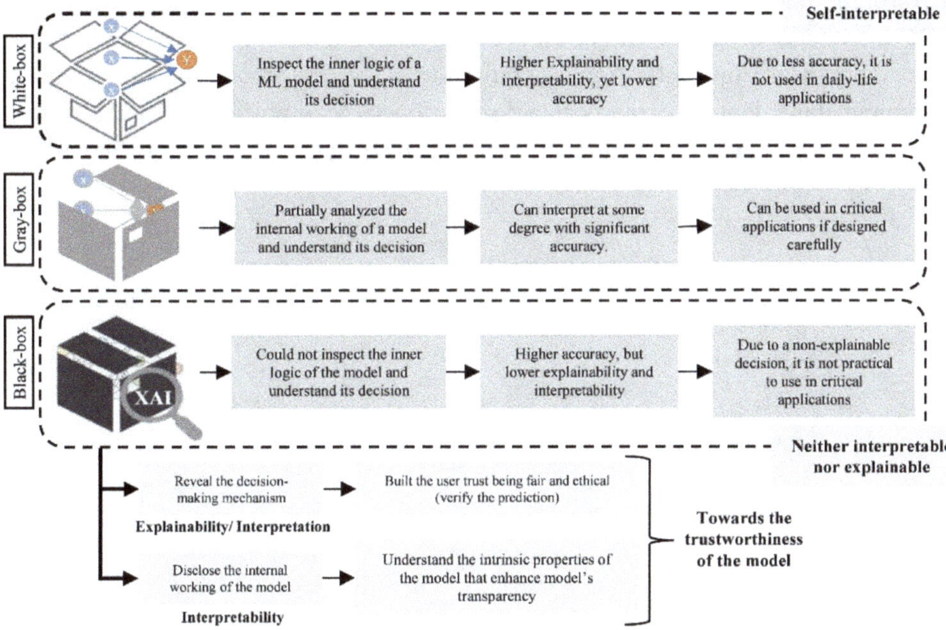

Usually, the simpler the AI models are, the more easily comprehensible and self-interpretable they are; the more accurate AI models might leave people with the aforementioned Black Box conundrum. Researchers categorize three situations in Figure 3 (Ali et al., 2023), where black-box AI models are more accurate but less interpretable, and white-box AI models are interpretable by design thus making their outputs easier to understand but decreasingly accurate. The grey-box AI models yield a balanced accuracy and interpretability trade-off. XAI aims at making AI more trustworthy and understandable, empowering individuals to combat any negative consequences of automated decision-making and to make more informed choices, while trying to integrate human-centered values throughout the process.

3.3 AI as Biomedical Technology

3.3.1 Conceptualizaion

Brain Computer Interface (BCI) or Brain-Machine Interface (BMI) refers to the technologies designed to communicate with the central nervous system and neural sensory organs, which establishes an independent channel between the brain and external muscle movement, benefiting people with neurodegenerative diseases like amyotrophic lateral sclerosis, or acquired brain injuries (Zhang et al., 2020). BCI or BMI, embedded with AI modules, is usually carried out through five successive stages (shown in Figure 4): signal acquisition stage, preprocessing or signal enhancement stage, feature extraction and selection stage, feature classification stage and the control interface or graphical user interface stage (Yadav et al., 2020).

Figure 4. Schematic of BCI process (Yadav et al., 2020)

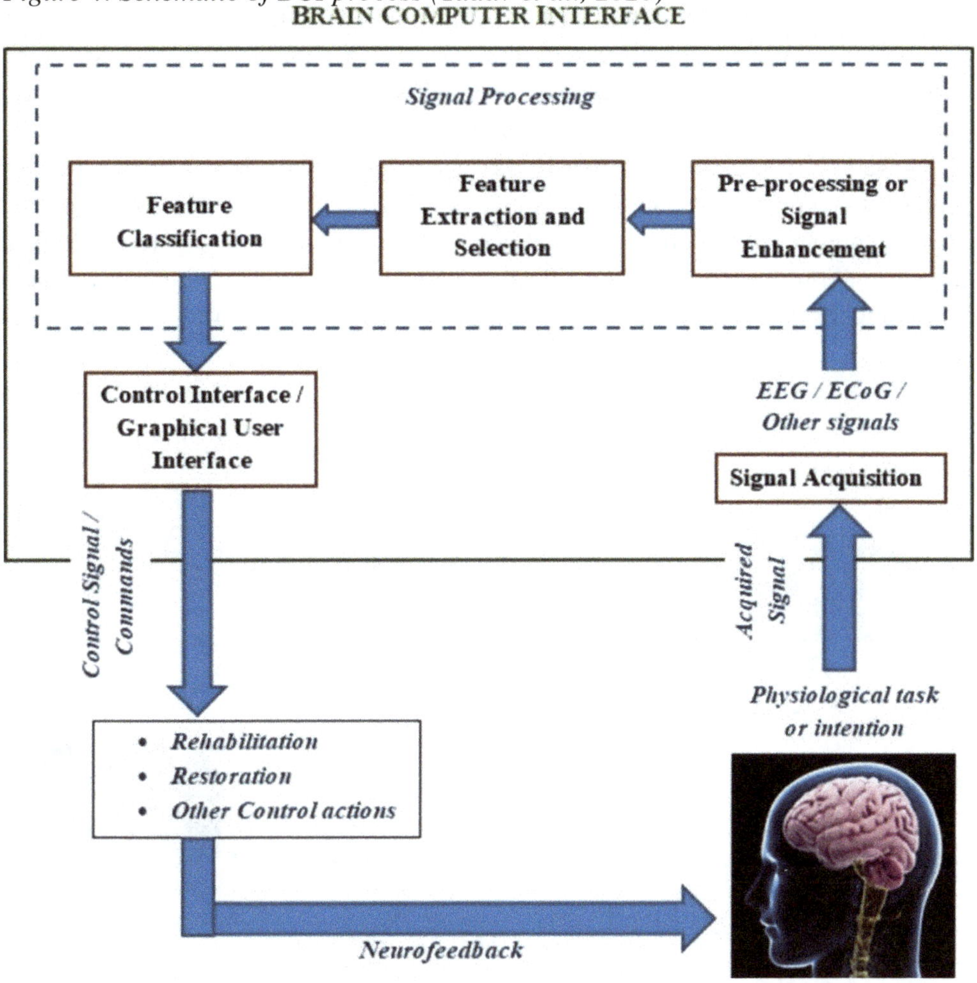

In the latest enrollment advertisement video of Tsinghua University 2024, named "Miracle," they introduced the first case where they helped a paraplegic patient recover movement by harnessing consciousness to control the impaired body (*Tsinghua University, 2024*). They successfully implanted brain-machine devices during the first clinical trial on October 24th, 2023. It is reported that after three months of brain-computer interface rehabilitation training, the patient could drive pneumatic gloves through brain electrical activity and perform brain-controlled functions such as drinking water independently. Additionally, the ASIA clinical score and sensory evoked potential response of the patient with spinal cord injury were significantly improved. So, what is the magic behind this cutting-edge technique? And how does AI contribute to this field?

The research and applications regarding BCI domain have grown rapidly and become increasingly matured over the past 20 years with the help of AI, especially the machine learning algorithms (Perdikis & Millan, 2020). According to Zhang et al. (2020), AI had notable advancements in the analysis and decoding of human neural activities, boosting the field of BCIs.

Nowadays, it is safe to say that BCIs have changed the game, altering the way human interact with computers and opening up new ways people understanding and utilizing human's brain power. Even it is now the dawn of digital and technological transformation, the combination of AI and BCIs is a glittering topic in research and clinical practices. AI has played an important role and served as an essential base for BCIs.

Figure 5. Graphic description of BCIs based on AI (Zhang et al., 2020)

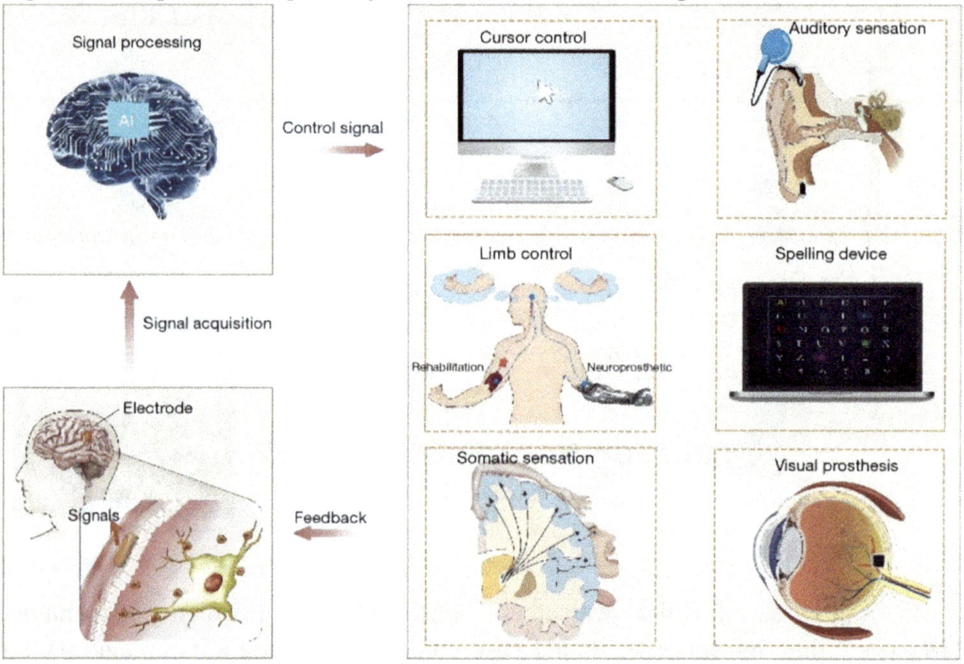

As shown in Figure 5, the circuit includes four procedures which combine BCIs and AI technologies (Zhang et al., 2020). The first step starts with the electrodes embedded in human brain, detecting the signals from central neural systems. Second, the electrodes send signal acquisition to AI algorithms to process the information. After decoding the instructions, AI systems output control signals to proceed with various actions, such as cursor control, limb control, somatic sensation, auditory sensation, spelling device, and visual prosthesis. Finally, the brain will receive feedbacks and make adjustments to instructions, where the cycle of AI and BCIs starts again.

3.3.2 Demonstration of BCI Classification

Previous scholars have classified BCIs according to three dimensions, which include the level of invasiveness, synchronization, and dependability. Additionally, BCIs are divided into two categories based on the origins of the input signals: exogenous and endogenous. Based on these criteria, a brief classification is illustrated below (in Figure 6).

Figure 6: Classification of BCIs

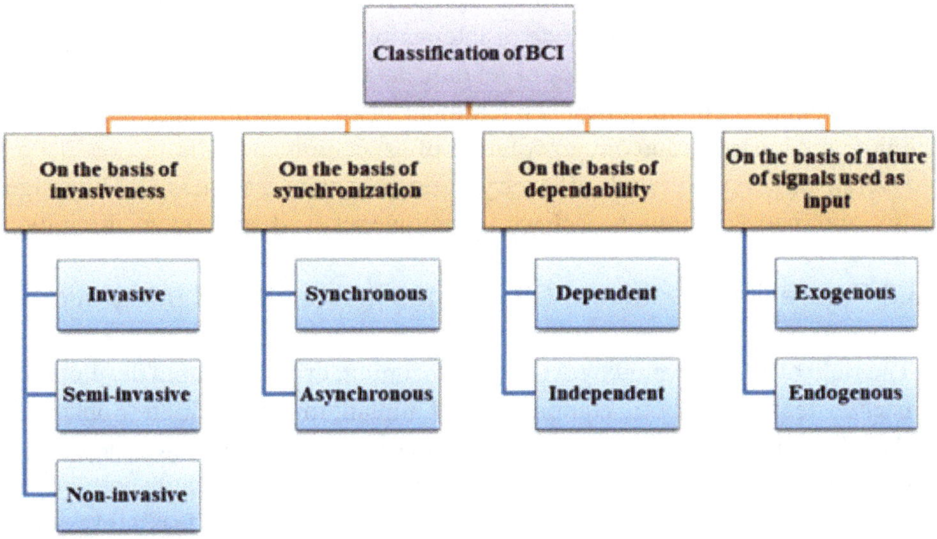

The measurement of brain activity offers choices ranging from invasive, semi-invasive, to non-invasive methods, each with its own advantages and disadvantages that cater to human-centric considerations. Invasive BCIs entail embedding microelectrodes into human brain beneath the skull during neurosurgical operation, offering exceptional signal quality but posing risks of tissue injury and limiting the measurement area. Alternatively, semi-invasive BCIs position electrodes beneath the skull, leveraging Electrocorticography (ECoG) for comparatively longer-term stability, superior spatial resolution, and reduced noise sensitivity. Non-invasive BCIs, on the other hand, capture brain signals from the scalp's surface, circumventing surgical risks of penetration yet compromising on signal quality and spatial resolution. Regardless of their poor quality, non-invasive BCIs still remain the most recommended option due to its minimal trauma to the brain, which adumbrates the human-centered principle that the human interests overweigh the potential shortages.

Based on the characteristics of synchronization and the natural modes of operation, BCIs can be defined as another two classifications: synchronous (cue-paced) and asynchronous (self-paced). In synchronous BCIs, individuals can control the system with the aid of some visual cues, with existing awareness of the exact time human brain will start working. This method bypassed antiquated facial expressions (i.e. blinks and eye movements) to analyze brain activities, where brain signals might be disregarded. While synchronous BCIs offer the advantage of easy performance evaluation, they also come with drawbacks. The reliance on visual cues can make them inconvenient for communication with external environments and can diminish the naturalness of interaction. The second one, asynchronous BCIs enable humans to perform mental activities at their own preferred pace without prompts from the machines, providing a natural mode of interaction. Given the freedom for users to decide their comfortable frequency of sending data, it puts pressure on the designers and programmers to distinguish the intentional and non-intentional control signals, adding to the intricacy and circumvolution of asynchronous BCIs.

Overall, these types of BCIs offer varying degrees of invasiveness, stability, signal quality, and spatial resolution, each with its unique set of advantages and limitations.

3.3.3 Future Prospects and Challenges in AI and BCI Integration

The field of BCI powered by AI is ever-changing, driven by rapid developments of machine learning, robotic equipment, and implant miniaturization (Sonko et al., 2024). With such techniques, people can better leverage BCIs to decode brain activity and output robotic performances. These enhancements include both invasive and non-invasive BCIs, with increased accuracy, robustness, and feasibility of BCIs and neural rehabilitation technologies.

While having a positive prospect, a spectrum of challenges comes along with it. Physiologically, people's neurological conditions are a rather complex variable, as they can be altered by age, gender, state of mind, memory capacity, and any other possible factors. Therefore, a good BCI design should take into account those variations and fluctuations so that it can be applied to a wider range of users. Technologically, BCIs face inevitable issues, such as wireless connectivity, signal decoding, and electrical stimulation. The current BCI paradigms need to improve the resolution of signals, while maintaining the intrinsic characteristics of BCIs, such as convenience, efficiency, safety, and mobility. Attention should also be paid to BCI illiteracy issues, as some people may have difficulty using the interface due to a lack of knowledge and guidance about it.

4. CASES

4.1 A Novel AI Distribution Service Platform

A successful AI-based service platform in a health center is named as Artificial Intelligence Distribution Interface for healthcare (AIDI). Building upon prior successful AI-based healthcare applications, AIDI has enhanced its capabilities to offer health assessment, healthcare evaluation, and cognitive assistance for researchers, healthcare service providers, clinicians, and patients (Väänänen et al., 2021).

This innovative AIDI platform is designed to offer a user-friendly interface, facilitating easy access for healthcare service providers, healthcare information technology companies, and researchers to employ cutting-edge third-party or proprietary AI methods applicable to specific healthcare scenarios. It comprises cloud-based AI services that seamlessly integrate with the healthcare service platforms of various end-user organizations through open application programming interfaces (APIs).

Figure 7. Basic architecture of AIDI (Väänänen et al., 2021)

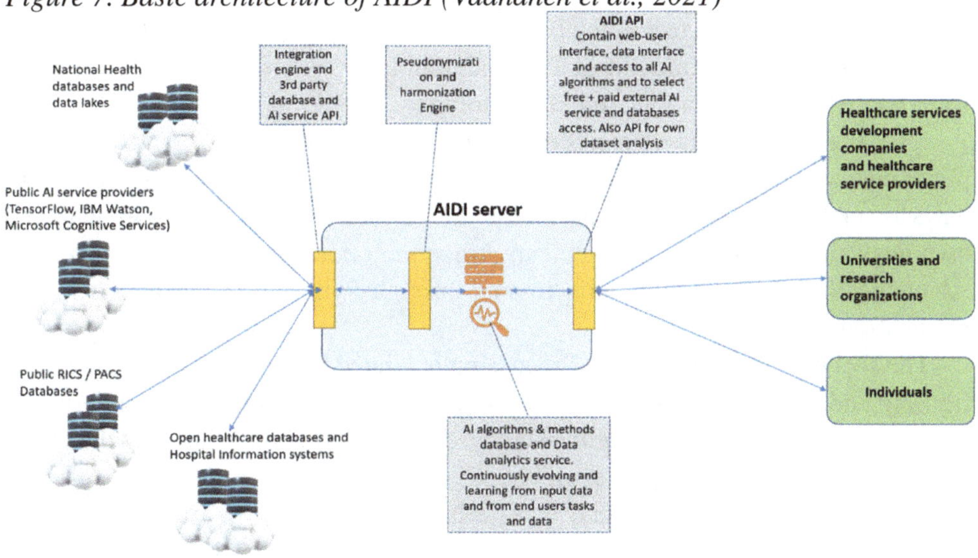

Figure 7 demonstrates the architectural framework of AIDI platform. The AIDI services are operated in the cloud-based environment like Microsoft Azur, gaining data repository interfaces from national health databases, public organization information systems, and AI service companies. Meanwhile, with AI algorithms and continuous evolution and learning, healthcare centers, research organizations, and individuals can get the results. The whole process showcases the human-in-the-loop principle, which is aligned with the original intention – being human-centered.

Figure 8. AIDI technology stack (Väänänen et al., 2021)

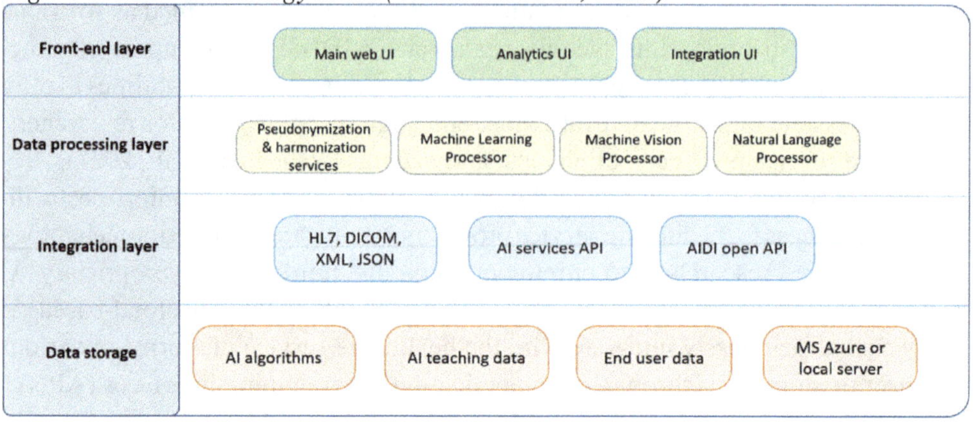

Figure 8 shows AIDI technology stack components, which enable AIDI platform to parallel process vast amounts of data with four layers of technologies: Front-End, Data Processing, Integration, and Data Storage.

First, the Front-end layer refers to a web-based user interface (UI) for main application features like graphic tools, database selection, and analytics. It then opens ways for analytical views for end users to analyze processed data and implement their own analysis. For developers, they can utilize the platform to check and compare AI methods, and made some adjustments through Python or other programming applications.

The second layer named Data Processing is related to processing and analyzing training and user data using AI-based processes. Pseudonymization and harmonization ensure data security and consistency, especially when dealing with data from various sources. Different processors handle tasks like machine learning, machine vision for image recognition, and natural language processing for tasks like text classification and machine translation. Various third-party machine learning platforms and technologies are used for analysis and processing.

The third one is Integration Layer, of which the application programming interfaces (APIs) facilitate integration with external databases, such as radiology imaging services and hospital information systems, using standard messaging formats. External data can be utilized for training AI methods. APIs also integrate with third-party AI algorithms and services, and AIDI offers an open API for users to upload their own data and AI methods. Streaming service platforms aid in integration and data streaming.

Finally, the Data Storage Layer provide spaces for repositories of AI algorithms and teaching data, including data retrieved from external databases. End user databases maintain user and organization information. AIDI offers services for importing/exporting virtual machines and databases, making it easy to install on cloud services like Microsoft Azure or other local servers, catering to specific company or organizational needs.

The AIDI platforms possesses various functions in different application scenarios, including but not limited to personalized healthcare, identifying clinical errors, health monitoring, and virtual medical assistant. To be more specific, personalized medicine, which tailors medical treatment to individual patient characteristics, aims to detect diseases at earlier stages for more effective treatment. AIDI utilizes patient diagnosis data to suggest personalized treatments based on pre-trained AI methods. Secondly, in healthcare, AI methods play a crucial role in detecting medication errors and improving medication adherence. AIDI offers these AI methods as a service for healthcare providers, including screening systems for medication errors and monitoring medication intake using machine vision and neural networks. Additionally, AI significantly enhances medical image diagnostics, surpassing human accuracy and efficiency. AIDI offers validated AI methods for instant image analysis in various medical imaging applications. Health monitoring and preventive health solutions utilize AI for continuous monitoring, healthcare assessment, and personalized suggestions based on user parameters. AIDI provides periodic analytics and analysis to healthcare service development companies using collected data. This function can be applied in epidemic management, where AIDI predicts outbreaks by analyzing spatial and behavioral data and provides solutions to manage ongoing outbreaks. What is also noteworthy is the virtual nursing assistants powered by AI assist healthcare services in reducing hospital visits and healthcare professionals' workload. These assistants provide pre-diagnosis based on patient history and assessment data, contributing to improved patient care efficiency. Last but not the least, from the perspective of clinical trials, AIDI can help to identify suitable patients as candidates, which is vital for comprehensive trial designs with reduced costs. AI aids in clinical trial design, patient selection, and monitoring, leading to increased enrollment. AIDI facilitates this process by leveraging AI to identify eligible patients for clinical trials.

With wide functions mentioned above, AIDI can showcase remarkable efficiency in various medical domains, for instance, curing eye diseases, breast cancer, skin cancer, and predicting glucose levels (De Fauw et al., 2018; McKinney et al., 2020). In addition, it shows promise in tuberculosis diagnostics and psychosis prediction. Leveraging these successful AI methods, the AIDI platform can offer direct access for customers and end users to utilize these diagnostic tools, which would be rather wise and sensible during some pandemic.

4.2 SepsisLab: An Improved Module of Human-AI Collaboration Throughout Sepsis Diagnosis and Medical Decision Making

Sepsis, an acute infectious disease, requires longitudinal monitoring and early warning, where clinical experts often struggle to provide precise answers, or the conditions of patients can get life-threatening in minutes.

One of the existing AI models adopted in sepsis-related healthcare, for instance, is the Epic Sepsis Module (ESM) (i.e. EPIC). The ESM (EPIC) is a proprietary tool for predicting sepsis. It works in four major steps (shown in Figure 9):

Figure 9. Four steps workflow in sepsis medical decision-making with module of ESM (EPIC)

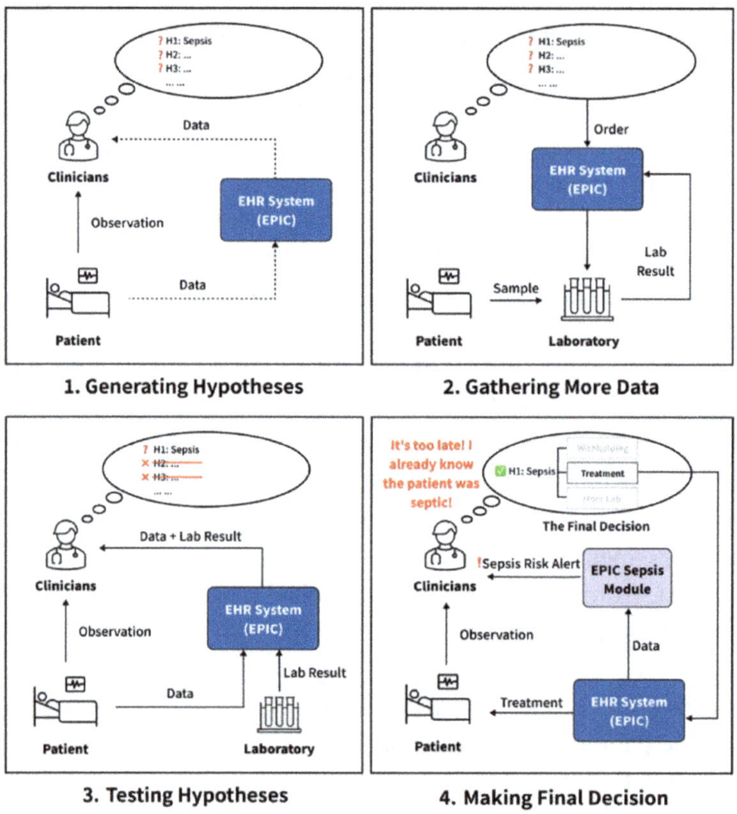

1. Generating Hypotheses: In the case of a patient at risk of sepsis, medical practitioners must frequently keep an eye on the individual's vital signs and current condition stored within the Electronic Health Record system. This initial

analysis generates a range of potential hypotheses, often clouded by significant uncertainty.

2. Gathering More Data: In light of the most plausible hypotheses, clinicians proceed to request specific laboratory examinations to gather additional data pertinent to these suppositions.
3. Testing Hypotheses: After receiving the results of the collected data and laboratory tests, physicians choose, refine or broaden their hypotheses based on the gathered data.
4. Making Final Decision: With the updated hypotheses, healthcare providers are tasked with selecting a course of action from three alternatives: initiating treatment, seeking further data, or adopting a wait-and-see approach for the evolution of the patient's condition.

Medical experts generally express optimism about the increased use of this AI model for medical decision-making in the future. However, there is a notable consensus regarding dissatisfaction with the current ESM. Some of the clinicians perceive this module as not only unhelpful but also contributing to superfluous work. Their discontent mainly stems from various factors:

1. Belated risk prefiguration: The timeliness of the risk prediction score within the ESM is often questioned, leading to potential issues in prompt intervention.
2. Lack of accuracy: Participants highlight inaccuracies in the predictions generated by the current ESM, potentially compromising personalized health care.
3. Lack of explanation: ESM only provide collected patients' information and experiment data, while the absence of transparent explanations regarding the ESM's predictions can leave clinicians without critical elaborations or actionable insights.
4. Erroneous focus, combined with the aforementioned shortcomings, leads to a sense of apprehension and disengagement among healthcare practitioners, ultimately resulting in the increased meaningless work and the disregard for the current sepsis AI module.

In response to the constant need in sepsis healthcare domain, scientists examined the drawbacks of the abandoned Sepsis AI module and have developed an improved and more human-centered AI-based model known as SepsisLab, which provides better human-machine collaboration paradigm to support experts in high-uncertainty, high-risk, and time-sensitive decision-making tasks. Those researchers designed five strategies of the new AI model:

Design Strategy 1: Performing Future Risk Score Prediction

According to their formative research findings, clinicians require accurate and timely risk score predictions rather than delayed and unreliable ones. Previous empirical studies on sepsis diagnosis have also emphasized the need to enhance the algorithm in the system's back-end to meet this requirement.

Design Strategy 2: Providing Accessible Model Explanation

Their interview results also signify the significance of an easy access to the explanations about the future risk score prediction. This issue is commonly highlighted in prior research. SepsisLab aims to implement a simple design that presents explanations in an easily accessible and comprehensible manner.

Design Strategy 3: Revealing Actionable Insights and Suggestions

Furthermore, predicting future risk scores alone is far from providing pragmatic insights. Clinicians rely on patients' physical signs and laboratory test values to make diagnostic decisions, with data collection (such as lab tests) being essential. Therefore, SepsisLab will offer meaningful recommendations by displaying potential lab tests.

Design Strategy 4: Displaying Uncertainty beyond the Risk Score

Apart from risk scores, sepsis diagnosis will also calculate and present the uncertainty during the decision-making process. While people take more factors into consideration, they tend to make more sensible decisions. This is in line with the encomium about Explainable AI, stating that

Design Strategy 5: Shifting AI from Suggesting the Final Decision to Supporting Intermediate Stages.

Lastly, a significant finding from their formative research prefigures the shifting power in AI related healthcare application. The AI-based sepsis modules mainly focus on final decisions, arousing friction with physicians and leading to module rejection. To step out of this dilemma, SepsisLab will support clinicians starting from intermediate decision-making stages, like hypothesis generation and data collection. This strategy fosters a new human-centered collaboration model, where AI prioritizes experts' and patients' needs.

The combined application of the five strategies is auspiciously depicted in the new AI module, as illustrated in Figures 9 and 10.

Figure 10. User interface of SepsisLab prototype system.

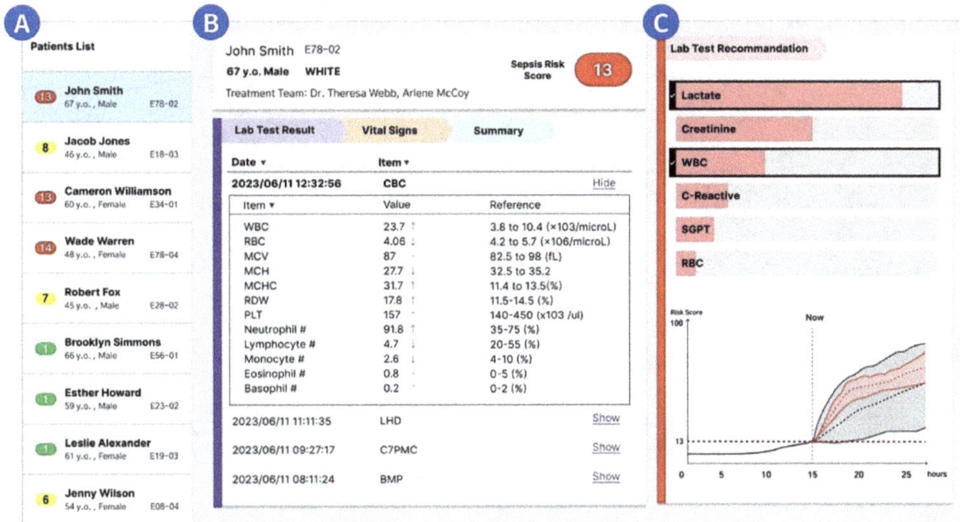

In Figure 10, it is noticeable that Column A is a set of patient's names with varying different risk prediction scores, ranging from no risk as Green, to medium risk as Yellow, to high risk as Red. In the middle of the user interface (Part B), patient's vital signs, lab test results, and medical history are displayed clearly. Part C is where SepsisLab system adds onto the existing electronic health records system, with visualized illustration of high-risk patient's data examined by experts 15 hours ago and to predict the next 25 hours, valuing uncertainty by showcasing lab test recommendations.

Figure 11. Four steps workflow in sepsis medical decision-making with support from SepsisLab

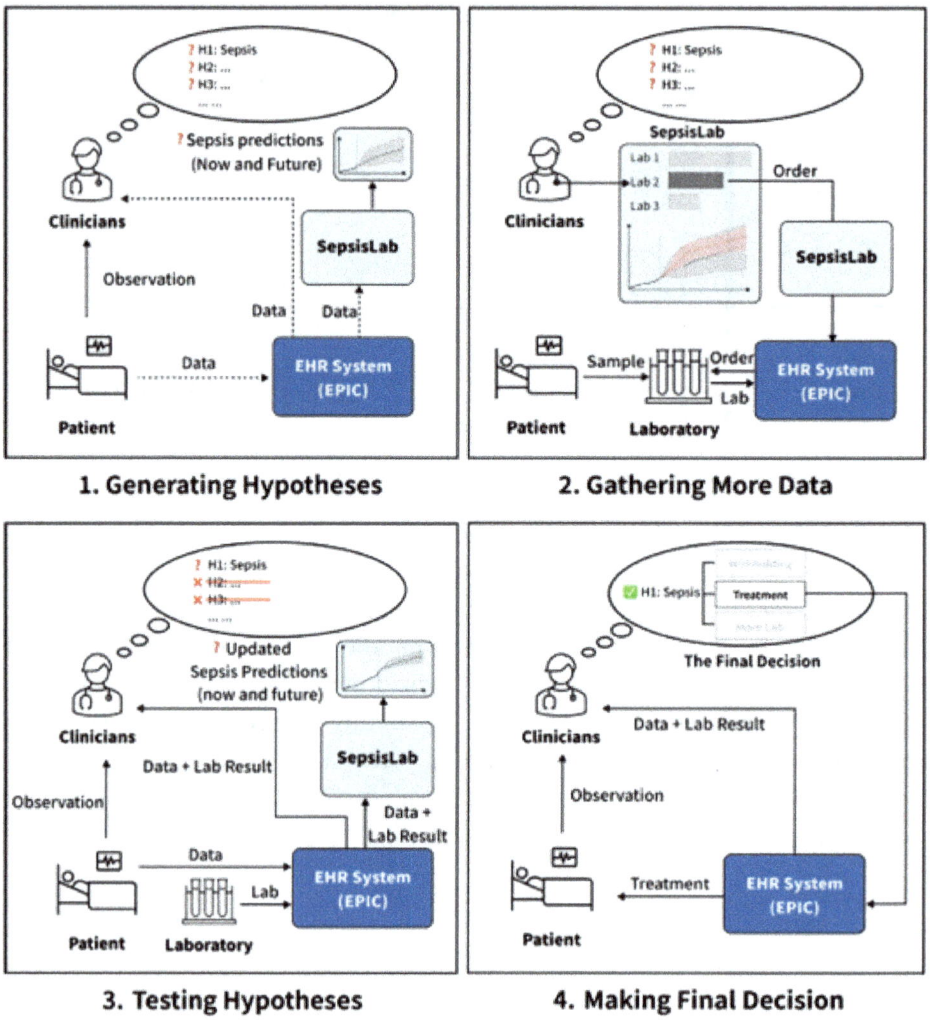

SepsisLab is built on a state-of-the-art AI algorithm, with extensive functions in aspects: the forecast of sepsis development, the visualization of prediction uncertainty, and the proposal of actionable suggestions, like offering additional information about laboratory tests to reduce uncertainties. The Figure 10 gives a clear demonstration of the workflow of SepsisLab, which integrated the human-centered design strategies and new functions of the AI module.

In the first step (in Figure 11), Sepsis generates predictions both for now and future, aligning with Design Strategy 1 and 4, analyzing future risk scores and uncertainty. Additionally, it suggests further lab tests based on their impact on model uncertainty, which aligns with Design Strategy 2. The second step generates interactive visualization which can aid clinicians in selecting the most valuable lab tests to support their decisions, displaying Design Strategy 3 and 4. Once new data are collected, the prediction visualization is updated (Step 3), enabling clinicians to test their hypotheses. This process is in accordance with Design Strategy 5, allowing clinicians to generate new hypotheses or reach final decisions, as demonstrated in Step 4. In this way, SepsisLab favorably meets experts needs in the intermediate stages of the medical decision-making process, rather than merely participating in arriving at the final decision. Beside benefits mentioned above, SepsisLab also provides counterfactual information by leading an alternative trajectory lab test, which will increase the decision-making transparency, saving time and effort for researchers in the thinking process and have a better understanding of its functions and processes.

Last but not the least, researchers still remind users of the potential risks and ethical concerns associated with the latest proposed AI-human collaborative model. For instance, interactive visualizations can cause additional cognitive burdens for clinicians, and some errors and biases are unavoidable in AI algorithms. Therefore, expert intelligence is required to minimize these defects. Additionally, researchers suggest that medical professionals should remain alert to over-dependency on AI systems, as this can foster complacency and reduce acumen in healthcare-related decision-making.

In a nutshell, with the guidance of educational and exploratory suggestions by clinicians using this new model, SepsisLab adumbrates a promising future where the AI-assisted and human-centered collaboration paradigm helps to address problems in sepsis diagnosis and other high-risks medical decision-making scenarios.

4.3 Convergence of AI and BCIs: A New Era of Brain-Machine Interface

As previously discussed, AI has played a pivotal role in brain-computer interfaces (BCIs), significantly facilitating disability empowerment and performance enhancement through movement restoration and mind-driven communication (Jaber et al., 2024).

There are several notable cases in the US demonstrating the pioneering role in BCIs realm (Sonko et al., 2024). There are notable projects in non-invasive BCIs, in which a notable case by Das and Nathan-Roberts (2021). They introduced the BCIs paradigms to assist motor impairment by using non-invasive devices, such as wearable headbands and earbuds. This process involved cross-field utilization, including neurobiology, neuroscience, cognitive psychology, robotics, computer science, biomedical engineering, and electrical engineering. Signals from human brain are detected by magnetic resonance imaging and electroencephalography. With those functions, motor impaired people may be able to communicate and move autonomously in a completely non-invasive manner.

Moreover, for the invasive devices, one representative project named the BrainGate Neural Interface System, concentrates on participants with quadriparesis, meaning a condition of partial motor impairment in four limbs (Figueiredo et al., 2013). Quadriparesis can result from spinal cord injury, brainstem stroke, and motor neuron disease. This study, part of the BrainGate feasibility study, is noted as the largest (12,203 days' records of safety experiences) and longest-running (over 17 years) clinical trial of invasive BCIs (Rubin et al., 2023). Those patients from seven healthcare centers underwent surgeries to implant the BrainGate devices, taking in the shape of 1 or 2 microelectrode arrays in the motor cortex of the dominant cerebral hemisphere. The BrainGate system consists of three components as illustrated in Figure 12.

Figure 12. Constituents of BrainGate system

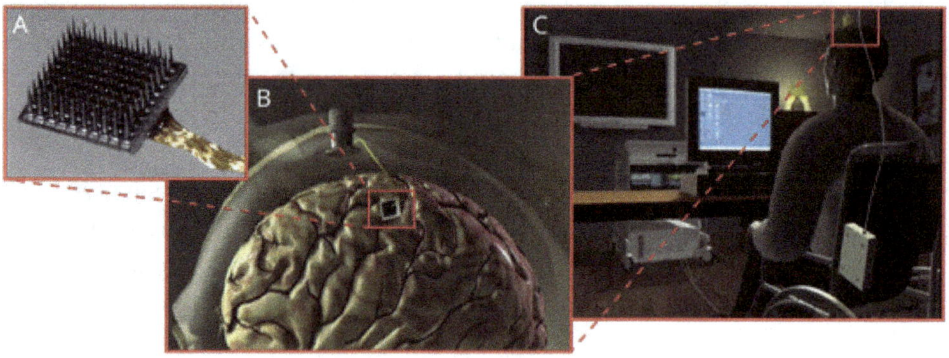

As illustrated in Figure 12, the system begins with a recording sensor that has 96 electrodes arranged on a small 4 × 4-mm platform (Part A), which is surgically implanted onto a specific area of the brain's surface (Part B). During the surgery, a pneumatic inserter wand will carefully apply an exact amount of force, aptly inserting the microelectrodes through the brain's outer layer and into the upper layers of the cortex. Then, a port is attached to the outer layer of the skull using medical titanium screws and connected to the microelectrode array with gold wires (Part B). When not in use, the port is covered with a disposable cap for protection purpose. Finally, brain signals are transmitted from the port to a decoding processor and then an output equipment, either wirelessly or through a cable (Part C), which completes the entire BCI circuit and exemplifies the principle of human-in-the-loop and human-centered AI applications.

A total of 14 patients, aged between 18 and 45 years old with quadriparesis, underwent implantation of BCI devices and experienced life with the BrainGate system for an average duration of 872 days. Among these participants, there were 68 device-related adverse events reported, including 6 serious adverse events. Common device-related or study-related adverse reactions included skin irritation around the percutaneous pedestal, infectious symptoms such as fever, and neurological issues like headaches, fatigue, seizures, and impaired hearing. Fortunately, it is noteworthy that there were no severe events leading to permanent disability or deaths associated with the BrainGate system. These results demonstrated that BrainGate is as safe as other long-term implantable medical equipment, providing both theoretical and empirical evidence for the long-term safety and efficacy of BCIs.

Researchers have noted both the advantages and disadvantages of invasive BrainGate devices. On the one hand, it is suggested that the BrainGate can improve the life quality of those individuals with paralysis. Firstly, it facilitates fast and convenient communication, allowing users of BrainGate to take control of a point-and-click interface with a highly accurate bidimensional censor at a speed of 30 to 40 correct characters per minute (CPM). Secondly, BrainGate is able to decode individual handwriting at a rate equivalent to a able-bodied person typing on a smartphone keyboard, reaching the rate of up to 90 CPM. Furthermore, apart from enhancing communication, the BrainGate system and other invasive BCIs have been employed to control assistive robotics and users' own arm and hand through functional electrical stimulation. Given this function, the intracortical system aims not only to restore interpersonal communication but also to empower mobility with individual autonomy and intuition, which sequently benefit human-centered control of functional electrical stimulation or wearable robotics. Additionally, its development may even contribute to closed-loop neuromodulation therapies for treating cure patients' disability in mental issues management, such as mood and cognition disorders. Nonetheless, the advantages can't overshadow the downsides that the current percutaneous component and substantial external hardware are suboptimal when compared to fully implanted or non-surgical approaches due to infection risks and the conspicuous electronic devices embedded in the head. Researchers have been and will continue to be committed to reducing adverse reactions and improving the cosmetic and aesthetic outcomes of the BrainGate system, with the propelling waves of the AI revolution.

Elon Musk, the well-known owner of Tesla and SpaceX, launched his AI company xAI last July, introducing the grandiose mission of "truthful, competent and maximally beneficial for all humanity." While the fulfillment of xAI's mission is yet to be seen, the company announced a $6 billion Series B funding round on May 26th this year for product research and development across various fields, including the healthcare sector, as reported by American Hospital Association in 2024. A healthcare analyst expresses his belief that xAI could revolutionize the healthcare domain, mirroring other tech giants' efforts to increase task automation, improve clinical workflows and optimize clinician productivity.

With the launch of the Grok-1 AI model in November, xAI began laying the groundwork for its system, boasting strong textual capability to answer almost any question. The company released an updated Grok-1.5 model and the GroK-1.5V with understanding of various images on April 12th, 2024. These and other tools create a training base model that can be adapted to everyday medical workflows.

Under Musk's ownership, he can bring parallel interests to another company, Neuralink, which has demonstrated achievement in its BCI technology. Similarly to BrainGate, Neuralink is working on enabling quadriplegics to control computers and mobile devices with their thoughts (*American Hospital Association, 2024*). In Neuralink's white paper of 2019, they described their first attempt toward a scalable high-bandwidth BCI system, which built arrays of small and flexible electrode "threads," with as many as 3072 electrodes per array distributed across 96 threads. They also designed a neurosurgical robot capable of inserting six threads (192 electrodes) per minute. Each thread can be individually inserted into the brain with micron precision for avoidance of surface vasculature and targeting specific brain regions. The electrode array is packaged into a small implantable device that contains custom chips for low-power on-board amplification and digitization. The package for 3072 channels occupying less than $23 \times 18.5 \times 2$ mm^3, marking unprecedented packaging density and scalability in a clinically relevant package (Musk, 2019).

In January of 2024, Neuralink announced its first implantation case of BCI technology in their PRIME study (Precise Robotically Implanted Brain-Computer Interface) to evaluate the safety of implants and surgical robots and assess the initial functionality of BCIs enabling patients with quadriplegia from spinal cord injury (SCI) or with amyotrophic lateral sclerosis (ALS) to intuitively control external devices. The first PRIME study was successfully performed in Barrow Neurological Institute in Phoenix, Arizona on a paralyzed adult, who was discharged from the ward the next day and underwent a smooth postsurgical recovery. Prior to the surgery, functional magnetic resonance imaging (fMRI) examinations were conducted to identify a specific area to embed the implants later. The fMRI study locates the targeted zone in the cortical regions that becomes significantly active when people performing certain movements. And on the official operation day, the surgery consisted of the exposure of the target region of the cortex by a professional neurosurgeon (e.g., scalp incision, craniectomy, durectomy), the insertion of threads and implants by a surgical robot, and the final stage of craniectomy and closing the scalp by the neurosurgeon.

It is reported that about 18 thousands American people suffered from SCI every year. The associate professor in Barrow Neurological Institute and an investigator of the PRIME Study Rory Murphy held supportive opinion, saying that "When an injury occurs to our human brain or spinal cord, it can disrupt the normal functioning of the entire nervous system. This can affect a person's ability to perform daily tasks. We remain hopeful that a BCI device may enable a digital bridge between the brain and spinal cord to potentially improve the quality of life for people with severe SCI." The first success of PRIME study and NeuraLink marks a significant milestone in AI's potential to address unmet medical needs and restore human autonomy. Forbes contributor Sai Balasubramanian, M.D., J.D., noted that while xAI and Neuralink are not directly related at present, there is significant potential for cross-pollination between the platforms.

The first user of Neuralink, Noland Arbaugh, is a 30-year-old Arizona resident. Arbaugh, who has been paralyzed below the middle of his neck since 2016, has shared his experience how the N1 chip (the Link) has helped him not only reconnect to the computer but also to the world (Leffer, 2024). He said that: "If I had lost my memory, and I woke up, and you told me there was something implanted in my brain, then I probably wouldn't believe you." This statement showed the minimal wound after the surgery that could be ignored. As for the outcomes, Arbaugh was able to move a digital cursor within a week after the surgery, with two methods—"attempted movement" and "imagined movement". Arbaugh said he used his device for hours at a time to browse the Web, send text messages, scroll social media, navigate apps and play video games. The device had one unavoidable drawback which needed to be regularly charged. However, the seamless experience with the N1 chip, namely the Link, stopped working in February. Arbaugh wasn't discouraged by the setback. In his view, everything he had gone through held one purpose: to improve the technology for others in future.

Most recently, Neuralink announced its second successful brain implant on August 6, 2024, which shows improvements of device allowing the user to control a computer cursor with their thoughts (Naddaf & Drew, 2024). Elon Musk predicted that there would be eight more BCI cases of Neuralink this year.

BrainGate and Neuralink represent pivotal advancements in AI-based BCI technology, each contributing uniquely to the evolution of neuroengineering. BrainGate's robust clinical validation and precise neural control capabilities underscore its effectiveness in restoring mobility and communication. In the meanwhile, Neuralink's innovative approach with precise implantation techniques and minimal invasive wounds promises a broader accessibility and integration into paralyzed people's daily life. Both of the BCI application cases display the human-centered principle by prioritizing user empowerment and enhancing quality of life, continuously fueling future innovations in the fields of neurotechnology and healthcare.

5. CONCLUSION

The chapter has studied and discussed multifaceted domains of human-centered AI in healthcare, shedding light on the transformative influence of this state-of-the art technology on various prominent aspects such as the AI-embedded service platform, decision-making process, and brain-machine interface biotechnology. These advancements signal a future where healthcare is not only more efficient and personalized but also more inclusive, with human involvement and ethical considerations placed at the forefront. The ongoing innovations may work on reducing costs and mitigating risks, making such AI-driven healthcare more accessible and reliable for the whole society. By prioritizing humanity and humanistic values, the application of AI in healthcare ensures that both patients and clinicians experience significant improvements, whether through dramatic breakthroughs or more subtle, yet still meaningful, enhancements.

As AI transitions from a conceptual possibility in literature or films, to a tangible reality in the current era where every unit of the society is digitally integrated, its impact on healthcare becomes unprecedentedly profound. This shift underscores the need for a broader and deeper commitment to AI from all sectors of society, including the government, academia, healthcare industry, and social welfare organizations. Their joint efforts are of great significance not only for reaping the immediate benefits that AI brings about but also for creating a sustainable and ethical framework that will allow AI to continue to evolve and enhance public health on a global scale. By fostering a culture of trust and collaboration around AI, we can ensure that its potential is fully realized, leading to a healthier, more equitable world for future generations.

Looking ahead, the integration of AI in healthcare will likely continue to push the boundaries of what is possible nowadays, from precisely predictive analytics to unique treatment. This evolution will require ongoing vigilance to ensure that the deployment of AI remains aligned with core human values, particularly as the technology becomes more pervasive. Moreover, as AI-driven tools and systems become increasingly popular in healthcare, greater importance should be attached to interdisciplinary collaboration, in which professionals in the fields of technology, medicine, ethics, and law will gather together and navigate the complex landscape of AI in a way that maximizes benefits while defending against potential harms.

In conclusion, the advent of AI in healthcare is not just a technological advancement but a paradigm shift that holds the promise of revolutionizing the way human approach health and well-being. The key to releasing the great potential lies in a cohesive contribution to embrace AI with a focus on human-centered values, ensuring that the technology unremittingly fuel the human experience rather than diminish it. As human continue to explore and refine the applications of AI in healthcare, it is necessary that people do so with a clear vision of how these advancements can conduce to a healthier, more equitable, and more humane world.

REFERENCES

Ali, S., Abuhmed, T., El-Sappagh, S., Muhammad, K., Alonso-Moral, J. M., Confalonieri, R., Guidotti, R., Del Ser, J., Díaz-Rodríguez, N., & Herrera, F. (2023). Explainable Artificial Intelligence (XAI): What we know and what is left to attain trustworthy artificial intelligence. *Information Fusion*, *99*, 101805. DOI: 10.1016/j.inffus.2023.101805

American Hospital Association. (2024). Can Elon Musk disrupt health care's booming AI field? American Hospital Association. https://www.aha.org/aha-center-health-innovation-market-scan/2024-06-04-can-elon-musk-disrupt-health-cares-booming-ai-field

Asgher, U., Ayaz, Y., & Taiar, R. (2023). Advances in artificial intelligence (AI) in brain computer interface (BCI) and Industry 4.0 for human machine interaction (HMI) [Editorial]. *Frontiers in Human Neuroscience*, *17*, 1320536. Advance online publication. DOI: 10.3389/fnhum.2023.1320536 PMID: 38116236

Barbierato, E., & Gatti, A. (2024). The challenges of machine Learning: A critical review. *Electronics (Basel)*, *13*(2), 416. DOI: 10.3390/electronics13020416

Benlian, A., Kettinger, W. J., Sunyaev, A., & Winkler, T. J. (2018). The transformative value of cloud computing: A decoupling, platformization, and recombination theoretical framework. *Journal of Management Information Systems*, *35*(3), 719–739. DOI: 10.1080/07421222.2018.1481634

Bohr, A., & Memarzadeh, K. (2020). The rise of artificial intelligence in healthcare applications. In Bohr, A., & Memarzadeh, K. (Eds.), *Artificial Intelligence in Healthcare* (pp. 25–60). Academic Press., DOI: 10.1016/B978-0-12-818438-7.00002-2

Buolamwini, J., & Gebru, T. (2018, January). Gender shades: Intersectional accuracy disparities in commercial gender classification. In Conference on fairness, accountability and transparency (pp. 77-91). PMLR.

Chen, M., & Decary, M. (2020). Artificial intelligence in healthcare: An essential guide for health leaders. *Healthcare Management Forum*, *33*(1), 10–18. DOI: 10.1177/0840470419873123 PMID: 31550922

Chong, J., Sin, C., & Kathiarayan, V. (2023). The role of artificial intelligence in strategic decision-making opportunities, challenges, and implications for managers in the digital age. https://www.researchgate.net/publication/370869247_The_Role_of_Artificial_Intelligence_in_Strategic_Decision-Making_Opportunities_Challenges_and_Implications_for_Managers_in_the_Digital_Age

Das, A., & Nathan-Roberts, D. (2021). Non-invasive brain–computer interfaces: Development and rehabilitation for motor disability. *Proceedings of the Human Factors and Ergonomics Society Annual Meeting*, *65*(1), 1264–1268. DOI: 10.1177/1071181321651299

De Fauw, J., Ledsam, J. R., Romera-Paredes, B., Nikolov, S., Tomasev, N., Blackwell, S., Askham, H., Glorot, X., O'Donoghue, B., Visentin, D., van den Driessche, G., Lakshminarayanan, B., Meyer, C., Mackinder, F., Bouton, S., Ayoub, K., Chopra, R., King, D., Karthikesalingam, A., & Ronneberger, O. (2018). Clinically applicable deep learning for diagnosis and referral in retinal disease. *Nature Medicine*, *24*(9), 1342–1350. DOI: 10.1038/s41591-018-0107-6 PMID: 30104768

Duan, Y., Edwards, J. S., & Dwivedi, Y. K. (2019). Artificial intelligence for decision making in the era of Big Data – evolution, challenges and research agenda. *International Journal of Information Management*, *48*, 63–71. DOI: 10.1016/j.ijinfomgt.2019.01.021

Dwivedi, Y. K., Hughes, L., Ismagilova, E., Aarts, G., Coombs, C., Crick, T., Duan, Y., Dwivedi, R., Edwards, J., Eirug, A., Galanos, V., Ilavarasan, P. V., Janssen, M., Jones, P., Kar, A. K., Kizgin, H., Kronemann, B., Lal, B., Lucini, B., & Williams, M. D. (2021). Artificial intelligence (AI): Multidisciplinary perspectives on emerging challenges, opportunities, and agenda for research, practice and policy. *International Journal of Information Management*, *57*, 101994. DOI: 10.1016/j.ijinfomgt.2019.08.002

Ferreira, J., & Monteiro, M. (2021). The human-AI relationship in decision-making: AI explanation to support people on justifying their decisions. https://doi.org//arXiv.2102.05460DOI: 10.48550

Figueiredo, N., Figueiredo, I. E., & Resnick, D. (2013). Tetraplegia or paraplegia with brachial diparesis? What is the most appropriate designation for the motor deficit in patients with lower cervical spinal cord injury? *Neurological Sciences*, *34*(2), 143–147. DOI: 10.1007/s10072-012-1160-4 PMID: 22825074

Giordano, C., Brennan, M., Mohamed, B., Rashidi, P., Modave, F., & Tighe, P. (2021). Accessing artificial intelligence for clinical decision-making. *Frontiers in Digital Health*, *3*, 645232. DOI: 10.3389/fdgth.2021.645232 PMID: 34713115

Jaber, W., Jaber, H. A., Jaber, R., & Saleh, Z. (2024). The convergence of AI and BCIs: A new era of brain-machine interfaces. *Artificial Intelligence in the Age of Nanotechnology*, 98-113. DOI: 10.4018/979-8-3693-0368-9.ch006

Javaid, M., Haleem, A., Pratap Singh, R., Suman, R., & Rab, S. (2022). Significance of machine learning in healthcare: Features, pillars and applications. *International Journal of Intelligent Networks*, *3*, 58–73. https://doi.org/doi.org/10.1016/j.ijin.2022.05.002. DOI: 10.1016/j.ijin.2022.05.002

Kaggwa, S., Eleogu, T. F., Okonkwo, F., Farayola, O. A., Uwaoma, P. U., & Akinoso, A. (2024). AI in decision making: Transforming business strategies. *International Journal of Innovation and Scientific Research*, *10*(12), 423–444. DOI: 10.51244/IJRSI.2023.1012032

Kaur, J., & Mann, K. S. (2018). AI based healthcare platform for real time, predictive and prescriptive analytics. In R. Sharma, A. Mantri, & S. Dua, *Computing, Analytics and Networks* Singapore. DOI: 10.1007/978-981-13-0755-3_11

Lee, C.-S., Wang, M.-H., Kuan, W.-K., Huang, S.-H., Tsai, Y.-L., Ciou, Z.-H., Yang, C.-K., & Kubota, N. (2023). BCI-based hit-loop agent for human and AI robot co-learning with AIoT application. *Journal of Ambient Intelligence and Humanized Computing*, *14*(4), 3583–3607. DOI: 10.1007/s12652-021-03487-0

Leffer, L. (2024). *What it's like to live with a brain chip, according to Neuralink's first user*. Scientific American. https://www.scientificamerican.com/article/neuralinks-first-user-describes-life-with-elon-musks-brain-chip/

Lins, S., Pandl, K. D., Teigeler, H., Thiebes, S., Bayer, C., & Sunyaev, A. (2021). Artificial intelligence as a service. *Business & Information Systems Engineering*, *63*(4), 441–456. DOI: 10.1007/s12599-021-00708-w

McKinney, S. M., Sieniek, M., Godbole, V., Godwin, J., Antropova, N., Ashrafian, H., Back, T., Chesus, M., Corrado, G. S., Darzi, A., Etemadi, M., Garcia-Vicente, F., Gilbert, F. J., Halling-Brown, M., Hassabis, D., Jansen, S., Karthikesalingam, A., Kelly, C. J., King, D., & Shetty, S. (2020). International evaluation of an AI system for breast cancer screening. *Nature*, *577*(7788), 89–94. DOI: 10.1038/s41586-019-1799-6 PMID: 31894144

Meissner, P., & Keding, C. (2021). *The Human Factor in AI-Based Decisions*. Massachusetts Institute of Technology. https://sloanreview.mit.edu/article/the-human-factor-in-ai-based-decision-making/

Meske, C., & Bunde, E. (2020). Transparency and trust in human-AI-interaction: The role of model-agnostic explanations in computer vision-based decision support. In H. Degen & L. Reinerman-Jones, *Artificial Intelligence in HCI* Cham.

Musk, E. (2019). An integrated Brain-Machine Interface platform with thousands of channels. *Journal of Medical Internet Research, 21*(10), e16194. DOI: 10.2196/16194 PMID: 31642810

Naddaf, M., & Drew, L. (2024). Second brain implant by Elon Musk's Neuralink: Will it fare better than the first? *Nature, 632*(8025), 481–482. DOI: 10.1038/d41586-024-02368-8 PMID: 39112576

O'Reilly-Shah, V. N., Gentry, K. R., Walters, A. M., Zivot, J., Anderson, C. T., & Tighe, P. J. (2020). Bias and ethical considerations in machine learning and the automation of perioperative risk assessment. *British Journal of Anaesthesia, 125*(6), 843–846. DOI: 10.1016/j.bja.2020.07.040 PMID: 32838979

Perdikis, S., & Millan, J. R. (2020). Brain-machine interfaces: A tale of two learners. *IEEE Systems, Man, and Cybernetics Magazine, 6*(3), 12–19. DOI: 10.1109/MSMC.2019.2958200

Pillai, A. S. (2023). AI-enabled hospital management systems for modern healthcare: An analysis of system components and interdependencies. *Journal of Advanced Analytics in Healthcare Management, 7*(1), 212–228. https://research.tensorgate.org/index.php/JAAHM/article/view/109

Rubin, D. B., Ajiboye, A. B., Barefoot, L., Bowker, M., Cash, S. S., Chen, D., Donoghue, J. P., Eskandar, E. N., Friehs, G., Grant, C., Henderson, J. M., Kirsch, R. F., Marujo, R., Masood, M., Mernoff, S. T., Miller, J. P., Mukand, J. A., Penn, R. D., Shefner, J., & Hochberg, L. R. (2023). Interim safety profile from the feasibility study of the BrainGate neural interface system. *Neurology, 100*(11), e1177–e1192. DOI: 10.1212/WNL.0000000000201707 PMID: 36639237

Russell, S. J., & Norvig, P. (2016). *Artificial intelligence: A modern approach.* Pearson.

Shaban-Nejad, A., Michalowski, M., Bianco, S., Brownstein, J. S., Buckeridge, D. L., & Davis, R. L. (2022). Applied artificial intelligence in healthcare: Listening to the winds of change in a post-COVID-19 world. *Experimental Biology and Medicine, 247*(22), 1969–1971. DOI: 10.1177/15353702221140406 PMID: 36426683

Sharma, D., Singh Aujla, G., & Bajaj, R. (2023). Evolution from ancient medication to human-centered Healthcare 4.0: A review on health care recommender systems. *International Journal of Communication Systems, 36*(12), e4058. DOI: 10.1002/dac.4058

Sonko, S., Fabuyide, A., Ibekwe, K. I., Etukudoh, E. A., & Ilojianya, V. I. (2024). Neural interfaces and human-computer interaction: A US review: Delving into the developments, ethical considerations, and future prospects of brain-computer interfaces. *International Journal of Science and Research Archive*, *11*(1), 702–717. DOI: 10.30574/ijsra.2024.11.1.0111

Sun, M., Wang, J., & Zhang, D. (2020). The progess that natural language processing has made towards human-level AI. *Journal of Artificial Intelligence Practice*, *3*(1), 38–47. DOI: 10.23977/jaip.2020.030107

Tsinghua University. (2024). 2024 Tsinghua University Admissions Film 'Miracle'. https://www.tsinghua.edu.cn/info/2160/112042.htm

Turchi, T., Prencipe, G., Malizia, A., Filogna, S., Latrofa, F., & Sgandurra, G. (2024). Pathways to democratized healthcare: Envisioning human-centered AI-as-a-service for customized diagnosis and rehabilitation. *Artificial Intelligence in Medicine*, *151*, 102850. DOI: 10.1016/j.artmed.2024.102850 PMID: 38555849

Väänänen, A., Haataja, K., Vehviläinen-Julkunen, K., & Toivanen, P. (2021). Proposal of a novel Artificial Intelligence Distribution Service platform for healthcare. *F1000 Research*, *10*, 245. DOI: 10.12688/f1000research.36775.1 PMID: 34804493

Weber, G. M., Adams, W. G., Bernstam, E. V., Bickel, J. P., Fox, K. P., Marsolo, K., Raghavan, V. A., Turchin, A., Zhou, X., Murphy, S. N., & Mandl, K. D. (2017). Biases introduced by filtering electronic health records for patients with "complete data". *Journal of the American Medical Informatics Association : JAMIA*, *24*(6), 1134–1141. DOI: 10.1093/jamia/ocx071 PMID: 29016972

Wijnberge, M., Geerts, B. F., Hol, L., Lemmers, N., Mulder, M. P., Berge, P., Schenk, J., Terwindt, L. E., Hollmann, M. W., Vlaar, A. P., & Veelo, D. P. (2020). Effect of a machine learning-derived early warning system for intraoperative hypotension VS standard care on depth and duration of intraoperative hypotension during elective noncardiac surgery: The hype randomized clinical trial. *Journal of the American Medical Association*, *323*(11), 1052–1060. DOI: 10.1001/jama.2020.0592 PMID: 32065827

Yadav, D., Yadav, S., & Veer, K. (2020). A comprehensive assessment of Brain Computer Interfaces: Recent trends and challenges. *Journal of Neuroscience Methods*, *346*, 108918. DOI: 10.1016/j.jneumeth.2020.108918 PMID: 32853592

Zhang, X., Ma, Z., Zheng, H., Li, T., Chen, K., Wang, X., Liu, C., Xu, L., Wu, X., Lin, D., & Lin, H. (2020). The combination of brain-computer interfaces and artificial intelligence: Applications and challenges. *Annals of Translational Medicine*, *8*(11), 712. DOI: 10.21037/atm.2019.11.109 PMID: 32617332

Chapter 7
Cyberchondria in the Age of Online Health Information

Mansour Amini
https://orcid.org/0000-0003-2149-4604
Universiti Sains Malaysia, Malaysia

Ashraf Sadat Ahadzadeh
https://orcid.org/0000-0002-3178-8684
Xiamen University Malaysia, Malaysia

ABSTRACT

Cyberchondria, characterised by escalating anxiety following online health information searches, has become increasingly relevant in the digital age, particularly with the growing reliance on digital platforms for self-diagnosis. Despite its significance, there is a lack of comprehensive literature addressing the psychological and social implications of cyberchondria. This book chapter aims to fill that gap by providing a detailed overview of cyberchondria, including demographic insights into its prevalence, conceptualization, and psychological impact. The chapter explores various factors that influence the development of cyberchondria, such as individual characteristics and the quality of online information. It examines the role of digital media in shaping cyberchondria and discusses coping strategies to mitigate its adverse effects. Emphasizing the importance of health education and digital literacy, the chapter highlights the need to empower individuals to use online health resources safely and effectively, particularly in light of the rise of cyberchondria.

DOI: 10.4018/979-8-3693-5837-5.ch007

1. INTRODUCTION

In the digital age, information and computer technologies (ICT) has become an indispensable tool for accessing health information. While this vast reservoir of resources has empowered individuals to take charge of their health, it has also given rise to a phenomenon known as cyberchondria. Cyberchondria refers to the increasing anxiety that individuals experience after searching for health-related information online (Vismara et al., 2020). This condition has become more prevalent as more people turn to the digital platforms for self-diagnosis and health advice, often resulting in heightened stress and concern about their health (Peng et al., 2021).

Despite the growing recognition of cyberchondria, there remains a significant gap in the literature regarding its psychological and social implications. The ease of access to medical information, coupled with the often alarming nature of online health content, can exacerbate fears and lead to a cycle of obsessive health-related searching (Bahadir & Dundar, 2024). This phenomenon not only impacts individuals' mental well-being but also strains healthcare systems as people seek unnecessary medical consultations based on their online findings (Varma & Singh, 2023). Understanding cyberchondria is crucial for developing effective strategies to manage its effects and improve overall health literacy and digital literacy.

In an era defined by the rapid proliferation of digital technologies and the transformation of healthcare paradigms, the convergence of digital literacy and health education emerges as an imperative discourse. As the contours of our knowledge society evolve, so too must our understanding of the competencies required to navigate its intricacies. Within the realm of higher education, the cultivation of digital literacy stands as a cornerstone, indispensable for future professionalisation and critical engagement (Arias López et al., 2023; Kim et al., 2024). For instance, the rapid advancement of artificial intelligence (AI) has significantly transformed the landscape of online health information, influencing both the accessibility and reliability of medical content and, consequently, the experience of cyberchondria. While these technologies have the potential to enhance healthcare accessibility and reduce uncertainty, they may also contribute to the intensification of cyberchondria. The ability of AI-powered tools to generate highly personalized yet sometimes alarmist health predictions can exacerbate health anxiety, leading users to engage in more frequent and compulsive health-related searches. Furthermore, the widespread use of AI in search engine algorithms influences the ranking and visibility of online health content, potentially exposing individuals to misleading or sensationalized medical information. As AI continues to reshape the digital health environment, it is essential to examine its role in both mitigating and exacerbating cyberchondria, ensuring that technological advancements prioritize accuracy, transparency, and responsible usage to minimize adverse psychological effects.

In the healthcare sphere, the influence of digital technologies goes beyond mere educational trends. These technologies have fundamentally altered the interaction between individuals and healthcare systems, revolutionising health promotion and disease management. Nonetheless, significant concerns arise about their potential to exacerbate existing inequalities in healthcare access and outcomes. This digital metamorphosis underscores the necessity for a thorough understanding of how personal, contextual, and technological factors interact to shape the adoption and use of digital health technologies, highlighting the intricate ways in which they can affect health outcomes.

Central to the efficacy of digital health technologies lies users' digital health literacy—a multifaceted competence encompassing the skills and resources necessary to navigate the digital health landscape effectively (Yuen et al., 2024). Yet, within this digital milieu lurks a phenomenon known as cyberchondria—a maladaptive pattern of behaviour characterised by excessive and distressing online health searches. Cyberchondria encapsulates the fusion of health anxiety with compulsive internet searches, amplifying distress and disrupting daily life. Furthermore, understanding cyberchondria requires an exploration of its antecedents, from individual traits to information quality, as well as the role of digital media in shaping its manifestation. Moreover, coping strategies to mitigate its adverse effects are imperative, acknowledging its nuanced relationship with health anxiety (Xu & Chen, 2024).

Cyberchondria, a condition characterised by excessive searches for health information online leading to heightened anxiety, may stem from various factors, including heightened health anxiety, diverse online search habits (such as the quantity, length, subjects, and selection of information sources), information overload, and insufficient e-health literacy (Peng et al., 2021). Despite growing recognition, research on cyberchondria remains nascent, with a notable lack of data on its prevalence and influencing factors (Vismara et al., 2020). On the other hand, in some cases, accessing credible online health information can facilitate early detection of medical issues, encourage proactive health behaviors, and enhance doctor-patient communication. Additionally, digital health platforms provide individuals with knowledge about new treatments, preventive care, and wellness strategies, fostering a sense of control over their health.

In this paper, we will emphasise that for navigating the vast expanse of online health information, a comprehensive understanding of digital literacy, health education, and the psychological impact of cyberchondria is indispensable for fostering informed and empowered individuals within our digital society.

2. LITERATURE REVIEW AND RELATED WORK

2.1. Demographic Insights into Cyberchondria and its Prevalence

The internet is a huge, constantly expanding platform that acts as a centre for a wide range of activities, services, and information. There were almost 1.11 billion websites on the internet as of 2023, ranging from business and personal blogs to e-commerce and educational portals (Pelchen, 2024). 5.44 billion people in general, or 67.1 percent of the world's population, were online as of April 2024. Of these, 5.07 billion people utilised social media, accounting for 62.6 percent of the world's population (Statista, 2024). In terms of geographic location, northern Europe has the highest internet penetration rate with nearly 97.4% of its population using the internet. Northern America came next, with 96.9 percent (Statista, 2024). Although the amount of time spent online varies depending on the age group, people use the internet for 6.5 hours a day on average (GlobalWebIndex, 2017).

The broad availability of the internet brought huge effects on the healthcare and health systems (Płaciszewski et al., 2022). Content related to health and well-being can easily be found on most major news websites worldwide. As a result of the abundance of readily available information, searching for health-related information online has become routine (Bujnowska-Fedak & Węgierek, 2020). According to many national and worldwide polls, between 70% and 80% of internet users particularly utilised the online to look up health-related information, get help, or get ready for a doctor's appointment (Vismara et al., 2020). The internet has occasionally taken the place of medical experts. Nearly half of participants in a survey of over 12,000 people from 12 countries self-diagnosed using the Google search engine (Vismara et al., 2020). In an online survey of 515 volunteers, approximately 20% of participants who described low levels of baseline health anxiety experienced frequent escalation of online worries, while 40% reported that interactions with the internet increased anxiety about medical problems (White & Horvitz, 2009).

This phenomenon is particularly pronounced in low- and middle-income countries where data is scarce. For instance, Makarla et al. (2019) investigated cyberchondria among employees in India's information technology sector. Their survey of 205 employees in Chennai revealed a significant prevalence of cyberchondria, with 55.6% exhibiting patterns of excessive searching, reassurance seeking, and distress. Participants were assessed via an online survey with the Cyberchondria Severity Scale (CSS)-15 items, with the subsequent exclusion of the "mistrust of medical professionals" factor. Notably, cyberchondria was inversely associated with general mental health, underscoring its relevance as a public mental health concern in India (Makarla et al., 2019). Besides, a survey of 300 outpatients in two Sri Lankan general hospitals using a self-report questionnaire (including CSS-33 items) showed a prevalence of cyberchondria of 16.3% (Wijesinghe et al., 2019).

Associations between age and gender and cyberchondria remain scarce and inconsistent in previous studies. A cross-sectional study among metabolic syndrome patients attending cardiology, endocrinology, and neurology outpatient clinics in a tertiary care hospital in South India showed no significant association between overall CSS scores and socio-demographic variables (e.g., gender, education level) except for suspected illness, which was significantly correlated with a history of myocardial infarction (Pawar et al., 2022). Similarly, Akhtar and Fatima (2019) found no significant gender differences in cyberchondria and its subscales. In their research, men had slightly higher overall CSS mean scores than women. Males scored higher on the obsessive-compulsive, distressing, excessive, and comforting scales, whereas females scored slightly higher than males on the "mistrust of the medical profession" scale.

However, socio-demographic variables, such as gender and age, have shown correlations with cyberchondria in other studies. A study designed to explore the prevalence of cyberchondria among students at Taif University, Saudi Arabia, and the impact of social media revealed that 651 participants had a mean CSS score of 2.73 ± 0.73, with a minimum score of 1.96 and a maximum score of 3.66. Females searched the internet for any unexplained bodily sensation significantly more often than males; that is, cyberchondria is more common in young adult females (Turkistani et al., 2020). Similarly, a web-based study conducted among 236 adult participants in Uttar Pradesh, India, revealed that cyberchondria constituted 45.3% of the participants, and the majority (56.4%) of the participants had varying degrees of depression. The study predicted the factors affecting cyberchondria through multiple regression analysis and found that female gender had an effect on the severity of cyberchondria (Tiwari et al., 2022). These results are not surprising, as data suggest that the prevalence of anxiety disorders is higher among females and findings suggest that females are more likely to seek health information than males (Jokić-Begić et al., 2019). Besides, health care worker occupation, and time spent watching television and social media for 1-3 hours per day all affect cyberchondria.

There were differences in the percentage of people in different age groups who had cyberchondria. According to a European survey, individuals between the ages of 30 and 44 were found to be the most frequent consumers of the internet for health-related information. The majority of them (66%) began their searches using general search engines like Google or Yahoo, with 27% began their searches on a specific health-related website (Turkistani et al., 2020). This might have reflected age-dependent patterns of general internet usage. Similarly, In an online survey of 565 young and older adults, it was discovered that those with severe cyberchondria were less accurate at identifying health misinformation because they were more likely to believe that the misinformation was accurate. On the other hand, as respondents' ages increased, they were more likely to believe that the misinformation was true. Additionally, after reading the partial information that they thought was correct, respondents were more likely to want to read more and look for more relevant information (Xiang et al., 2023). This is a consequence of the increased risk of cyberchondria in the elderly population.

What's more, Agrawal et al. (2024) confirmed that there is also a relationship between being a medical professional and the prevalence of cyberchondria. The study's findings demonstrated the disparities in information interpretation between medical and non-medical staff, which in turn caused differences in the prevalence of cyber-susceptibility. Of the individuals, 58.5% were enrolled in a program leading to a medical or paramedical degree, whereas the remaining 41.5% were not in the medical field. Furthermore, according to Agrawal et al. (2024), the cumulative CSS of the medical cohort was substantially lower than that of the non-medical cohort. According to these results, people with medical expertise and training may be less anxious about their health and less likely to look up health-related information online. These findings may be explained by medical students' high degree of medical concept understanding and the development of critical appraisal skills, which may lessen their susceptibility to cyberchondria.

Given the extensive demographic insights into cyberchondria and its prevalence, it is essential to explore how this phenomenon is conceptualized and understood in academic discourse. The increasing reliance on online health information, coupled with psychological factors such as health anxiety, has shaped various interpretations of cyberchondria over time. The following section delves into its definitions, theoretical foundations, and measurement approaches, providing a clearer understanding of how cyberchondria is framed within the broader landscape of health-related internet behaviors.

2.2. Conceptualisations of Cyberchondria

Cyberchondria is becoming more and more prevalent in the current modern era as the internet has become widely accessible. The term was derived from the terms "cyber" and "hypochondriasis" and was proposed by news media during the mid-1990s (Loos, 2013; Vismara et al., 2020). As per Merriam-Webster, the term hypochondriasis is defined as "excessive concern about one's health especially when accompanied by imagined physical l ailments". On the other hand, the most widely used description of cyberchondria at the moment was offered by Starcevic and Berle (2013), who defined it as "an obsessive search for health-related material on the internet brought on by anxiety over health issues, which increases psychological distress." The conceptual framework previously mentioned has since been widely accepted and applied in various scholarly research.

The first self-report measure for cyberchondria was conducted by McElroy and Shevlin (2014). The Cyberchondria Severity Scale (CSS) was designed during this process. Originally, 43 items that describe behaviours, emotions, and related anxiety disorders were generated from previous research on cyberchondria, however following an exploratory factor analysis on 190 subjects, 10 items were eliminated. The final version contained 33 items with five-point rating scale responses (1 - Never, 2 - Rarely, 3 - Sometimes, 4 - Often, 5 - Always) and is divided into 5 factors: (1) Compulsion, describing the negative effects of online medical searches interfering daily activities; (2) Distress, related to negative emotional responses; (3) Excessiveness, describing the repeated nature of research for medical information; (4) Reassurance, where people seek professional medical advice after the heightened anxiety after medical research on the internet; (5) Mistrust of Medical Professionals, which reflects the situation where people trust medical advice from the internet more than medical professionals (McElroy & Shevlin, 2014).

However, a number of scholars have questioned the validity of the original CSS, pointing out that the final factor—Mistrust of Medical Professionals—did not exhibit a strong correlation with the other four variables. This is further supported by Fergus (2014), who used second-order confirmatory factor analysis (CFA) to gather data from a community sample of 539 adults in order to support the assertion. Fergus suggested eliminating the final component from the CSS, but the results of the Short Health Anxiety Inventory (SHAI) indicated a link between health anxiety problems and "Mistrust of Medical Professionals." In subsequent studies, CSS without the last factor had been used, where it was further simplified using just 12 items, where 3 questions were asked for the remaining 4 original factors left. The shortened CSS-12 was approved in a sample of 661 undergraduate students and had shown excellent consistency.

CSS was then translated into various languages, which included Polish, Turkish, German, and Portuguese (Bajcar & Babiak, 2019; Barke et al., 2016; Da Silva et al., 2016; Selvi et al., 2018). The "Mistrust of Medical Professionals" items of the CSS were taken out of the Polish version and acquired with inconsistent results from the Turkish version of CSS (Bajcar & Babiak, 2019; Selvi et al., 2018). On the other hand, the German version of the CSS had received excellent consistency, including the "Mistrust of Medical Professionals" items (Da Silva et al., 2016). As a result, CSS-15—a condensed version of the standard—was created, containing just three item that loaded at the highest level across all five elements. However, a different scale called the Cyberchondria scale has been developed in Turkey. It contains 27 items with similar 1 to 5 Likert scales, which include 5 factors: (1) increasing anxiety; (2) hypochondria; (3) decreasing anxiety; (4) doctor-patient interaction; (5) dysfunctional internet use. However, more studies are required to verify its psychometric properties, although it might serve as an alternative tool to measure cyberchondria.

Other than that, a newly created assessment tool called the Short Cyberchondria Scale (SCS) is used to measure cyberchondria, which is defined as the condition in which people experience increased health worry as a result of excessively surfing the internet for health information (Jokić-Begić et al., 2019). The CSS is one of the current leading measurements; but the SCS seeks to improve upon it by being more brief, valid, and dependable across a range of demographics.

The SCS has been validated through extensive research involving multiple participant samples and has demonstrated satisfactory psychometric properties. Key findings indicate that the SCS captures the core elements of cyberchondria—specifically the amplification of anxiety resulting from excessive online health searches—while also showing good reliability and validity when compared to other relevant constructs like health anxiety and anxiety sensitivity (Jokić-Begić et al., 2019).

As the conceptual understanding of cyberchondria continues to evolve, it is essential to examine the underlying factors that contribute to its development. Beyond individual tendencies and measurement approaches, cyberchondria is shaped by a complex interplay of psychological, social, and technological influences. The following section explores these determinants, highlighting how cognitive biases, emotional regulation, digital engagement, and sociocultural factors contribute to the manifestation and severity of cyberchondria.

2.3. Determinants of Cyberchondria Development

Cyberchondria, an increasingly recognised phenomenon characterised by excessive searches for health-related information online, reflects not only an individual's psychological state but also encompasses broader familial and social dynamics (Bajcar & Babiak, 2019). The development of cyberchondria is influenced by a range of psychological, social, technological and personal factors. In other words, as a pattern of cognitive, emotional, and behavioural components, cyberchondria may be influenced by subjective emotional and behavioural factors such as fear of missing out (FoMO) and excessive use of social media for online communication (Wang et al., n.d.). These factors interact with each other in complex ways, leading to the widespread emergence. In navigating the intricate interplay between individual characteristics and the quality of health information accessed online, recent studies such as Nasiri et al. (2023) propose that health-related metacognition, cognitive biases, and emotional dysregulation may play an adequate mediating role in the correlation between personality traits and cyberchondria. Building upon this framework, Müller et al. (2022) advocate for a targeted treatment approach, emphasising the importance of challenging maladaptive assumptions and beliefs regarding health while simultaneously addressing problematic internet usage and enhancing eHealth literacy among individuals affected by cyberchondria. This multifaceted perspective underscores the imperative outlined by Varma and Singh (2023) for further research aimed at deepening our understanding of cyberchondria and developing tailored interventions to cultivate a healthier online health environment and optimise the utilisation of healthcare resources. Besides, McMullan et al. (2019) found a direct link between health anxiety and both the search for online health information and cyberchondria. They suggested that future investigations should delve into the circumstances surrounding these connections and work towards overcoming the limitations noted in the existing body of literature. Yang et al. (2022) also conducted a systematic review aimed at identifying key psychological predictors of cyberchondria. Their review highlights the significant role of individual metacognition, uncertainty regarding online information, and biassed algorithm-driven content in fuelling cyberchondria. They propose a holistic framework that emphasises psychoeducation, screening, and support for vulnerable groups, suggesting that interventions should address the multifaceted nature of cyberchondria.

This growing body of research highlights the multifaceted nature of cyberchondria, illustrating how individual psychological traits, cognitive biases, and external digital influences intertwine to shape health-related online behaviors. While previous studies have primarily focused on metacognitive factors and personality traits, emerging research expands the scope by considering the impact of digital environments, such as online advertisements and smartphone addiction, on cyberchondria. These insights underscore the necessity of addressing both psychological predispositions and technological factors to develop comprehensive strategies for mitigating the adverse effects of excessive health-related internet use.

Zhang et al. (2024) identified a direct and positive correlation between cyberchondria and health-related advertisement interference, exploring both direct and indirect links through a stress-strain-outcome (SSO) model. Their findings revealed that information overload and information irrelevance not only contributed to advertisement interference but also intensified mistrust of the internet as a reliable health resource. This mistrust can lead individuals to approach online information with skepticism, which may exacerbate feelings of anxiety related to health concerns. Additionally, the role of smartphone addiction in mental health was highlighted, with Agrawal et al. (2024) investigating the prevalence of cyberchondria among both medical and non-medical personnel. Their research indicated a positive correlation between the severity of cyberchondria and smartphone addiction across both groups. This suggests that individuals with problematic smartphone usage patterns—whether they are in the healthcare field or not—are more prone to engage in compulsive health-related internet searches, further influencing their perceptions of health information online. Distrust of the internet is closely linked to cyberchondria, where excessive online health searches heighten anxiety due to selective information seeking, misinformation, and repetitive symptom-checking. People skeptical of mainstream medical sources often turn to unreliable alternatives, reinforcing their fears and misconceptions. This distrust also exacerbates healthcare inequalities, as individuals may avoid telemedicine, struggle with distinguishing credible health information, and delay or mismanage treatment, particularly among those with lower digital literacy. Ultimately, mistrust in digital health resources not only fuels anxiety but also restricts access to essential medical care, worsening health disparities.

Cyberchondria has also been linked to the sharing of unvalidated COVID-19 materials on social media. A research model based on theories of health perception and cognitive load was built and tested to investigate why people engaged in this behavior, with a focus on personal attributes. This study examined cyberchondria during the COVID-19 pandemic (Laato et al., 2020). The findings imply that key determinants of unverified information sharing include an individual's perception of information overload and their level of trust in online sources.

Cyberchondria will be greatly influenced by these variables as well as an individual's assessment of the severity and vulnerability to COVID-19.

The influence of the family on the individual is crucial. Studies, such as that conducted by Liu et al. (2022), underscore the critical role of family functioning in the context of cyberchondria, particularly among adolescents. Their research among Chinese adolescents revealed a positive association between family dysfunction and cyberchondria, with health anxiety acting as a partial mediator. Furthermore, the study found that optimism played a moderating role, suggesting the complexity of factors influencing cyberchondria among youths. These findings emphasise the importance of comprehensive intervention programs that consider both individual and family dynamics.

Similarly, in a Chinese cultural context, Hu et al. (2020) delved into cyberchondria, identifying risk factors and potential negative consequences. Through exploratory factor analysis, they discerned differences between Western and Chinese contexts, leading to the development of a Chinese version of the Cyberchondria Severity Scale (C-CSS) with demonstrated reliability and validity. Regression analysis highlighted three predictors of cyberchondria, and the C-CSS was found to correlate with relevant outcomes, indicating its efficacy in assessing cyberchondria severity among Chinese undergraduates. This study illustrates the utility of cultural adaptation in understanding and addressing cyberchondria within diverse populations.

As cyberchondria is shaped by a range of psychological, social, and technological influences, it is also deeply intertwined with cultural and socioeconomic factors that determine how individuals interact with online health information. The prevalence and severity of cyberchondria are not uniform across populations, as variations in healthcare accessibility, cultural perceptions of illness, and digital literacy levels contribute to differing experiences. Understanding these broader influences provides valuable context for assessing the global implications of cyberchondria and highlights the need for tailored interventions. The following section explores how cultural beliefs, socioeconomic status, and healthcare systems shape cyberchondria, offering a more comprehensive perspective on the condition's diverse manifestations.

2.4 The Role of Cultural and Socioeconomic Factors in Shaping Experiences of Cyberchondria

Cultural and socioeconomic factors play a crucial role in shaping individuals' experiences of cyberchondria (e.g., Infanti et al., 2022; Starcevic et al., 2021), yet they remain underexplored in existing discussions. Cultural attitudes toward illness, healthcare systems, and trust in medical professionals significantly influence how people seek and interpret online health information. For instance, in cultures where discussing health concerns is stigmatized, individuals may turn to the internet as a primary source of information (e.g., Xu, 2024), potentially exacerbating anxiety-driven health searches. Similarly, socioeconomic status affects access to reliable healthcare and digital literacy, which in turn impacts how individuals engage with online medical content. Research comparing different cultural contexts highlights variations in cyberchondria prevalence, suggesting that factors such as collectivism versus individualism, healthcare affordability, and the perceived credibility of online sources all contribute to differing levels of cyberchondria across populations (e.g., Abdulrahman et al., 2024; Mestre-Bach & Potenza, 2023); Szawłoga et al., 2024). Including such perspectives can provide a more nuanced understanding of how cyberchondria manifests in diverse settings.

Understanding the role of cultural and socioeconomic factors in shaping cyberchondria provides a crucial foundation for examining its broader psychological and behavioral consequences. While societal attitudes, healthcare access, and digital literacy influence how individuals engage with online health information, the psychological toll of excessive health-related internet searches extends beyond cultural boundaries. The distress associated with cyberchondria can manifest in both mental and physical health outcomes, further complicating individuals' well-being. As cyberchondria continues to shape health behaviors, it is important to explore its psychological and behavioral effects, including its impact on anxiety levels, healthcare decision-making, and overall quality of life. The following section delves into these implications, emphasizing the necessity of holistic approaches to understanding and addressing the condition.

2.5 Psychological and Behavioural Implications of Cyberchondria

Cyberchondria has tangible effects on physical health that warrant further attention. Prolonged anxiety and stress associated with excessive online health searches can trigger physiological responses such as increased cortisol levels, which may contribute to chronic conditions like hypertension, digestive disorders, and sleep disturbances. Studies have shown that individuals who frequently engage in health-related internet searches are more likely to report somatic symptoms, even in the absence of an underlying medical condition, due to heightened stress and hyperawareness of bodily sensations. Furthermore, disrupted sleep patterns caused by late-night health searches and constant worry can further deteriorate physical well-being. Addressing the physical health implications of cyberchondria alongside its psychological impact offers a more comprehensive view of the condition, emphasizing the need for holistic interventions that incorporate both mental and physical health strategies. As cyberchondria creeps into people's lives and negatively impacts their daily lives, it has caused psychological and behavioural changes towards people suffering from it. It has been proven to inject depression, anxiety, and stress into people, adults or teenagers. As an example, after COVID-19 had spread around the world, people often searched the internet to verify whether the perceived symptoms were related to COVID-19 or not (Yam et al., 2021). Yam et al. (2021) found out that cyberchondria had both moderating and mediating roles on smartphone addictions and, most importantly, the fear of infecting the coronavirus itself. In another study, the authors showed that cyberchondria had negatively affected the academic performances of students, where they surveyed 302 undergraduate dental students using CSS-15 and compared the results with the percentage of marks obtained in their examinations (Patanapu et al., 2022).

Moreover, cyberchondria has been proven to negatively impact trust in physicians and also positively affect the propensity to self-medicate (Khan & Pandey, 2022). This is very dangerous, as seeking health information increases online information overload, which triggers cyberchondria (Zheng et al., 2023). Other than that, the distress and anxiety caused by cyberchondria had also decreased the quality of life (QOL) of people (Rahme et al., 2021). Rahme and her colleagues studied 449 adults in Lebanon during the COVID-19 pandemic. The results indicated that higher physical QOL scores were significantly correlated with older age and tertiary education, while lower mental QOL scores were significantly correlated with higher levels of stress and anxiety. All of this demonstrated how exposure to a large quantity of health information, whether from reputable websites or not, can cause people to experience symptoms of anxiety, which will often devolve into a decrease in life quality, or possibly even worse, addictions and distrust in medical professionals, which feed into the vicious circle of cyberchondria (Tarabay et al., 2023).

The psychological impact of cyberchondria extends beyond individual distress to encompass teenagers across cognitive, affective, and behavioural domains (Indreswari et al., 2023). Their study underscores the pervasive nature of cyberchondria, noting its potential to induce non-specific somatic complaints among adolescents. This highlights the importance of early detection and intervention strategies to mitigate the adverse effects of cyberchondria on teenage mental health.

By integrating both the benefits and risks of online health searches, a more balanced perspective can be presented, allowing for a critical evaluation of how digital health literacy and responsible information-seeking behaviors can mitigate the adverse effects of cyberchondria. Cognitive-behavioral therapy (CBT), for example, has been widely used to help individuals with health anxiety by challenging maladaptive thought patterns and reducing compulsive health-related searches. Digital literacy programs aimed at improving individuals' ability to assess online health information critically can also play a key role in mitigating cyberchondria. Additionally, support groups and community-based initiatives provide social and psychological support for individuals struggling with excessive health concerns. Highlighting successful intervention programs and their effectiveness, such as structured CBT programs or educational workshops on digital health literacy, can offer valuable guidance for individuals, healthcare professionals, and policymakers in addressing cyberchondria more comprehensively.

Further emphasising the real-world implications of cyberchondria, Özkent et al. (2023) investigated its prevalence and impact among patients attending a urology clinic. Their findings revealed a significant correlation between the severity of cyberchondria and health anxiety. This underscores the importance for healthcare professionals to recognise and address the burden of cyberchondria in clinical settings, ensuring that patients receive appropriate support and intervention to effectively manage their health-related anxieties. These insights emphasise the urgent need for tailored approaches in both clinical and community settings to address the multifaceted challenges posed by cyberchondria and its impact on mental health and well-being.

The significant psychological and behavioral implications of cyberchondria highlight the urgent need for effective strategies to mitigate its negative effects. While excessive online health searches can lead to heightened anxiety, misinformation, and decreased quality of life, digital literacy and health education play a crucial role in addressing these challenges. By equipping individuals with the skills to critically evaluate online health information, digital literacy can help prevent unnecessary distress and promote informed decision-making. Furthermore, structured health education initiatives can enhance public awareness of responsible online health-seeking behaviors, ultimately reducing the likelihood of cyberchondria. The following section explores the importance of digital literacy and health education as key tools in fostering a more balanced and informed approach to online health information consumption.

2.6 Importance of Digital Literacy and Health Education

The advent of the knowledge society heralds a paradigm shift, emphasising the cultivation and adept application of a repertoire of competencies for discerning and judiciously utilising knowledge. Within this framework, higher education assumes the pivotal role of nurturing these competencies, with digital literacy emerging as a cornerstone deemed indispensable for successful professionalisation in the future (Santos & Serpa, 2017). Moreover, Reddy et al. (2020) assert that the seamless integration of cutting-edge digital technologies into higher education pedagogies has fundamentally altered teaching methodologies and reshaped the learning landscape for students.

In the realm of healthcare, the pervasive influence of digital technologies is reshaping the dynamics between individuals and healthcare systems, profoundly influencing health promotion and disease management. However, concerns regarding their potential to exacerbate existing inequalities in healthcare access are gaining prominence within the public health discourse (Azzopardi-Muscat & Sørensen, 2019). It is recognised that the uptake and utilisation of digital health technologies are influenced by a myriad of personal, contextual, and technological factors, underscoring the intricate interplay shaping their impact on health outcomes. The efficacy and benefits of digital health technologies hinge significantly on users' digital health literacy, which encompasses the capabilities and resources requisite for individuals to effectively utilise and derive benefits from digital health resources. This fusion of health and digital literacy underscores the multifaceted nature of competence necessary for navigating the digital health landscape (Kemp et al., 2020).

Not only that, digital literacy serves as a stepping stone to enable individuals to connect with other people through social media, email, and other online platforms (Hague & Payton, 2011). It has been shown that it fosters communication between people and helps sustain not only personal relationships but also professional partnerships across great distances (Park et al., 2014). However, there exist concerns regarding its adverse effects on people's communication skills, especially nonverbal decoding skills (Ruben et al., 2021). Thus, one should utilise technology in a more passive and observational manner instead of an active and self-centred manner.

Other than that, in a world with copious amounts of online information, digital literacy is indispensable, as it helps people to assess the credibility of information from sources on the internet effectively. Yet a report showed that students, the future of our world, still exhibit a startling lack of skill to determine the validity of data available online (Wineburg & McGrew, 2016). People all throughout the world have been impacted by misinformation and disinformation, such as fake news, which has eroded confidence, caused confusion, and posed dangers to democracy and the right to free speech (Gaillard et al., 2021). Therefore, future generations should be nurtured since youth need to improve their digital literacy skills in order to survive and be independent in the present era.

Digital literacy also promotes ethical online behaviour and reminds people that they hold full responsibility for their words and actions on the internet. Skills that digital literacy encompasses include mastering the knowledge about privacy settings, learning technical aspects of the internet, and the legal implications of one's online actions (Park, 2011). It has demonstrated effectiveness in preventing hacking, particularly phishing. (Kumar, 2021). We can browse the internet worry-free only when internet users acquire digital literacy and are sensitive to suspicious behaviour on the web.

As digital literacy becomes increasingly vital in navigating the vast landscape of online health information, it is equally important to examine how digital media influences individuals' perceptions and behaviors related to health. While digital literacy can empower users to critically evaluate medical content and reduce misinformation susceptibility, the growing presence of algorithm-driven search engines and social media platforms has introduced new challenges. The accessibility and personalization of online health information, while beneficial in some cases, can also reinforce biased search patterns, leading to heightened health anxiety and compulsive searching behaviors. The following underscores the need to explore the influence of digital media on the development of cyberchondria, shedding light on how technological advancements shape health information consumption and its psychological consequences.

2.7 Influence of Digital Media on the Development of Cyberchondria

In the contemporary era dominated by digital media, the phenomenon of cyberchondria, characterised by excessive internet searches for medical information leading to heightened health anxiety, has garnered increasing attention. Fergus and Dolan (2014) dove into this complex interplay between digital connectivity and health anxiety, exploring how problematic internet use (PIU) correlates with cyberchondria among a sizable cohort of medically healthy adults in the United States. Their research revealed that individuals experiencing escalated health anxiety subsequent to online medical enquiries were prone to manifesting problematic internet use, even after accounting for search frequency and negative emotional impact influences

(Fergus & Dolan, 2014). These findings underscore the critical need for a nuanced understanding of cyberchondria's dynamics and suggest avenues for its therapeutic intervention within the evolving digital landscape.

Based on these findings, a number of studies have analysed the role digital media plays in exacerbating health anxiety and cyberchondria. For example, Yang et al. (2022) illustrate that the algorithms of digital media's search engines may create biassed information landscapes, as these algorithm-driven technologies tend to prioritise worrisome or serious health-related content, leading to the increased compulsion to search. This interplay between technology and user behaviour suggests that online health information searches are not neutral but rather shaped by manipulated algorithms, leading to disproportionate exposure of users to distressing information, thereby exacerbating cyberchondria. Search engines can be dangerous to users who have faith in them but are unable to properly assess search results (Schultheiß & Lewandowski, 2021). Users that have higher levels of trust are more inclined to use search engines and rely on the system, but they are also more prone to mistake common benign symptoms for important medical conditions (Yang et al., 2022). Besides, constant social media exposure exacerbates the phenomenon of information overload, in which large amounts of information lead to confusion and avoidance. Information obtained from social media sources contributes to cyberchondria and information overload, presumably because the news on these platforms is less impartial and less rigorous than that of journalists, making it more prone to personal opinions (Farooq et al., 2020).

In the post-pandemic era, there is a growing body of relevant research on the role of digital media. Wu et al. (2021) provided examples of how the epidemic's prolonged usage of online media exacerbated people's anxiety and panic, which in turn caused cyberchondria. Their emphasis on excessive and repetitive online health searches highlights the contradictory role of the internet during the period of socialised isolation at a distance. Zhang et al. (2023) also demonstrated that individuals who regularly use social media might become more anxious during an outbreak, and while this anxiety may not directly translate into holding more rumours, it can affect how they perceive and respond to health-related misinformation. Meanwhile, social media use amplifies this effect, creating a feedback loop where increased anxiety leads to more frequent media consumption (Zhang et al., 2023).

The increasing influence of digital media on cyberchondria highlights the need for effective coping strategies to mitigate its adverse effects. While digital platforms provide vast amounts of health-related information, their unregulated nature can fuel anxiety and reinforce compulsive health-searching behaviors. As individuals become more reliant on online sources for medical guidance, the challenge lies in equipping them with the skills and resources necessary to navigate digital health information responsibly. Addressing cyberchondria requires a multifaceted approach that includes psychological interventions, digital literacy initiatives, and support systems to help individuals manage their health concerns in a balanced and informed manner. The following section explores various coping strategies and evidence-based interventions that have been proposed to alleviate the psychological distress associated with excessive online health searching.

2.8 Coping Strategies to Mitigate Adverse Effects of Cyberchondria

Understanding the relationship between health anxiety and cyberchondria is crucial for informing clinical practice and intervention strategies. By addressing underlying cognitive processes, promoting healthy coping mechanisms, and guiding responsible internet use, healthcare professionals can more effectively help individuals manage both health anxiety and cyberchondria. Raising awareness about the risks of excessive online health searching and encouraging critical evaluation of online information can potentially reduce the risk of cyberchondria and help individuals navigate digital health resources with greater confidence.

Research highlights the complexity of this relationship. Afrin and Prybutok (2022) found that intolerance for unpredictability, associated with cyberchondria, is mediated by health anxiety and affective responses. This insight is valuable for healthcare educators and practitioners aiming to manage cyberchondria effectively. Bajcar and Babiak (2019) revealed that obsessive-compulsive symptoms and health anxiety mediate the link between self-esteem and cyberchondria, suggesting that health anxiety, obsessive-compulsive symptoms, and low self-esteem may be risk factors for cyberchondria. They also indicated that obsessive-compulsive symptoms and health anxiety resulting from cyberchondria could predict self-esteem both directly and indirectly.

Further, Fergus and Russell (2016) established that while health anxiety and cyberchondria are related, they differ in significant ways. Health anxiety involves excessive worry about one's health, whereas cyberchondria is characterized by compulsive online health searches, often exacerbating health concerns. Dhamija (2022) highlighted that the COVID-19 pandemic has intensified health-related anxiety, with cyberchondria emerging as a coping mechanism through online searches, despite the associated mental health challenges. Additionally, Sohail and Zafar (2022) investigated the role of cyberchondria in the relationship between fear of COVID-19 and stress among university students. Their study, involving 205 students from Pakistan, found a positive correlation between fear of COVID-19 and cyberchondria, which in turn correlates with creative coping strategies and academic stress. Cyberchondria was a significant predictor of stress, mediated by fear of COVID-19 and moderated by creative coping strategies and social support.

In summary, As cyberchondria continues to evolve in the digital era, its development is influenced by a range of psychological, social, and technological factors. The widespread accessibility of online health information has led to varying conceptualizations of cyberchondria, highlighting its complex nature and the need for standardized assessment tools. Additionally, research has identified key determinants such as cognitive biases, emotional regulation, and excessive engagement with digital media, which collectively shape individuals' susceptibility to cyberchondria. Digital media, in particular, plays a pivotal role in exacerbating health anxiety through algorithm-driven content, misinformation, and information overload, making it crucial to explore its impact on compulsive health-related searches. In response to these challenges, various coping strategies have been proposed, including cognitive-behavioral therapy, digital literacy programs, and community-based interventions, which offer potential pathways for mitigating the adverse effects of cyberchondria. By examining these interconnected aspects, it becomes evident that cyberchondria requires a multifaceted approach, integrating psychological insights, technological awareness, and targeted intervention strategies.

3 CONCLUSION

The psychological impact of cyberchondria spans individual, familial, and clinical domains, underscoring the need for comprehensive approaches to address its complexities. Studies highlight the intricate interplay between factors such as family dynamics, individual cognition, and online information environments in shaping cyberchondria. By recognising these multifaceted influences and implementing tailored intervention strategies, healthcare professionals can better support individuals affected by cyberchondria and mitigate its adverse effects on mental health and well-being. Individuals with high levels of health anxiety may be more prone to developing cyberchondria, as the accessibility of online health information can exacerbate existing worries and fuel maladaptive coping behaviours. However, it's important to recognise that not all individuals with health anxiety engage in cyberchondria, and vice versa. Factors such as personality traits, coping styles, and cognitive biases may influence the likelihood of experiencing one or both phenomena. As world citizens, one should give an emphasis to mastering digital literacy and obtain health information from trustworthy websites in order to obtain a more enhanced comprehension of cyberchondria.

Despite growing recognition of cyberchondria and its impact on mental health and healthcare, several research gaps remain. Future studies should adopt a multifaceted approach to understand its development, influences, and possible interventions. Longitudinal research is needed to track how cyberchondria evolves over time and its long-term psychological effects. Additionally, exploring individual differences—such as personality traits and coping mechanisms—can help identify those most vulnerable. Cultural and socioeconomic factors also play a role in shaping cyberchondria experiences, necessitating further research into how beliefs and financial constraints influence health anxiety. Digital literacy training has been proposed as a potential solution, with future studies needed to determine its effectiveness in reducing cyberchondria through improved health information navigation. Furthermore, technological advancements, including algorithms, social media, and online advertising, may contribute to cyberchondria by directing users toward distressing health information, warranting further exploration. Clinical interventions should also be developed to help healthcare professionals identify and manage cyberchondria in patients. Research on coping strategies could uncover effective techniques for mitigating health-related anxiety. Additionally, the relationship between health misinformation and cyberchondria remains underexplored, highlighting the need to examine how misinformation exacerbates distress. Addressing these gaps through interdisciplinary research and collaboration among healthcare providers, digital platform developers, and educators could lead to better strategies for managing cyberchondria and improving mental health outcomes.

While cyberchondria is often associated with increased anxiety and distress, it is important to acknowledge that online health information can also have positive effects. Many individuals find reassurance and empowerment through online medical resources, enabling them to better understand their symptoms and potential health conditions. A critical gap is the need for cross-cultural studies examining how different sociocultural contexts influence the prevalence and manifestation of cyberchondria. Additionally, research on the role of artificial intelligence in shaping health information-seeking behaviors, particularly how AI-driven chatbots and search algorithms impact cyberchondria, is necessary. Investigating the long-term effects of cyberchondria on physical health outcomes, such as chronic stress-related conditions, would also provide a more comprehensive picture of its impact. Furthermore, future studies should assess the effectiveness of various intervention strategies, including digital literacy training, structured therapy programs, and technological solutions designed to improve online health information accuracy. By addressing these research gaps, scholars and practitioners can develop more effective strategies for managing cyberchondria and promoting responsible digital health engagement.

REFERENCES

Abdulrahman, K. A. B., Musfir, S. K. A., Alforaih, A. S., Alshehri, A., Aldossari, A. K., & Dawood, F. D. B. (2024). The prevalence of cyberchondria and the impact of skepticism on medical decisions among Imam Mohammed Ibn Saud Islamic university students, riyadh, Saudi Arabia. *Journal of Family Medicine and Primary Care, 13*(11), 5334–5340. DOI: 10.4103/jfmpc.jfmpc_640_24 PMID: 39722934

Afrin, R., & Prybutok, G. (2022). Insights into the antecedents of cyberchondria: A perspective from the USA. *Health Promotion International, 37*(4), daac108. Advance online publication. DOI: 10.1093/heapro/daac108 PMID: 36047641

Agrawal, V., Khulbe, Y., Singh, A., & Kar, S. K. (2024). The digital health dilemma: Exploring cyberchondria, well-being, and smartphone addiction in medical and non-medical undergraduates. *Indian Journal of Psychiatry, 66*(3), 256–262. DOI: 10.4103/indianjpsychiatry.indianjpsychiatry_570_23 PMID: 39100122

Akhtar, M., & Fatima, T. (2019). Exploring cyberchondria and worry about health among individuals with no diagnosed medical condition. *JPMA. The Journal of the Pakistan Medical Association, 0*(0), 1. DOI: 10.5455/JPMA.8682 PMID: 31954030

Arias López, M. D. P., Ong, B. A., Borrat Frigola, X., Fernández, A. L., Hicklent, R. S., Obeles, A. J., Rocimo, A. M., & Celi, L. A. (2023). Digital literacy as a new determinant of health: A scoping review. *PLOS Digital Health, 2*(10), e0000279. DOI: 10.1371/journal.pdig.0000279 PMID: 37824584

Bahadir, O., & Dundar, C. (2024). The impact of online health information source preference on intolerance to uncertainty and cyberchondria in a youthful generation. *Indian Journal of Psychiatry, 66*(4), 360–366. DOI: 10.4103/indianjpsychiatry.indianjpsychiatry_715_23 PMID: 38778859

Bajcar, B., & Babiak, J. (2019). Self-esteem and cyberchondria: The mediation effects of health anxiety and obsessive–compulsive symptoms in a community sample. *Current Psychology (New Brunswick, N.J.), 40*(6), 2820–2831. DOI: 10.1007/s12144-019-00216-x

Barke, A., Bleichhardt, G., Rief, W., & Doering, B. K. (2016). The Cyberchondria Severity Scale (CSS): German validation and development of a short form. *International Journal of Behavioral Medicine, 23*(5), 595–605. DOI: 10.1007/s12529-016-9549-8 PMID: 26931780

Bujnowska-Fedak, M. M., & Węgierek, P. (2020). The impact of online health information on patient health behaviours and making decisions concerning health. *International Journal of Environmental Research and Public Health*, *17*(3), 880. DOI: 10.3390/ijerph17030880 PMID: 32023828

Da Silva, F. G., Andrade, R., Silva, I., & Cardoso, A. (2016). Cross-cultural adaptation of the Cyberchondria Severity Scale for Brazilian Portuguese. *Trends in Psychiatry and Psychotherapy*, *38*(2), 90–95. DOI: 10.1590/2237-6089-2015-0063 PMID: 27409134

Farooq, A., Laato, S., & Islam, A. K. M. N. (2020). Impact of online Information on Self-Isolation Intention during the COVID-19 Pandemic: Cross-Sectional Study. *Journal of Medical Internet Research*, *22*(5), e19128. DOI: 10.2196/19128 PMID: 32330115

Fergus, T. A. (2014). The Cyberchondria Severity Scale (CSS): An examination of structure and relations with health anxiety in a community sample. *Journal of Anxiety Disorders*, *28*(6), 504–510. DOI: 10.1016/j.janxdis.2014.05.006 PMID: 24956357

Fergus, T. A., & Dolan, S. L. (2014). Problematic internet use and internet searches for medical information: The role of health anxiety. *Cyberpsychology, Behavior, and Social Networking*, *17*(12), 761–765. DOI: 10.1089/cyber.2014.0169 PMID: 25412398

Fergus, T. A., & Russell, L. H. (2016). Does cyberchondria overlap with health anxiety and obsessive–compulsive symptoms? An examination of latent structure and scale interrelations. *Journal of Anxiety Disorders*, *38*, 88–94. DOI: 10.1016/j.janxdis.2016.01.009 PMID: 26851749

Gaillard, S., Oláh, Z. A., Venmans, S., & Burke, M. (2021). Countering the cognitive, linguistic, and psychological underpinnings behind susceptibility to fake news: A review of current literature with special focus on the role of age and digital literacy. *Frontiers in Communication*, *6*, 661801. Advance online publication. DOI: 10.3389/fcomm.2021.661801

Global Web Index. (2017). Digital vs. traditional media consumption. In *Global Web Index* (Q1 2017). https://www.gwi.com/hubfs/Digital_vs_Traditional_Media_Consumption.pdf

Hague, C., & Payton, S. (2011). *Digital Literacy Across The Curriculum*. Curriculum Leadership Journal.

Infanti, A., Starcevic, V., Schimmenti, A., Khazaal, Y., Karila, L., Giardina, A., Flayelle, M., Hedayatzadeh Razavi, S. B., Baggio, S., Vögele, C., & Billieux, J. (2022). Predictors of Cyberchondria during the COVID-19 pandemic: Cross-sectional study using supervised machine learning. *JMIR Formative Research, 7*, e42206. Advance online publication. DOI: 10.2196/42206 PMID: 36947575

Jokić-Begić, N., Mikac, U., Čuržik, D., & Jokić, C. S. (2019). The development and validation of the Short Cyberchondria Scale (SCS). *Journal of Psychopathology and Behavioral Assessment, 41*(4), 662–676. DOI: 10.1007/s10862-019-09744-z

Khan, A. W., & Pandey, J. (2022). Dark side consequences of cyberchondria: An empirical investigation. *Aslib Journal of Information Management, 74*(5), 801–817. DOI: 10.1108/AJIM-08-2021-0222

Kim, J., Livingston, M. A., Jin, B., Watts, M., & Hwang, J. (2024). Fundamentals of digital health literacy: A scoping review of identifying core competencies to use in practice. *Adult Learning, 35*(3), 131–142. DOI: 10.1177/10451595231178298

Kumar, A. (2021). Role of digital literacy in preventing hacking. *IJIRT, 8*(1), 1392–1399. https://www.ijirt.org/master/publishedpaper/IJIRT157666_PAPER.pdf

Laato, S., Islam, A. K. M. N., Islam, M. N., & Whelan, E. (2020). What drives unverified information sharing and cyberchondria during the COVID-19 pandemic? *European Journal of Information Systems, 29*(3), 288–305. DOI: 10.1080/0960085X.2020.1770632

Loos, A. (2013). Cyberchondria: Too much information for the health anxious patient? *Journal of Consumer Health on the Internet, 17*(4), 439–445. DOI: 10.1080/15398285.2013.833452

Makarla, S., Gopichandran, V., & Tondare, D. (2019). Prevalence and correlates of cyberchondria among professionals working in the information technology sector in Chennai, India. *Journal of Postgraduate Medicine, 65*(2), 87–92. DOI: 10.4103/jpgm.JPGM_293_18 PMID: 31036778

McElroy, E., & Shevlin, M. (2014). The development and initial validation of the cyberchondria severity scale (CSS). *Journal of Anxiety Disorders, 28*(2), 259–265. DOI: 10.1016/j.janxdis.2013.12.007 PMID: 24508033

McMullan, R., Berle, D., Arnáez, S., & Starčević, V. (2019). The relationships between health anxiety, online health information seeking, and cyberchondria: Systematic review and meta-analysis. *Journal of Affective Disorders, 245*, 270–278. DOI: 10.1016/j.jad.2018.11.037 PMID: 30419526

Mestre-Bach, G., & Potenza, M. N. (2023). Cyberchondria: A growing concern during the covid-19 pandemic and a possible addictive disorder? *Current Addiction Reports, 10*(1), 77–96. DOI: 10.1007/s40429-022-00462-3 PMID: 36785757

Müller, A., Baumann, E., & Dierks, M. (2022). Cyberchondria. *The International Encyclopedia of Health Communication,* 1-6. DOI: 10.1002/9781119678816.iehc0624

Nasiri, M. M., Mohammadkhani, S., Akbari, M., & Alilou, M. M. (2023). The structural model of cyberchondria based on personality traits, health-related metacognition, cognitive bias, and emotion dysregulation. *Frontiers in Psychiatry, 13,* 960055. Advance online publication. DOI: 10.3389/fpsyt.2022.960055 PMID: 36699479

Özkent, M. S., Kılınç, M. T., Hamarat, M. B., Yılmaz, B., Göger, Y. E., Özkent, Y., & Pişkin, M. M. (2023). Digitalization and urological diseases: Severity of cyberchondria and level of health anxiety in patients visiting outpatient urology clinics. *Cyberpsychology, Behavior, and Social Networking, 26*(1), 28–34. DOI: 10.1089/cyber.2022.0089 PMID: 36454182

Park, S., Kim, E., & Na, E. (2014). Online activities, digital media literacy, and networked individualism of Korean youth. *Youth & Society, 47*(6), 829–849. DOI: 10.1177/0044118X14561008

Park, Y. J. (2011). Digital literacy and privacy behavior online. *Communication Research, 40*(2), 215–236. DOI: 10.1177/0093650211418338

Patanapu, S., Sreeja, C., Veeraboina, N., Reddy, K., Voruganti, S., & Anusha, P. (2022). Prevalence and effect of cyberchondria on academic performance among undergraduate dental students: An institutional based study. *Industrial Psychiatry Journal, 31*(2), 228–234. DOI: 10.4103/ipj.ipj_272_21 PMID: 36419676

Pawar, P., Kamat, A., Salimath, G., Jacob, K. R., & Kamath, R. (2022). Prevalence of Cyberchondria among Outpatients with Metabolic Syndrome in a Tertiary Care Hospital in Southern India. *TheScientificWorldJournal, 1–5,* 1–5. Advance online publication. DOI: 10.1155/2022/3211501 PMID: 36199439

Płaciszewski, K., Wierzba, W., Ostrowski, J., Pinkas, J., & Jankowski, M. (2022). Use of the Internet for health purposes—A national web-based cross-sectional survey among adults in Poland. *International Journal of Environmental Research and Public Health, 19*(23), 16315. DOI: 10.3390/ijerph192316315 PMID: 36498389

Rahme, C., Akel, M., Obeid, S., & Hallit, S. (2021). Cyberchondria severity and quality of life among Lebanese adults: The mediating role of fear of COVID-19, depression, anxiety, stress and obsessive–compulsive behavior—a structural equation model approach. *BMC Psychology*, *9*(1), 169. Advance online publication. DOI: 10.1186/s40359-021-00674-8 PMID: 34715930

Ruben, M. A., Stosic, M. D., Correale, J., & Blanch-Hartigan, D. (2021). Is technology enhancing or hindering interpersonal communication? A framework and preliminary results to examine the relationship between technology use and nonverbal decoding skill. *Frontiers in Psychology*, *11*, 611670. Advance online publication. DOI: 10.3389/fpsyg.2020.611670 PMID: 33519627

Selvi, Y., Turan, S. G., Sayin, A. A., Boysan, M., & Kandeger, A. (2018). The Cyberchondria Severity Scale (CSS): Validity and reliability study of the Turkish version. *Sleep and Hypnosis*, •••, 241–246. DOI: 10.5350/Sleep.Hypn.2018.20.0157

Sohail, M., & Zafar, N. (2022). Fear of COVID-19 and stress in university students: Mediating role of cyberchondria and moderating role of creative coping and social supports. *JPMA. The Journal of the Pakistan Medical Association*. Advance online publication. DOI: 10.47391/JPMA.4350 PMID: 36280920

Starcevic, V., & Berle, D. (2013). Cyberchondria: Towards a better understanding of excessive health-related Internet use. *Expert Review of Neurotherapeutics*, *13*(2), 205–213. DOI: 10.1586/ern.12.162 PMID: 23368807

Starcevic, V., Schimmenti, A., Billieux, J., & Berle, D. (2021). Cyberchondria in the time of the COVID-19 pandemic. *Human Behavior and Emerging Technologies*, *3*(1), 53–62. DOI: 10.1002/hbe2.233 PMID: 33363277

Statista. (May 22, 2024). Number of internet and social media users worldwide as of April 2024 (in billions). In *Statista*. Retrieved April 2024, from https://www-statista-com.ezproxy.lib.hkmu.edu.hk/forecasts/1146659/social-media-users-in-the-world

Statista. (May 7, 2024). Global internet penetration rate as of April 2024, by region. In *Statista*. Retrieved April 2024, from https://www.statista.com/statistics/269329/penetration-rate-of-the-internet-by-region/#:~:text=Internet%20penetration%20rate%20worldwide%202024%2C%20by%20region&text=As%20of%20April%202024%2C%20Northern,rate%20was%20roughly%2067.1%20percent

Szawłoga, T., Soroka, K., & Śliwińska, M. (2024). Cyberchondria in students: An eHealth related problem. A review. *Medical Science Pulse*, *18*(2, SUPPLEMENT 3), 12–21. DOI: 10.5604/01.3001.0054.5653

Tarabay, C., Bitar, Z., Akel, M., Hallit, S., Obeid, S., & Soufia, M. (2023). Cyberchondria Severity and quality of life among Lebanese adults. *The Primary Care Companion for CNS Disorders*, *25*(2). Advance online publication. DOI: 10.4088/PCC.22m03252 PMID: 37115149

Tiwari, S., Srivastava, S., & Negi, M. (2022). Prevalence and predictors of cyberchondria and depression amid COVID-19 pandemic in adult population of Uttar Pradesh, India. *Archives of Medicine and Health Sciences*, *10*(2), 200–206. DOI: 10.4103/amhs.amhs_95_22

Turkistani, A., Mashaikhi, A., Bajaber, A., Alghamdi, W., Althobaity, B., Alharthi, N., & Alhomaiani, S. (2020). The prevalence of cyberchondria and the impact of social media among the students in Taif University. *International Journal of Medicine in Developing Countries*, 1759–1765. https://doi.org/DOI: 10.24911/IJMDC.51-1598363146

Varma, R., & Singh, T. (2023). Cyberchondria and health: Exploring the linkages. *Mind & Society*, *12*(02), 29–34. DOI: 10.56011/mind-mri-122-20233

Vismara, M., Caricasole, V., Starcevic, V., Cinosi, E., Dell'Osso, B., Martinotti, G., & Fineberg, N. A. (2020). Is cyberchondria a new transdiagnostic digital compulsive syndrome? A systematic review of the evidence. *Comprehensive Psychiatry*, *99*, 152167. DOI: 10.1016/j.comppsych.2020.152167 PMID: 32146315

Wang, P., Li, L., & Chen, W. (n.d.). *Exploring Antecedents of Cyberchondria During Pandemics: An integration of Stress and Coping and SOR*. AIS Electronic Library (AISeL). https://aisel.aisnet.org/pacis2023/112

White, R. W., & Horvitz, E. (2009). Cyberchondria. *ACM Transactions on Information Systems*, *27*(4), 1–37. DOI: 10.1145/1629096.1629101

Wijesinghe, C. A., Liyanage, U. L. N. S., Kapugama, K. G. C. L., Warsapperuma, W. N. P., Williams, S. S., Kuruppuarachchi, K. L. A., & Rodrigo, A. (2019). "Muddling by googling" – Cyberchondria among outpatient attendees of two hospitals in Sri Lanka. *Sri Lanka Journal of Psychiatry*, *10*(1), 11–15. DOI: 10.4038/sljpsyc.v10i1.8202

Wineburg, S., & McGrew, S. (2016). Evaluating Information: The cornerstone of civic online reasoning. *Stanford Digital Repository*. https://apo.org.au/resource/evaluating-information-cornerstone-civic-online-reasoning

Wu, X., Nazari, N., & Griffiths, M. D. (2021). Using fear and anxiety related to COVID-19 to predict cyberchondria: Cross-sectional survey study. *Journal of Medical Internet Research*, *23*(6), e26285. DOI: 10.2196/26285 PMID: 34014833

Xiang, H., Zhou, J., & Liu, M. (2023). Judging online health misinformation: Effects of cyberchondria and age. In *Lecture notes in computer science* (pp. 284–301). https://doi.org/DOI: 10.1007/978-3-031-34866-2_22

Xu, R. H., & Chen, C. (2024). Moderating effect of coping strategies on the association between the infodemic-driven overuse of health care services and Cyberchondria and anxiety: Partial Least Squares Structural Equation Modeling Study. *Journal of Medical Internet Research*, *26*, e53417. https://doi.org/doi:10.2196/53417. DOI: 10.2196/53417 PMID: 38593427

Xu, Z. (2024). The impact of online resources on reducing mental health stigma among international college students: A case study. *Lecture Notes in Education Psychology and Public Media*, *58*(1), 141–147. DOI: 10.54254/2753-7048/58/20241770

Yam, F. C., Korkmaz, O., & Griffiths, M. D. (2021). The association between fear of Covid-19 and smartphone addiction among individuals: The mediating and moderating role of cyberchondria severity. *Current Psychology (New Brunswick, N.J.)*, *42*(3), 2377–2390. DOI: 10.1007/s12144-021-02324-z PMID: 34690474

Yang, Y., Ta, N., & Li, Z. (2022). Investigating the obsessive and compulsive features of cyberchondria: A Holistic review. *Frontiers in Psychology*, *13*, 897426. Advance online publication. DOI: 10.3389/fpsyg.2022.897426 PMID: 35859839

Yuen, E., Winter, N., Savira, F., Huggins, C. E., Nguyen, L., Cooper, P., Peeters, A., Anderson, K., Bhoyroo, R., Crowe, S., & Ugalde, A. (2024). Digital health literacy and its association with sociodemographic characteristics, health resource use, and health outcomes: Rapid review. *Interactive Journal of Medical Research*, *13*(1), e46888. DOI: 10.2196/46888 PMID: 39059006

Zhang, X., Liu, Y., Qin, Z., Ye, Z., & Meng, F. (2023). Understanding the role of social media usage and health self-efficacy in the processing of COVID-19 rumors: A SOR perspective. *Data and Information Management*, *7*(2), 100043. DOI: 10.1016/j.dim.2023.100043 PMID: 37304677

Chapter 8

Timeliness and Appropriateness of Cross-Sectional Study Design in the Study of Online Health Information Seeking Using AI

Shujin Lin
https://orcid.org/0009-0009-2840-7316
Xiamen University Malaysia, Malaysia

ABSTRACT

Users using AI such as ChatGPT and Gemini for health consultation and self-diagnosis is becoming a popular way of health information-seeking for the public, which marks a noticeable change in the ways people interact with health information. Under such a status quo, it leads to a need to systematically study on the users' behaviour in key factors including perceived trust, motivations and levels of satisfaction. This study proposes that the Cross-sectional Study Design is the timely and appropriate approach to explore in this new-appearing phenomenon. In addition, to sufficiently explain the use of cross-sectional studies in the research of using AI for health information-seeking, this study also constructs a preliminary conceptual research framework based on the Planned Risk Information Seeking Model (PRISM) and Health Belief Model (HBM) with several exemplary research questions, aiming to discuss how factors from different groups including perceived

DOI: 10.4018/979-8-3693-5837-5.ch008

trust on AI-generated information, usage motivations and the perceived accuracy of information affect their behavioural intentions.

1. INTRODUCTION

In recent years, Artificial Intelligence (AI) technologies have experienced rapid development and shown enormous implemental potential in different fields, the healthcare field is no exception. Traditional medical research and clinical practices often rely on experienced professionals and structured data, which requires a huge amount of human material resources, and even leads to lower efficiency and higher expenditure (Wang et al., 2024). To solve these issues, researchers have started to study on the possibility of using AI to improve the quality and efficiency of medical services.

During the COVID-19 pandemic, the increasing pressure on the healthcare system accelerated a new form of "doctor" – digital symptom checkers. The emergence of COVID-19 quickly rose people's interests in remote medical assessment tools. Such rapid increase of interest was also based on the growing demand of obtaining immediate and convenient information (Esmaeilzadeh et al., 2025). Although the traditional online platforms such as the search engines and social media hold comparatively high accessibility and various contents, these platforms are generally lack for real-time interaction, contextual guidance and personalised support, which makes it functionally limited in dealing with complicated health issues (Jibril & Adzovie, 2022). The web-based symptom checkers are artificial intelligence-supported software which function as chatbots in supporting diagnosis and classification (Morse et al., 2020). OpenAI introduced ChatGPT on December 22, 2022, which is a large language model AI trained based on a large amount of text data and is able to generate responses just like humans. By February 2025, the worldwide weekly active users of ChatGPT have reached 400 million (Backlinko, 2025). Shen et al. (2024) suggested that compared to traditional web search, ChatGPT had a more outstanding performance in answering the questions from patients which were related to symptom-based diagnoses, and has an equivalent result in providing medical knowledge and established policies. ChatGPT can effectively deliver information and support to the patient in multiple scenarios, such as mental health assessment, consultation, education, and medication management (Cascella et al., 2023). Instead of treating AI as a pure technical tool, it is more like an interactive object which holds impact on human behaviour, decision-making and health information processing styles. As the promising performance in searching for healthcare knowledge, there underlines a big possibility that AI tools like ChatGPT may replace traditional search engines such as Google Search in the coming future (Duarte, 2025; Incerti Parenti et al.,

2024). While most patients had rather high confidence in health information generated by AI (Shahsavar & Choudhury, 2023; Ye et al., 2024), the LLM chatbot is, however, tested to be not as accurate as professionals (Makhoul et al., 2024; Ye et al., 2024). This is because ChatGPT was not professionally and specifically trained for medical literature, which underlines big risks in the application of self-diagnosis from patients, as research found that some of the patients tend to trust the answers generated by AI and determined for self-diagnosis (Shahsavar & Choudhury, 2023).

At the same time, the behaviour patterns of the public in using AI as an online health information tool differ. Users from different age groups, with different educational backgrounds and health information literacy, tend to vary widely in terms of the trust level of health suggestions from AI, ways of evaluating information and usage frequency, some of the users showed a high reliance on AI suggestions and even regarded it as an "alternative doctor", while other users remain skeptical and take it as only references (Ayo-Ajibola et al., 2024). These shifts have brought new challenges and reflections on public health communication, the justification for obtaining healthcare services and healthcare ethics. Facing the differences and complexity, a systematic methodology is needed for more comprehensive, structuralised capture and explanation of the patterns behind, especially in analysing the interactive relationship between the users and AI health information at a group level. This will not only benefit in understanding the public level of acceptance on AI-generated health care information, but also provide a basic support for improving digital health literacy, optimising platform design and public health communication strategies. Comparing to the pure evaluation on the accuracy of AI tools, more urgent problems are that "Under what motivations do the public choose to turn to these AI tools for healthcare information-seeking?", "What subjective judgements do their perceived trust of AI-generated suggestions build on?"

Under the discussed context, this study proposed the Cross-sectional Study as one of the core research methodologies in studying the public online health information-seeking behaviour on AI platforms. Compared to longitudinal research or experimental research, the cross-sectional study has the advantage of being rapid, efficient, and cost-controllable, especially suitable for capturing the general character and relationship between variables of the user groups at a certain time point (Kesmodel, 2018; Wang & Cheng, 2020). By this methodology, researchers will be able to obtain the cross-sectional data about usage frequency, trust level, ways of evaluating information and the preference in choosing AI tools. By analysing on different user groups, the usage landscape of AI health information-seeking in real life will be presented. This research design not only suits the swift evolution of the current digital healthcare environment, but also provides a methodological basis for the future research in the cross field of AI and public health communication.

2. LITERATURE REVIEW

2.1 What is a Cross-Sectional Study?

A cross-sectional study is an observational research design that collects the data of studied subjects at a specific time to measure both exposure factors and study outcomes simultaneously. Unlike the case-control study, which chooses its subjects based on the results, and the cohort study, which chooses its subjects based on exposure factors, the mechanism of a cross-sectional study is similar to capturing a snapshot of the targeted population. Without a prospective or retrospective follow-up, researchers often randomly choose the subjects from the related groups whilst analysing the relationship between exposure and result (Wang & Cheng, 2020). This study is often used to evaluate disease prevalence, perception and knowledge of healthcare, validation of measurement tools and study on reliabilities. However, due to the fixed time point of the study, researchers are not able to induct the cause-and-effect relationship, and the result may be affected by complex factors such as selection and information bias (Kesmodel, 2018).

The two subtypes under cross-sectional study are descriptive and analytical study, which depends specifically on whether the study involves the evaluation of relationships between outcome variables and exposure or risk factors. A descriptive cross-sectional study is mostly used to represent the prevalence of one or more health conditions in a certain group of people but does not encompass the association analysis between variables. While the analytical cross-sectional study is to simultaneously collect the exposure and result data at a certain time point, such that a difference between the exposed group and non-exposed group is compared. However, as the data is collected at the same time, it can be hard to tell whether the exposure is before the result, which means it a hard to determine the causal relationship (Wang & Cheng, 2020).

2.2 Strengths and Weakness of Cross-Sectional Study

Wang and Cheng (2020) argued, in their study, that the advantage of the cross-sectional study lies in its rapid implementation with a relatively low cost, making it a cost-effective research methodology. As the data are usually collected at the same point of time, researchers can simultaneously examine multiple exposure factors and results, such that the breadth and applicability are improved. Furthermore, a cross-sectional study can be applied to estimate the disease prevalence and provide critical evidence for epidemiological surveys, public health policy-making and further longitudinal studies. Compared to cohort studies and case-control studies, cross-sectional studies would not face ethical dilemmas as artificial intervention is not involved here, that is saying the studied subjects will not be intentionally exposed to certain factors or receive certain treatments. Besides, as a long-term follow-up is not needed, a cross-sectional study minimizes the influence of data lost, making the research comparatively easier to conduct, especially for a bigger target group.

As the cross-sectional study only focuses on a certain point of time, it is not able to evaluate the incidence from the process where the subject transformed from healthy to diseased. A causal relationship is also unable to be identified from such limited data as the result may differ under another time-frame (Levin, 2006). Without longitudinal data, a cause-and-effect relationship cannot be built (Solem, 2015). Another important limit lies in the unavailability of studying on the temporal sequences, which means it can be hard to explain the research result. For example, when studying the relationship between some diseases and certain risk factors, it is unsure whether it is the risk factor that leads to the disease or, whether the disease itself affects the subject's behaviours and physical conditions. The reliability of a cross-sectional study may be affected by sampling bias, nonresponse bias and memory bias from the subject. Particularly, in the study of a long-term disease, individuals who passed away prematurely due to a more severe condition may be excluded, leading to the underestimation of certain risk factors, which is called prevalence-incidence bias (Neyman bias) (Levin, 2006).

2.3 The Application of Cross-Sectional Study

As a popular observational research design, the cross-sectional study has vital applications in epidemiological and public health research. First of all, a cross-sectional study can be effective in the evaluation of prevalence studies, especially for the mass-scale screening of the target group at a certain point in time to obtain the cross-sectional snapshot of the disease distribution. Secondly, it is often applied in the discussion of attitudes, knowledge and health behaviour among patients and health professionals and is widely used in health education and public health policy studies. Other than that, cross-sectional studies have important applications in the evaluation of validation and reliability of measurement instruments, namely the comparison of accuracy and consistency between different measurement instruments and questionnaires. It is also worth mentioning that the cross-sectional study can also be utilised as a base for producing assumptions, which provides basic data support for further longitudinal studies (e.g. Cohort study and randomized controlled trial). Due to its convenience in conduction, effectiveness and cost-friendliness, cross-sectional studies have been widely applied in multiple research fields such as epidemiological research, public health planning and healthcare service evaluation (Kesmodel, 2018).

Bodani et al. (2023) invited 525 participants who are residing in Karachi, Pakistan to fill out the online questionnaire via different social media platforms from January to March 2023 to determine the knowledge, attitude and practices of ChatGPT, where they had the result of 76.2% of participants were familiar with ChatGPT, and demonstrated positive perception and confidence in its accuracy. However, the participants also showed cautious concerns about over-dependence and different levels of concern on privacy and security issues of ChatGPT. On the other aspect, a cross-sectional study was conducted by Parikh et al. (2023) to compare the perceptions of ChatGPT between healthcare workers and other professionals. A survey was sent out to 210 participants including 157 healthcare professionals and 53 from other fields on February 2023. Although healthcare workers owned a lower percentage in the usage of ChatGPT, they were more positive about the possible impact from ChatGPT on their future career life and more likely to consider a shift of career due to its appearance. Most of the participants thought the influence of ChatGPT would not exceed 50% before the year of 2050, but the healthcare professionals were more conservative on this aspect, which showed an obvious difference on professional backgrounds on the acceptance of artificial intelligence. Shahsavar and Choudhury (2-23) tested the users' intentions on using ChatGPT for self-diagnosis and other health-related purposes with a cross-sectional study by collecting data from 607 participants. They found that 78.4% of respondents had the intention to use ChatGPT for self-diagnosis with a partial least squares structural equation modelling (PLS-SEM). Another study in 2024 also examined the factors which affect users in the perspective of using ChatGPT as an assistant technology in healthcare decision-making (Choudhury et al., 2024). Their findings suggested that trustworthiness was the paramount concern in healthcare as the decisions were directly linked to health implications, which emphasises an accurate, clear and secure AI system. While for non-healthcare contexts, although trustworthiness was still important, it includes a broader range of factors namely efficiency, user experience and novelty.

2.4 Cross-Sectional Studies on Health Information Seeking Behaviour and AI

Cross-sectional studies were widely adopted in the research of health information-seeking behaviours and artificial intelligence. A cross-sectional study was conducted by Carmona et al. (2022) to research on the users of a web-based intelligent symptom checker (Bouy) for health information. The research found that among the users of Bouy, individuals who received a college degree or higher were up to 81%, and white female was the majority. Most of the users had medical insurance and regular healthcare providers. Bouy was seen by the majority of users as reliable, useful and easy to understand, and showed a positive effect in relieving medical anxiety and enhancing self-care ability. Ayo-Ajibola et al. (2024) studied the adoption and experience of users who utilised AI to generate health information in the United States with a cross-sectional questionnaire. Among the 2406 respondents, there were 21.5% who used ChatGPT for online health information. The 21.5% of respondents showed characteristics of younger ages, a lower percentage of higher educational background, tended to use transient healthcare (ED or urgent care), and had a higher frequency of searching general online health information as well. Approximately 39.3% of ChatGPT users used this platform twice to thrice or more every week with the primary usage of determining whether a medical consultation is necessary or searching for alternative treatments. Most users regarded ChatGPT and other online health information resources as equally useful or even more useful than a medical doctor, and about one-third of users would ask for a referral or change of medication under the suggestion of ChatGPT. Even though, 67.9% of users kept skeptical about the results given by ChatGPT and 67.5% expressed they would make further confirmation with the doctor. Similarly, Ye et al. (2023) conducted the research based on the evaluation from patients and physicians on Large Language Model responses to Rheumatology patients' questions with a single-centre cross-sectional survey. Seventeen patients from Edmonton, Alberta, Canada evaluated between the answers of the LLM chatbot and physician for comprehensiveness and readability, and four rheumatologists evaluated the accuracy of the answers, too. From the patient side, the results showed similarity to the AI-generated responses and physician-generated responses. Yet the rheumatologists rated AI responses much lower than the ones the physician gave. This indicated that the patients might not be aware of the inferiority of LLM-generated responses to physician-generated responses. More specifically, Ayo-Ajibola et al. (2025) designed a cross-sectional national survey to research on the influential factors which can affect access to care such as owning a usual source of primary care (USPC), and their effect on the use of ChatGPT and other OHI platforms. Among the 2406 respondents, 56% reported owning a usual source of primary care. Those respondents who aged older than those who didn't, use English as a primary language, had a higher income level, and had more formal education. This indicated that those people with regular primary care access, tend to rely less on ChatGPT, suggesting that a usual source of primary care may weaken the need or motive to use artificial intelligence for online health information.

2.5 Theoretical Background of the Conceptual Framework

The Health Belief Model (HBM) has been widely used as a research framework in studying the reason why patients take proactive health behaviours in history (Orji et al., 2012; Zhao et al., 2022b). It provides the theoretical basis in improving the cognition of the public in terms of healthcare issues, health risks, and taking precautionary measures, or being part of related interventional strategies. In its subsequent versions, the Health Belief Model further stresses the importance of enhancing self-efficacy, with the aim of facilitating necessary behavioural changes. Although this model focuses on an individual level, it also takes the social environment where the healthcare behaviour is surrounded into consideration (Green et al., 2020). This model assumes that the intention of taking proactive healthcare behaviour is more dependent on the personal belief of certain situations instead of the objective fact of the condition. The deciding factors may include the perceived susceptibility on the disease, the perceived severity of the consequences of the disease and related conditions, the perceived benefits of the behaviours in eliminating the threat brought by disease, and the perceived barriers in front of the negative aspect of those healthcare behaviours (Janz & Becker, 1984).

The Planned Risk Information Seeking Model is brought up by Kahlor (2010) to explain how individuals seek for information when individuals are facing health risks. This is a model which integrates multiple information seeking models including the theory of planned behaviour, the risk information seeking and processing model (RISP) and the augmented RSIP model (Niu et al., 2020). The core of the PRISM model is the individual's subjective norms, attitudes in information seeking and the perceived control of information seeking will create positive influences on his/her intention in information seeking. Other than that, the model also noted that the emotional response an individual has to health risks and the perceived lack of knowledge will also enhance his/her intention for information seeking (Kahlor, 2010). PRISM has been proven to be effective in predicting the intention of information seeking and showed a well performance in the application in multiple health sectors such as sexual healthcare, vaccine information avoidance and cancer risk communication (Hovick et al., 2014; Link & Kahlor, 2024; Niu et al., 2020).

The Health Belief Model (HBM) has shown outstanding explanatory and applicability as one of the widely adopted theoretical frameworks that has been used to understand individuals' health behaviours. Previous empirical studies have proved that the HBM is able to effectively predict and explain multiple health behaviours, such as healthy diets, vaccination, cancer screening, health-seeking behaviours and precautionary behaviours in public health incidents (Zhao et al., 2022a). Those studies have tested the predictive capacity of the key variables in HBM, including perceived susceptibility, perceived severity, perceived benefits and perceived benefits. For example, in the study of the acceptance of COVID-19 vaccination, the perceived severity of infection and the perceived benefits of vaccination have tangibly increased the willingness to receive vaccination (Wong et al., 2021). Other than that, the theoretical logic of HBM is especially suitable for the explanation of why individuals would make health behaviours under the circumstances where symptoms and external pressure are lacking. This aspect makes the HBM especially suitable for the psychological mechanism of online health information-seeking (Ahadzadeh et al., 2015). For high-risk groups with chronic diseases, their perceptions on self-health risks will have a direct influence on whether to proactively search for related information to control the disease or prevent complications. Under these conditions, this study believes that the HBM can provide an analytical angle which is more suitable for the research subjects. More importantly, an existing meta-analysis by Carpenter (2010) further supported the obvious advantage of HBM in predicting "precautionary health behaviours." Despite the fact that certain variables have a comparatively weak effect in predicting health behaviours such as the perceived susceptibility, the predictive capacity of the model was obviously strengthened when the research subjects were set to engage in precautionary behaviours, including information seeking and vaccination, instead of treatment behaviours. Such a conclusion has provided a strong support for the applications of the Health Belief Model in the research of health information seeking behaviours. To sum up, considering the systematic structure in the aspect of the explanation of individuals' health behaviour, the suitability among high-risk groups and the theoretical advantages in predicting precautionary behaviours, the choice of using the HBM as the theoretical basis of this study is built on solid previous empirical and logical evidence. Compared to other models, which concentrate on technologies and the media such as the Technology Acceptance Model, these models place more emphasis on the channel of information, the use of medium and the information avoidance tendency instead of taking the health motivation as the fundamental point of departure. While the HBM can be closer to the psychological variables such as health motivations and perceived risks. The health information-seeking behaviour driven under the context of the popularity of AI discussed in this study is deeply rooted in the perceptual and psychological motivations of individuals on health risks in the essence (Davidhizar, 1983). Such that the Health Belief Model is more suitable for the discussion of online health information-seeking behaviours within the current context of the wide adoptions of AI platforms. It not only provides a precise theoretical framework for this study, but also enables the deeper research on the behavioural change of individuals facing health risk perceptions, which further valuably guides the practical health behaviour interventions and health communication strategies.

2.6 Existing Literature on Theoretical Integrations in Health Information Studies

With the wider application of AI technologies in obtaining health information day to day, a traditional single theoretical model might be not adequate enough to explain the complicated behaviours of users under such a new emerging scenario. To achieve a more precise capture of individuals' information-seeking motivations, technological acceptance process and behavioural feedback when facing health risks, researchers gradually tend to make integrative use of several theoretical models.

With the generalisation of social media, search engines and intelligent devices, the information reception ways are becoming more complicated and varied in the modern society. The public was not only relying on proactive searching to obtain health information, but also unconsciously exposed to relative information in more cases. Such passive information reception channels were also playing an equally important role in influencing the individuals' healthcare decision-making and behaviours. As the existing health information-seeking studies are over-focusing on the proactive information-seeking behaviour from individuals while neglecting the passive nature of information reception, Longo (2005) suggested an extensive health information-seeking model which differentiated the two ways of information reception including proactively seeking and passively receiving. The model conducted a deeper analysis on the effect of different information resources including social media, health applications and intelligent devices. Other than that, the framework also emphasised on the influence of the socio-economic background of the individual, pointing out the differences between different socio-economic groups in obtaining information and interpretation. The framework proposed by Longo aimed to provide a new angle for understanding the communicational mechanism of health information but also offer theoretical support for optimising healthcare policies.

Ahadzadeh et.al. (2015) suggested that the single use of the Technology Acceptance Model or the Health Belief Model was not able to fully explain the health-related internet usage behaviour in past studies. The TAM is mainly used to predict the use of technology yet without a full consideration of health motivational factors, while the HBM only explain the healthcare-related internet use from a healthcare perspective yet without explanations of the behaviour process. Thus, an integrative model based on TAM and HBM is suggested. The participants chosen in this study were the women who were internet users living in the state of Selangor, Malaysia. Detailed results showed that among the 293 participants, the perceived health risks had tangibly affected their internet use and health awareness also drove health information-seeking behaviours. In particular, the perceived health risks and the influences from health internet use on health awareness were more presented through the individuals' perceptions and emotional attitudes on the Internet. The study found that women are more intended to use the Internet to obtain health information when they perceive health risks and are equipped with health awareness. The perceived benefits, usability and positive attitudes to health purposes were the key factors to driving the use.

Another research proposed a consumer acceptance model which integrated the usability and social cognitive theories into the Technology Acceptance Model to understand the acceptance level of young Internet users on health information portals (Tao et al., 2020). By sending out questionnaires to 201 participants in China, the study found that the young consumers' acceptance of health information portals was affected primarily by the attitudes they had on the portal, while the attitudes were affected by the perceived usability and perceived usefulness. The young consumers were more focused on the practicality of the portals in healthcare instead of the convenience of using, as the perceived usefulness was more capable of explaining the differences in the attitudes of use than the perceived usability. Other than that, the subjective usability has noticeable influences on perceived usability and perceived usefulness, with the self-efficacy set by the portal playing an important role in driving the consumers' usage intentions as well. The study also showed that the usability design of the portals had a significant effect in enhancing the consumers' usage intentions, especially in terms of increasing self-efficacy and optimising user experiences.

Zhao et al. (2022a) integrated the Health Belief Model and the Social Support Theory and a critical health literacy perspective in their study with the aim of understanding the online health information-seeking behaviour of patients who suffer from chronic conditions. Their research found that the integrative model based on the HBM and SST is capable of predicting the online health information-seeking behaviours of patients. And the perceived susceptibility and severity can further contribute to the prediction and explain the perceived risks. The perceived benefits were facilitated by the informational support and emotional support which positively affected the behaviour. Other than that, the study also proved the important negative moderating influences that critical health literacy has on the relationship between perceived risks and online health information-seeking behaviours.

2.7 Gap Identification

Even though there is more and more research focusing on the application of AI in online health information seeking, especially with the rapid development of artificial intelligence technologies in the healthcare field, a greater number of users started to use AI as tools for online health information seeking, diagnosis and suggestions. However, current studies are more focused on the accuracy, ethical considerations and application scenarios of AI technologies, yet lack a systematic analysis of user behaviour and the global adoption of this phenomenon. As utilising AI for online health information is a growing trend, the situation calls for a more detailed analysis. From the examined past studies, single variables were focused on by each study, such as perceived trust, user motivations, and information evaluation standards. Questions like "how the sense of trust affect the willingness to use", "how is the relationship between the willingness to use and satisfaction level", and "how the perceived trust and motivation of AI-generated health information from different groups of people differ" calls for a deeper research and understanding.

As a quantitative research methodology, cross-sectional study has the characteristics of being able to systematically, rapidly and effectively capture the behaviours, attitudes, and cognitions of different groups at the same point of time. It provides the researchers with a chance to analyse the prevalence of health information-seeking behaviour using AI, at the same time revealing the differences between users in terms of perceived trust and usage motivation. By cross-sectional study, researchers will be able to discuss the perceived trust and motivations of different groups of people, and further the internal relationship between those variables such as trustworthiness – willingness to use – satisfaction level. Such structural analysis can benefit the understanding of behaviour patterns and psychological motivations of users' usage of AI for health information seeking. Under the need to shift the research focus to further understand the phenomenon of using AI for health information seeking, cross-sectional study can be one contextually appropriate and time-sensitive, as there's no more need to prove the existence and importance of this phenomenon, which is already widely existed in different social groups. The implementation of cross-sectional studies in this field can quickly obtain the data of the status quo of using AI for health information-seeking, and provide a base for future longitudinal research.

To sum up, although there are studies that focus on the relationship between AI and health information seeking, the analysis of motivation differences and variable relations remains weak. Thus, adopting cross-sectional studies to systematically analyse this situation can be a way to fill up the gap.

3. CONCEPTUAL FRAMEWORK AND RESEARCH PROPOSAL

3.1 The Construction of Conceptual Framework

In this study, a conceptual model is constructed with the aim of researching the users' behaviour and attitudes in the process of using AI for health information-seeking, providing preliminary validation of this methodology design for future empirical studies. This model tries to integrate the Health Belief Model and the

Planned Risk Information Seeking Model as the theoretical base, explaining why, when, and where the users would use the AI tools for health information-seeking in multiple aspects namely risk perception, individual belief, social norms and information-seeking behaviour. It's worth noting that this model can be only one of the theoretical models, the core goal of which is to present how cross-sectional studies can be applied to this topic. By using one-time data collection, it is able to catch the interactive relationship between multiple variables and explore the psychology and cognitive mechanism behind.

Under the theoretical framework of PRISM, in a situation where individuals are facing uncertainty or health risks, whether to proactively obtain information is affected by multiple reasons. Among those, the subjective norms reflect the expectations that an individual perceived from other individuals in the society (such as family members, friends and doctors); the perceived control of information seeking describes whether the individual believes that he/she has adequate abilities or resources to obtain information; and the perceived risk and concern constructs the basic motivation that drives actions. With the joint effects of the mentioned factors, an individual's information-seeking intention will be affected. While in the HBM, the health behaviour often runs above the perceived threats about health issues (i.e. the perceived susceptibility and perceived severity) and the trade-off between the benefits and barriers after taking action. This model on the other hand emphasises on: if one believes that they are at certain health risk, the use of AI will contribute to tangible benefits such as timely and reliable information, and that the barriers like the untrust of AI and difficulties in usage are relatively low, such that they are more likely to proactively conduct information-seeking behaviours.

3.2 Proposed Research Questions

Based on the mentioned theoretical basis, this study focuses on the exemplary formation pathway of the users' perceived trust mechanism, motivation structure and behavioural intention under the context of the growing tendency of AI applications to obtain health information. Considering the fact that the users' using AI tools for health information-seeking is presenting a tendency of large-scale and normalisation, this study proposes to use the cross-sectional study design to collect and compare presentational differences between the related psychological variables and behavioural variables from various user groups at a single point of time. A cross-sectional research design will not only effectively capture the users' attitudes and behaviours under "current conditions", but also benefits in recognising the structural relationship between different variables, such that it is much more suitable for testing the following research questions:

- RQ1: What are the key factors that influence the perceived trust of users in AI-generated health information?

This study aims at exploring the factors including perceived risks, emotional responses, information judgmental standards and subjective norms, and how these factors mutually affect the trust level of the user to AI-generated health information. By cross-sectional study, it is able to systematically analyse the formation mechanism of perceived trust, and reveal the cognitive model of users in the reliability and accuracy of AI.

- RQ2: What are the differences in motivations and intentions between users with various demographic characteristics in using AI for health information-seeking?

In view of variables like age, gender, educational background and health conditions that may affect the intention of individuals' digital literacy and health behaviour tendencies, this study tries to discuss the motivational differences and intensity of intentions of different user groups in the use of AI tools by intergroup comparative analysis, such that provides the basis for a more precise user profile and service optimisation.

- RQ3: What kind of pathways are presented between the users' willingness to use and satisfaction level under the influences of factors such as perceived barriers, perceived benefits and subjective norms?

This study wishes to recognise a pathway chain which starts from the perceived factors to the formation of usage intentions, and further to the factors that influence realistic experiential satisfaction levels. The cross-sectional study is able to describe the direct and indirect effects between different variables through modelling analysis, providing quantitative pieces of evidence to the understanding of the psychological mechanism from trust to action.

The three research questions mentioned above not only present the vital topics in the convergence point of AI technologies and health communication behaviours, but also show the strong analytic potential that cross-sectional studies have in revealing behavioural structures, group differences and perceived trust mechanisms. Through the empirical examination of those research questions, it will be possible to more comprehensively understand the interactive logics between the users and AI health information systems.

3.3 Conceptual Research Model Design

In the detailed construction of the model, the perceived health risk will be seen as the basic variable that triggers health information-seeking motivations. According to the HBM, when an individual perceives that they are facing health threats, especially under a higher perceived susceptibility to a certain disease or a higher perceived severity of the disease consequences, they will tend to seek related health information to relieve the anxiety or make corresponding strategies (RQ1). At the same time, based on the logic of PRISM, the emotional responses users had on potential health issues such as worry and unease will further strengthen the behavioural motivation of information-seeking. These motivations have constructed the psychological basis of why the individual proactively does information seeking. While the perceived barrier and perceived control form the key factors of "abilities to seek for information": If the user believes that AI tools are difficult to operate, lack for information credibility or are not capable of meeting personal demands, the perceived barrier will restrain his/her behavioural intention; On the contrary, when the user with a higher digital literacy or holds the full sense of control during the process of using AI tools, he/she will more likely to start proactive information-seeking (RQ3). Besides, the subjective norms are also indispensable, which refer to the perceived attitudes and expectations from important others on using AI to obtain health information. Such perceived pressure or support from the social network will regulate whether the user acts on information-seeking to a great extent.

More importantly, with the generalisation of AI applications in the healthcare field, the perceived trust of AI-generated content has become one of the key deciding variables that determine users' using behaviours (RQ1). If the user believes that the health suggestions generated by AI tools are reliable, professional and objective, they will be more willing to rely on these tools; While if the trust basis is weak, even if there exists motivations, the information-seeking may also be restrained. Furtherly, the perceived benefits such as the immediacy of information and the comprehensiveness of answers are also positive factors that trigger intentions. With all variables mentioned above eventually create a joint effect in the users' information-seeking intentions, this intention further transforms into realistic behaviours and satisfaction evaluation. On such basis, this study also incorporates demographic variables namely age, gender, educational background and health conditions, to discuss the differences in model pathways of various groups, which leads to the next-step understanding of the applicability and variability of behavioural mechanisms within different groups of people. It should be noted that due to the fact that cross-sectional studies can manage to achieve the general and systematic measurement of all mentioned variables, such that it has a high applicability and practicality within this research question.

In summary, the integrated model of PRISM and HBM suggested by this study not only provides a theoretical operatable framework to understand the behavioural mechanism of users in using AI for health information-seeking, but also presents a strong applicability and application values. Through the one-time questionnaire that facing a large sample size, it is able to quantitatively reveal the potential causal relationship and pathway direction between different variables, clarifying the position inside the behavioural chain where perceived trust, motivations, social influences and cognitive appraisal are, and providing theoretical references for conducting further longitudinal research or interventional design. It is necessary to stress that the model suggested by this study is only one of the exemplary applications of cross-sectional studies in this research field. In the future, the variable settings and pathway structure can be adjusted according to the research objectives. Thus, cross-sectional studies are not only suitable for the understanding of current AI applications in health information-seeking behaviour, but also lay a solid foundation for the following research stages such as tracking, comparing and intervening, which suggests a higher academic extensibility and realistic meaning.

3.4 Justification for the Application of the Cross-Sectional Study

The cross-sectional study has been selected as the core research design of this study due to its advantage in effectively collecting massive size of sample data and comprehensively reflecting the user behaviours within a limited time. In a global context where AI is gradually penetrating into the health information-seeking and communication fields, current existing user behaviour patterns and trust mechanisms are still in the exploratory stage, especially in the analysis of motivations and behaviours of different groups in using AI for health information-seeking. By cross-sectional study, it is manageable to capture factors including the perceived trust, searching motivations and usage intentions at one time, and systematically analyse the relations between these variables at a single point of time, such that the universality and differences of current behavioural patterns are revealed.

3.4.1 Effectiveness and Extensiveness

The cross-sectional study is a rapid and economic methodology with a wide representation, which is able to obtain massive samples within a short period of time and reveal the general behavioural patterns through descriptive analysis. Compared to longitudinal analysis, cross-sectional studies are capable of avoiding long-term tracking and data collection, releasing the pressure on cost and time, which can be especially suitable for the preliminary exploration in the rapidly developing technology sector. In this study, the cross-sectional study enables us to swiftly capture key variables including the perceived trust (RQ1), differences in motivations (RQ2) and behavioural pathways (RQ3), providing further data basis and theoretical support for the longitudinal research in the future.

3.4.2 Strong Adaptability

With the rapid adoption of AI technologies, health information-seeking behaviour and trust mechanism are also swiftly changing, which makes the traditional qualitative analytic methodologies hard to capture such massive social phenomenon. While the cross-sectional studies are able to precisely capture the user behaviour conditions at this point, helping researchers understand current trends and pattern. In this study, an exemplary cross-sectional study model is applied to analyse the behavioural pattern at a single point of time and discuss the motivations, behaviours, levels of satisfaction of different groups in using AI for health information-seeking. Due to its high efficiency, timeliness and wide applicability, cross-sectional studies provide a current "snapshot" for understanding the application of AI in health information-seeking, revealing the noticeable differences of different groups in aspects such as perceived trust and willingness to use.

3.4.3 Multi-variables Exploration

Another important advantage of the cross-sectional study is to identify the relationship between different variables within a single point in time, such as how the factors including perceived trust, perceived benefits and subjective norms jointly affect the formation of willingness to use and satisfaction level. This methodology is able to reveal the structural relations between different variables and provide a theoretical basis for further quantitative research. In this study, the planned obtained data will help answer the research questions including the RQ1 – factors that affect the perceived trust of users in AI-generated information, and RQ3 – the pathway relationship that affects users' willingness to use. By the cross-sectional intergroup analysis, it will be able to identify the differences between different groups in the perceived trust and willingness to use AI for health information-seeking, such that provides scientific shreds of evidence for designing targeted information communication strategies.

3.4.4 A Basis for Further Research

Despite that the cross-sectional study is not available for a causal induction, it still lays a solid foundation for longitudinal research and intervention design in the future. Through the data obtained from the cross-sectional study, a preliminary assumptive framework for a follow-up study is constructed. For example, whether the perceived trust of different groups will change over time, or whether the behavioural intentions of users will change under certain intervention measures. Thus, the cross-sectional study is not only able to provide a timely reflection on the current phenomenon, but also offers a strong foundation for future research, supporting more in-depth discussion on the causal relationships.

In conclusion, cross-sectional studies are capable of systematically and economically presenting the multi-dimensional characteristics under the general context of increasing application of AI in health information-seeking, and solving the existing research gaps among current literature as well. This research method not only provides a profound understanding in current behavioural phenomena, but also offers a theoretical basis and empirical evidence for more in-depth longitudinal research in the future. Thus, the choice of cross-sectional studies in this study is a reasonable response to the current research situation as well as a workable research direction for the academic extension and practical application in the future.

4. IMPLICATIONS

This study provides valuable insights into theoretical, methodological and practical implementations, holding importance to the further research of Artificial Intelligence technologies in the health communication field. Theoretically speaking, with the day-to-day wider application of AI tools in healthcare information communication, traditional health communication theories – such as the Technology Acceptance Model (TAM), Health Belief Model (HBM) and Theory of Planned Behaviour (TPB) are facing certain theoretical bottleneck and applicability challenge. By trying to construct an expandable user behavioural analysis model with psychological variables namely perceived trust, health anxiety level and information evaluation ability included into consideration, this study tried to build an explanation research framework that is more aligned with the realistic implementations in the current digital era. This model not only expands the theoretical broader of the cross-research on AI and health behaviour, but also provides a new angle in understanding the health information-seeking behaviour under the context of machine-human interaction. Furthermore, with an understanding of the differences in cognition and behaviour patterns from different groups in using AI for healthcare consultation, this study solidified the base for the future research in user psychology.

Next, at the methodological level, this study highlighted characteristics of cross-sectional studies such as lower expenditure, ease of conduct and rich information, showing its unique value in digital healthcare communication. Compared to traditional experiences or longitudinal tracking methods, cross-sectional design can systematically capture user characteristics and behavioural state at a certain time point within a short period, which is suitable for the preliminary explorative analysis under the context of the early-stage application or rapid evolution of a new-emerged technology. Although cross-sectional studies are somehow limited in deducting the causal relationship, this methodology still outperforms in the aspects of recognising behaviour tendencies, exploring variable relationships and analysing stratified samples. By introducing the interactive analysis of demographic variables, psychological factors and behavioural variables, this study also presents the flexibility and suitability of cross-sectional study in health communication data construction.

Lastly, the result of this study provides a realistic pathway for designing and optimising the AI system especially in the healthcare aspect. According to the result of different groups in perceived trust difference, evaluation strategies and usage motivation, developers will be able to targetedly improve the system based on the user profiles. For example, the system can provide in-depth functionality like more high-level visualised data and professional data source attribution for users with higher health information literacy. While for beginners or users with a high tendency to healthcare anxiety, the system should add in more differentiation prompts between the AI-generated suggestions and professional physicians' suggestions to eliminate the risk of overdependence. Besides, AI platforms can also optimise the service accuracy and user satisfaction level through personalised recommendations, audience segmentation strategies and deeper training on professional healthcare standards of procedures (SOPs), and thus enhance the overall literacy of public health.

5. LIMITATIONS AND FUTURE STUDIES

This study also holds certain limitations. First of all, the data collection in a cross-sectional study is limited within a certain point of time or short period, which makes it hard to reveal the tendency and causal mechanism of user behaviour along with the changes of time. Next, the examined samples in cross-sectional studies are always constrained within users from the same region, language and cultural backgrounds, which may lead to the limitations in the wider application under the context of globalisation. Thirdly, the self-reported data may be affected by social desirability bias especially when being asked about healthcare and perceived trust in new technologies, "ideal" answers from the respondents are possible, where future research should try and introduce in the behaviour tracking data or in-depth interview to fill in the blanks of cross-sectional methodology.

For future research, further studies in several aspects are suggested: (1) Incorporate longitudinal research or a mix of research methodologies with cross-sectional studies, track the changes in user behaviour and analyse the effect of using AI for health information-seeking on perceived trust and decision-making, which can benefit in tracking the evolution of user behaviour as well as analysing the chain of causality. (2) Combine experimental design and test the influence of intervention actions. By combining experiences and creating stimulus on different intervention measures (such as resource attribution and risk notification), users' perceived trust and judgement ability are thus tested, benefiting the optimisation of AI platforms and increasing their trustworthiness and user satisfaction level. (3)Intercultural comparison. Studying the users' trust mechanism and usage preferences on using AI for healthcare consultation under different cultural and regional backgrounds and discussing the influence of cultural differences on healthcare decision-making will provide valuable references for global healthcare platforms and more localised responses from AI platforms. (4) Explore the collaborative effect of AI and medical professionals. Further research on the collaboration system of AI and healthcare workers and understanding how users diffuse perceived trust and make decisions will provide practical and evidential support in helping improve AI platforms, and facilitating the development of the digital healthcare field. These are the suggested future research angles which may help deepen the understanding of the application of AI in health information-seeking, providing empirical support for the optimisation of digital healthcare platforms and public health policies.

6. CONCLUSION

Under the conjunction where Artificial Intelligence technologies are rapidly developing and being widely applied, AI has dived deeply into people's ways of health information-seeking, which is gradually evolving from traditional search engines to intelligent assistants who rely on natural language processing, context recognition and knowledge generation ability. The public's perceptions of health risks are tangibly increasing especially after the outbreak of COVID-19. However, despite the fact that using AI in health information is becoming more and more common from day to day, a systematic and mass-scale empirical understanding of how users evaluate information, build up trust, generate motivation and form behavioural intentions during the process is still left in a blank.

Starting from this aspect, this study proposed the necessity and appropriateness of applying a Cross-sectional Study Design in the study of using AI for health information-seeking. Compared to other research designs, cross-sectional studies have the unique advantages of being effective in obtaining massive sample data and suitable for multi-variable modelling, which makes it especially applicable in portraying the structural distribution of a social phenomenon at a certain point of time. Under the complicated context where AI and health information are intersecting, the application of cross-sectional studies makes it manageable to rapidly capture the behavioural profile of users, recognise the differences in behaviours between different user groups, and reveal the psychological pattern at an individual level, laying a solid foundation for deeper research in the future.

To illustrate the applicability and values of cross-sectional in a more detailed manner, this study further constructed a preliminary conceptual research framework based on the Planned Risk Information Seeking Model (PRISM) and the Health Belief Model (HBM). The PRISM emphasises that the information-seeking behaviour which people conduct when facing potential health risks is a planned behaviour restrained by the combined effect of multiple variables including a sense of information insufficiency, perceived risks, trust expectations and subjective norms. While the HBM starts from the psychological premise where the healthcare behaviour takes place, focusing on the individual's judgements on perceived severity, perceived susceptibility, behavioural efficacy and barriers. Combining these two models, this study creates a research model which includes variables like the usage frequency, perceived trust, perceived accuracy, usage motivations, subjective norms, behavioural intention and satisfaction level, with the aim of revealing the pathway relationship and structural distributions between variables through the cross-sectional study.

Other than that, this study also proposes several theoretically and practically valuable research questions including:

- RQ1: What are the key factors that influence the perceived trust of users in AI-generated information?
- RQ2: What are the differences in motivations and intentions between users with various demographic characteristics in using AI for health information-seeking?
- RQ3: What kind of pathways are presented between the users' willingness to use and satisfaction level under the influences of factors such as perceived barriers, perceived benefits and subjective norms?

These research questions hold not only the potential for exploration, but also provide clear guidance for the practical application in the future. Whether it is in the product optimisation, user education, or platform design and policy-making, cross-sectional studies make it possible to facilitate a more precise and responsible development of the AI platforms through the research findings.

More importantly, the meaning of cross-sectional study design in this research topic is not only restricted to its applicability but also more to its necessity in doing so. In other words, when a technological behaviour is widely appearing, possessing obvious social influences and so far has not been systematically understood, cross-sectional studies as a research design that is closer to reality and clear in structure, can be the most tailored choice for the current situation. Instead of waiting for the confirmation of a causal relationship, it sets off from observing the structure and understanding the relations between variables, providing unshakeable foundations for theoretical construction and longitudinal tracking research in the future.

To sum up, the research topic of using AI for health information-seeking is the microcosm of a technological trend, as well as the psychological and behavioural responses made by the public under the context where information credibility is more blurred from day to day. The application of cross-sectional study design is not only limited to a choice of research methodology, but also the embodiment of research ethics in the response of issues in the conjunction. In the coming future, with the accumulation of this kind of research, it is hopeful to construct a health communication theoretical system facing the AI era step by step, at the same time, guiding the development of digital technology to focus more on human-oriented care and the equity in knowledge.

REFERENCES

Ahadzadeh, A. S., Sharif, S. P., Ong, F. S., & Khong, K. W. (2015). Integrating Health Belief Model and Technology Acceptance Model: An Investigation of Health-Related Internet Use. *Journal of Medical Internet Research*, *17*(2), e3564. DOI: 10.2196/jmir.3564 PMID: 25700481

Ayo-Ajibola, O., Davis, R. J., Lin, M. E., Riddell, J., & Kravitz, R. L. (2024). Characterizing the Adoption and Experiences of Users of Artificial Intelligence–Generated Health Information in the United States: Cross-Sectional Questionnaire Study. *Journal of Medical Internet Research*, *26*(1), e55138. DOI: 10.2196/55138 PMID: 39141910

Ayo-Ajibola, O., Julien, C., Lin, M. E., Riddell, J., Duan, N., & Kravitz, R. L. (2025). Association of Primary Care Access with Health-Related ChatGPT Use: A National Cross-Sectional Survey. *Journal of General Internal Medicine*. Advance online publication. DOI: 10.1007/s11606-025-09406-9 PMID: 39930155

Backlinko. (2025, March 31). *ChatGPT Statistics 2025: How Many People Use ChatGPT?* Retrieved April 1, 2025, https://backlinko.com/chatgpt-stats

Bodani, N., Lal, A., Maqsood, A., Altamash, S., Ahmed, N., & Heboyan, A. (2023). Knowledge, Attitude, and Practices of General Population Toward Utilizing ChatGPT: A Cross-sectional Study. *SAGE Open*, *13*(4), 21582440231211079. DOI: 10.1177/21582440231211079

Carmona, K. A., Chittamuru, D., Kravitz, R. L., Ramondt, S., & Ramírez, A. S. (2022). Health Information Seeking From an Intelligent Web-Based Symptom Checker: Cross-sectional Questionnaire Study. *Journal of Medical Internet Research*, *24*(8), e36322. DOI: 10.2196/36322 PMID: 35984690

Carpenter, C. J. (2010). A meta-analysis of the effectiveness of health belief model variables in predicting behavior. *Health Communication*, *25*(8), 661–669. DOI: 10.1080/10410236.2010.521906 PMID: 21153982

Cascella, M., Montomoli, J., Bellini, V., & Bignami, E. (2023). Evaluating the Feasibility of ChatGPT in Healthcare: An Analysis of Multiple Clinical and Research Scenarios. *Journal of Medical Systems*, *47*(1), 33. DOI: 10.1007/s10916-023-01925-4 PMID: 36869927

Choudhury, A., Elkefi, S., & Tounsi, A. (2024). Exploring factors influencing user perspective of ChatGPT as a technology that assists in healthcare decision making: A cross sectional survey study. *PLoS One*, *19*(3), e0296151. DOI: 10.1371/journal.pone.0296151 PMID: 38457373

Davidhizar, R. (1983). Critique of the health-belief model. *Journal of Advanced Nursing*, *8*(6), 467–472. DOI: 10.1111/j.1365-2648.1983.tb00473.x PMID: 6558081

Duarte, F. (2025, March 26). *Number of CHatGPT Users (March 2025)*. Exploding Topics. Retrieved April 1, 2025, from https://explodingtopics.com/blog/chatgpt-users

Esmaeilzadeh, P., Maddah, M., & Mirzaei, T. (2025). Using AI chatbots (e.g., CHATGPT) in seeking health-related information online: The case of a common ailment. *Computers in Human Behavior Artificial Humans*, *100127*, 100127. Advance online publication. DOI: 10.1016/j.chbah.2025.100127

Green, E. C., Murphy, E. M., & Gryboski, K. (2020). The Health Belief Model. In *The Wiley Encyclopedia of Health Psychology* (pp. 211–214). John Wiley & Sons, Ltd., DOI: 10.1002/9781119057840.ch68

Hovick, S. R., Kahlor, L., & Liang, M.-C. (2014). Personal Cancer Knowledge and Information Seeking Through PRISM: The Planned Risk Information Seeking Model. *Journal of Health Communication*, *19*(4), 511–527. DOI: 10.1080/10810730.2013.821556 PMID: 24433251

Incerti Parenti, S., Bartolucci, M. L., Biondi, E., Maglioni, A., Corazza, G., Gracco, A., & Alessandri-Bonetti, G. (2023). Online Patient Education in Obstructive Sleep Apnea: ChatGPT versus Google Search. *Health Care*, *12*(17), 1781. DOI: 10.3390/healthcare12171781 PMID: 39273804

Janz, N. K., & Becker, M. H. (1984). The Health Belief Model: A decade later. *Health Education Quarterly*, *11*(1), 1–47. DOI: 10.1177/109019818401100101 PMID: 6392204

Jibril, A. B., & Adzovie, D. E. (2022). Understanding the moderating role of E-WoM and traditional media advertisement toward fast-food joint selection: A uses and gratifications theory. *Journal of Foodservice Business Research*, *27*(1), 1–25. DOI: 10.1080/15378020.2022.2070450

Kahlor, L. (2010). PRISM: A planned risk information seeking model. *Health Communication*, *25*(4), 345–356. DOI: 10.1080/10410231003775172 PMID: 20512716

Kesmodel, U. S. (2018). Cross-sectional studies – what are they good for? *Acta Obstetricia et Gynecologica Scandinavica*, *97*(4), 388–393. DOI: 10.1111/aogs.13331 PMID: 29453895

Levin, K. A. (2006). Study design III: Cross-sectional studies. *Evidence-Based Dentistry*, *7*(1), 24–25. DOI: 10.1038/sj.ebd.6400375 PMID: 16557257

Link, E., & Kahlor, L. A. (2024). The Planned Risk Information Seeking Model Applied to Vaccine Information Avoidance and the Role of Affect, Emotion and Perceived Benefits. *Health Communication*, *39*(11), 2376–2389. DOI: 10.1080/10410236.2023.2268912 PMID: 37872691

Longo, D. R. (2005). Understanding health information, communication, and information seeking of patients and consumers: A comprehensive and integrated model. *Health Expectations*, *8*(3), 189–194. DOI: 10.1111/j.1369-7625.2005.00339.x PMID: 16098149

Makhoul, M., Melkane, A. E., Khoury, P. E., Hadi, C. E., & Matar, N. (2024). A cross-sectional comparative study: ChatGPT 3.5 versus diverse levels of medical experts in the diagnosis of ENT diseases. *European Archives of Oto-Rhino-Laryngology*, *281*(5), 2717–2721. DOI: 10.1007/s00405-024-08509-z PMID: 38365990

Morse, K. E., Ostberg, N. P., Jones, V. G., & Chan, A. S. (2020). Use Characteristics and Triage Acuity of a Digital Symptom Checker in a Large Integrated Health System: Population-Based Descriptive Study. *Journal of Medical Internet Research*, *22*(11), e20549. DOI: 10.2196/20549 PMID: 33170799

Niu, Z., Willoughby, J. F., Mei, J., Li, S., & Hu, P. (2020). A Cross-Cultural Comparison of an Extended Planned Risk Information Seeking Model on Mental Health Among College Students: Cross-Sectional Study. *Journal of Medical Internet Research*, *22*(5), e15817. DOI: 10.2196/15817 PMID: 32441654

Orji, R., Vassileva, J., & Mandryk, R. (2012). Towards an Effective Health Interventions Design: An Extension of the Health Belief Model. *Online Journal of Public Health Informatics*, *4*(3), e61050. DOI: 10.5210/ojphi.v4i3.4321 PMID: 23569653

Parikh, P. M., Talwar, V., & Goyal, M. (2023). ChatGPT: An online cross-sectional descriptive survey comparing perceptions of healthcare workers to those of other professionals. *Cancer Research, Statistics, and Treatment*, *6*(1), 32–36. DOI: 10.4103/crst.crst_40_23

Shahsavar, Y., & Choudhury, A. (2023). User Intentions to Use ChatGPT for Self-Diagnosis and Health-Related Purposes: Cross-sectional Survey Study. *JMIR Human Factors*, *10*(1), e47564. DOI: 10.2196/47564 PMID: 37195756

Shen, S. A., Perez-Heydrich, C. A., Xie, D. X., & Nellis, J. C. (2024). ChatGPT vs. web search for patient questions: What does ChatGPT do better? *European Archives of Oto-Rhino-Laryngology*, *281*(6), 3219–3225. DOI: 10.1007/s00405-024-08524-0 PMID: 38416195

Solem, R. C. (2015). Limitation of a cross-sectional study. *American Journal of Orthodontics and Dentofacial Orthopedics*, *148*(2), 205. DOI: 10.1016/j.ajodo.2015.05.006 PMID: 26232823

Tao, D., Shao, F., Wang, H., Yan, M., & Qu, X. (2020). Integrating usability and social cognitive theories with the technology acceptance model to understand young users' acceptance of a health information portal. *Health Informatics Journal*, *26*(2), 1347–1362. DOI: 10.1177/1460458219879337 PMID: 31603378

Wang, X., & Cheng, Z. (2020). Cross-Sectional Studies: Strengths, Weaknesses, and Recommendations. *Chest*, *158*(1, Supplement), S65–S71. DOI: 10.1016/j.chest.2020.03.012 PMID: 32658654

Wang, Y., Chen, Y., & Sheng, J. (2024). Assessing ChatGPT as a Medical Consultation Assistant for Chronic Hepatitis B: Cross-Language Study of English and Chinese. *JMIR Medical Informatics*, *12*(1), e56426. DOI: 10.2196/56426 PMID: 39115930

Wong, M. C. S., Wong, E. L. Y., Huang, J., Cheung, A. W. L., Law, K., Chong, M. K. C., Ng, R. W. Y., Lai, C. K. C., Boon, S. S., Lau, J. T. F., Chen, Z., & Chan, P. K. S. (2021). Acceptance of the COVID-19 vaccine based on the health belief model: A population-based survey in Hong Kong. *Vaccine*, *39*(7), 1148–1156. DOI: 10.1016/j.vaccine.2020.12.083 PMID: 33461834

Ye, C., Zweck, E., Ma, Z., Smith, J., & Katz, S. (2024). Doctor Versus Artificial Intelligence: Patient and Physician Evaluation of Large Language Model Responses to Rheumatology Patient Questions in a Cross-Sectional Study. *Arthritis & Rheumatology (Hoboken, N.J.)*, *76*(3), 479–484. DOI: 10.1002/art.42737 PMID: 37902018

Zhao, Y. C., Zhao, M., & Song, S. (2022a). Online Health Information Seeking Among Patients With Chronic Conditions: Integrating the Health Belief Model and Social Support Theory. *Journal of Medical Internet Research*, *24*(11), e42447. DOI: 10.2196/42447 PMID: 36322124

Zhao, Y. C., Zhao, M., & Song, S. (2022b). Online Health Information Seeking Behaviors Among Older Adults: Systematic Scoping Review. *Journal of Medical Internet Research*, *24*(2), e34790. DOI: 10.2196/34790 PMID: 35171099

Conclusion

The exploration of AI's role in healthcare, as detailed in this book, reveals a landscape marked by extraordinary promise and profound responsibility. The chapters collectively illuminate how AI can revolutionize health information access, diagnosis, and treatment, while also highlighting the ethical, cultural, and psychological challenges that accompany its adoption. As we synthesize these insights, three overarching imperatives emerge: the need for ethical governance, cultural competence, and human-centric design.

AI's potential to transform medical tourism through robotics, telemedicine, and genomics exemplifies its capacity to bridge global health divides. Yet, this progress must be tempered with regulatory vigilance to address privacy concerns and ensure equitable access. Similarly, emotionally intelligent AI offers groundbreaking mental health support but risks depersonalizing care if not balanced with human empathy—a theme echoed in discussions of human-centered design, where AI's role is to enhance, not replace, clinical judgment.

Ethical considerations permeate every application. AI-powered health communities must prioritize data governance to prevent exploitation, while culturally competent systems require diverse datasets to mitigate bias. Concurrently, the rise of AI-driven disinformation and cyberchondria underscores the urgency of fostering digital literacy, enabling users to discern credible information amidst algorithmic noise.

The path forward demands interdisciplinary collaboration. Policymakers, technologists, and healthcare providers must co-create frameworks that address gaps in existing regulations, such as the lack of global standards for AI in medical tourism or emotional AI. Ethical guidelines should mandate transparency in AI algorithms, ensuring users understand how decisions are made and data is utilized. Moreover, cultural competence must be embedded into AI development cycles, involving stakeholders from diverse backgrounds in design processes to counteract systemic biases.

Education emerges as a cornerstone. Public health campaigns and digital literacy programs can mitigate cyberchondria and disinformation risks, equipping individuals with skills to critically evaluate AI-generated content. Similarly, training healthcare professionals in AI literacy will foster informed collaboration with AI tools, enhancing clinical outcomes without eroding patient trust.

The integration of cross-sectional studies into AI health research offers a blueprint for evidence-based policy. By examining user behavior through models like PRISM and HBM, researchers can identify determinants of trust and satisfaction, informing interventions that align AI tools with user needs. Future studies should expand into longitudinal analyses to track AI's long-term societal impacts, particularly in vulnerable populations.

Technologically, the evolution of AI must prioritize explainability and accessibility. Tools like BrainGate and Neuralink, while revolutionary, require stringent ethical oversight to prevent misuse. Similarly, blockchain applications in medical tourism must balance innovation with patient confidentiality.

As AI continues to reshape healthcare, stakeholders must remain vigilant guardians of ethical principles. This entails not only addressing current challenges but anticipating future dilemmas—such as the implications of AI in genetic engineering or global health crises. The chapters in this book advocate for a proactive approach: designing AI systems that are not only intelligent but also compassionate, inclusive, and accountable.

In closing, *Navigating Health Information in the Age of Artificial Intelligence* underscores that the true measure of progress lies not in technological prowess alone, but in our ability to harness it for the collective good. By championing human dignity, equity, and transparency, we can ensure that AI serves as a force for healing, uniting innovation with the timeless values of care and empathy. The journey ahead is complex, but with collaborative effort and moral clarity, a future where AI empowers holistic health and wellbeing is within reach.

Compilation of References

Abdullah, Y., Schuman, J., Shabsigh, R., Caplan, A., & Al-Aswad, L. (2021). Ethics of artificial intelligence in medicine and ophthalmology. *Asia-Pacific Journal of Ophthalmology*, *10*(3), 289–298. DOI: 10.1097/APO.0000000000000397 PMID: 34383720

Abdulrahman, K. A. B., Musfir, S. K. A., Alforaih, A. S., Alshehri, A., Aldossari, A. K., & Dawood, F. D. B. (2024). The prevalence of cyberchondria and the impact of skepticism on medical decisions among Imam Mohammed Ibn Saud Islamic university students, riyadh, Saudi Arabia. *Journal of Family Medicine and Primary Care*, *13*(11), 5334–5340. DOI: 10.4103/jfmpc.jfmpc_640_24 PMID: 39722934

Aboujaoude, E., Gega, L., Parish, M. B., & Hilty, D. M. (2020). Editorial: Digital interventions in mental health: Current status and future directions. *Frontiers in Psychiatry*, *11*, 111. Advance online publication. DOI: 10.3389/fpsyt.2020.00111 PMID: 32174858

Afrin, R., & Prybutok, G. (2022). Insights into the antecedents of cyberchondria: A perspective from the USA. *Health Promotion International*, *37*(4), daac108. Advance online publication. DOI: 10.1093/heapro/daac108 PMID: 36047641

Agarwal, S. (2022). Iot applications for health care. *Advanced Technologies and Societal Change*, 91-97. DOI: 10.1007/978-981-19-0770-8_8

Aggarwal, A., Tam, C. C., Wu, D., Li, X., & Qiao, S. (2022). Artificial intelligence (ai)-based chatbots in promoting health behavioral changes: A systematic review. *Journal of Medical Internet Research*, *25*. Advance online publication. DOI: 10.1101/2022.07.05.22277263

Agrawal, V., Khulbe, Y., Singh, A., & Kar, S. K. (2024). The digital health dilemma: Exploring cyberchondria, well-being, and smartphone addiction in medical and non-medical undergraduates. *Indian Journal of Psychiatry*, *66*(3), 256–262. DOI: 10.4103/indianjpsychiatry.indianjpsychiatry_570_23 PMID: 39100122

Ahadzadeh, A. S., Sharif, S. P., Ong, F. S., & Khong, K. W. (2015). Integrating Health Belief Model and Technology Acceptance Model: An Investigation of Health-Related Internet Use. *Journal of Medical Internet Research, 17*(2), e3564. DOI: 10.2196/jmir.3564 PMID: 25700481

Akhavan, P., Azizi, N., Akhtari, S., Haass, O., Jan, T., & Sajeev, S. (2023). Understanding critical success factors for implementing medical tourism in a multi-case analysis. *Knowledge Management and E-Learning*, 15(1).

Akhtar, M., & Fatima, T. (2019). Exploring cyberchondria and worry about health among individuals with no diagnosed medical condition. *JPMA. The Journal of the Pakistan Medical Association, 0*(0), 1. DOI: 10.5455/JPMA.8682 PMID: 31954030

Akter, S., McCarthy, G., Sajib, S., Michael, K., Dwivedi, Y. K., D'Ambra, J., & Shen, K. N. (2021). Algorithmic bias in data-driven innovation in the age of AI. *International Journal of Information Management, 60*, 102387. Advance online publication. DOI: 10.1016/j.ijinfomgt.2021.102387

Alam, M. N., Kaur, M., & Kabir, M. S. (2023). Explainable AI in healthcare: Enhancing transparency and trust upon legal and ethical consideration. *International Research Journal of Engineering and Technology, 10*(6), 828–835.

Alaziz, S. N., Albayati, B., El-Bagoury, A. A. A. H., & Shafik, W. (2023). Clustering of COVID-19 Multi-Time Series-Based K-Means and PCA With Forecasting. *International Journal of Data Warehousing and Mining, 19*(3), 1–25. DOI: 10.4018/IJDWM.317374

Al-Hwsali, A., Alsaadi, B., Abdi, N., Khatab, S., Alzubaidi, M., Solaiman, B., & Househ, M. (2023). Scoping review: Legal and ethical principles of artificial intelligence in public health. *Studies in Health Technology and Informatics*. Advance online publication. DOI: 10.3233/SHTI230579 PMID: 37387113

Ali, S., Abuhmed, T., El-Sappagh, S., Muhammad, K., Alonso-Moral, J. M., Confalonieri, R., Guidotti, R., Del Ser, J., Díaz-Rodríguez, N., & Herrera, F. (2023). Explainable Artificial Intelligence (XAI): What we know and what is left to attain trustworthy artificial intelligence. *Information Fusion, 99*, 101805. DOI: 10.1016/j.inffus.2023.101805

Allen, C., Payne, B., Abegaz, T., & Robertson, C. (2023). What you see is not what you know: Studying deception in deepfake video manipulation. *Journal of Cybersecurity Education Research and Practice, 2024*(1). Advance online publication. DOI: 10.32727/8.2023.25

Al-Tamimi, F., & Aziz, A. M. (2022). Evaluating the impact of transparency and accountability measures on the ethical implementation of artificial intelligence applications in healthcare. *International Journal of Responsible Artificial Intelligence, as*(as), 27–34.

Amann, J., Blasimme, A., Vayena, E., Frey, D., & Madai, V. I. (2020). Explainability for Artificial Intelligence in healthcare: A multidisciplinary perspective. *BMC Medical Informatics and Decision Making*, *20*(1), 310. Advance online publication. DOI: 10.1186/s12911-020-01332-6 PMID: 33256715

American College of Obstetricians and Gynecologists. (2011). Committee opinion no. 493: Cultural sensitivity and awareness in the delivery of health care. *Obstetrics and Gynecology*, *117*(5), 1258–1261. DOI: 10.1097/AOG.0b013e31821d7db0

American Hospital Association. (2024). Can Elon Musk disrupt health care's booming AI field? American Hospital Association. https://www.aha.org/aha-center-health-innovation-market-scan/2024-06-04-can-elon-musk-disrupt-health-cares-booming-ai-field

American Psychological Association. (November, 2022). *Psychologists struggle to meet demand amid mental health crisis: 2022 COVID-19 Practitioner Impact Survey.* Retrieved from https://www.apa.org/pubs/reports/practitioner/2022-covid-psychologist-workload

Amershi, S., Weld, D., Vorvoreanu, M., Fourney, A., Nushi, B., Collisson, P., & Horvitz, E. (2019). Guidelines for human-ai interaction. *Proceedings of the 2019 CHI Conference on Human Factors in Computing Systems*. DOI: 10.1145/3290605.3300233

Amiri, Z. (2024). Ai-Driven Decision-Making in Healthcare Information Systems: A Comprehensive Review. Available at *SSRN* 4756316. DOI: 10.2139/ssrn.4756316

Ananya, S. A. (2021). Technology Based Service Offers and Tourist Experience Generation in the Tourism and Hospitality Industry in Bangladesh. In *Technology Application in the Tourism and Hospitality Industry of Bangladesh.* DOI: 10.1007/978-981-16-2434-6_20

Angerschmid, A., Zhou, J., Theuermann, K., Chen, F., & Holzinger, A. (2022). Fairness and explanation in AI-informed decision making. *Machine Learning and Knowledge Extraction*, *4*(2), 556–579. DOI: 10.3390/make4020026

Ansari, T. M. (2022). Conversational AI assistant. *International Journal for Research in Applied Science and Engineering Technology*, *10*(11), 1169–1172. DOI: 10.22214/ijraset.2022.47554

Anthes, E. (2016). Mental health: There's an app for that. *Nature, 532*(7597), 20–23. DOI: 10.1038/532020a PMID: 27078548

Apuke, O. D., Omar, B., Tunca, E. A., & Gever, C. V. (2022). Information overload and misinformation sharing behaviour of social media users: Testing the moderating role of cognitive ability. *Journal of Information Science, 01655515221121 9.* Advance online publication. DOI: 10.1177/01655515221121942

Araujo, T., Helberger, N., Kruikemeier, S., & de Vreese, C. H. (2020). In ai we trust? perceptions about automated decision-making by Artificial Intelligence. *AI & Society*, *35*(3), 611–623. DOI: 10.1007/s00146-019-00931-w

Arestad, K., MacPhee, D., Lim, C., & Khetani, M. (2017). Cultural adaptation of a pediatric functional assessment for rehabilitation outcomes research. *BMC Health Services Research, 17*(1), 658. Advance online publication. DOI: 10.1186/s12913-017-2592-6 PMID: 28915817

Arias López, M. D. P., Ong, B. A., Borrat Frigola, X., Fernández, A. L., Hicklent, R. S., Obeles, A. J., Rocimo, A. M., & Celi, L. A. (2023). Digital literacy as a new determinant of health: A scoping review. *PLOS Digital Health*, *2*(10), e0000279. DOI: 10.1371/journal.pdig.0000279 PMID: 37824584

Aronsson, J., Lu, P., Strüber, D., & Berger, T. (2021). A maturity assessment framework for conversational AI development platforms. *Proceedings of the 36th Annual ACM Symposium on Applied Computing*. DOI: 10.1145/3412841.3442046

Arrioja-Castrejón, E., López-Fernández, A. M., Ramírez-Pérez, H. X., & Dávila-Aragón, G. (2023). Digital consumer behavior and medical tourism: A regional analysis in Mexico. *Contaduría y Administración*, *68*(4), 419. DOI: 10.22201/fca.24488410e.2023.4968

Arvindhan, M., Gupta, R., Priyadharshini, S., & Anbananthen, K. S. M. (2022). The scope and future outlook of artificial intelligence in healthcare systems. *Applications of Artificial Intelligence in E-Healthcare Systems,* 19-36. DOI: 10.1049/PBHE040E_ch2

Aryan, J., & Shashank, K. (2023). Leveraging Generative AI Models for Synthetic Data Generation in Healthcare: Balancing Research and Privacy. *2023 International Conference on Smart Applications, Communications and Networking (SmartNets),* Istanbul, Turkiye, 1-4. DOI: 10.1109/SmartNets58706.2023.10215825

Asgher, U., Ayaz, Y., & Taiar, R. (2023). Advances in artificial intelligence (AI) in brain computer interface (BCI) and Industry 4.0 for human machine interaction (HMI) [Editorial]. *Frontiers in Human Neuroscience*, *17*, 1320536. Advance online publication. DOI: 10.3389/fnhum.2023.1320536 PMID: 38116236

Assunção, G., Patrão, B., Castelo-Branco, M., & Menezes, P. (2022). An overview of emotion in artificial intelligence. *IEEE Transactions on Artificial Intelligence*, *3*(6), 867–886. DOI: 10.1109/TAI.2022.3159614

Awad, S. H., & Wagoner, B. (2014). Agency and creativity in the midst of social change. *Constraints of Agency*, 229–243. DOI: 10.1007/978-3-319-10130-9_14

Ayo-Ajibola, O., Davis, R. J., Lin, M. E., Riddell, J., & Kravitz, R. L. (2024). Characterizing the Adoption and Experiences of Users of Artificial Intelligence–Generated Health Information in the United States: Cross-Sectional Questionnaire Study. *Journal of Medical Internet Research*, *26*(1), e55138. DOI: 10.2196/55138 PMID: 39141910

Ayo-Ajibola, O., Julien, C., Lin, M. E., Riddell, J., Duan, N., & Kravitz, R. L. (2025). Association of Primary Care Access with Health-Related ChatGPT Use: A National Cross-Sectional Survey. *Journal of General Internal Medicine*. Advance online publication. DOI: 10.1007/s11606-025-09406-9 PMID: 39930155

Backlinko. (2025, March 31). *ChatGPT Statistics 2025: How Many People Use ChatGPT?* Retrieved April 1, 2025, https://backlinko.com/chatgpt-stats

Bader, V., & Kaiser, S. (2019). Algorithmic decision-making? the user interface and its role for human involvement in decisions supported by Artificial Intelligence. *Organization*, *26*(5), 655–672. DOI: 10.1177/1350508419855714

Baghramian, M., & Caprioglio Panizza, S. (2022). Scepticism and the value of distrust. *Inquiry (Oslo, Norway)*, •••, 1–28. DOI: 10.1080/0020174X.2022.2135821

Bahadir, O., & Dundar, C. (2024). The impact of online health information source preference on intolerance to uncertainty and cyberchondria in a youthful generation. *Indian Journal of Psychiatry*, *66*(4), 360–366. DOI: 10.4103/indianjpsychiatry.indianjpsychiatry_715_23 PMID: 38778859

Baigi, S., Sarbaz, M., Ghaddaripouri, K., Ghaddaripouri, M., Mousavi, A., & Kimiafar, K. (2023). Attitudes, knowledge, and skills towards artificial intelligence among healthcare students: A systematic review. *Health Science Reports*, *6*(3), e1138. Advance online publication. DOI: 10.1002/hsr2.1138 PMID: 36923372

Bajcar, B., & Babiak, J. (2019). Self-esteem and cyberchondria: The mediation effects of health anxiety and obsessive–compulsive symptoms in a community sample. *Current Psychology (New Brunswick, N.J.)*, *40*(6), 2820–2831. DOI: 10.1007/s12144-019-00216-x

Balachandran, P., Karuveettil, V., & Janakiram, C. (2022). Development and validation of cultural competence assessment tool for healthcare professionals, India. *Frontiers in Public Health*, *10*, 919386. Advance online publication. DOI: 10.3389/fpubh.2022.919386 PMID: 36081476

Balasubrahmanyam, S., & Prasad, K. (2024). Disruptive Customer Value Propositions in the Global Health and Medical Tourism Industry. *International Journal of Business and Globalisation*, *1*(1), 10053643. DOI: 10.1504/IJBG.2024.10053643

Balcombe, L. (2023, October). AI chatbots in digital mental health. [). MDPI.]. *Informatics (MDPI)*, *10*(4), 82. DOI: 10.3390/informatics10040082

Baptista, J. P., Gradim, A., & Correla, E. (2022). Bullshit receptivity: What matters is who said it, not what is said. *Journal of Digital Media & Interaction*, *5*(12), 7–23. DOI: 10.34624/jdmi.v5i12.28717

Barbey, A. K., & Sloman, S. A. (2007). Base-rate respect: From ecological rationality to dual processes. *Behavioral and Brain Sciences*, *30*(3), 241–254. DOI: 10.1017/S0140525X07001653 PMID: 17963533

Barbierato, E., & Gatti, A. (2024). The challenges of machine Learning: A critical review. *Electronics (Basel)*, *13*(2), 416. DOI: 10.3390/electronics13020416

Barke, A., Bleichhardt, G., Rief, W., & Doering, B. K. (2016). The Cyberchondria Severity Scale (CSS): German validation and development of a short form. *International Journal of Behavioral Medicine*, *23*(5), 595–605. DOI: 10.1007/s12529-016-9549-8 PMID: 26931780

Baron, J., Scott, S., Fincher, K., & Emlen Metz, S. (2015). Why does the Cognitive Reflection Test (sometimes) predict utilitarian moral judgment (and other things)? *Journal of Applied Research in Memory and Cognition*, *4*(3), 265–284. DOI: 10.1016/j.jarmac.2014.09.003

Bayer, J., Bitiukova, N., Bard, P., Szakács, J., Alemanno, A., & Uszkiewicz, E. (2021). Disinformation and propaganda – impact on the functioning of the rule of law in the EU and its Member States. SSRN *Electronic Journal*. DOI: 10.2139/ssrn.3409279

Beladi, H., Chao, C. C., Ee, M. S., & Hollas, D. (2023). Welfare-improving policy on medical tourism and labor productivity: A theoretical analysis. *Economic Systems*, *47*(1), 101052. DOI: 10.1016/j.ecosys.2022.101052

Benlian, A., Kettinger, W. J., Sunyaev, A., & Winkler, T. J. (2018). The transformative value of cloud computing: A decoupling, platformization, and recombination theoretical framework. *Journal of Management Information Systems, 35*(3), 719–739. DOI: 10.1080/07421222.2018.1481634

Beretta. (2024). *The impact of AI literacy on the emotional reaction to AI mistakes in human-AI collaboration* (thesis). *University of Twente*. Retrieved 2024, from https://essay.utwente.nl/98115/

Bernal, J., & Mazo, C. (2022). Transparency of artificial intelligence in Healthcare: Insights from professionals in computing and Healthcare Worldwide. *Applied Sciences (Basel, Switzerland), 12*(20), 10228. DOI: 10.3390/app122010228

Bhargava, A., Bhargava, D., & Rana, A. (2023). Edge-AI-empowered blockchain: A game-changer for the medical tourism industry. In *Edge-AI in Healthcare*. Trends and Future Perspectives. DOI: 10.1201/9781003244592-16

Bhatnagr, P., Rajesh, A., & Misra, R. (2024). Continuous intention usage of artificial intelligence enabled Digital Banks: A review of expectation confirmation model. *Journal of Enterprise Information Management, 37*(6), 1763–1787. Advance online publication. DOI: 10.1108/JEIM-11-2023-0617

Bickmore, T. W., Schulman, D., & Sidner, C. (2011). A reusable framework for health counseling dialogue systems based on a behavioral medicine ontology. *Journal of Biomedical Informatics, 44*(2), 183–197. DOI: 10.1016/j.jbi.2010.12.006 PMID: 21220044

Bjerring, J. C., & Busch, J. (2020). Artificial Intelligence and patient-centered decision-making. *Philosophy &amp. Philosophy & Technology, 34*(2), 349–371. DOI: 10.1007/s13347-019-00391-6

Bodani, N., Lal, A., Maqsood, A., Altamash, S., Ahmed, N., & Heboyan, A. (2023). Knowledge, Attitude, and Practices of General Population Toward Utilizing ChatGPT: A Cross-sectional Study. *SAGE Open, 13*(4), 21582440231211079. DOI: 10.1177/21582440231211079

Bohr, A., & Memarzadeh, K. (2020). The rise of Artificial Intelligence in healthcare applications. *Artificial Intelligence in Healthcare*, 25–60. DOI: 10.1016/B978-0-12-818438-7.00002-2

Bonnet, G. W. and D. (2015, February 18). *Revamping your business through Digital Transformation*. MIT Sloan Management Review. https://sloanreview.mit.edu/article/revamping-your-business-through-digital-transformation/

Bottomley, D., & Thaldar, D. (2023a). Liability for harm caused by ai in Healthcare: An overview of the core legal concepts. *Frontiers in Pharmacology*, *14*, 1297353. Advance online publication. DOI: 10.3389/fphar.2023.1297353 PMID: 38161692

Bouderhem, R. (2022, December). AI regulation in healthcare: new paradigms for a legally binding treaty under the World Health Organization. In *2022 14th International Conference on Computational Intelligence and Communication Networks (CICN)* (pp. 277-281). IEEE. DOI: 10.1109/CICN56167.2022.10008303

Bovsh, L. A., Hopkalo, L. M., & Rasulova, A. M. (2023). *Digital relationship marketing strategies of medical tourism entities*. In Integrating Digital Health Strategies for Effective Administration. DOI: 10.4018/978-1-6684-8337-4.ch008

BOŽİĆ, V. (2023). Integrated risk management and artificial intelligence in hospital. *Journal of AI, 7*(1), 63-80. DOI: 10.61969/jai.1329224

Braun, P. S., & Kloss, B. (2017). Wellness programs – Emotional wellness. *Employee Benefit Plan Review*, *72*(1), 27–28. https://link.gale.com/apps/doc/A504543974/ITOF?u=unilanc&sid=bookmark-ITOF&xid=fc2665b0

Brown, J. E., & Halpern, J. (2021). AI chatbots cannot replace human interactions in the pursuit of more inclusive mental healthcare. *SSM. Mental Health*, *1*, 100017. DOI: 10.1016/j.ssmmh.2021.100017

Bryanov, K., & Vziatysheva, V. (2021). Determinants of individuals' belief in fake news: A scoping review determinants of belief in fake news. *PLoS One*, *16*(6), e0253717. Advance online publication. DOI: 10.1371/journal.pone.0253717 PMID: 34166478

Bujnowska-Fedak, M. M., & Węgierek, P. (2020). The impact of online health information on patient health behaviours and making decisions concerning health. *International Journal of Environmental Research and Public Health*, *17*(3), 880. DOI: 10.3390/ijerph17030880 PMID: 32023828

Buolamwini, J., & Gebru, T. (2018, January). Gender shades: Intersectional accuracy disparities in commercial gender classification. In Conference on fairness, accountability and transparency (pp. 77-91). PMLR.

Burgess, D. J., Bokhour, B. G., Cunningham, B. A., Do, T., Gordon, H. S., Jones, D. M., Pope, C., Saha, S., & Gollust, S. E. (2019). Healthcare providers' responses to narrative communication about racial healthcare disparities. *Health Communication*, *34*(2), 149–161. DOI: 10.1080/10410236.2017.1389049 PMID: 29068701

Calanzone, D., Coppari, A., Tedoldi, R., Olivato, G., & Casonato, C. (2023). *An open source perspective on AI and alignment with the EU AI Act*. CEUR Workshop Proceedings. https://halixness.github.io/assets/pdf/calanzone_coppari_tedoldi.pdf

Calvo, R. A., D'Mello, S., Gratch, J., & Kappas, A. (2014). *The Oxford handbook of affective computing*. Oxford University Press.

Campinha-Bacote, J. (2018). Cultural competemility: A paradigm shift in the cultural competence versus cultural humility debate – part i. *Online Journal of Issues in Nursing*, *24*(1). Advance online publication. DOI: 10.3912/OJIN.Vol24No01PPT20

Carmona, K. A., Chittamuru, D., Kravitz, R. L., Ramondt, S., & Ramírez, A. S. (2022). Health Information Seeking From an Intelligent Web-Based Symptom Checker: Cross-sectional Questionnaire Study. *Journal of Medical Internet Research*, *24*(8), e36322. DOI: 10.2196/36322 PMID: 35984690

Carpenter, C. J. (2010). A meta-analysis of the effectiveness of health belief model variables in predicting behavior. *Health Communication*, *25*(8), 661–669. DOI: 10.1080/10410236.2010.521906 PMID: 21153982

Cascella, M., Montomoli, J., Bellini, V., & Bignami, E. (2023). Evaluating the Feasibility of ChatGPT in Healthcare: An Analysis of Multiple Clinical and Research Scenarios. *Journal of Medical Systems*, *47*(1), 33. DOI: 10.1007/s10916-023-01925-4 PMID: 36869927

Castañeda-Garza, G., Ceballos, H. G., & Mejía-Almada, P. G. (2023). Artificial Intelligence for Mental Health: A Review of AI Solutions and Their Future. *What AI Can*, 373-399.

Čebron, U., & Huber, I. (2020). Cultural competence and healthcare. *Etnološka Tribina*, *50*(43), 68–88. DOI: 10.15378/1848-9540.2020.43.02

Celi, L. A., Cellini, J., Charpignon, M.-L., Dee, E. C., Dernoncourt, F., Eber, R., Mitchell, W. G., Moukheiber, L., Schirmer, J., Situ, J., Paguio, J., Park, J., Wawira, J. G., & Yao, S. (2022). Sources of bias in artificial intelligence that perpetuate healthcare disparities—A global review. *PLOS Digital Health*, *1*(3), e0000022. Advance online publication. DOI: 10.1371/journal.pdig.0000022 PMID: 36812532

Chaney, M. A. (2021). So you want to write a narrative review article? *Journal of Cardiothoracic and Vascular Anesthesia*, *35*(10), 3045–3049. DOI: 10.1053/j.jvca.2021.06.017 PMID: 34272117

Chatterjee, A., Gerdes, M. W., & Martinez, S. (2019, October). eHealth initiatives for the promotion of healthy lifestyle and allied implementation difficulties. In *2019 International Conference on Wireless and Mobile Computing, Networking and Communications (WiMob)* (pp. 1-8). IEEE. DOI: 10.1109/WiMOB.2019.8923324

Cheng, J., Sabour, S., Sun, H., Chen, Z., & Huang, M. (2022). Pal: Persona-augmented emotional support conversation generation. *Findings of the Association for Computational Linguistics: ACL, 2023*, 535–554. DOI: 10.18653/v1/2023.findings-acl.34

Chen, M., & Decary, M. (2020). Artificial intelligence in healthcare: An essential guide for health leaders. *Healthcare Management Forum*, *33*(1), 10–18. DOI: 10.1177/0840470419873123 PMID: 31550922

Chesney, R., & Citron, D. (2019). Deepfakes and the new disinformation war: The coming age of post-truth geopolitics. *Foreign Affairs*, *98*(1), 147.

Chong, J., Sin, C., & Kathiarayan, V. (2023). The role of artificial intelligence in strategic decision-making opportunities, challenges, and implications for managers in the digital age. https://www.researchgate.net/publication/370869247_The_Role_of_Artificial_Intelligence_in_Strategic_Decision-Making_Opportunities_Challenges_and_Implications_for_Managers_in_the_Digital_Age

Choudhury, A., Elkefi, S., & Tounsi, A. (2024). Exploring factors influencing user perspective of ChatGPT as a technology that assists in healthcare decision making: A cross sectional survey study. *PLoS One*, *19*(3), e0296151. DOI: 10.1371/journal.pone.0296151 PMID: 38457373

Choung, H., David, P., & Ross, A. (2022). Trust and ethics in ai. *AI & Society*, *38*(2), 733–745. DOI: 10.1007/s00146-022-01473-4

Clair, R., Gordon, M., Kroon, M., & Reilly, C. (2021). The effects of social isolation on well-being and life satisfaction during pandemic. *Humanities & Social Sciences Communications*, *8*(28), 28. Advance online publication. DOI: 10.1057/s41599-021-00710-3

Coiro, J. (2010). *Handbook of Research on new literacies*. Lawrence Erlbaum Associates.

Corrigan, P. W. (2004). How stigma interferes with mental health care. *The American Psychologist*, *59*(7), 614–625. DOI: 10.1037/0003-066X.59.7.614 PMID: 15491256

Crigger, E., Reinbold, K., Hanson, C., Kao, A., Blake, K., & Irons, M. (2022). Trustworthy augmented intelligence in health care. *Journal of Medical Systems*, *46*(2), 12. DOI: 10.1007/s10916-021-01790-z PMID: 35020064

Crossnohere, N. L., Elsaid, M., Paskett, J., Bose-Brill, S., & Bridges, J. F. (2022a). Guidelines for Artificial Intelligence in Medicine: Literature Review and Content Analysis of Frameworks. *Journal of Medical Internet Research, 24*(8), e36823. Advance online publication. DOI: 10.2196/36823 PMID: 36006692

Curiel, R. P., & Ramirez, H. G. (2021). Vaccination strategies against covid-19 and the diffusion of anti-vaccination views. *Scientific Reports, 11*(1), 6626. Advance online publication. DOI: 10.1038/s41598-021-85555-1 PMID: 33758218

Da Silva, F. G., Andrade, R., Silva, I., & Cardoso, A. (2016). Cross-cultural adaptation of the Cyberchondria Severity Scale for Brazilian Portuguese. *Trends in Psychiatry and Psychotherapy, 38*(2), 90–95. DOI: 10.1590/2237-6089-2015-0063 PMID: 27409134

Dalkıran, G. B. (2023). Health Tourism Components and Intermediary Institutions as Supplier Businesses in the Context of Health 4.0. *In Accounting, Finance, Sustainability, Governance and Fraud.*

Das, A., & Nathan-Roberts, D. (2021). Non-invasive brain–computer interfaces: Development and rehabilitation for motor disability. *Proceedings of the Human Factors and Ergonomics Society Annual Meeting, 65*(1), 1264–1268. DOI: 10.1177/1071181321651299

Davey, O. M., & Sauerwein, L. (2023). Deepfake in online fraud cases: The haze of artificial intelligence's accountability based on the international law. *Sriwijaya Crimen and Legal Studies, 1*(2), 89–99. DOI: 10.28946/scls.v1i2.2654

Davidhizar, R. (1983). Critique of the health-belief model. *Journal of Advanced Nursing, 8*(6), 467–472. DOI: 10.1111/j.1365-2648.1983.tb00473.x PMID: 6558081

Dávila-Aragón, G., & Arrioja-Castrejón, E. (2021). Medical Tourism in Mexico. Analysis of the Economic and Technological Model in the COVID-19 Pandemic Era. *In The Future of Companies in the Face of a New Reality: Impact and Development in Latin America.*

De Carlo, M., Ferilli, G., d'Angella, F., & Buscema, M. (2021). Artificial intelligence to design collaborative strategy: An application to urban destinations. *Journal of Business Research, 129*, 129. DOI: 10.1016/j.jbusres.2020.09.013

De Fauw, J., Ledsam, J. R., Romera-Paredes, B., Nikolov, S., Tomasev, N., Blackwell, S., Askham, H., Glorot, X., O'Donoghue, B., Visentin, D., van den Driessche, G., Lakshminarayanan, B., Meyer, C., Mackinder, F., Bouton, S., Ayoub, K., Chopra, R., King, D., Karthikesalingam, A., & Ronneberger, O. (2018). Clinically applicable deep learning for diagnosis and referral in retinal disease. *Nature Medicine, 24*(9), 1342–1350. DOI: 10.1038/s41591-018-0107-6 PMID: 30104768

De Neys, W., & Glumicic, T. (2008). Conflict monitoring in dual process theories of thinking. *Cognition, 106*(3), 1248–1299. DOI: 10.1016/j.cognition.2007.06.002 PMID: 17631876

Dechene, A., Stahl, C., Hansen, J., & Wänke, M. (2010). The truth about the truth: A meta-analytic review of the truth effect. *Personality and Social Psychology Review, 14*(2), 238–257. DOI: 10.1177/1088868309352251 PMID: 20023210

de-Manuel-Vicente, C. (2024). A development framework for trustworthy artificial intelligence in health with example code pipelines. DOI: 10.1101/2024.07.17.24310418

Denecke, K., Abd-Alrazaq, A., & Househ, M. (2021). Artificial intelligence for chatbots in mental health: opportunities and challenges. *Multiple perspectives on artificial intelligence in healthcare: Opportunities and challenges*, 115-128.

Diaz-Asper, C., Hauglid, M. K., Chandler, C., Cohen, A. S., Foltz, P. W., & Elvevåg, B. (2024). A framework for language technologies in behavioral research and clinical applications: Ethical challenges, implications, and solutions. *The American Psychologist, 79*(1), 79–91. DOI: 10.1037/amp0001195 PMID: 38236217

Doss, C., Mondschein, J., Shu, D., Wolfson, T., Kopecky, D., Fitton-Kane, V. A., Bush, L., & Tucker, C. (2023). Deepfakes and scientific knowledge dissemination. *Scientific Reports, 13*(1), 13429. Advance online publication. DOI: 10.1038/s41598-023-39944-3 PMID: 37596384

Drukker, K., Chen, W., Gichoya, J., Gruszauskas, N., Kalpathy–Cramer, J., Koyejo, S., Myers, K., Sá, R. C., Sahiner, B., Whitney, H., Zhang, Z., & Giger, M. (2023). Toward fairness in artificial intelligence for medical image analysis: Identification and mitigation of potential biases in the roadmap from data collection to model deployment. *Journal of Medical Imaging (Bellingham, Wash.), 10*(06). Advance online publication. DOI: 10.1117/1.JMI.10.6.061104 PMID: 37125409

Drukker, L., Noble, J. A., & Papageorghiou, A. T. (2020). Introduction to artificial intelligence in ultrasound imaging in obstetrics and gynecology. *Ultrasound in Obstetrics & Gynecology, 56*(4), 498–505. DOI: 10.1002/uog.22122 PMID: 32530098

Duan, Y., Edwards, J. S., & Dwivedi, Y. K. (2019). Artificial intelligence for decision making in the era of Big Data – evolution, challenges and research agenda. *International Journal of Information Management*, *48*, 63–71. DOI: 10.1016/j.ijinfomgt.2019.01.021

Duarte, F. (2025, March 26). *Number of CHatGPT Users (March 2025).* Exploding Topics. Retrieved April 1, 2025, from https://explodingtopics.com/blog/chatgpt-users

Duke, D., & Fiacconi, C. M., & KÃ¶hler, S. (. (2014). Parallel effects of processing fluency and positive affect on familiarity-based recognition decisions for faces. *Frontiers in Psychology*, *5*. Advance online publication. DOI: 10.3389/fpsyg.2014.00328 PMID: 24795678

Dunne, R. (2016). *Decision making is caused by information processing and emotion: A synthesis of two approaches to explain the phenomenon of confirmation bias* (thesis). Belfield.

Dwivedi, Y. K., Hughes, L., Ismagilova, E., Aarts, G., Coombs, C., Crick, T., Duan, Y., Dwivedi, R., Edwards, J., Eirug, A., Galanos, V., Ilavarasan, P. V., Janssen, M., Jones, P., Kar, A. K., Kizgin, H., Kronemann, B., Lal, B., Lucini, B., & Williams, M. D. (2021). Artificial intelligence (ai): Multidisciplinary perspectives on emerging challenges, opportunities, and agenda for research, practice and policy. *International Journal of Information Management*, *57*, 101994. DOI: 10.1016/j.ijinfomgt.2019.08.002

Ediansyah, A., Arief, M., Hamsal, M., & Abdinagoro, S. B. (2023). Interplay between Networking Capability and Hospital Performance in Indonesia's Medical Tourism Sector. *International Journal of Environmental Research and Public Health*, *20*(1), 374. DOI: 10.3390/ijerph20010374 PMID: 36612699

Elendu, C., Amaechi, D. C., Elendu, T. C., Jingwa, K. A., Okoye, O. K., John Okah, M., Ladele, J. A., Farah, A. H., & Alimi, H. A. (2023). Ethical implications of AI and robotics in healthcare: A review. *Medicine*, *102*(50), e36671. DOI: 10.1097/MD.0000000000036671 PMID: 38115340

Esmaeilzadeh, P., Maddah, M., & Mirzaei, T. (2025). Using AI chatbots (e.g., CHATGPT) in seeking health-related information online: The case of a common ailment. *Computers in Human Behavior Artificial Humans*, *100127*, 100127. Advance online publication. DOI: 10.1016/j.chbah.2025.100127

Evans, A., Sleegers, W., & Mlakar, Ž. (2020). Individual differences in receptivity to scientific bullshit. *Judgment and Decision Making*, *15*(3), 401–412. DOI: 10.1017/S1930297500007191

Fahim, K. E., Kalinaki, K., & Shafik, W. (2023). Electronic Devices in the Artificial Intelligence of the Internet of Medical Things (AIoMT). In *Handbook of Security and Privacy of AI-Enabled Healthcare Systems and Internet of Medical Things* (pp. 41-62). CRC Press.

Familoni, B.Babajide Tolulope Familoni. (2024). Ethical frameworks for AI in healthcare entrepreneurship: A theoretical examination of challenges and approaches. *International Journal of Frontiers in Biology and Pharmacy Research*, *5*(1), 57–65. DOI: 10.53294/ijfbpr.2024.5.1.0032

Farooq, A., Laato, S., & Islam, A. K. M. N. (2020). Impact of online Information on Self-Isolation Intention during the COVID-19 Pandemic: Cross-Sectional Study. *Journal of Medical Internet Research*, *22*(5), e19128. DOI: 10.2196/19128 PMID: 32330115

Fazio, L. K., Brashier, N. M., Payne, B. K., & Marsh, E. J. (2015). Knowledge does not protect against illusory truth. *Journal of Experimental Psychology. General*, *144*(5), 993–1002. DOI: 10.1037/xge0000098 PMID: 26301795

Fergus, T. A. (2014). The Cyberchondria Severity Scale (CSS): An examination of structure and relations with health anxiety in a community sample. *Journal of Anxiety Disorders*, *28*(6), 504–510. DOI: 10.1016/j.janxdis.2014.05.006 PMID: 24956357

Fergus, T. A., & Dolan, S. L. (2014). Problematic internet use and internet searches for medical information: The role of health anxiety. *Cyberpsychology, Behavior, and Social Networking*, *17*(12), 761–765. DOI: 10.1089/cyber.2014.0169 PMID: 25412398

Fergus, T. A., & Russell, L. H. (2016). Does cyberchondria overlap with health anxiety and obsessive–compulsive symptoms? An examination of latent structure and scale interrelations. *Journal of Anxiety Disorders*, *38*, 88–94. DOI: 10.1016/j.janxdis.2016.01.009 PMID: 26851749

Fernández-López, M., & Perea, M. (2020). Language does not modulate fake news credibility, but emotion does. *Psicológica Journal*, *41*(2), 84–102. DOI: 10.2478/psicolj-2020-0005

Figueiredo, N., Figueiredo, I. E., & Resnick, D. (2013). Tetraplegia or paraplegia with brachial diparesis? What is the most appropriate designation for the motor deficit in patients with lower cervical spinal cord injury? *Neurological Sciences*, *34*(2), 143–147. DOI: 10.1007/s10072-012-1160-4 PMID: 22825074

Flynn, D. J., Nyhan, B., & Reifler, J. (2017). The nature and origins of misperceptions: Understanding false and unsupported beliefs about politics. *Political Psychology*, *38*(S1), 127–150. DOI: 10.1111/pops.12394

Fournier-Tombs, E., & McHardy, J. (2023). A medical ethics framework for conversational artificial intelligence. *Journal of Medical Internet Research*, *25*, e43068. DOI: 10.2196/43068 PMID: 37224277

Frankfurt, H. G. (2005). *On bullshit.* Princeton University Press. DOI: 10.1515/9781400826537

Fu, Z., Burger, H., Arjadi, R., & Bockting, C. L. H. (2020). Effectiveness of digital psychological interventions for mental health problems in low-income and middle-income countries: A systematic review and meta-analysis. *The Lancet. Psychiatry*, *7*(10), 851–864. DOI: 10.1016/S2215-0366(20)30256-X PMID: 32866459

Gaillard, S., Oláh, Z. A., Venmans, S., & Burke, M. (2021). Countering the cognitive, linguistic, and psychological underpinnings behind susceptibility to fake news: A review of current literature with special focus on the role of age and digital literacy. *Frontiers in Communication*, *6*, 661801. Advance online publication. DOI: 10.3389/fcomm.2021.661801

Galtier, M., & Meadon, D. (2023). *Applying AI to real-world health-care settings and the life sciences: Tackling data privacy, security and policy challenges with federated learning.* In artificial intelligence in science: Challenges, opportunities and the future of research. OECD Publishing. DOI: 10.1787/058a23d0-en

Gamble, A. (2020). Artificial intelligence and mobile apps for mental healthcare: A social informatics perspective. *Aslib Journal of Information Management*, *72*(4), 509–523. DOI: 10.1108/AJIM-11-2019-0316

Gandhi, T. K., Classen, D., Sinsky, C. A., Rhew, D. C., Vande Garde, N., Roberts, A., & Federico, F. (2023). How can artificial intelligence decrease cognitive and work burden for front line practitioners? *JAMIA Open*, *6*(3), ooad079. Advance online publication. DOI: 10.1093/jamiaopen/ooad079 PMID: 37655124

Gerke, S., Minssen, T., & Cohen, G. (2020a). Ethical and legal challenges of artificial intelligence-driven healthcare. *Artificial Intelligence in Healthcare*, 295–336. DOI: 10.1016/B978-0-12-818438-7.00012-5

Gerke, S., Minssen, T., & Cohen, G. Ethical and legal challenges of artificial intelligence-driven health care In: *Artificial Intelligence in Health Care.* 1st ed. 2020:295–336. DOI: 10.2139/ssrn.3570129

Ghosh, S., Bagai, S., & Westner, M. M. (2023). *Replika: Embodying AI.* Harvard Business School Case 823-090. https://www.hbs.edu/faculty/Pages/item.aspx?num=63508

Giannake, G., Economou, A., Metaxas, T., & Geitona, M. (2023). Medical Tourism in the Region of Thessaly, Greece: Opinions and Perspectives from Healthcare Providers. *Sustainability (Basel), 15*(10), 7864. DOI: 10.3390/su15107864

Giordano, C., Brennan, M., Mohamed, B., Rashidi, P., Modave, F., & Tighe, P. (2021). Accessing artificial intelligence for clinical decision-making. *Frontiers in Digital Health, 3*, 645232. DOI: 10.3389/fdgth.2021.645232 PMID: 34713115

Giustini, D., & Dastyar, V. (2024). *Critical AI literacy for interpreting in the age of AI.* Interpreting and Society., DOI: 10.1177/27523810241247259

Global Web Index. (2017). Digital vs. traditional media consumption. In *Global Web Index* (Q1 2017). https://www.gwi.com/hubfs/Digital_vs_Traditional_Media_Consumption.pdf

Goirand, M., Austin, E., & Clay-Williams, R. (2023). Mapping the flow of knowledge as guidance for ethics implementation in medical AI: A qualitative study. *PLoS One, 18*(11), e0288448. DOI: 10.1371/journal.pone.0288448 PMID: 37917735

Gomes, N., Pato, M., Lourenco, A. R., & Datia, N. (2023). A survey on wearable sensors for mental health monitoring. *Sensors (Basel), 23*(3), 1330. DOI: 10.3390/s23031330 PMID: 36772370

Gonzalez, J. L. B., González Gámez, M., Mendoza Enciso, E. A., Esparza Maldonado, R. J., Hernández Palacios, D., Dueñas Campos, S., Robles, I. O., Macías Guzmán, M. J., García Díaz, A. L., Gutiérrez Peña, C. M., Martinez Medina, L., Monroy Colin, V. A., & Arreola Guerra, J. M. (2022). Efficacy and safety of ivermectin and hydroxychloroquine in patients with severe COVID-19: A randomized controlled trial. *Infectious Disease Reports, 14*(2), 160–168. DOI: 10.3390/idr14020020 PMID: 35314650

González-Prendes, A., Hindo, C., & Pardo, Y. (2011). Cultural values integration in cognitive-behavioral therapy for a Latino with depression. *Clinical Case Studies, 10*(5), 376–394. DOI: 10.1177/1534650111427075

Gopichandran, V., & Chetlapalli, S. (2013). Factors influencing trust in doctors: A community segmentation strategy for quality improvement in healthcare. *BMJ Open, 3*(12), e004115. DOI: 10.1136/bmjopen-2013-004115 PMID: 24302512

Govere, L., & Govere, E. (2016). How effective is cultural competence training of healthcare providers on improving patient satisfaction of minority groups? A systematic review of literature. *Worldviews on Evidence-Based Nursing, 13*(6), 402–410. DOI: 10.1111/wvn.12176 PMID: 27779817

Green, E. C., Murphy, E. M., & Gryboski, K. (2020). The Health Belief Model. In *The Wiley Encyclopedia of Health Psychology* (pp. 211–214). John Wiley & Sons, Ltd., DOI: 10.1002/9781119057840.ch68

Guan, J. (2019). Artificial Intelligence in Healthcare and medicine: Promises, ethical challenges, and governance. *Chinese Medical Sciences Journal, 0*(0), 99. DOI: 10.24920/003611 PMID: 31315747

Guidance, W. H. O. (2021). *Ethics and governance of artificial intelligence for health.* World Health Organization.

Gulati, S., & Weir, C. (2022). Cultural competence in healthcare leadership education and development. *Societies (Basel, Switzerland), 12*(2), 39. DOI: 10.3390/soc12020039

Habli, I., Lawton, T., & Porter, Z. (2020). Artificial Intelligence in health care: Accountability and safety. *Bulletin of the World Health Organization, 98*(4), 251–256. DOI: 10.2471/BLT.19.237487 PMID: 32284648

Hadjiiski, L., Cha, K., Chan, H., Drukker, K., Morra, L., Näppi, J., Sahiner, B., Yoshida, H., Chen, Q., Deserno, T. M., Greenspan, H., Huisman, H., Huo, Z., Mazurchuk, R., Petrick, N., Regge, D., Samala, R., Summers, R. M., Suzuki, K., & Armato, S.III. (2023). Aapm task group report 273: Recommendations on best practices for AI and machine learning for computer-aided diagnosis in medical imaging. *Medical Physics, 50*(2). Advance online publication. DOI: 10.1002/mp.16188 PMID: 36565447

Hagendorff, T. (2020). The ethics of AI Ethics: An evaluation of guidelines. *Minds and Machines, 30*(1), 99–120. DOI: 10.1007/s11023-020-09517-8

Hague, C., & Payton, S. (2011). *Digital Literacy Across The Curriculum.* Curriculum Leadership Journal.

Haleem, A., Javaid, M., Singh, R. P., & Suman, R. (2022). Medical 4.0 technologies for healthcare: Features, capabilities, and applications. *Internet of Things and Cyber-Physical Systems, 2*, 12–30. DOI: 10.1016/j.iotcps.2022.04.001

Hall, W. J., Chapman, M. V., Lee, K. M., Merino, Y. M., Thomas, T. W., Payne, B. K., Eng, E., Day, S. H., & Coyne-Beasley, T. (2015). Implicit Racial/Ethnic Bias Among Health Care Professionals and Its Influence on Health Care Outcomes: A Systematic Review. *American Journal of Public Health, 105*(12), 60–76. DOI: 10.2105/AJPH.2015.302903 PMID: 26469668

Handtke, O., Schilgen, B., & Mösko, M. (2019). Culturally competent healthcare – a scoping review of strategies implemented in healthcare organizations and a model of culturally competent healthcare provision. *PLoS One, 14*(7), e0219971. DOI: 10.1371/journal.pone.0219971 PMID: 31361783

Harding, N., Azim, M. I., Jidin, R., & Muir, J. P. (2016). A consideration of literature on trust and distrust as they relate to auditor professional scepticism. *Australian Accounting Review, 26*(3), 243–254. DOI: 10.1111/auar.12126

Harrison, R., Walton, M., Chauhan, A., Manias, E., Chitkara, U., Latanik, M., & Leone, D. (2019). What is the role of cultural competence in ethnic minority consumer engagement? An analysis in community healthcare. *International Journal for Equity in Health, 18*(1), 191. Advance online publication. DOI: 10.1186/s12939-019-1104-1 PMID: 31801565

Hassan, V., & Bellos, G. (2022). COVID-19: Reshaping Medical Tourism through Artificial Intelligence (AI) and Robotics. *Athens Journal of Tourism,* 9(2).

Ha, T., & Kim, S. (2023). Improving trust in AI with mitigating confirmation bias: Effects of explanation type and debiasing strategy for decision-making with explainable AI. *International Journal of Human-Computer Interaction,* •••, 1–12. DOI: 10.1080/10447318.2023.2285640

Hautekiet, P., Saenen, N. D., Martens, D. S., Debay, M., Van der Heyden, J., Nawrot, T. S., & De Clercq, E. M. (2022). A healthy lifestyle is positively associated with mental health and well-being and core markers in ageing. *BMC Medicine, 20*(1), 328. Advance online publication. DOI: 10.1186/s12916-022-02524-9 PMID: 36171556

Heinz, T., Eidmann, A., Jakuscheit, A., Laux, T., Rudert, M., & Stratos, I. (2023). Demographics and Trends for Inbound Medical Tourism in Germany for Orthopedic Patients before and during the COVID-19 Pandemic. *International Journal of Environmental Research and Public Health, 20*(2), 1209. DOI: 10.3390/ijerph20021209 PMID: 36673964

Hoek, S., Metselaar, S., Ploem, C., & Bak, M. (2024). Promising for patients or deeply disturbing? the ethical and legal aspects of Deepfake Therapy. *Journal of Medical Ethics*, jme-2024-109985. Advance online publication. DOI: 10.1136/jme-2024-109985 PMID: 38981659

Holohan, M., & Fiske, A. (2021). “Like I’m talking to a real person”: Exploring the meaning of transference for the use and design of AI-based applications in psychotherapy. *Frontiers in Psychology, 12*, 720476. Advance online publication. DOI: 10.3389/fpsyg.2021.720476 PMID: 34646209

Hoop, J. G., DiPasquale, T., Hernandez, J. M., & Roberts, L. W. (2008). Ethics and Culture in Mental Health Care. *Ethics & Behavior, 18*(4), 353–372. DOI: 10.1080/10508420701713048

Hovick, S. R., Kahlor, L., & Liang, M.-C. (2014). Personal Cancer Knowledge and Information Seeking Through PRISM: The Planned Risk Information Seeking Model. *Journal of Health Communication, 19*(4), 511–527. DOI: 10.1080/10810730.2013.821556 PMID: 24433251

Hristovska, A. (2023). Fostering media literacy in the age of AI: Examining the impact on digital citizenship and ethical decision-making. *Media and Communication Review, 2*(2).

Hu, B. (2022). Status Quo and Key Technologies of Artificial Intelligence. *Lecture Notes on Data Engineering and Communications Technologies,* 103.

Huang, Q., Lei, S., & Ni, B. (2022). Perceived information overload and unverified information sharing on WeChat amid the covid-19 pandemic: A moderated mediation model of anxiety and perceived herd. *Frontiers in Psychology, 13*, 837820. Advance online publication. DOI: 10.3389/fpsyg.2022.837820 PMID: 35185742

Hulsen, T. (2021). Literature analysis of artificial intelligence in biomedicine. https://doi.org/DOI: 10.20944/preprints202105.0056.v1

Huñis, A. (2023). Addressing cancer disparities in the Hispanic population in the US and LMICs. *Acta Scientific Cancer Biology, 7*(6), 8–21. DOI: 10.31080/ASCB.2023.07.0428

Huriye, A. (2023). The ethics of artificial intelligence: Examining the ethical considerations surrounding the development and use of AI. *American Journal of Technology, 2*(1), 37–45. DOI: 10.58425/ajt.v2i1.142

Iacobucci, S., & Cicco, R. D. (2022). A literature review of bullshit receptivity: Perspectives for an informed policy making against misinformation. *Journal of Behavioral Economics for Policy, 6*(1), 23–40.

Iacobucci, S., De Cicco, R., Michetti, F., Palumbo, R., & Pagliaro, S. (2021). Deepfakes Unmasked: The effects of information priming and bullshit receptivity on deepfake recognition and sharing intention. *Cyberpsychology, Behavior, and Social Networking, 24*(3), 194–202. DOI: 10.1089/cyber.2020.0149 PMID: 33646046

Incerti Parenti, S., Bartolucci, M. L., Biondi, E., Maglioni, A., Corazza, G., Gracco, A., & Alessandri-Bonetti, G. (2023). Online Patient Education in Obstructive Sleep Apnea: ChatGPT versus Google Search. *Health Care*, *12*(17), 1781. DOI: 10.3390/healthcare12171781 PMID: 39273804

Infanti, A., Starcevic, V., Schimmenti, A., Khazaal, Y., Karila, L., Giardina, A., Flayelle, M., Hedayatzadeh Razavi, S. B., Baggio, S., Vögele, C., & Billieux, J. (2022). Predictors of Cyberchondria during the COVID-19 pandemic: Cross-sectional study using supervised machine learning. *JMIR Formative Research*, *7*, e42206. Advance online publication. DOI: 10.2196/42206 PMID: 36947575

Iniesta, R. (2023). The human role to guarantee an ethical AI in healthcare: A five-facts approach. *AI and Ethics*, •••, 1–13.

Institution of Safe Medication Practice. (2017). (rep.). *Understanding human over-reliance on technology* (Vol. 5, Ser. 5).

Ipsos. (2020). *More than 1 in 3 Americans believe a 'deep state' is working to undermine Trump*. https://www.ipsos.com/en-us/news-polls/npr-misinformation-123020

Jaber, W., Jaber, H. A., Jaber, R., & Saleh, Z. (2024). The convergence of AI and BCIs: A new era of brain-machine interfaces. *Artificial Intelligence in the Age of Nanotechnology*, 98-113. DOI: 10.4018/979-8-3693-0368-9.ch006

Jacovi, A., Marasović, A., Miller, T., & Goldberg, Y. (2021). Formalizing trust in artificial intelligence. *Proceedings of the 2021 ACM Conference on Fairness, Accountability, and Transparency*. DOI: 10.1145/3442188.3445923

Janz, N. K., & Becker, M. H. (1984). The Health Belief Model: A decade later. *Health Education Quarterly*, *11*(1), 1–47. DOI: 10.1177/109019818401100101 PMID: 6392204

Javaid, M., Haleem, A., Pratap Singh, R., Suman, R., & Rab, S. (2022). Significance of machine learning in healthcare: Features, pillars and applications. *International Journal of Intelligent Networks*, *3*, 58–73. https://doi.org/doi.org/10.1016/j.ijin.2022.05.002. DOI: 10.1016/j.ijin.2022.05.002

Jeong, S.-H., Cho, H., & Hwang, Y. (2012). Media Literacy Interventions: A meta-analytic review. *Journal of Communication*, *62*(3), 454–472. DOI: 10.1111/j.1460-2466.2012.01643.x PMID: 22736807

Jiang, F., Jiang, Y., Zhi, H., Dong, Y., Li, H., Ma, S., Wang, Y., Dong, Q., Shen, H., & Wang, Y. (2017). Artificial Intelligence in healthcare: Past, present and future. *Stroke and Vascular Neurology*, *2*(4), 230–243. DOI: 10.1136/svn-2017-000101 PMID: 29507784

Jibril, A. B., & Adzovie, D. E. (2022). Understanding the moderating role of E-WoM and traditional media advertisement toward fast-food joint selection: A uses and gratifications theory. *Journal of Foodservice Business Research, 27*(1), 1–25. DOI: 10.1080/15378020.2022.2070450

Jobin, A., Ienca, M., & Vayena, E. (2019). The global landscape of AI ethics guidelines. *Nature Machine Intelligence, 1*(9), 389–399. DOI: 10.1038/s42256-019-0088-2

Jokić-Begić, N., Mikac, U., Čuržik, D., & Jokić, C. S. (2019). The development and validation of the Short Cyberchondria Scale (SCS). *Journal of Psychopathology and Behavioral Assessment, 41*(4), 662–676. DOI: 10.1007/s10862-019-09744-z

Jones-Jang, S. M., Mortensen, T., & Liu, J. (2019a). Does Media Literacy help identification of fake news? information literacy helps, but other literacies don't. *The American Behavioral Scientist, 65*(2), 371–388. DOI: 10.1177/0002764219869406

Jongen, C., McCalman, J., & Bainbridge, R. (2018). Health workforce cultural competency interventions: A systematic scoping review. *BMC Health Services Research, 18*(1), 232. Advance online publication. DOI: 10.1186/s12913-018-3001-5 PMID: 29609614

Jung, W., Lee, K., Suh, B., Seok, H., & Lee, D. (2021). Deep learning for osteoarthritis classification in temporomandibular joint. *Oral Diseases, 29*(3), 1050–1059. DOI: 10.1111/odi.14056 PMID: 34689379

Jun, Y., Craig, A., Shafik, W., & Sharif, L. (2021). Artificial intelligence application in cybersecurity and cyberdefense. *Wireless Communications and Mobile Computing, 2021*(1), 1–10. DOI: 10.1155/2021/3329581

Kaas, M. H., Porter, Z., Lim, E., Higham, A., Khavandi, S., & Habli, I. (2023, July). Ethics in conversation: Building an ethics assurance case for autonomous AI-enabled voice agents in healthcare. In *Proceedings of the First International Symposium on Trustworthy Autonomous Systems* (pp. 1-13). DOI: 10.1145/3597512.3599713

Kabir, M. (2023). Machine learning-based security and privacy protection approach to handle physiological data. A*rtificial Intelligence for Disease Diagnosis and Prognosis in Smart Healthcare*, 287-304. DOI: 10.1201/9781003251903-16

Kaggwa, S., Eleogu, T. F., Okonkwo, F., Farayola, O. A., Uwaoma, P. U., & Akinoso, A. (2024). AI in decision making: Transforming business strategies. *International Journal of Innovation and Scientific Research, 10*(12), 423–444. DOI: 10.51244/IJRSI.2023.1012032

Kahlor, L. (2010). PRISM: A planned risk information seeking model. *Health Communication, 25*(4), 345–356. DOI: 10.1080/10410231003775172 PMID: 20512716

Kalinaki, K., Fahadi, M., Alli, A. A., Shafik, W., Yasin, M., & Mutwalibi, N. (2023). Artificial Intelligence of Internet of Medical Things (AIoMT) in Smart Cities: A Review of Cybersecurity for Smart Healthcare. *Handbook of Security and Privacy of AI-Enabled Healthcare Systems and Internet of Medical Things*, 271-292.

Kapoor, A., & Goel, S. (2022). *Applications of conversational AI in mental health: A survey.* 2022 6th International Conference on Trends in Electronics and Informatics (ICOEI). DOI: 10.1109/ICOEI53556.2022.9777127

Karadayi-Usta, S., & Serdarasan, S. (2023). Supplier selection and capacity allocation in medical tourism service supply chain. *OPSEARCH*.

Karnouskos, S. (2020). Artificial Intelligence in digital media: The Era of Deepfakes. *IEEE Transactions on Technology and Society*, *1*(3), 138–147. DOI: 10.1109/TTS.2020.3001312

Kasinidou, M. (2024). Development of personalised educational tools for AI literacy using participatory design. *Adjunct Proceedings of the 32nd ACM Conference on User Modeling, Adaptation and Personalization*. DOI: 10.1145/3631700.3664917

Kaur, J., & Mann, K. S. (2018). AI based healthcare platform for real time, predictive and prescriptive analytics. In R. Sharma, A. Mantri, & S. Dua, *Computing, Analytics and Networks* Singapore. DOI: 10.1007/978-981-13-0755-3_11

Keefer, L., Bedell, A., Norton, C., & Hart, A. L. (2022). How should pain, fatigue, and emotional wellness be incorporated into treatment goals for optimal management of inflammatory bowel disease? *Gastroenterology*, *162*(5), 1439–1451. DOI: 10.1053/j.gastro.2021.08.060 PMID: 34995528

Kertysova, K. (2018). Artificial Intelligence and disinformation. *Security and Human Rights*, *29*(1–4), 55–81. DOI: 10.1163/18750230-02901005

Kesmodel, U. S. (2018). Cross-sectional studies – what are they good for? *Acta Obstetricia et Gynecologica Scandinavica*, *97*(4), 388–393. DOI: 10.1111/aogs.13331 PMID: 29453895

Khaksar Shahmirzadi, E., Saner, T., Attaeyan, A., Abdolahi, S., Mohammadi, M., & Heydari, S. (2022). Evaluation of the use of robotic surgery with remote simulation for use in the field of Medical Tourism and Pro-Tourism development. *In Journal of Simulation and Analysis of Novel Technologies in Mechanical Engineering*, vol. 14(1).

Khan, A. W., & Pandey, J. (2022). Dark side consequences of cyberchondria: An empirical investigation. *Aslib Journal of Information Management*, *74*(5), 801–817. DOI: 10.1108/AJIM-08-2021-0222

Khan, M. A., Asadi, H., Zhang, L., Qazani, M. R., Oladazimi, S., Loo, C. K., Lim, C. P., & Nahavandi, S. (2024). Application of artificial intelligence in cognitive load analysis using functional near-infrared spectroscopy: A systematic review. *Expert Systems with Applications*, *249*, 123717. DOI: 10.1016/j.eswa.2024.123717

Khare, S. K., Blanes-Vidal, V., Nadimi, E. S., & Acharya, U. R. (2024). Emotion recognition and artificial intelligence: A systematic review (2014–2023) and research recommendations. *Information Fusion*, *102*, 102019. DOI: 10.1016/j.inffus.2023.102019

Khullar, D., Casalino, L. P., Qian, Y., Lu, Y., Chang, E., & Aneja, S. (2021). Public vs physician views of liability for Artificial Intelligence in health care. *Journal of the American Medical Informatics Association : JAMIA*, *28*(7), 1574–1577. DOI: 10.1093/jamia/ocab055 PMID: 33871009

Kim, B., Xiong, A., Lee, D., & Han, K. (2021). A systematic review on fake news research through the lens of news creation and consumption: Research efforts, challenges, and Future Directions. *PLoS One*, *16*(12), e0260080. Advance online publication. DOI: 10.1371/journal.pone.0260080 PMID: 34882703

Kim-Godwin, Y., Clarke, P., & Barton, L. (2001). A model for the delivery of culturally competent community care. *Journal of Advanced Nursing*, *35*(6), 918–925. DOI: 10.1046/j.1365-2648.2001.01929.x PMID: 11555040

Kim, J., Aryee, L. M. D., Bang, H., Prajogo, S., Choi, Y. K., Hoch, J. S., & Prado, E. L. (2023). Effectiveness of digital mental health tools to reduce depressive and anxiety symptoms in low- and middle-income countries: Systematic review and meta-analysis. *JMIR Mental Health*, *10*, e43066. DOI: 10.2196/43066 PMID: 36939820

Kim, J., Livingston, M. A., Jin, B., Watts, M., & Hwang, J. (2024). Fundamentals of digital health literacy: A scoping review of identifying core competencies to use in practice. *Adult Learning*, *35*(3), 131–142. DOI: 10.1177/10451595231178298

Kiseleva, A. (2020). Ai as a medical device: Is it enough to ensure performance transparency and accountability? *European Pharmaceutical Law Review*, *4*(1), 5–16. DOI: 10.21552/eplr/2020/1/4

Kompton, A. M., & Vassilakopoulou, P. (2021). *Accountability, Transparency and Explainability in AI for Healthcare*. DOI: 10.18420/ihc2021_018

Kostic, E. J., Pavlović, D. A., & Živković, M. D. (2019). Applications of artificial intelligence in medicine and pharmacy – ethical aspects. *Acta Medica Medianae*, *58*(3), 128–137. DOI: 10.5633/amm.2019.0319

Kumar, A. (2021). Role of digital literacy in preventing hacking. *IJIRT, 8*(1), 1392–1399. https://www.ijirt.org/master/publishedpaper/IJIRT157666_PAPER.pdf

Kumar, S., Sajnani, M., & Chopra, A. (2023). Analysis of RAISA (Robotics, Artificial Intelligence & Service Automation) and Dubai Tourism. *Proceedings of 3rd IEEE International Conference on Computational Intelligence and Knowledge Economy,* 2023. DOI: 10.1109/ICCIKE58312.2023.10131791

Kundu, R., Shi, X., Morrison, J., Barrett, J., & Mukherjee, B. (2024). A framework for understanding selection bias in real-world healthcare data. *Journal of the Royal Statistical Society. Series A, (Statistics in Society), 187*(3), qnae039. DOI: 10.1093/jrsssa/qnae039 PMID: 39281782

Kurian, N. (2023). AI's empathy gap: The risks of conversational Artificial Intelligence for young children's well-being and key ethical considerations for early childhood education and care. *Contemporary Issues in Early Childhood,* •••, 14639491231206004.

Kusuma, A., Praja, A., Chairuddin, B., & Dewi, M. P. (2023). The Role of Stakeholders In Supporting The Hospital Towards Medical Tourism Services. *The Seybold Report,* 17(11).

Kwiatkoski, D., Mantovani, M., Pereira, E., Bortolato-Major, C., & Peres, A. (2017). Translation and cross-cultural adaptation of the clinical competence questionnaire for use in Brazil. *Revista Latino-Americana de Enfermagem, 25*(0). Advance online publication. DOI: 10.1590/1518-8345.1757.2898 PMID: 28591303

Laato, S., Islam, A. K., Islam, M. N., & Whelan, E. (2020). What drives unverified information sharing and cyberchondria during the covid-19 pandemic? *European Journal of Information Systems, 29*(3), 288–305. DOI: 10.1080/0960085X.2020.1770632

Land, M. K., & Aronson, J. D. (2020). Human Rights and Technology: New challenges for justice and Accountability. *Annual Review of Law and Social Science, 16*(1), 223–240. DOI: 10.1146/annurev-lawsocsci-060220-081955

Lattie, E. G., Stiles-Shields, C., & Graham, A. K. (2022). An overview of and recommendations for more accessible digital mental health services. *Nature Reviews Psychology, 1*(2), 87–100. DOI: 10.1038/s44159-021-00003-1 PMID: 38515434

Lee, J., Lee, S., & Kim, D. (2022). *Problems and issues of emotional computing and artificial emotional intelligence: A review of Rosalind w. picard's thesis "affective computing: challenges"*. 2022 IEEE/ACIS 7th International Conference on Big Data, Cloud Computing, and Data Science (BCD). DOI: 10.1109/BCD54882.2022.9900683

Lee, C., Houssami, N., Elmore, J., & Buist, D. (2020). Pathways to breast cancer screening artificial intelligence algorithm validation. *The Breast : Official Journal of the European Society of Mastology*, *52*, 146–149. DOI: 10.1016/j.breast.2019.09.005 PMID: 31540699

Lee, C.-S., Wang, M.-H., Kuan, W.-K., Huang, S.-H., Tsai, Y.-L., Ciou, Z.-H., Yang, C.-K., & Kubota, N. (2023). BCI-based hit-loop agent for human and AI robot co-learning with AIoT application. *Journal of Ambient Intelligence and Humanized Computing*, *14*(4), 3583–3607. DOI: 10.1007/s12652-021-03487-0

Leffer, L. (2024). *What it's like to live with a brain chip, according to Neuralink's first user.* Scientific American. https://www.scientificamerican.com/article/neuralinks-first-user-describes-life-with-elon-musks-brain-chip/

Legaspi, R., He, Z., & Toyoizumi, T. (2019). Synthetic Agency: Sense of agency in Artificial Intelligence. *Current Opinion in Behavioral Sciences*, *29*, 84–90. DOI: 10.1016/j.cobeha.2019.04.004

Le, L. H., Hoang, P. A., & Pham, H. C. (2023). Sharing health information across online platforms: A systematic review. *Health Communication*, *38*(8), 1550–1562. DOI: 10.1080/10410236.2021.2019920 PMID: 34978235

Leung, R. (2023, June). Using ai–ml to augment the capabilities of social media for telehealth and remote patient monitoring. [). MDPI.]. *Health Care*, *11*(12), 1704. PMID: 37372822

Leung, Y., Park, B., Heo, R., Adikari, A., Chackochan, S., Wong, J., Alie, E., Gancarz, M., Kacala, M., Hirst, G., de Silva, D., French, L., Bender, J., Mishna, F., Gratzer, D., Alahakoon, D., & Esplen, M. J. (2022). Providing care beyond therapy sessions with a natural language processing–based recommender system that identifies cancer patients who experience psychosocial challenges and provides self-care support: Pilot study. *JMIR Cancer*, *8*(3), e35893. DOI: 10.2196/35893 PMID: 35904877

Levin, K. A. (2006). Study design III: Cross-sectional studies. *Evidence-Based Dentistry*, *7*(1), 24–25. DOI: 10.1038/sj.ebd.6400375 PMID: 16557257

Liao, F., Adelaine, S., Afshar, M., & Patterson, B. W. (2022). Governance of clinical AI applications to facilitate safe and equitable deployment in a large health system: Key elements and early successes. *Frontiers in Digital Health*, *4*, 931439. Advance online publication. DOI: 10.3389/fdgth.2022.931439 PMID: 36093386

Li, H., Du, Y., Xue, T., & Jenkins, C. L. (2023). Chinese medical tourism: Review and research agenda. *Journal of Quality Assurance in Hospitality & Tourism*, *24*(5), 663–687. DOI: 10.1080/1528008X.2022.2073939

Li, J., Dada, A., Kleesiek, J., & Egger, J. (2023). *Chatgpt in Healthcare: A Taxonomy and Systematic Review*. DOI: 10.1101/2023.03.30.23287899

Lin, B., Cecchi, G., & Bouneffouf, D. (2023, March 13). *Psychotherapy AI Companion with Reinforcement Learning Recommendations and Interpretable Policy Dynamics.* Companion Proceedings of the ACM Web Conference 2023 (WWW '23 Companion). DOI: 10.1145/3543873.3587623

Ling, E. C., Tussyadiah, I., Tuomi, A., Stienmetz, J., & Ioannou, A. (2021). Factors influencing users' adoption and use of conversational agents: A systematic review. *Psychology &amp. Psychology and Marketing*, *38*(7), 1031–1051. DOI: 10.1002/mar.21491

Link, B. G., & Phelan, J. C. (2001). Conceptualizing stigma. *Annual Review of Sociology*, *27*(1), 363–385. DOI: 10.1146/annurev.soc.27.1.363

Link, E., & Kahlor, L. A. (2024). The Planned Risk Information Seeking Model Applied to Vaccine Information Avoidance and the Role of Affect, Emotion and Perceived Benefits. *Health Communication*, *39*(11), 2376–2389. DOI: 10.1080/10410236.2023.2268912 PMID: 37872691

Lins, S., Pandl, K. D., Teigeler, H., Thiebes, S., Bayer, C., & Sunyaev, A. (2021). Artificial intelligence as a service. *Business & Information Systems Engineering*, *63*(4), 441–456. DOI: 10.1007/s12599-021-00708-w

Liu, Y., Wang, R., & Zhao, T. (2022). Interaction Design in Residence Mode of Health and Tourism. *Lecture Notes in Computer Science (Including Subseries Lecture Notes in Artificial Intelligence and Lecture Notes in Bioinformatics),* 13325 LNCS.

Liu, J., Chen, C., Qu, Y., Yang, S., & Xu, L. (2023). Rass: Enabling privacy-preserving and authentication in online AI-driven healthcare applications. *ISA Transactions*, *141*, 20–29. DOI: 10.1016/j.isatra.2023.03.049 PMID: 37059673

Lockey, S., Gillespie, N., Holm, D., & Someh, I. A. (2021a). A review of trust in artificial intelligence: Challenges, vulnerabilities and future directions. In *54th Hawaii International Conference on System Sciences*. DOI: 10.24251/HICSS.2021.664

Lomiguen, C., Rosete, I., & Chin, J. (2020). Providing culturally competent care for covid-19 intensive care unit delirium: A case report and review. *Cureus*. Advance online publication. DOI: 10.7759/cureus.10867 PMID: 33178520

Longo, D. R. (2005). Understanding health information, communication, and information seeking of patients and consumers: A comprehensive and integrated model. *Health Expectations*, *8*(3), 189–194. DOI: 10.1111/j.1369-7625.2005.00339.x PMID: 16098149

Loos, A. (2013). Cyberchondria: Too much information for the health anxious patient? *Journal of Consumer Health on the Internet, 17*(4), 439–445. DOI: 10.1080/15398285.2013.833452

Loveys, K., Prina, M., Axford, C., Domènec, Ò. R., Weng, W., Broadbent, E., Pujari, S., Jang, H., Han, Z. A., & Thiyagarajan, J. A. (2022). Artificial intelligence for older people receiving long-term care: A systematic review of acceptability and effectiveness studies. *The Lancet. Healthy Longevity, 3*(4), e286–e297. DOI: 10.1016/S2666-7568(22)00034-4 PMID: 35515814

Luca, C., Casu, F., Manunta, M., Onorato, G., & Lanari, R. (2021). Comment on "Study of systematic bias in measuring surface deformation with SAR interferometry" by Ansari et al. (2021). DOI: 10.36227/techrxiv.14691333

Lukyanenko, R., Maass, W., & Storey, V. C. (2022). Trust in artificial intelligence: From a foundational trust framework to emerging research opportunities. *Electronic Markets, 32*(4), 1993–2020. DOI: 10.1007/s12525-022-00605-4

Lun, V. M.-C., Yeung, J. C., & Ku, K. Y. (2023a). Effects of mood on critical thinking. *Thinking Skills and Creativity, 47*, 101247. DOI: 10.1016/j.tsc.2023.101247

Lysaght, T., Lim, H. Y., Xafis, V., & Ngiam, K. Y. (2019). Ai-assisted decision-making in Healthcare. *Asian Bioethics Review, 11*(3), 299–314. DOI: 10.1007/s41649-019-00096-0 PMID: 33717318

Maharjan, B., Li, J., Kong, J., & Tao, C. (2019, October). Alexa, what should I eat?: A personalized virtual nutrition coach for native American diabetes patients using Amazon's smart speaker technology. In *2019 IEEE International Conference on E- health Networking, Application & Services (HealthCom)* (pp. 1-6). IEEE. DOI: 10.1109/HealthCom46333.2019.9009613

Mahlknecht, A., Engl, A., Piccoliori, G., & Wiedermann, C. J. (2023). Supporting primary care through symptom checking artificial intelligence: A study of patient and physician attitudes in Italian general practice. *BMC Primary Care, 24*(1), 174. Advance online publication. DOI: 10.1186/s12875-023-02143-0 PMID: 37661285

Makarla, S., Gopichandran, V., & Tondare, D. (2019). Prevalence and correlates of cyberchondria among professionals working in the information technology sector in Chennai, India. *Journal of Postgraduate Medicine, 65*(2), 87–92. DOI: 10.4103/jpgm.JPGM_293_18 PMID: 31036778

Makhoul, M., Melkane, A. E., Khoury, P. E., Hadi, C. E., & Matar, N. (2024). A cross-sectional comparative study: ChatGPT 3.5 versus diverse levels of medical experts in the diagnosis of ENT diseases. *European Archives of Oto-Rhino-Laryngology*, *281*(5), 2717–2721. DOI: 10.1007/s00405-024-08509-z PMID: 38365990

Mak, R. H., Endres, M. G., Paik, J. H., Sergeev, R. A., Aerts, H., Williams, C. L., Lakhani, K. R., & Guinan, E. C. (2019). Use of crowd innovation to develop an artificial intelligence–based solution for radiation therapy targeting. *JAMA Oncology*, *5*(5), 654–661. DOI: 10.1001/jamaoncol.2019.0159 PMID: 30998808

Mandler, G. (2008). Familiarity breeds attempts: A critical review of dual-process theories of recognition. *Perspectives on Psychological Science*, *3*(5), 390–399. DOI: 10.1111/j.1745-6924.2008.00087.x PMID: 26158957

Mantello, P., & Ho, T. (2022). Why we need to be weary of emotional AI. *AI & Society*. Advance online publication. DOI: 10.1007/s00146-022-01576-y

Manyika, J., Chui, M., Miremadi, M., Bughin, J., George, K., Willmott, P., & Dewhurst, M. (2017). A future that works: AI, automation, employment, and productivity. *McKinsey Global Institute Research. Tech. Rep*, *60*, 1–135.

Martel, C., Pennycook, G., & Rand, D. G. (2020). Reliance on emotion promotes belief in fake news. *Cognitive Research: Principles and Implications*, *5*(1), 47. Advance online publication. DOI: 10.1186/s41235-020-00252-3 PMID: 33026546

Marzo, R. R. (2024). Bridging the Digital Divide: AI Solutions for Health Literacy in Underserved Populations. In *Modern Management Science Practices in the Age of AI* (pp. 151-180). IGI Global.

Maslach, C., & Leiter, M. P. (2016). Understanding the burnout experience: Recent research and its implications for psychiatry. *World Psychiatry; Official Journal of the World Psychiatric Association (WPA)*, *15*(2), 103–111. DOI: 10.1002/wps.20311 PMID: 27265691

Mason, A., Spencer, E., Barnett, K., & Bouchie, J. (2023). Examining the prominence and congruence of organizational corporate social responsibility (CSR) communication in medical tourism provider websites. *Journal of Hospitality and Tourism Insights*, *6*(1), 1–17. DOI: 10.1108/JHTI-06-2021-0136

Matinkhah, S. M., Shafik, W., & Ghasemzadeh, M. (2019). Emerging artificial intelligence application: reinforcement learning issues on current internet of things. In *2019 16th international Conference in information knowledge and Technology (ikt2019)* (p. 2019).

Maulida, S., & Marlina, L. (2023). Halal Medical Tourism. Halal Tourism and Pilgrimage, 2(2).

Mays, K., Lei, Y., Giovanetti, R., & Katz, J. (2021). AI as a boss? A national US survey of predispositions governing comfort with expanded AI roles in society. *AI & Society*, *37*(4), 1587–1600. DOI: 10.1007/s00146-021-01253-6

McCalman, J., Jongen, C., & Bainbridge, R. (2017). Organisational systems' approaches to improving cultural competence in healthcare: A systematic scoping review of the literature. *International Journal for Equity in Health*, *16*(1), 78. Advance online publication. DOI: 10.1186/s12939-017-0571-5 PMID: 28499378

McCradden, M. D., Baba, A., Saha, A., Ahmad, S., Boparai, K., Fadaiefard, P., & Cusimano, M. D. (2020). Ethical concerns around use of artificial intelligence in health care research from the perspective of patients with meningioma, caregivers and health care providers: A qualitative study. *CMAJ Open*, *8*(1), E90–E95. DOI: 10.9778/cmajo.20190151 PMID: 32071143

McElroy, E., & Shevlin, M. (2014). The development and initial validation of the cyberchondria severity scale (CSS). *Journal of Anxiety Disorders*, *28*(2), 259–265. DOI: 10.1016/j.janxdis.2013.12.007 PMID: 24508033

McEwen, B. S. (2007). Physiology and neurobiology of stress and adaptation: Central role of the brain. *Physiological Reviews*, *87*(3), 873–904. DOI: 10.1152/physrev.00041.2006 PMID: 17615391

McKinney, S. M., Sieniek, M., Godbole, V., Godwin, J., Antropova, N., Ashrafian, H., Back, T., Chesus, M., Corrado, G. S., Darzi, A., Etemadi, M., Garcia-Vicente, F., Gilbert, F. J., Halling-Brown, M., Hassabis, D., Jansen, S., Karthikesalingam, A., Kelly, C. J., King, D., & Shetty, S. (2020). International evaluation of an AI system for breast cancer screening. *Nature*, *577*(7788), 89–94. DOI: 10.1038/s41586-019-1799-6 PMID: 31894144

McKivigan, J. (2020). Evaluation of the American physical therapy association's guidelines for training culturally competent physical therapists. *Higher Education Research*, *5*(4), 154. DOI: 10.11648/j.her.20200504.16

McMullan, R., Berle, D., Arnáez, S., & Starčević, V. (2019). The relationships between health anxiety, online health information seeking, and cyberchondria: Systematic review and meta-analysis. *Journal of Affective Disorders*, *245*, 270–278. DOI: 10.1016/j.jad.2018.11.037 PMID: 30419526

McStay, A. (2024). *Automating empathy: Decoding technologies that gauge intimate life*. Oxford University Press., DOI: 10.1093/oso/9780197615546.001.0001

Meissner, P., & Keding, C. (2021). *The Human Factor in AI-Based Decisions*. Massachusetts Institute of Technology. https://sloanreview.mit.edu/article/the-human-factor-in-ai-based-decision-making/

Meng, J., Rheu, M., Zhang, Y., Dai, Y., & Peng, W. (2023). *Mediated social support for distress reduction: ai chatbots vs. human*. Proceedings of the ACM on Human-Computer Interaction, 7(CSCW1), 1-25. DOI: 10.1145/3579505

Mensah, G. B. (2024). Ai ethics. *Africa Journal For Regulatory Affairs*. DOI: 10.62839/AJFRA/2024.v1.I1.32-45

Meske, C., & Bunde, E. (2020). Transparency and trust in human-AI-interaction: The role of model-agnostic explanations in computer vision-based decision support. In H. Degen & L. Reinerman-Jones, *Artificial Intelligence in HCI* Cham.

Mesko, B., & Topol, E. J. (2023). The imperative for regulatory oversight of large language models (or generative AI) in healthcare. *NPJ Digital Medicine*, *6*(1), 120. Advance online publication. DOI: 10.1038/s41746-023-00873-0 PMID: 37414860

Mestre-Bach, G., & Potenza, M. N. (2023). Cyberchondria: A growing concern during the covid-19 pandemic and a possible addictive disorder? *Current Addiction Reports*, *10*(1), 77–96. DOI: 10.1007/s40429-022-00462-3 PMID: 36785757

Mihailidis, P., & Viotty, S. (2017). Spreadable spectacle in Digital Culture: Civic expression, fake news, and the role of media literacies in "Post-fact" society. *The American Behavioral Scientist*, *61*(4), 441–454. DOI: 10.1177/0002764217701217

Mishima, M., Hayashida, K., Fukasaku, Y., Ogata, R., Ohsawa, K., Iwai, K., Wen, W., & Morioka, S. (2023). Adaptability of the sense of agency in healthy young adults in sensorimotor tasks for a short term. *Behavioral Sciences (Basel, Switzerland)*, *13*(2), 132. DOI: 10.3390/bs13020132 PMID: 36829361

Mogaji, E., Olaleye, S. A., & Ukpabi, D. C. (2019). Using AI to personalise emotionally appealing advertisement. *Digital and Social Media Marketing*, 137-150. DOI: 10.1007/978-3-030-24374-6_10

Möller, J., Trilling, D., Helberger, N., & van Es, B. (2018). Do not blame it on the algorithm: An empirical assessment of multiple recommender systems and their impact on content diversity. *Information Communication and Society*, *21*(7), 959–977. DOI: 10.1080/1369118X.2018.1444076

Monlezun, D. (2023). The future's (ai) thinking healthcare system. *The Thinking Healthcare System*, 263-303. DOI: 10.1016/B978-0-443-18906-7.00008-8

Monteleone, S. (2019). Artificial Intelligence, data protection, and elections. *Ser.*, *637*, 952.

Moore, C. M. (2022). The challenges of health inequities and ai. *Intelligence-Based Medicine*, *6*, 100067. DOI: 10.1016/j.ibmed.2022.100067

Morse, K. E., Ostberg, N. P., Jones, V. G., & Chan, A. S. (2020). Use Characteristics and Triage Acuity of a Digital Symptom Checker in a Large Integrated Health System: Population-Based Descriptive Study. *Journal of Medical Internet Research*, *22*(11), e20549. DOI: 10.2196/20549 PMID: 33170799

Muetunda, F., Jamil, M. L., Pais, S., Sabry, S., Dias, G., Pombo, N., & Cordeiro, J. (2023). Exploring the role of artificial intelligence in mental health. *2023 IEEE International Conference on Data Mining Workshops (ICDMW)*, 1289–1298. DOI: 10.1109/ICDMW60847.2023.00166

Müller, A., Baumann, E., & Dierks, M. (2022). Cyberchondria. *The International Encyclopedia of Health Communication,* 1-6. DOI: 10.1002/9781119678816.iehc0624

Murdoch, B. (2021). Privacy and artificial intelligence: Challenges for protecting health information in a new era. *BMC Medical Ethics*, *22*(1), 122. Advance online publication. DOI: 10.1186/s12910-021-00687-3 PMID: 34525993

Murphy, K., Ruggiero, E., Upshur, R., Willison, D., Malhotra, N., Cai, J., & Gibson, J. (2021). Artificial intelligence for good health: A scoping review of the ethics literature. *BMC Medical Ethics*, *22*(1), 14. Advance online publication. DOI: 10.1186/s12910-021-00577-8 PMID: 33588803

Musk, E. (2019). An integrated Brain-Machine Interface platform with thousands of channels. *Journal of Medical Internet Research*, *21*(10), e16194. DOI: 10.2196/16194 PMID: 31642810

Naddaf, M., & Drew, L. (2024). Second brain implant by Elon Musk's Neuralink: Will it fare better than the first? *Nature*, *632*(8025), 481–482. DOI: 10.1038/d41586-024-02368-8 PMID: 39112576

Naik, N., Hameed, B. M., Shetty, D. K., Swain, D., Shah, M., Paul, R., Aggarwal, K., Ibrahim, S., Patil, V., Smriti, K., Shetty, S., Rai, B. P., Chlosta, P., & Somani, B. K. (2022). Legal and ethical consideration in artificial intelligence in Healthcare: Who takes responsibility? *Frontiers in Surgery*, *9*, 862322. Advance online publication. DOI: 10.3389/fsurg.2022.862322 PMID: 35360424

Naja, B. (2018). (rep.). *Computation propaganda techniques. Ser.*, *628*, 284.

Na, S. A., Nee, A. Y. H., & Onn, C. Y. (2017). Medical tourism: The effects of perceived benefits, perceived risks and geographic region. *Pertanika Journal of Social Science & Humanities*, •••, 25.

Na, S. A., Onn, C. Y., & Meng, C. L. (2016). Travel Intentions among Foreign Tourists for Medical Treatment in Malaysia: An Empirical Study. *Procedia: Social and Behavioral Sciences*, *224*, 224. DOI: 10.1016/j.sbspro.2016.05.434

Nasiri, M. M., Mohammadkhani, S., Akbari, M., & Alilou, M. M. (2023). The structural model of cyberchondria based on personality traits, health-related metacognition, cognitive bias, and emotion dysregulation. *Frontiers in Psychiatry*, *13*, 960055. Advance online publication. DOI: 10.3389/fpsyt.2022.960055 PMID: 36699479

Nazer, L. H., Zatarah, R., Waldrip, S., Ke, J. X. C., Moukheiber, M., Khanna, A. K., Hicklen, R. S., Moukheiber, L., Moukheiber, D., Ma, H., & Mathur, P. (2023). Bias in artificial intelligence algorithms and recommendations for mitigation. *PLOS Digital Health*, *2*(6), e0000278. DOI: 10.1371/journal.pdig.0000278 PMID: 37347721

Nelson, G. S. (2019). Bias in artificial intelligence. *North Carolina Medical Journal*, *80*(4), 220–222. DOI: 10.18043/ncm.80.4.220 PMID: 31278182

Ng, D. T., Leung, J. K., Chu, S. K., & Qiao, M. S. (2021). Conceptualizing ai literacy: An exploratory review. *Computers and Education: Artificial Intelligence*, *2*, 100041. DOI: 10.1016/j.caeai.2021.100041

Nicolescu, L., & Tudorache, M. T. (2022). Human-Computer Interaction in Customer Service: The experience with AI Chatbots—a systematic literature review. *Electronics (Basel)*, *11*(10), 1579. DOI: 10.3390/electronics11101579

Niu, Z., Willoughby, J. F., Mei, J., Li, S., & Hu, P. (2020). A Cross-Cultural Comparison of an Extended Planned Risk Information Seeking Model on Mental Health Among College Students: Cross-Sectional Study. *Journal of Medical Internet Research*, *22*(5), e15817. DOI: 10.2196/15817 PMID: 32441654

Norcross, J. C., & Wampold, B. E. (2011). Evidence-based therapy relationships: Research conclusions and clinical practices. *Psychotherapy (Chicago, Ill.)*, *48*(1), 98–102. DOI: 10.1037/a0022161 PMID: 21401280

Nowaskie, D., & Najam, S. (2022). Lesbian, gay, bisexual, and/or transgender (lgbt) cultural competency across the intersectionalities of gender identity, sexual orientation, and race among healthcare professionals. *PLoS One*, *17*(11), e0277682. DOI: 10.1371/journal.pone.0277682 PMID: 36367906

O'Reilly-Shah, V. N., Gentry, K. R., Walters, A. M., Zivot, J., Anderson, C. T., & Tighe, P. J. (2020). Bias and ethical considerations in machine learning and the automation of perioperative risk assessment. *British Journal of Anaesthesia, 125*(6), 843–846. DOI: 10.1016/j.bja.2020.07.040 PMID: 32838979

Oberauer, K. (2018). On the automaticity of familiarity in short-term recognition: A test of the dual-process assumption with the PRP paradigm. *Journal of Cognition, 1*(1), 20. Advance online publication. DOI: 10.5334/joc.21 PMID: 31517194

Okoro, Y. O., Ayo-Farai, O., Maduka, C. P., Okongwu, C. C., & Sodamade, O. T. (2024). A review of health misinformation on Digital Platforms: Challenges and countermeasures. *International Journal of Applied Research in Social Sciences, 6*(1), 23–36. DOI: 10.51594/ijarss.v6i1.689

Ong, D. C. (2021, September). An ethical framework for guiding the development of affectively-aware artificial intelligence. *9th International Conference on Affective Computing and Intelligent Interaction (ACII)*, Nara, Japan, 2021, 1-8. DOI: 10.1109/ACII52823.2021.9597441

Orji, R., Vassileva, J., & Mandryk, R. (2012). Towards an Effective Health Interventions Design: An Extension of the Health Belief Model. *Online Journal of Public Health Informatics, 4*(3), e61050. DOI: 10.5210/ojphi.v4i3.4321 PMID: 23569653

Ouédraogo, I. (2024). *Mobile technology and artificial intelligence for improving health literacy among underserved communities* (Doctoral dissertation, Université de Bordeaux; Université Nazi Boni (Bobo-Dioulasso, Burkina Faso)).

Özkent, M. S., Kılınç, M. T., Hamarat, M. B., Yılmaz, B., Göger, Y. E., Özkent, Y., & Pişkin, M. M. (2023). Digitalization and urological diseases: Severity of cyberchondria and level of health anxiety in patients visiting outpatient urology clinics. *Cyberpsychology, Behavior, and Social Networking, 26*(1), 28–34. DOI: 10.1089/cyber.2022.0089 PMID: 36454182

Ozmen Garibay, O., Winslow, B., Andolina, S., Antona, M., Bodenschatz, A., Coursaris, C., Falco, G., Fiore, S. M., Garibay, I., Grieman, K., Havens, J. C., Jirotka, M., Kacorri, H., Karwowski, W., Kider, J., Konstan, J., Koon, S., Lopez-Gonzalez, M., Maifeld-Carucci, I., & Xu, W. (2023). Six human-centered artificial intelligence grand challenges. *International Journal of Human-Computer Interaction, 39*(3), 391–437. DOI: 10.1080/10447318.2022.2153320

Pagliari, M., Chambon, V., & Berberian, B. (2022). What is new with Artificial Intelligence? human–agent interactions through the lens of Social Agency. *Frontiers in Psychology, 13*, 954444. Advance online publication. DOI: 10.3389/fpsyg.2022.954444 PMID: 36248519

Pannu, A. (2015). Artificial intelligence and its application in different areas. *Artificial Intelligence*, *4*(10), 79–84.

Parikh, P. M., Talwar, V., & Goyal, M. (2023). ChatGPT: An online cross-sectional descriptive survey comparing perceptions of healthcare workers to those of other professionals. *Cancer Research, Statistics, and Treatment*, *6*(1), 32–36. DOI: 10.4103/crst.crst_40_23

Park, S., Kim, E., & Na, E. (2014). Online activities, digital media literacy, and networked individualism of Korean youth. *Youth & Society*, *47*(6), 829–849. DOI: 10.1177/0044118X14561008

Park, Y. J. (2011). Digital literacy and privacy behavior online. *Communication Research*, *40*(2), 215–236. DOI: 10.1177/0093650211418338

Patanapu, S., Sreeja, C., Veeraboina, N., Reddy, K., Voruganti, S., & Anusha, P. (2022). Prevalence and effect of cyberchondria on academic performance among undergraduate dental students: An institutional based study. *Industrial Psychiatry Journal*, *31*(2), 228–234. DOI: 10.4103/ipj.ipj_272_21 PMID: 36419676

Patel, S., & Fan, J. (2023). Identification and description of emotions by current large language models. *bioRxiv*. DOI: 10.1101/2023.07.17.549421

PATIL. (2021). *S.* India–A Pivotal Centre for Medical Tourism. PalArch's Journal of Archaeology of Egypt/Egyptology.

Paton, C., & Kobayashi, S. (2019). An open science approach to artificial intelligence in Healthcare. *Yearbook of Medical Informatics, 28*(01), 047–051. DOI: 10.1055/s-0039-1677898

Patricia, H. (2005). Improving patient–provider communication: Insights from interpreters. *Family Practice*, *22*(3), 311–316. DOI: 10.1093/fampra/cmi015 PMID: 15805131

Paulhus, D. L., Harms, P. D., Bruce, M. N., & Lysy, D. C. (2003). The over-claiming technique: Measuring self-enhancement independent of ability. *Journal of Personality and Social Psychology*, *84*(4), 890–904. DOI: 10.1037/0022-3514.84.4.890 PMID: 12703655

Pautasso, M. (2019). The structure and conduct of a narrative literature review. *A guide to the scientific career: Virtues, communication, research and academic writing*, 299-310.

Pawar, P., Kamat, A., Salimath, G., Jacob, K. R., & Kamath, R. (2022). Prevalence of Cyberchondria among Outpatients with Metabolic Syndrome in a Tertiary Care Hospital in Southern India. *TheScientificWorldJournal, 1–5*, 1–5. Advance online publication. DOI: 10.1155/2022/3211501 PMID: 36199439

Pennycook, G., & Rand, D. G. (2017). Assessing the effect of "disputed" warnings and source salience on perceptions of fake news accuracy. SSRN *Electronic Journal*. DOI: 10.2139/ssrn.3035384

Pennycook, G., Cannon, T. D., & Rand, D. G. (2018). Prior exposure increases perceived accuracy of fake news. *Journal of Experimental Psychology. General, 147*(12), 1865–1880. DOI: 10.1037/xge0000465 PMID: 30247057

Pennycook, G., Fugelsang, J. A., & Koehler, D. J. (2015). What makes us think? A three-stage dual-process model of analytic engagement. *Cognitive Psychology*, *80*, 34–72. DOI: 10.1016/j.cogpsych.2015.05.001 PMID: 26091582

Pennycook, G., & Rand, D. G. (2019). Who falls for fake news? the roles of bullshit receptivity, overclaiming, familiarity, and analytic thinking. *Journal of Personality*, *88*(2), 185–200. DOI: 10.1111/jopy.12476 PMID: 30929263

Perdikis, S., & Millan, J. R. (2020). Brain-machine interfaces: A tale of two learners. *IEEE Systems, Man, and Cybernetics Magazine*, *6*(3), 12–19. DOI: 10.1109/MSMC.2019.2958200

Pereira, T. C., Costa, E., Borges, I., Silva, F. M., Pinto, A. S., & Vázquez-Justo, E. (2022). Health Tourism Monitor System Model. *Smart Innovation, Systems and Technologies,* 284.

Perlis, R. H., Lunz Trujillo, K., Green, J., Safarpour, A., Druckman, J. N., Santillana, M., Ognyanova, K., & Lazer, D. (2023). Misinformation, trust, and use of ivermectin and hydroxychloroquine for covid-19. *JAMA Health Forum*, *4*(9), e233257. Advance online publication. DOI: 10.1001/jamahealthforum.2023.3257 PMID: 37773507

Pesapane, F., Bracchi, D. A., Mulligan, J. F., Linnikov, A., Maslennikov, O., Lanzavecchia, M. B., Tantrige, P., Stasolla, A., Biondetti, P., Giuggioli, P. F., Cassano, E., & Carrafiello, G. (2021). Legal and regulatory framework for AI solutions in Healthcare in EU, US, China, and Russia: New scenarios after a pandemic. *Radiation*, *1*(4), 261–276. DOI: 10.3390/radiation1040022

Pettersson, S., Holstein, J., Jirwe, M., Jaarsma, T., & Klompstra, L. (2021). Cultural competence in healthcare professionals, specialised in diabetes, working in primary healthcare—A descriptive study. *Health & Social Care in the Community*, *30*(3). Advance online publication. DOI: 10.1111/hsc.13442 PMID: 34145649

Petty, R. E., Brinol, P., McCaslin, M. J., & Loerch, C. (2009). The need for cognition. In *Handbook of individual differences in social behavior* (pp. 318–329). essay.

Peuter, S. D., Oulasvirta, A., & Kaski, S. (2023). Toward AI assistants that let designers design. *AI Magazine*, *44*(1), 85–96. DOI: 10.1002/aaai.12077

Picard, R. W., & Klein, J. (2002). Computers that recognize and respond to user emotion: Theoretical and practical implications. *Interacting with Computers*, *14*(2), 141–169. DOI: 10.1016/S0953-5438(01)00055-8

Pillai, A. S. (2023). AI-enabled hospital management systems for modern healthcare: An analysis of system components and interdependencies. *Journal of Advanced Analytics in Healthcare Management*, *7*(1), 212–228. https://research.tensorgate.org/index.php/JAAHM/article/view/109

Płaciszewski, K., Wierzba, W., Ostrowski, J., Pinkas, J., & Jankowski, M. (2022). Use of the Internet for health purposes—A national web-based cross-sectional survey among adults in Poland. *International Journal of Environmental Research and Public Health*, *19*(23), 16315. DOI: 10.3390/ijerph192316315 PMID: 36498389

Ponnusamy, V., Vasuki, A., Clement, J. C., & Eswaran, P. (2022). AI-Driven Information and Communication Technologies, Services, and Applications for Next-Generation Healthcare System. Smart Systems for Industrial Applications, 1-32.

Prabhakaran, V., Qadri, R., & Hutchinson, B. (2022). *Cultural incongruencies in artificial intelligence*. arXiv. https://doi.org//arXiv.2211.13069DOI: 10.48550

Pranckutė, R. (2021). Web of science (WoS) and Scopus: The titans of bibliographic information in today's academic world. *Publications/MDPI*, *9*(1), 12. DOI: 10.3390/publications9010012

Pullman, D., & Etchegary, H. (2021). Ethical, legal, and social issues (ELSI) in clinical genetics research. *Clinical Epidemiology: Practice and Methods*, 65-82.

Qadri, R., Shelby, R., Bennett, C. L., & Denton, E. (2023). AI's regimes of representation: a community-centered study of text-to-image models in South Asia. *2023 ACM Conference on Fairness, Accountability, and Transparency*. DOI: 10.1145/3593013.3594016

Queiroz, M., & Wamba, S. (2021). A structured literature review on the interplay between emerging technologies and covid-19 – insights and directions to operations fields. *Annals of Operations Research*, *335*(3), 937–963. DOI: 10.1007/s10479-021-04107-y PMID: 34226781

Qureshi, J., & Khan, S. (2024). *Artificial Intelligence (AI) Deepfakes in Healthcare Systems: A Double-Edged Sword? Balancing Opportunities and Navigating Risks*. DOI: 10.20944/preprints202402.0176.v1

Rahman, M. M. (2023). Ensuring halal compliance in AI-driven healthcare solutions. *Advances in Healthcare Information Systems and Administration*, •••, 298–320. DOI: 10.4018/979-8-3693-1082-3.ch015

Rahme, C., Akel, M., Obeid, S., & Hallit, S. (2021). Cyberchondria severity and quality of life among Lebanese adults: The mediating role of fear of COVID-19, depression, anxiety, stress and obsessive–compulsive behavior—a structural equation model approach. *BMC Psychology*, *9*(1), 169. Advance online publication. DOI: 10.1186/s40359-021-00674-8 PMID: 34715930

Rajpurkar, P., Chen, E., Banerjee, O., & Topol, E. J. (2022). Ai in Health and Medicine. *Nature Medicine*, *28*(1), 31–38. DOI: 10.1038/s41591-021-01614-0 PMID: 35058619

Rastogi, C., Zhang, Y., Wei, D., Varshney, K. R., Dhurandhar, A., & Tomsett, R. (2022). Deciding fast and slow: The role of cognitive biases in AI-assisted decision-making. *Proceedings of the ACM on Human-Computer Interaction, 6*(CSCW1), 1–22. DOI: 10.1145/3512930

Rauck, R., Loudermilk, E., Paez, J., Bojrab, L., Noles, J., Turley, T., Ibrahim, M., Patwardhan, A., Scowcroft, J., Przkora, R., Miller, N., Chaiban, G., Hershey, B., Lechleiter, K., Woon, R., Huynh, D., Tchrakian, T., Rodgers, J., & McDonald, M. (2022). O045 / #626 artificial intelligence-driven closed-loop SCS: Early patient feedback on personalized therapy recommendations from a digital-health assistant. *Neuromodulation*, *25*(7), S72–S73. DOI: 10.1016/j.neurom.2022.08.083

Razzaq, N., Farzeen Khan, E., & Razzaq, S. (2023). Analyzing the role of language and religion in culturally competent healthcare: An interdisciplinary perspective. *AIM*, *1*(3). Advance online publication. DOI: 10.59652/aim.v1i3.61

Reddy, S., Allan, S., Coghlan, S., & Cooper, P. (2019). A governance model for the application of AI in health care. *Journal of the American Medical Informatics Association : JAMIA*, *27*(3), 491–497. DOI: 10.1093/jamia/ocz192 PMID: 31682262

Redrup Hill, E., Mitchell, C., Brigden, T., & Hall, A. (2023). Ethical and legal considerations influencing human involvement in the implementation of artificial intelligence in a clinical pathway: A multi-stakeholder perspective. *Frontiers in Digital Health*, *5*, 1139210. DOI: 10.3389/fdgth.2023.1139210 PMID: 36999168

Roberts, M. J., & Newton, E. J. (2010). Inspection Times, the change task, and the rapid-response selection task. *The Quarterly Journal of Experimental Psychology. A, Human Experimental Psychology*, *54*(4), 1031–1048. DOI: 10.1080/713756016 PMID: 11765731

Robertson, C., Woods, A., Bergstrand, K., Findley, J., Balser, C., & Slepian, M. (2023). Diverse patients' attitudes towards artificial intelligence (AI) in diagnosis. *PLOS Digital Health*, *2*(5), e0000237. DOI: 10.1371/journal.pdig.0000237 PMID: 37205713

Rodríguez, N. R., Cote, L., Fuentes, C., Jaramillo, E., Arana, S., Castro, A., Behrens, E., Ramos, A., & Zerrweck, C. (2023). First National Consensus on the Safe Practice of Medical Tourism for Bariatric Surgery in Mexico. *Obesity Surgery*, *33*(4), 1060–1072. DOI: 10.1007/s11695-023-06468-8 PMID: 36729365

Ruben, M. A., Stosic, M. D., Correale, J., & Blanch-Hartigan, D. (2021). Is technology enhancing or hindering interpersonal communication? A framework and preliminary results to examine the relationship between technology use and nonverbal decoding skill. *Frontiers in Psychology*, *11*, 611670. Advance online publication. DOI: 10.3389/fpsyg.2020.611670 PMID: 33519627

Rubin, D. B., Ajiboye, A. B., Barefoot, L., Bowker, M., Cash, S. S., Chen, D., Donoghue, J. P., Eskandar, E. N., Friehs, G., Grant, C., Henderson, J. M., Kirsch, R. F., Marujo, R., Masood, M., Mernoff, S. T., Miller, J. P., Mukand, J. A., Penn, R. D., Shefner, J., & Hochberg, L. R. (2023). Interim safety profile from the feasibility study of the BrainGate neural interface system. *Neurology*, *100*(11), e1177–e1192. DOI: 10.1212/WNL.0000000000201707 PMID: 36639237

Rubin, V. L. (2022). *Misinformation and disinformation: Detecting fakes with the eye and ai*. Springer. DOI: 10.1007/978-3-030-95656-1

Russell, R. D., Black, L. J., Pham, N. M., & Begley, A. (2020). The effectiveness of emotional wellness programs on mental health outcomes for adults with multiple sclerosis: A systematic review and meta-analysis. *Multiple Sclerosis and Related Disorders*, *44*, 102171. DOI: 10.1016/j.msard.2020.102171 PMID: 32554283

Russell, S. J., & Norvig, P. (2016). *Artificial intelligence: A modern approach*. Pearson.

Ryff, C. D., & Singer, B. (1998). The contours of positive human health. *Psychological Inquiry*, *9*(1), 1–28. DOI: 10.1207/s15327965pli0901_1

Ryndach, M. A., Kargina, L. A., Lebedeva, S. L., & Chernyshova, L. A. (2021). Artificial intelligence in accessible tourism. *CEUR Workshop Proceedings*, ●●●, 2914.

Sakipov, N., & Vikhnin, O. (2021). The Modern Symbolic Artificial Intelligence and Its Use in Medical Tourism. *15th IEEE International Conference on Application of Information and Communication Technologies,* AICT 2021. DOI: 10.1109/AICT52784.2021.9620321

Saleh, S., & Battseren, B. (2023). Ai-driven solutions for sustainable environment monitoring. *Embedded Selforganising Systems, 10*(8), 1-2. https://doi.org/DOI: 10.14464/ess.v10i8.615

Salih, S. (2024). Perceptions of faculty and students about use of artificial intelligence in medical education: A qualitative study. *Cureus*. Advance online publication. DOI: 10.7759/cureus.57605 PMID: 38707183

Sallam, M. (2023). *The Utility of Chatgpt as an Example of Large Language Models in Healthcare Education, Research and Practice: Systematic Review on the Future Perspectives and Potential Limitations*. DOI: 10.1101/2023.02.19.23286155

Samson, K., & Kostyszyn, P. (2015a). Effects of cognitive load on trusting behavior – an experiment using the Trust game. *PLoS One*, *10*(5), e0127680. Advance online publication. DOI: 10.1371/journal.pone.0127680 PMID: 26010489

Sankaran, K. S., Tai-Hoon, K., & Renjith, P. N. (2023). An improved AI-based secure m-trust privacy protocol for medical internet of things in smart healthcare system. *IEEE Internet of Things Journal*, *10*(21), 18477–18485. DOI: 10.1109/JIOT.2023.3280592

Sasmal, S. (2024). Data warehousing revolution: AI-driven solutions. International Research *Journal Of Engineering & Applied Sciences, 12*(1), 01-06. https://doi.org/DOI: 10.55083/irjeas.2024.v12i01001

Schmälzle, R., & Wilcox, S. (2022). Harnessing artificial intelligence for health message generation: The folic acid message engine. *Journal of Medical Internet Research*, *24*(1), e28858. DOI: 10.2196/28858 PMID: 35040800

Schonberger, D. (2019). Artificial Intelligence in healthcare: A critical analysis of the legal and ethical implications. *International Journal of Law and Information Technology*, *27*(2), 171–203. DOI: 10.1093/ijlit/eaz004

Schyff, E. L. d., Ridout, B., Amon, K. L., Forsyth, R., & Campbell, A. (2023). *Providing self-led mental health support through an artificial intelligence–powered chatbot (leora) to meet the demand of mental health care* (preprint). DOI: 10.2196/preprints.46448

Sedlakova, J., & Trachsel, M. (2023). Conversational artificial intelligence in psychotherapy: A new therapeutic tool or agent? *The American Journal of Bioethics*, *23*(5), 4–13. DOI: 10.1080/15265161.2022.2048739 PMID: 35362368

Selvi, Y., Turan, S. G., Sayin, A. A., Boysan, M., & Kandeger, A. (2018). The Cyberchondria Severity Scale (CSS): Validity and reliability study of the Turkish version. *Sleep and Hypnosis*, •••, 241–246. DOI: 10.5350/Sleep.Hypn.2018.20.0157

Seow, A. N., Choong, C. K., Chen, I. C., & Choong, Y. O. (2022). Can protection motivation theory explain the perception of international tourists' on medical tourism? *Journal of Hospitality and Tourism Insights*, *5*(2), 394–412. DOI: 10.1108/JHTI-10-2020-0189

Seow, A. N., Choong, Y. O., & Chan, L. M. (2018). What Influences The Behavioural Intention In Medical Tourism? *A Threat and Coping Perspective.Global Business and Management Research, 10*(3).

Seow, A. N., Choong, Y. O., Moorthy, K., & Chan, L. M. (2017). Intention to visit Malaysia for medical tourism using the antecedents of Theory of Planned Behaviour: A predictive model. *International Journal of Tourism Research, 19*(3), 383–393. DOI: 10.1002/jtr.2120

Seow, A. N., Choong, Y. O., Moorthy, K., & Choong, C. K. (2021). Predicting medical tourism behavioural intention using social cognition models. *Tourism Review*, *76*(2), 374–391. DOI: 10.1108/TR-06-2019-0267

Sequeiros, H., Oliveira, T., & Thomas, M. A. (2022). The impact of IoT smart home services on psychological well-being. *Information Systems Frontiers*, *24*(3), 1009–1026. DOI: 10.1007/s10796-021-10118-8

Shaban-Nejad, A., Michalowski, M., Bianco, S., Brownstein, J. S., Buckeridge, D. L., & Davis, R. L. (2022). Applied artificial intelligence in healthcare: Listening to the winds of change in a post-COVID-19 world. *Experimental Biology and Medicine*, *247*(22), 1969–1971. DOI: 10.1177/15353702221140406 PMID: 36426683

Shafik, W. (2023d). Making Cities Smarter: IoT and SDN Applications, Challenges, and Future Trends. In *Opportunities and Challenges of Industrial IoT in 5G and 6G Networks* (pp. 73-94). IGI Global.

Shafik, W. (2024b). Wearable Medical Electronics in Artificial Intelligence of Medical Things. *Handbook of Security and Privacy of AI-Enabled Healthcare Systems and Internet of Medical Things,* 21-40.

Shafik, W., & Kalinaki, K. (2023). Smart City Ecosystem: An Exploration of Requirements, Architecture, Applications, Security, and Emerging Motivations. In *Handbook of Research on Network-Enabled IoT Applications for Smart City Services* (pp. 75-98). IGI Global.

Shafik, W. (2023a). A Comprehensive Cybersecurity Framework for Present and Future Global Information Technology Organizations. In *Effective Cybersecurity Operations for Enterprise-Wide Systems* (pp. 56–79). IGI Global. DOI: 10.4018/978-1-6684-9018-1.ch002

Shafik, W. (2023b). Artificial intelligence and Blockchain technology enabling cybersecurity in telehealth systems. [IET.]. *Artificial Intelligence and Blockchain Technology in Modern Telehealth Systems*, *1*, 285–326. DOI: 10.1049/PBHE061E_ch11

Shafik, W. (2023c). Cyber Security Perspectives in Public Spaces: Drone Case Study. In *Handbook of Research on Cybersecurity Risk in Contemporary Business Systems* (pp. 79–97). IGI Global. DOI: 10.4018/978-1-6684-7207-1.ch004

Shafik, W. (2024a). Predicting Future Cybercrime Trends in the Metaverse Era. In *Forecasting Cyber Crimes in the Age of the Metaverse* (pp. 78–113). IGI Global.

Shafik, W. (2024c). Introduction to ChatGPT. In *Advanced Applications of Generative AI and Natural Language Processing Models* (pp. 1–25). IGI Global.

Shahsavar, Y., & Choudhury, A. (2023). User intentions to use CHATGPT for self-diagnosis and health-related purposes: Cross-sectional survey study. *JMIR Human Factors*, *10*, e47564. Advance online publication. DOI: 10.2196/47564 PMID: 37195756

Sharma, D., Singh Aujla, G., & Bajaj, R. (2023). Evolution from ancient medication to human-centered Healthcare 4.0: A review on health care recommender systems. *International Journal of Communication Systems*, *36*(12), e4058. DOI: 10.1002/dac.4058

Shen, S. A., Perez-Heydrich, C. A., Xie, D. X., & Nellis, J. C. (2024). ChatGPT vs. web search for patient questions: What does ChatGPT do better? *European Archives of Oto-Rhino-Laryngology*, *281*(6), 3219–3225. DOI: 10.1007/s00405-024-08524-0 PMID: 38416195

Shimada, K. (2023). The role of artificial intelligence in mental health: A Review. *Science Insights*, *43*(5), 1119–1127. DOI: 10.15354/si.23.re820

Shinners, L., Aggar, C., Grace, S., & Smith, S. (2019, September 30). Exploring healthcare professionals' understanding and experiences of artificial intelligence technology use in the delivery of healthcare: An integrative review. *Health Informatics Journal*, *26*(2), 1225–1236. DOI: 10.1177/1460458219874641 PMID: 31566454

Shi, X., & Gan, L. (2023). Equilibrium in Competitive Insurance Markets with Medical Tourism. *Studies in Microeconomics*, *11*(2), 246–269. DOI: 10.1177/23210222211051439

Sidaoui, K., Jaakkola, M., & Burton, J. (2020). Ai feel you: Customer experience assessment via chatbot interviews. *Journal of Service Management*, *31*(4), 745–766. DOI: 10.1108/JOSM-11-2019-0341

Smith, H. (2020). Clinical AI: Opacity, accountability, responsibility and liability. *AI & Society*, *36*(2), 535–545. DOI: 10.1007/s00146-020-01019-6

Smolin, V. S. (2020). The prospects of the mankind in the era of technological singularity. *Epistemol Philos Sci*, *57*(2), 192–207. DOI: 10.5840/eps202057230

Sodiya, E. O., Amoo, O. O., Umoga, U. J., & Atadoga, A. (2024). AI-driven personalization in web content delivery: A comparative study of user engagement in the USA and the UK. *World Journal of Advanced Research and Reviews*, *21*(2), 887–902. DOI: 10.30574/wjarr.2024.21.2.0502

Sohail, M., & Zafar, N. (2022). Fear of COVID-19 and stress in university students: Mediating role of cyberchondria and moderating role of creative coping and social supports. *JPMA. The Journal of the Pakistan Medical Association*. Advance online publication. DOI: 10.47391/JPMA.4350 PMID: 36280920

Solanki, P., Grundy, J., & Hussain, W. (2022). Operationalising Ethics in Artificial Intelligence for Healthcare: A framework for AI developers. *AI and Ethics*, *3*(1), 223–240. DOI: 10.1007/s43681-022-00195-z

Solem, R. C. (2015). Limitation of a cross-sectional study. *American Journal of Orthodontics and Dentofacial Orthopedics*, *148*(2), 205. DOI: 10.1016/j.ajodo.2015.05.006 PMID: 26232823

Solez, K., Bernier, A., Crichton, J., Graves, H., Kuttikat, P., Lockwood, R., Marovitz, W. F., Monroe, D., Pallen, M., Pandya, S., Pearce, D., Saleh, A., Sandhu, N., Sergi, C., Tuszynski, J., Waugh, E., White, J., Woodside, M., Wyndham, R., & Zakus, D. (2013). Bridging the gap between the technological singularity and mainstream medicine: Highlighting a course on technology and the future of medicine. *Global Journal of Health Science*, *5*(6), 112–125. DOI: 10.5539/gjhs.v5n6p112 PMID: 24171879

Sonko, S., Fabuyide, A., Ibekwe, K. I., Etukudoh, E. A., & Ilojianya, V. I. (2024). Neural interfaces and human-computer interaction: A US review: Delving into the developments, ethical considerations, and future prospects of brain-computer interfaces. *International Journal of Science and Research Archive*, *11*(1), 702–717. DOI: 10.30574/ijsra.2024.11.1.0111

Srinivasan, V. (2020, April 2). *Context, language, and reasoning in AI: Three key challenges*. MIT Technology Review. https://www.technologyreview.com/2016/10/14/156968/context-language-and-reasoning-in-ai-three-key-challenges/

St. Evans, J. (2008). Dual-processing accounts of reasoning, judgment, and social cognition. *Annual Review of Psychology*, *59*(1), 255–278. DOI: 10.1146/annurev.psych.59.103006.093629 PMID: 18154502

St. Evans, J., & Curtis-Holmes, J. (2005). Rapid responding increases belief bias: Evidence for the dual-process theory of reasoning. *Thinking &amp. Thinking & Reasoning*, *11*(4), 382–389. DOI: 10.1080/13546780542000005

St. Evans, J., & Stanovich, K. E. (2013). Dual-process theories of higher cognition. *Perspectives on Psychological Science*, *8*(3), 223–241. DOI: 10.1177/1745691612460685 PMID: 26172965

Stanovich, K. E., & West, R. F. (1998). Individual differences in rational thought. *Journal of Experimental Psychology. General*, *127*(2), 161–188. DOI: 10.1037/0096-3445.127.2.161

Stanovich, K. E., & West, R. F. (2000). Individual differences in reasoning: Implications for the rationality debate? *Behavioral and Brain Sciences*, *23*(5), 645–665. DOI: 10.1017/S0140525X00003435 PMID: 11301544

Stanton, B., & Jensen, T. (2021). Trust and artificial intelligence. *National Institute of Standards and Technology*. https://doi.org/https://doi.org/10.6028/NIST.IR.8332-draft

Starcevic, V., & Berle, D. (2013). Cyberchondria: Towards a better understanding of excessive health-related Internet use. *Expert Review of Neurotherapeutics*, *13*(2), 205–213. DOI: 10.1586/ern.12.162 PMID: 23368807

Starcevic, V., Schimmenti, A., Billieux, J., & Berle, D. (2021). Cyberchondria in the time of the COVID-19 pandemic. *Human Behavior and Emerging Technologies*, *3*(1), 53–62. DOI: 10.1002/hbe2.233 PMID: 33363277

Stark, L., & Hoey, J. (2019). The ethics of emotion in AI systems. *AoIR Selected Papers of Internet Research*. DOI: 10.5210/spir.v2019i0.11039

Statista. (May 22, 2024). Number of internet and social media users worldwide as of April 2024 (in billions). In *Statista*. Retrieved April 2024, from https://www-statista-com.ezproxy.lib.hkmu.edu.hk/forecasts/1146659/social-media-users-in-the-world

Statista. (May 7, 2024). Global internet penetration rate as of April 2024, by region. In *Statista*. Retrieved April 2024, from https://www.statista.com/statistics/269329/penetration-rate-of-the-internet-by-region/#:~:text=Internet%20penetration%20rate%20worldwide%202024%2C%20by%20region&text=As%20of%20April%202024%2C%20Northern,rate%20was%20roughly%2067.1%20percent

Strauss, A., & Corbin, J. (1990). *Basics of qualitative research* (Vol. 15). Newbury Park, CA: sage.

Subasi, A., Ozaltin, O., Mitra, A., Subasi, M. E., & Sarirete, A. (2023). Trustworthy artificial intelligence in healthcare. In *Accelerating Strategic Changes for Digital Transformation in the Healthcare Industry* (pp. 145–177). Academic Press. DOI: 10.1016/B978-0-443-15299-3.00015-4

Subasinghe, M., Magalage, D., Amadoru, N., Amarathunga, L., Bhanupriya, N., & Wijekoon, J. L. (2020). Effectiveness of artificial intelligence, decentralized and distributed systems for prediction and secure channelling for Medical Tourism. *11th Annual IEEE Information Technology, Electronics and Mobile Communication Conference,* IEMCON 2020.

Sujan, M., Furniss, D., Grundy, K., Grundy, H., Nelson, D., Elliott, M., White, S., Habli, I., & Reynolds, N. (2019). Human factors challenges for the safe use of artificial intelligence in patient care. *BMJ Health & Care Informatics*, *26*(1), e100081. DOI: 10.1136/bmjhci-2019-100081 PMID: 31780459

Sukhera, J. (2022). Narrative reviews: Flexible, rigorous, and practical. *Journal of Graduate Medical Education*, *14*(4), 414–417. DOI: 10.4300/JGME-D-22-00480.1 PMID: 35991099

Sun, G., & Zhou, Y.-H. (2023). AI in healthcare: Navigating opportunities and challenges in digital communication. *Frontiers in Digital Health*, *5*, 1291132. DOI: 10.3389/fdgth.2023.1291132 PMID: 38173911

Sun, M., Wang, J., & Zhang, D. (2020). The progess that natural language processing has made towards human-level AI. *Journal of Artificial Intelligence Practice*, *3*(1), 38–47. DOI: 10.23977/jaip.2020.030107

Sweller, J. (2011). Cognitive load theory. *Psychology of Learning and Motivation*, *55*, 37–76. DOI: 10.1016/B978-0-12-387691-1.00002-8

Sylvester, S. M. (2021). Covid-19 and motivated reasoning: The influence of knowledge on covid-related policy and Health Behavior. *Social Science Quarterly*, *102*(5), 2341–2359. DOI: 10.1111/ssqu.12989 PMID: 34226771

Szawłoga, T., Soroka, K., & Śliwińska, M. (2024). Cyberchondria in students: An eHealth related problem. A review. *Medical Science Pulse*, *18*(2, SUPPLEMENT 3), 12–21. DOI: 10.5604/01.3001.0054.5653

Taddeo, M., & Floridi, L. (2018). How AI can be a force for good. *Science*, *361*(6404), 751–752. DOI: 10.1126/science.aat5991 PMID: 30139858

Talwar, S., Dhir, A., Kaur, P., Zafar, N., & Alrasheedy, M. (2019). Why do people share fake news? associations between the Dark Side of social media use and fake news sharing behavior. *Journal of Retailing and Consumer Services*, *51*, 72–82. DOI: 10.1016/j.jretconser.2019.05.026

Tao, D., Shao, F., Wang, H., Yan, M., & Qu, X. (2020). Integrating usability and social cognitive theories with the technology acceptance model to understand young users' acceptance of a health information portal. *Health Informatics Journal*, *26*(2), 1347–1362. DOI: 10.1177/1460458219879337 PMID: 31603378

Tarabay, C., Bitar, Z., Akel, M., Hallit, S., Obeid, S., & Soufia, M. (2023). Cyberchondria Severity and quality of life among Lebanese adults. *The Primary Care Companion for CNS Disorders*, *25*(2). Advance online publication. DOI: 10.4088/PCC.22m03252 PMID: 37115149

Tejeda, H., Kumar, A., Smyth, P., & Steyvers, M. (2022). Ai-assisted decision-making: A cognitive modeling approach to infer latent Reliance Strategies. *Computational Brain &amp. Computational Brain & Behavior*, *5*(4), 491–508. DOI: 10.1007/s42113-022-00157-y

Thompson, S. A., & Tsu, T. (2023, February 8). *Disinformation researchers raise alarms about A.I. Chatbots*. The New York Times. https://www.nytimes.com/2023/02/08/technology/ai-chatbots-disinformation.html

Thompson, V. A. (2013). Why it matters. *Perspectives on Psychological Science*, *8*(3), 253–256. DOI: 10.1177/1745691613483476 PMID: 26172968

Thoo, A. C., Khairuddin, A. I. N., Tat, H. H., Sulaiman, Z., Lai, L. Y., & Masâ€T-Mod, A. (2018). Factors Affecting Medical Tourists to Malaysia. *Asia Proceedings of Social Sciences*, 2(3).

Thoo, A. C., Khairuddin, A. I. N., Tat, H. H., Sulaiman, Z., Lai, L. Y., & Mas'od, A. (2020). Why medical tourists must go to Malaysia! *International Journal of Business Continuity and Risk Management*, *10*(2–3), 224. DOI: 10.1504/IJBCRM.2020.108510

Timmons, A. C., Duong, J. B., Fiallo, N. S., Lee, T., Vo, H. P. Q., Ahle, M. W., & Chaspari, T. (2022). A call to action on assessing and mitigating bias in artificial intelligence applications for mental health. *Perspectives on Psychological Science, 18*(5), 1062–1096. DOI: 10.1177/17456916221134490 PMID: 36490369

Tiwari, S., Srivastava, S., & Negi, M. (2022). Prevalence and predictors of cyberchondria and depression amid COVID-19 pandemic in adult population of Uttar Pradesh, India. *Archives of Medicine and Health Sciences, 10*(2), 200–206. DOI: 10.4103/amhs.amhs_95_22

Tom, E., Keane, P. A., Blazes, M., Pasquale, L. R., Chiang, M. F., Lee, A. Y., & Lee, C. S. (2020). Protecting data privacy in the age of ai-enabled ophthalmology. *Translational Vision Science &amp. Technology, 9*(2), 36. DOI: 10.1167/tvst.9.2.36 PMID: 32855840

Trabelsi, Z., Alnajjar, F., Parambil, M. M. A., Gochoo, M., & Ali, L. (2023). Real-time attention monitoring system for classroom: A deep learning approach for student's behavior recognition. *Big Data and Cognitive Computing, 7*(48), 48. Advance online publication. DOI: 10.3390/bdcc7010048

Tran, B. X., Vu, G. T., Ha, G. H., Vuong, Q.-H., Ho, M.-T., Vuong, T.-T., La, V.-P., Ho, M.-T., Nghiem, K.-C. P., Nguyen, H. L. T., Latkin, C. A., Tam, W. W. S., Cheung, N.-M., Nguyen, H.-K. T., Ho, C. S. H., & Ho, R. C. M. (2019). Global evolution of research in artificial intelligence in health and medicine: A bibliometric study. *Journal of Clinical Medicine, 8*(3), 360. DOI: 10.3390/jcm8030360 PMID: 30875745

Trivedi, B., Mares, A. C., & Mukherjee, D.. (2023). Effectiveness of a social justice curriculum intervention on cultural competency among internal medicine residents. *Research Square*. DOI: 10.21203/rs.3.rs-3426316/v1

Tsinghua University. (2024). 2024 Tsinghua University Admissions Film 'Miracle'. https://www.tsinghua.edu.cn/info/2160/112042.htm

Turchi, T., Prencipe, G., Malizia, A., Filogna, S., Latrofa, F., & Sgandurra, G. (2024). Pathways to democratized healthcare: Envisioning human-centered AI-as-a-service for customized diagnosis and rehabilitation. *Artificial Intelligence in Medicine, 151*, 102850. DOI: 10.1016/j.artmed.2024.102850 PMID: 38555849

Turkistani, A., Mashaikhi, A., Bajaber, A., Alghamdi, W., Althobaity, B., Alharthi, N., & Alhomaiani, S. (2020). The prevalence of cyberchondria and the impact of social media among the students in Taif University. *International Journal of Medicine in Developing Countries*, 1759–1765. https://doi.org/DOI: 10.24911/IJMDC.51-1598363146

Twenge, J. M., Joiner, T. E., Rogers, M. L., & Martin, G. N. (2018). Increases in depressive symptoms, suicide-related outcomes, and suicide rates among US adolescents after 2010 and links to increased new media screen time. *Clinical Psychological Science*, *6*(1), 3–17. DOI: 10.1177/2167702617723376

Väänänen, A., Haataja, K., Vehviläinen-Julkunen, K., & Toivanen, P. (2021). Proposal of a novel Artificial Intelligence Distribution Service platform for healthcare. *F1000 Research*, *10*, 245. DOI: 10.12688/f1000research.36775.1 PMID: 34804493

Varma, P., Junge, M., Meaklim, H., & Jackson, M. L. (2021). Younger people are more vulnerable to stress, anxiety and depression during COVID-19 pandemic: A global cross-sectional survey. *Progress in Neuro-Psychopharmacology & Biological Psychiatry*, *109*, 110236. DOI: 10.1016/j.pnpbp.2020.110236 PMID: 33373680

Varma, R., & Singh, T. (2023). Cyberchondria and health: Exploring the linkages. *Mind & Society*, *12*(02), 29–34. DOI: 10.56011/mind-mri-122-20233

Vellido, A. (2019). Societal issues concerning the application of artificial intelligence in medicine. *Kidney Diseases*, *5*(1), 11–17. DOI: 10.1159/000492428 PMID: 30815459

Verdejo Espinosa, A., Lopez, J. L., Mata Mata, F., & Estevez, M. E. (2021). Application of IoT in healthcare: Keys to implementation of the sustainable development goals. *Sensors (Basel)*, *21*(7), 2330. DOI: 10.3390/s21072330 PMID: 33810606

Victor, T. W., Tivesten, E., Gustavsson, P., Johansson, J., Sangberg, F., & Ljung Aust, M. (2018). Automation expectation mismatch: Incorrect prediction despite eyes on threat and hands on wheel. *Human Factors*, *60*(8), 1095–1116. DOI: 10.1177/0018720818788164 PMID: 30096002

Vigneswaran, A. J. G., & Aakash, B. (2022). Artificial intelligence-based voice assistant. *International Journal for Research in Applied Science and Engineering Technology*, *10*(12), 1130–1133. DOI: 10.22214/ijraset.2022.48147

Vilela, A., Costa, C., Souza, M., Fiaccadori, F., Leles, C., & Costa, N. (2021). Validity and reliability of immunochromatographic IGM/IGG rapid tests for covid-19 salivary diagnosis. *Oral Diseases*, *28*(S2), 2465–2473. DOI: 10.1111/odi.14059 PMID: 34695290

Vismara, M., Caricasole, V., Starcevic, V., Cinosi, E., Dell'Osso, B., Martinotti, G., & Fineberg, N. A. (2020). Is cyberchondria a new transdiagnostic digital compulsive syndrome? A systematic review of the evidence. *Comprehensive Psychiatry*, *99*, 152167. DOI: 10.1016/j.comppsych.2020.152167 PMID: 32146315

Vyas, S., Gupta, S., & Shukla, V. K. (2023). Towards edge AI and varied approaches of digital wellness in healthcare administration: a study. *2023 International Conference on Computational Intelligence and Knowledge Economy (ICCIKE)*. DOI: 10.1109/ICCIKE58312.2023.10131857

Wang, P., Li, L., & Chen, W. (n.d.). *Exploring Antecedents of Cyberchondria During Pandemics: An integration of Stress and Coping and SOR*. AIS Electronic Library (AISeL). https://aisel.aisnet.org/pacis2023/112

Wang, Q., Fan, K., & Li, P. (2022). Effect of the use of home and community care services on the multidimensional health of older adults. *International Journal of Environmental Research and Public Health*, *19*(22), 15402. DOI: 10.3390/ijerph192215402 PMID: 36430119

Wang, Q., Peng, S., Zha, Z., Han, X., Deng, C., Hu, L., & Hu, P. (2023). Enhancing the conversational agent with an emotional support system for mental health digital therapeutics. *Frontiers in Psychiatry*, *14*, 1148534. Advance online publication. DOI: 10.3389/fpsyt.2023.1148534 PMID: 37139323

Wang, X., & Cheng, Z. (2020). Cross-Sectional Studies: Strengths, Weaknesses, and Recommendations. *Chest*, *158*(1, Supplement), S65–S71. DOI: 10.1016/j.chest.2020.03.012 PMID: 32658654

Wang, Y., Chen, Y., & Sheng, J. (2024). Assessing ChatGPT as a Medical Consultation Assistant for Chronic Hepatitis B: Cross-Language Study of English and Chinese. *JMIR Medical Informatics*, *12*(1), e56426. DOI: 10.2196/56426 PMID: 39115930

Wang, Y., Shafik, W., Seong, J. T., Al Mutairi, A., Mustafa, M. S., & Mouhamed, M. R. (2023). Service delay and optimization of the energy efficiency of a system in fog-enabled smart cities. *Alexandria Engineering Journal*, *84*, 112–125. DOI: 10.1016/j.aej.2023.10.034

Weber, G. M., Adams, W. G., Bernstam, E. V., Bickel, J. P., Fox, K. P., Marsolo, K., Raghavan, V. A., Turchin, A., Zhou, X., Murphy, S. N., & Mandl, K. D. (2017). Biases introduced by filtering electronic health records for patients with "complete data". *Journal of the American Medical Informatics Association : JAMIA*, *24*(6), 1134–1141. DOI: 10.1093/jamia/ocx071 PMID: 29016972

Wen, W., Ishii, H., Ohata, R., Yamashita, A., Asama, H., & Imamizu, H. (2021). Perception and control: Individual difference in the sense of agency is associated with learnability in sensorimotor adaptation. *Scientific Reports*, *11*(1), 20542. Advance online publication. DOI: 10.1038/s41598-021-99969-4 PMID: 34654878

Whelan, E., Islam, A. K. M. N., & Brooks, S. (2020a). Applying the SOBC paradigm to explain how social media overload affects academic performance. *Computers &amp. Computers & Education, 143*, 103692. DOI: 10.1016/j.compedu.2019.103692

White, R. W., & Horvitz, E. (2009). Cyberchondria. *ACM Transactions on Information Systems, 27*(4), 1–37. DOI: 10.1145/1629096.1629101

Whyte, C. (2020). Deepfake News: AI-enabled disinformation as a multi-level public policy challenge. *Journal of Cyber Policy, 5*(2), 199–217. DOI: 10.1080/23738871.2020.1797135

Wijesinghe, C. A., Liyanage, U. L. N. S., Kapugama, K. G. C. L., Warsapperuma, W. N. P., Williams, S. S., Kuruppuarachchi, K. L. A., & Rodrigo, A. (2019). "Muddling by googling" – Cyberchondria among outpatient attendees of two hospitals in Sri Lanka. *Sri Lanka Journal of Psychiatry, 10*(1), 11–15. DOI: 10.4038/sljpsyc.v10i1.8202

Wijnberge, M., Geerts, B. F., Hol, L., Lemmers, N., Mulder, M. P., Berge, P., Schenk, J., Terwindt, L. E., Hollmann, M. W., Vlaar, A. P., & Veelo, D. P. (2020). Effect of a machine learning-derived early warning system for intraoperative hypotension VS standard care on depth and duration of intraoperative hypotension during elective noncardiac surgery: The hype randomized clinical trial. *Journal of the American Medical Association, 323*(11), 1052–1060. DOI: 10.1001/jama.2020.0592 PMID: 32065827

Williams, D. R., & Mohammed, S. A. (2009). Discrimination and racial disparities in health: Evidence and needed research. *Journal of Behavioral Medicine, 32*(1), 20–47. DOI: 10.1007/s10865-008-9185-0 PMID: 19030981

Williamson, S. M., & Prybutok, V. (2024). Balancing privacy and progress: A review of privacy challenges, systemic oversight, and patient perceptions in AI-driven healthcare. *Applied Sciences (Basel, Switzerland), 14*(2), 675. DOI: 10.3390/app14020675

Wilmink, G., Dupey, K., Alkire, S., Grote, J., Zobel, G., Fillit, H., & Movva, S. (2020). Artificial intelligence–powered digital health platform and wearable devices improve outcomes for older adults in assisted living communities: Pilot intervention study. *JMIR Aging, 3*(2), e19554. DOI: 10.2196/19554 PMID: 32723711

Wilson, J. M., Lee, J., Fitzgerald, H. N., Oosterhoff, B., Sevi, B., & Shook, N. J. (2020). Job insecurity and financial concern during the COVID-19 pandemic are associated with worse mental health. *Journal of Occupational and Environmental Medicine, 62*(9), 686–691. DOI: 10.1097/JOM.0000000000001962 PMID: 32890205

Wimbarti, S., Kairupan, B. H., & Tallei, T. E. (2024). Critical review of self-diagnosis of mental health conditions using artificial intelligence. *International Journal of Mental Health Nursing, 33*(2), 344–358. DOI: 10.1111/inm.13303 PMID: 38345132

Wineburg, S., & McGrew, S. (2016). Evaluating Information: The cornerstone of civic online reasoning. *Stanford Digital Repository.* https://apo.org.au/resource/evaluating-information-cornerstone-civic-online-reasoning

Wong, M. C. S., Wong, E. L. Y., Huang, J., Cheung, A. W. L., Law, K., Chong, M. K. C., Ng, R. W. Y., Lai, C. K. C., Boon, S. S., Lau, J. T. F., Chen, Z., & Chan, P. K. S. (2021). Acceptance of the COVID-19 vaccine based on the health belief model: A population-based survey in Hong Kong. *Vaccine, 39*(7), 1148–1156. DOI: 10.1016/j.vaccine.2020.12.083 PMID: 33461834

World Health Organisation. (n.d.). *Constitution of the World Health Organization.* World Health Organization. https://www.who.int/about/governance/constitution

World Health Organization. (2021). Ethics and governance of artificial intelligence for health: WHO guidance: executive summary.

Wright, D. W. M., & Zascerinska, S. (2023). Becoming immortal: Future wellness and medical tourism markets. *Journal of Tourism Futures, 9*(2), 168–195. DOI: 10.1108/JTF-05-2021-0119

Wu, X., Nazari, N., & Griffiths, M. D. (2021). Using fear and anxiety related to COVID-19 to predict cyberchondria: Cross-sectional survey study. *Journal of Medical Internet Research, 23*(6), e26285. DOI: 10.2196/26285 PMID: 34014833

Xafis, V., Schaefer, G. O., Labude, M. K., Brassington, I., Ballantyne, A., Lim, H. Y., Lipworth, W., Lysaght, T., Stewart, C., Sun, S., Laurie, G. T., & Tai, E. S. (2019). An ethics framework for big data in health and research. *Asian Bioethics Review, 11*(3), 227–254. DOI: 10.1007/s41649-019-00099-x PMID: 33717314

Xiang, H., Zhou, J., & Liu, M. (2023). Judging online health misinformation: Effects of cyberchondria and age. In *Lecture notes in computer science* (pp. 284–301). https://doi.org/DOI: 10.1007/978-3-031-34866-2_22

Xiaoling, P., & Xuan, Z. (2022). The transformation of artificial intelligence in the 5G era and the impact on education. *2022 IEEE 2nd International Conference on Electronic Technology, Communication and Information,* ICETCI 2022.

Xu, X. (2022). *Towards future health and well-being: bridging behavior modeling and intervention.* Adjunct Proceedings of the 35th Annual ACM Symposium on User Interface Software and Technology. DOI: 10.1145/3526114.3558524

Xu, A., Johari, S. A., Khademolomoom, A. H., Khabaz, M. T., Umurzoqovich, R. S., Hosseini, S., & Semiromi, D. T. (2023). Investigation of management of international education considering sustainable medical tourism and entrepreneurship. *Heliyon, 9*(1), e12691. DOI: 10.1016/j.heliyon.2022.e12691 PMID: 36685466

Xu, R. H., & Chen, C. (2024). Moderating effect of coping strategies on the association between the infodemic-driven overuse of health care services and Cyberchondria and anxiety: Partial Least Squares Structural Equation Modeling Study. *Journal of Medical Internet Research, 26*, e53417. https://doi.org/doi:10.2196/53417. DOI: 10.2196/53417 PMID: 38593427

Xu, W., Dainoff, M. J., Ge, L., & Gao, Z. (2022). Transitioning to human interaction with AI systems: New challenges and opportunities for HCI professionals to enable human-centered AI. *International Journal of Human-Computer Interaction, 39*(3), 494–518. DOI: 10.1080/10447318.2022.2041900

Xu, Z. (2024). The impact of online resources on reducing mental health stigma among international college students: A case study. *Lecture Notes in Education Psychology and Public Media, 58*(1), 141–147. DOI: 10.54254/2753-7048/58/20241770

Yadav, D., Yadav, S., & Veer, K. (2020). A comprehensive assessment of Brain Computer Interfaces: Recent trends and challenges. *Journal of Neuroscience Methods, 346*, 108918. DOI: 10.1016/j.jneumeth.2020.108918 PMID: 32853592

Yam, F. C., Korkmaz, O., & Griffiths, M. D. (2021). The association between fear of Covid-19 and smartphone addiction among individuals: The mediating and moderating role of cyberchondria severity. *Current Psychology (New Brunswick, N.J.), 42*(3), 2377–2390. DOI: 10.1007/s12144-021-02324-z PMID: 34690474

Yang, T., Zhao, L., Li, W., Wu, J., & Zomaya, A. Y. (2021). Towards healthy and cost-effective indoor environment management in smart homes: A deep reinforcement learning approach. *Applied Energy, 300*, 117335. DOI: 10.1016/j.apenergy.2021.117335

Yang, Y., Ta, N., & Li, Z. (2022). Investigating the obsessive and compulsive features of cyberchondria: A Holistic review. *Frontiers in Psychology, 13*, 897426. Advance online publication. DOI: 10.3389/fpsyg.2022.897426 PMID: 35859839

Yang, Z., Zhou, Q., Lei, L., Zheng, K., & Xiang, H. (2016). An IoT-cloud based wearable ECG monitoring system for smart healthcare. *Journal of Medical Systems, 40*(286), 286. Advance online publication. DOI: 10.1007/s10916-016-0644-9 PMID: 27796840

Ye, C., Zweck, E., Ma, Z., Smith, J., & Katz, S. (2024). Doctor Versus Artificial Intelligence: Patient and Physician Evaluation of Large Language Model Responses to Rheumatology Patient Questions in a Cross-Sectional Study. *Arthritis & Rheumatology (Hoboken, N.J.)*, *76*(3), 479–484. DOI: 10.1002/art.42737 PMID: 37902018

Yoo, B., Thelen, S. T., & Harrison, K. (2023). Patient consideration of local hospital, center of excellence, and medical tourism options for surgery. *Health Marketing Quarterly*, *40*(2), 119–140. DOI: 10.1080/07359683.2021.1994171 PMID: 34736359

Yousefi, Y. (2022). Data sharing as a debiasing measure for AI systems in healthcare: new legal basis. *15th International Conference on Theory and Practice of Electronic Governance*. DOI: 10.1145/3560107.3560116

Yuen, E., Winter, N., Savira, F., Huggins, C. E., Nguyen, L., Cooper, P., Peeters, A., Anderson, K., Bhoyroo, R., Crowe, S., & Ugalde, A. (2024). Digital health literacy and its association with sociodemographic characteristics, health resource use, and health outcomes: Rapid review. *Interactive Journal of Medical Research*, *13*(1), e46888. DOI: 10.2196/46888 PMID: 39059006

Yunus, S., Puteh, S., Ali, A., & Daud, F. (2021). The covid impact to public healthcare utilization among urban low-income subsidized community in Klang Valley Malaysia. *Health Services Research and Managerial Epidemiology*, *8*, 23333928211002407. https://doi.org. DOI: 10.1177/23333928211002407 PMID: 33796627

Zaidan, A. M. (2023). The leading global health challenges in the artificial intelligence era. *Frontiers in Public Health*, *11*, 1328918. DOI: 10.3389/fpubh.2023.1328918 PMID: 38089037

Zakaria, M., Islam, M. A., Islam, M. K., Begum, A., Poly, N. A., Cheng, F., & Xu, J. (2023). Determinants of Bangladeshi patients' decision-making process and satisfaction toward medical tourism in India. *Frontiers in Public Health*, *11*, 11. DOI: 10.3389/fpubh.2023.1137929 PMID: 37200988

Zeng, L., Li, R. Y. M., & Zeng, H. (2023). Weibo users and Academia's foci on tourism safety: Implications from institutional differences and digital divide. *Heliyon*, *9*(3), e12306. DOI: 10.1016/j.heliyon.2022.e12306 PMID: 36923855

Zhang, H., Kuhnle, A., Zhang, H., & Thai, M. T. (2016). Detecting misinformation in online social networks before it is too late. *2016 IEEE/ACM International Conference on Advances in Social Networks Analysis and Mining (ASONAM)*. DOI: 10.1109/ASONAM.2016.7752288

Zhang, J., & Zhang, Z. M. (2023). Ethics and governance of trustworthy medical artificial intelligence. *BMC Medical Informatics and Decision Making*, *23*(1), 7. DOI: 10.1186/s12911-023-02103-9 PMID: 36639799

Zhang, L., & Sun, Z. (2019). The Application of Artificial Intelligence Technology in the Tourism Industry of Jinan. *Journal of Physics: Conference Series*, *1302*(3), 032005. DOI: 10.1088/1742-6596/1302/3/032005

Zhang, Q. (2024). Online health communities provide important support in China. *Nature Human Behaviour*, *8*(1), 8–8. DOI: 10.1038/s41562-023-01766-8 PMID: 37923912

Zhang, X., Liu, Y., Qin, Z., Ye, Z., & Meng, F. (2023). Understanding the role of social media usage and health self-efficacy in the processing of COVID-19 rumors: A SOR perspective. *Data and Information Management*, *7*(2), 100043. DOI: 10.1016/j.dim.2023.100043 PMID: 37304677

Zhang, X., Ma, Z., Zheng, H., Li, T., Chen, K., Wang, X., Liu, C., Xu, L., Wu, X., Lin, D., & Lin, H. (2020). The combination of brain-computer interfaces and artificial intelligence: Applications and challenges. *Annals of Translational Medicine*, *8*(11), 712. DOI: 10.21037/atm.2019.11.109 PMID: 32617332

Zhao, H., Fu, S., & Chen, X. (2020). Promoting users' intention to share online health articles on social media: The role of Confirmation Bias. *Information Processing &amp. Management*, *57*(6), 102354. DOI: 10.1016/j.ipm.2020.102354 PMID: 32834400

Zhao, L., Zhu, D., Shafik, W., Matinkhah, S. M., Ahmad, Z., Sharif, L., & Craig, A. (2022). Artificial intelligence analysis in cyber domain: A review. *International Journal of Distributed Sensor Networks*, *18*(4), 15501329221084882. DOI: 10.1177/15501329221084882

Zhao, Y. C., Zhao, M., & Song, S. (2022a). Online Health Information Seeking Among Patients With Chronic Conditions: Integrating the Health Belief Model and Social Support Theory. *Journal of Medical Internet Research*, *24*(11), e42447. DOI: 10.2196/42447 PMID: 36322124

Zhao, Y. C., Zhao, M., & Song, S. (2022b). Online Health Information Seeking Behaviors Among Older Adults: Systematic Scoping Review. *Journal of Medical Internet Research*, *24*(2), e34790. DOI: 10.2196/34790 PMID: 35171099

Zhao, Y., Chen, K., Peng, J., Wang, J., & Song, N. (2022). Diverse needs and cooperative deeds: Comprehending users' identities in online health communities. *Information Processing & Management*, *59*(5), 103060. DOI: 10.1016/j.ipm.2022.103060

About the Contributors

Ahadzadeh Ashrafsadat (Jeyran) holds the position of Associate Professor at the School of Communication, Xiamen University Malaysia. With ten years of experience teaching at international tertiary institutions in Malaysia, Dr. Jeyran has cultivated advanced pedagogical competencies tailored to the evolving demands of modern academia. Dr. Jeyran's research expertise spans digital health, emerging technologies, and their intersection with psychological frameworks. Her scholarly work is distinguished by a commitment to transcending conventional research paradigms, driven by an unwavering dedication to multidisciplinary inquiry. This intellectual rigor fuels her exploration of uncharted territories, positioning her at the forefront of pioneering innovative investigations into technology-mediated human behavior.

Mansour Amini is an interdisciplinary researcher and a senior lecturer from the School of Languages, Literacies, and Translation, Universiti Sains Malaysia (USM). He has a Diploma in Mathematics and Physics, a B.A. in English Language and Literature, an M.A. in English Language Teaching, and a PhD in Translation Studies. Formerly, he served as the Head of Research and Postgraduate Studies, Faculty of Social Sciences and Liberal Arts, at UCSI University Malaysia. He has published articles in Translation, Education, Humanities, and Social Sciences, and is the principal investigator of several research projects. He has conducted workshops, seminars, and talks on Thesis Writing and Research Methodology in Malaysia, Thailand, Indonesia, Iran, and China. Dr. Mansour Amini is a reviewer, editing manager, and editorial board member of several academic journals. He has tried to link research with teaching practice by applying the lessons learned from authentic research outputs into teaching scenarios.

Wu Shin Ling obtained both her bachelor's degree in Human Development and doctorate in Psychology of Child Development from Universiti Putra Malaysia. Her postgraduate research focused on the risk and protective factors of suicidal ideation specifically among adolescents. She has presented on topics such as mental health issues, suicidal ideation and happiness at various international conferences. She is a member of the Malaysian Psychological Association (PSIMA), and Golden Key International Honour Society.

***

Michael Jenkins is a Senior Lecturer at Sunway University who focuses on conducting EEG research. He completed his PhD at Birkbeck University of London in 2017, followed by a postdoctoral fellowship at McMaster University until 2022. His research employs experimental techniques to cover a range of topics in cognitive psychology and cognitive neuroscience. Currently, he is pursuing research questions related to the sense of agency, joint action, healthy ageing, and cognitive frailty. Additionally, he is interested in research exploring the implications of diversity for cognition, psychology, and behaviour.

Lin Mei-Hua is an Industrial and Organisational Psychologist and a Professor in the Department of Psychology at Sunway University. She obtained her MSc and PhD in Human Factor/Industrial-Organizational Psychology from Wright State University, USA. Her research focuses on trust and distrust in the workplace, employability, national differences in cognition and work behaviors, and job attitudes. She has experience managing research involving multinational groups, working with various international researchers in multiple disciplines in research such as cross-cultural cognition, performance measures, group processes, decision-making, and multinational teamwork. Dr. Lin was involved in a cross-cultural research effort that included seven nations from the regions of North America, South Asia, East Asia, and Southeast Asia. She has published over 40 articles, book chapters, and technical reports.

Wasswa Shafik (Member, IEEE) received a Bachelor of Science degree in information technology engineering with a minor in mathematics from Ndejje University, Kampala, Uganda, a Master of Engineering degree in information technology engineering (MIT) from Yazd University, Iran, and a Ph.D. degree in computer science with the School of Digital Science, Universiti Brunei Darussalam, Brunei Darussalam. He is also the Founder and a Principal Investigator of the Dig Connectivity Research Laboratory (DCRLab) after serving as a Research Associate at Network Interconnectivity Research Laboratory, Yazd University. Prior to this, he worked as a Community Data Analyst at Population Services International (PSI-Uganda), Community Data Officer at Programme for Accessible Health Communication (PACE-Uganda), Research Assistant at the Socio-Economic Data

Centre (SEDC-Uganda), Prime Minister's Office, Kampala, Uganda, an Assistant Data Officer at TechnoServe, Kampala, IT Support at Thurayya Islam Media, Uganda, and Asmaah Charity Organization. He has 70+ publications in renowned journals and conferences. His research interests include AI, smart agriculture, health computing and ecological informatics.

Adam Kah Jjin Wee is a PhD candidate in the Department of Psychology at Sunway University. His PhD project focuses on human-AI interactions and its influences on people cognitive skills. He is also a teaching assistant in Sunway University, assisting lecturers in delivering classes. With experience as a research assistant in Sunway University, HELP University, and Epitome Global, Adam has exposure to multiple disciplines of research, including construal level theory, anonymous discourses, visual discomfort, and work-values. Moreover, he is interested in research exploring the realms of AI-Psychology, social-cognition, and industrial organizational psychology.

Wu Yushan earned her Bachelor of Arts degree in Journalism at the School of Communication, Xiamen University Malaysia (XMUM), and is preparing to pursue a Master of Journalism degree at the Faculty of Social Sciences, the University of Hong Kong (HKU). Her undergraduate research explored the psychological and behavioral patterns of Chinese individuals in the context of social media and health communication. She has published papers and presented her findings at various academic conferences. Moving forward, her research will focus on the intersection of AI, social media, journalism, and healthcare, with particular emphasis on the global advancements in AI and the integration of AI-powered innovations into contemporary journalistic practices.

Ali Zahabi, PhD, is a lecturer at School of Liberal Arts, King Mongkut's University of Technology Thonburi (KMUTT), Thailand. He is a PhD graduate in Applied Linguistics from Universiti Sains Malaysia. He has more than 15 years of teaching experience at the academic level mostly in Southeast Asia (Malaysia, Thailand). His research interests include task-based language teaching, semiotics, and language assessment.ali.zaha@kmutt.ac.th

Index

I

L

M

N

O

P

S

T

www.ingramcontent.com/pod-product-compliance
Lightning Source LLC
LaVergne TN
LVHW080641011026
849160LV00014B/1284